Simplicity

# *Simply the Best*

# SEWING BOOK

## The essential reference for all home sewers

**Simplicity**

# *Simply the Best*
# SEWING BOOK

The essential reference for all home sewers

**Simplicity**
BOOKS

## SIMPLICITY
## SEWING BOOK

First published in the United Kingdom in 2011 by
Simplicity Books
10 Southcombe Street
London W14 0RA

An imprint of Anova Books Company Ltd

Illustrations by Kuo Kang Chen

ISBN 978-1-84340-557-3

A CIP catalogue for this book is available from the British Library.

10 9 8 7 6 5 4 3 2 1

Reproduction by Repro by Mission, Hong Kong
Printed and bound by 1010 Printing International Ltd, China

This book can be ordered direct from the publisher at
www.anovabooks.com

## Acknowledgments

Judy Raymond, Simplicity Creative Group Senior Vice President,
inspired, supported and guided the direction of this book
at every step. Without her, the *Simplicity Simply the Best
Sewing Book* would not have its fresh new approach to
creative home sewing.

Deborah Kreiling, Simplicity Creative Group Design
Development Director, provided expert technical guidance
and supported the creation of materials and projects included
in this book.

Laura Corbett, Simplicity Creative Group Merchandising
Associate, aided in the editing of materials, giving a practical
home-sewing and merchandising eye to the content and
projects contained in this book.

Carin Blankoff, Simplicity Creative Group Fabric Director,
researched many of the products referred to in this book,
ensuring the accuracy of fabrics, notions and products
available in the marketplace.

# CONTENTS

# BEFORE YOU BEGIN

The aim of this book is to be the most comprehensive source of information for both new and experienced sewers, as well as for those who are rediscovering the joys of this rewarding craft. It has been compiled by working closely with the Simplicity Consumer Relations Department, which deals with requests for specific information.

OPPOSITE **By perfecting your sewing skills you can learn how to easily construct those details that make garments as unique as the person who is wearing them.**

## SIMPLICITY® SEWING BOOK KEY FEATURES

✂ Access to the very latest techniques and advice you can trust from the leaders in home sewing.

✂ Designed for quick and easy reference at every stage of your dressmaking journey.

✂ Conventional and serger sewing presented step-by-step and side-by-side – pick and choose to suit you.

✂ Tips provided throughout to help save time and to ensure the very best results every time.

✂ A selection of patternless projects is provided so you can get started on a project today.

## HOW TO USE THIS BOOK

This book is designed to give you all the information you need to make your own clothes, with confidence. It is for all of you who have ever been tempted to make a garment, but thought: "Oh, but I could never sew something like that!" The truth is that most garments, including the ones you love best, are well within your sewing abilities. Loose-fitting, tailored, very casual or elegant – there's a wide range of style, fabric, color and fit combinations to be discovered once you know how.

### Chapter by chapter

✂ **Sewing for Today:** This chapter helps you to decide what to sew, to ensure that your wardrobe is your most complementary yet.

✂ **Understanding Patterns:** Learn how to select the right pattern to suit your sewing priorities and dressmaking skills; and truly understand the information your pattern can provide you with.

✂ **A Buyer's Guide:** The information in this chapter will enable you to select fabrics and notions with confidence and to make informed choices about the tools and equipment you invest in.

✂ **A Perfect Fit:** This will guide you through the basics to make sure that you select the right size pattern for your body measurements, and offers advice for making adjustments to standard patterns to ensure the perfect fit for your figure.

✂ **Universal Basics:** Discover the fundamentals that apply to almost any project you make, no matter what style pattern you choose, what fabric catches your eye, or what your sewing skill level may be.

✂ **Sewing Techniques:** The information in this chapter is designed to support the techniques included on your pattern's instruction sheet; it provides more detailed information on the key elements used in garment construction and the variations on them. The easy-to-follow instructions include options for both conventional and serger sewing, and for combining the two to achieve professional results in the least possible time.

✂ **Sewing on Special Fabrics:** This chapter contains helpful information to transform challenging fabrics into sewer-friendly fabrics.

✂ **Patternless Projects:** To get you started on your sewing adventure, this chapter has four easy, self-contained projects. As none needs a pattern, you can begin today.

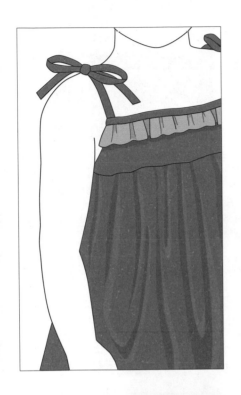

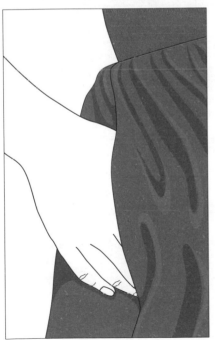
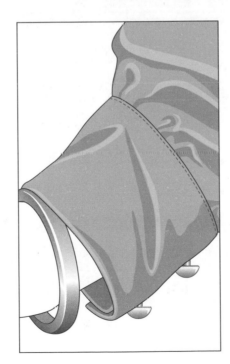

# SEWING FOR TODAY

# INTRODUCTION

With today's easy sewing techniques, helpful notions and new sewing machine technology, anyone can turn out a professional-looking garment. There are many different reasons to sew your own clothes, from saving money to providing you with an outlet for your creativity. This chapter helps you to establish what your sewing priorities are. Regardless of why you sew or what sewing philosophy you adopt, how do you combine fabric, pattern and fit to achieve the most flattering wardrobe ever? This is the question that challenges everyone who sews her own clothes, and the second half of this chapter will help you to find the answer.

# REASONS TO SEW

**Sewing provides you with the opportunity to combine good fit, complementary color, suitable fabric and flattering style all in one garment. When you sew, every garment in your closet can rate a 10. Discover why others sew, then decide on your sewing priorities.**

## SEWING SOLUTIONS

Not long ago, if you asked a group of people why they sewed, you would probably get one of two answers. The first would be "to save money." The second would be "because there is nothing suitable in the stores." Ask that same question today, and you'll get many different answers.

**"When I sew, I get to be the designer, the one who picks the style, the fabric and the color for my garment"**
It doesn't matter if you shop in a department store, an expensive boutique or a discount chain, when you buy ready-made clothes you run the risk of running into someone wearing the same outfit.

Those chances are almost non-existent if you sew.

**"Sewing is a way to express myself"**
In this age of advanced technology and mass production, sewing provides the means for expressing individuality. If you sew your own outfits you can say to yourself, "I may not have designed this garment, but through my choice of fabric color and pattern, and finishing trims and techniques, I can express myself as an individual."

**"Sewing gives me time to unwind"**
Sewing is the perfect antidote for stress. As sewing is an activity that occupies both your hands and your brain, it demands your complete attention and

offers you the opportunity to escape from the cares and pressures of the day, even if only for half an hour. When sewing time is over, you can go back to the "real" world with a clearer head.

### "The garments I sew are better made, in better fabric, than the ones I could afford to buy"

Buttons fall off, seams aren't finished, hems come undone, even on the most expensive ready-to-wear garments. If you invest that same amount of money in quality fabric and a flattering pattern, you'll end up with a garment that will look better and last longer than the one you would have bought.

In fact, the more you sew, the more discriminating a buyer you will become. You'll be able to recognize quality construction when you see it, which means you'll ultimately get more for your money when you do buy ready-to-wear outfits, too.

### "I have small children and buying clothes for them is so expensive"

Sewing children's clothes is a great way to save money and a great way to create children's outfits with irresistible appeal. Since children's clothes take relatively little fabric, you may be able to use the leftovers from the clothes you sew for yourself. Remnant tables, with yardages that are frequently insufficient for adult garments, provide countless bargains for children's sewing. Sewing children's garments is also a great way to experiment with new techniques, such as stitching details, appliqués and trims.

A small child won't notice, or even care, if the plaids don't match perfectly or the buttonholes aren't exactly straight.

### "Sewing is great fun and now it's so easy"

If you learned to sew back in the days when finishing the seams on a garment was a real task, when making a jacket meant hours of laborious padstitching or when reading pattern instructions was like learning a foreign language, you're in for a pleasant surprise. "State-of-the-art" sewing has never been easier.

> **TIP** Chapters 5, 6 and 7 are full of tips and techniques for using timesaving notions.

## CHOOSING YOUR SEWING PRIORITIES

Who, in this busy world of ours, has time to sew everything she needs? With so many beautiful fabrics and patterns to choose from, it makes good sense to adopt a sewing philosophy to help you decide where your sewing priorities lie.

### Buy hard, sew easy
Sew simple, easy-fitting garments that don't have a lot of complicated details, in fabrics that don't require special handling. For example, you might make the top and the skirt, but buy the coordinating tailored jacket to complete the outfit. If you're short on time or sewing experience, this may be the best option for you.

### Buy easy, sew hard
Put your time and money into the luxury fabrics and special details that greatly increase the cost of a ready-to-wear garment. With this approach, you would buy the top and the pants, and use your sewing time to create the jacket.

### Sew the classics
Choose traditional styles that won't go out of fashion for several seasons. If you're sewing mostly for pleasure, it may not matter how soon the project is finished. Concentrate on seasonless fabrics so that the garment can go straight into your wardrobe regardless of when it's finished.

### Sew the "fad" styles
If you want to be the first with the newest fashions, keep up-to-date on all of the latest shortcut techniques. Because you sew a style for today with the understanding that tomorrow it may be passé, timesaving patterns and techniques are essential to making this sewing objective a success.

### SEW-FRIENDLY EQUIPMENT ON THE MARKET

✂ **Computerized sewing machines:** These require no more than a light touch of the finger to change stitch length, width or configuration, allowing you to go from straight stitch to zigzag stitch to stretch stitch in a matter of seconds. For more on sewing machines, see page 37.

✂ **Serger (overlock) sewing machines:** Once the exclusive property of the garment industry, these are now widely available for home use and are the perfect complement to the conventional sewing machine. They stitch, trim and overcast a seam all in one operation. For more on sergers, see page 40.

✂ **Sewing patterns:** These are easier to use than ever before, and now there are even special pattern groups, each identified by its own unique logo, which focus on the needs of the beginner, on overlock sewing, and on quick, easy sewing, among others. For more on patterns, see Chapter 2.

✂ **Fusible interfacings:** Those that really stay fused through repeated washings or dry cleanings take the work out of shaping a garment, whether you are merely adding interfacing to the collar and cuffs of a blouse, or constructing a tailored jacket.

✂ **Sewing aids and notions:** From basting thread that dissolves in the wash to disappearing marking pens that make it possible to mark directly on the right side of the fabric; from a lightweight, sheer seam binding that automatically curls around the edge of the fabric as you apply it to a liquid that invisibly seals the raw edges of seams, trim or buttonholes – advancements such as these have simplified sewing in ways your grandmother couldn't have dreamed possible.

### Sew for special occasions
If you love to dress to impress, you may want to devote your sewing time exclusively to the very satisfying sewing category of evening wear. Not only are the fabrics for formal clothes wonderful and inspiring to work with, but you can also save money by sewing the glamorous parts of your wardrobe.

### Sew simply because you love to
If you enjoy the opportunity to experiment with different types of fabrics and patterns, sewing anything that catches your eye, then you're someone who enjoys sewing for the pure pleasure of it. If you're not in this category now, with a little sewing experience you soon will be!

# FINDING WHAT FLATTERS

**How do you combine fabric, pattern and fit to achieve the most flattering wardrobe ever? The answer, believe it or not, can be found in the clothes you already own. Your first job is to open your closet and pull out the items you wear most often.**

## ANALYZING YOUR FAVORITE GARMENTS

The chances are you wear only 10 percent of your clothes 90 percent of the time. While not immediately apparent, there are some very good reasons why this is so. Examine each garment carefully and try it on – you're going to analyze what it is that makes each one a favorite by assessing it against five different categories.

### The five categories

You'll need a pen and notebook, and a full-length mirror. As you go through the list of the five categories below, award the garment two points if it's a success, one point if it's just okay, no points if it's a flop. Some of the garments in your 10 percent group will score high marks in all five categories. Others will have only one or two features that make them favorites, such as great fit and/or comfortable fabric, but they may be in a color that does nothing special for you. Pay closest attention to the garments that get the highest scores.

### FABRIC

Perhaps you like the look and feel of natural fiber or the easy care of a synthetic. Do you wear this garment because it keeps you very warm or very cool? Does the fabric have some "give" (for example, is it a knit or is it cut on the bias) that enhances the fit and adds to the comfort?

### COLOR

If it's an outfit that brings you lots of compliments, it may just be the color. Even the simplest of garments in a flattering color will win rave reviews.

### STYLE

Do you like the garment because it makes you look taller, shorter or thinner? Or because it camouflages wide hips, a thick waist, narrow shoulders, a large bust or a flat chest?

### FIT

You won't feel comfortable in a garment unless it fits well. Notice what features provide you with a good fit. Are the sleeves cut full in the upper arm? Is the dress a no-waistline or elasticized-waist style? Do the trousers have front pleats? Pay particular attention to the proportions. Do many of your favorite jackets and tops end at the waistline or high hipbone, or do you prefer styles that cover up the fullest part of your hips and bottom? What shirt lengths enhance your proportions and provide the most comfort?

### COMPATIBILITY

Do some garments get a lot of wear because they coordinate well with other items in your wardrobe?

### The analysis

Now go back to your closet and take a look at the things that you seldom wear. As you compare the two sets of clothes, certain themes will begin to emerge. Notice how, when you shopped, you were attracted to a variety of styles, fabrics and colors. However, once you got those garments home, you only wore certain ones; the others were relegated to the far corners of your closet – a waste of time and money.

Analyzing the good and bad points of your current wardrobe gives you clues about where to concentrate your sewing efforts. If you focus on the clothes you love, pinpointing fabric type, color, style and fit, you will have established valuable guidelines to use in choosing patterns, fabrics and sewing techniques.

The purpose of a wardrobe analysis is not to look for clothes to duplicate (although that's not a bad idea), but rather to give you information about your best personal style. It will help you to make wise choices about what to sew and to avoid repeating the mistakes you found in the clothes you've purchased.

**TIP** Write down the good points and bad points you've discovered about the clothes from your closet. Keep the points handy as you read and act on the information in Chapters 2 and 3 on selecting patterns and fabric.

# UNDERSTANDING PATTERNS

# INTRODUCTION

Leafing through the pages of a pattern catalog is like being turned loose in a candy store. There are so many goodies to choose from, how do you select the ones that are right for you? This chapter includes some helpful tips to ensure that you make the best choices. Once selected, a pattern will include everything you need to know to make up the design, from choosing the fabric to useful sewing tips, as well as specialized fitting information. There is advice here on what you can expect from your pattern before you begin.

# SELECTING A PATTERN

One of the advantages of sewing your own clothes is that the ultimate choice of pattern-and-fabric combinations is all your own. Explore designer inspirations and learn how to make confident choices. Start your own fashion file, clipping from magazines those outfits that catch your eye. Keep a look out for pleasing design lines, great color combinations, unusual fabric mixes, and interesting trim details.

## MAKING A CHOICE

For some, sifting through the pattern catalog with its wide range of choices is pure delight; for others, choosing a pattern can be a bit overwhelming. It's really very easy if you just keep three simple criteria in mind. One, choose a style that you like. Two, choose design lines that are flattering to your figure. Three, look for design details that are compatible with your sewing skills.

### Choose a style that you like

Don't select a pattern just because the style is "in" or just because it's easy. Make sure you really like what you select. After all, half the fun of sewing is being able to show off what you have made.

### Choose a style that flatters

Be sure that the style you love is also a style that flatters. If the style you're considering is a radical departure from anything you've ever worn, it might be wise to spend some time trying on a few similar ready-to-wear garments before you purchase your fabric and pattern.

### Choose a style to match your skills

If you were learning to cook you probably wouldn't begin by making a soufflé. Instead, you'd start with something basic and gradually work your way up to more complicated recipes. Learning to sew is much the same.

### Learn to be adaptable

Occasionally it may not be possible to find a pattern that matches exactly the garment that you have selected and fallen in love with from your inspirations fashion file. So you will need to be adaptable. For example, a skirt and blouse combination may give you the same look as a dress, and have the added advantage of being able to be worn separately. Alternatively, pants and a top made from the same fabric may make a good substitute for a jumpsuit, and be easier to fit and more versatile than a one-piece garment. And, one final example, a blouse pattern that has the right lines can be lengthened to make a dress, but do be sure to buy sufficient extra fabric to accommodate the longer length.

---

**FASHION INSPIRATIONS**

✂ **The pattern catalog in-store:** This is full of ideas for coordinating separates, combining colors and prints, and picking fabrics. By studying the photographs and sketches carefully, you'll also pick up some good ideas about how to accessorize your finished garment.

✂ **The pattern catalog on subscription:** Some pattern companies make their catalogs available to sewers on a subscription basis, delivered to your door.

✂ **The pattern catalog on-line:** Also, catalogs may be available for viewing on-line so you can choose your sewing projects from a selection of the newest patterns in the comfort of your own home. (See www.simplicity.com)

✂ **Sewing magazines:** Turn to these for regular features on new patterns and fabrics.

## THE PATTERN CATALOG

As you thumb through the Simplicity® pattern catalog, you will notice how the patterns are grouped together in various ways. You'll find color bars printed along the bottom and side of each catalog page. These indicate garment or other categories, such as "Dresses", "Evening, Prom, Bridal", "Sportswear", "Home Decorating" or "Crafts", as well as special size and age ranges such as "Plus Sizes" and "Children". For easy reference, the entire color bar is printed on the extension of the back inside cover. It also appears on the inside front cover and first page of every Simplicity catalog, along with the page numbers that are assigned to each category.

In addition, there are two other pattern categories, one based on fitting techniques and the other on sewing techniques. These may have their own tabs or they may be found under the tabs for particular garment, size or age range categories.

### FIT

Patterns with logos such as FIT *for* PETITE™ are designed to help solve certain fitting dilemmas. (See Chapter 4 for more information.)

### SEWING LEVEL

If you're just learning to sew, if you're experimenting with a difficult-to-handle fabric, or if you need to sew something fast, look at patterns with logos such as 1 HOUR™ or 2 HOUR™ (which indicate sewing time, not cutting and marking time) or EASY TO SEW™. Patterns marked OVERLOCK/SERGER include instructions for sewing on the serger as well as on the conventional machine. Although these are certainly not the only patterns you can use with a serger, they're a great help when you're just learning to use this fabulous machine.

> **TIP** Every major pattern company has its own set of terms or logos to indicate its specialized patterns. If you're not sure what the terms mean, turn to the back of the pattern catalog. You'll usually find a page that includes an explanation of each category. If the category doesn't have its own section, you'll often find an index that includes a listing of the specialized patterns and their appropriate page numbers.

## THE CATALOG PAGE

The catalog page is a treasure trove of information. If you know how to read it properly, you'll be able to pick the pattern that's just right for your needs. Here's the information you will find there, keyed by number to its location on the sample catalog page that is shown overleaf.

**❶ FASHION PHOTO**
One of the views shows how the pattern will look when it is sewn. The garment may have been altered slightly to fit the model's individual proportions, but no more so than for anyone else. Therefore, you can consider the photograph an accurate guide as to how the pattern should fit. It also provides you with visual clues about what fabric weights and textures are suitable for the design.

**❷ FASHION DRAWINGS**
These show what other views or versions are included in the pattern. They may be illustrated in different colors, prints or fabric types from the photo to inspire you with more fashion and fabric ideas that are compatible with the design.

**❸ IDENTIFICATION INFORMATION**
This includes the pattern number and the price.

**❹ LOGO**
This identifies any special category for the pattern (such as EASY TO SEW™, 6 MADE EASY!™, or, as shown in the illustration on page 18, AMAZING FIT COLLECTION™).

**❺ CHART**
This gives details of the sizes the pattern comes in, a brief list of suggested fabrics and the approximate amount of fabric needed for the size range. This chart is handy if you've come to the store for fabric and you've forgotten to bring your pattern, or if you're looking for a pattern to go with a piece of fabric you already have available.

**❻ BACK VIEWS**
These show you fashion details, such as zipper, pocket or button locations, seams and darts that are not visible from the front.

NECKLINE
LAYS FLAT
AGAINST
THE BODY

BODICE
FRONT

FOLLOWS
CONTOURS
OF THE
BUST
SMOOTHLY

WAIST-
LINE
SEAM

SITS AT
THE
NATURAL
WAISTLINE

SKIRT
SEAMS

FIT
SMOOTHLY
OVER THE
BODY
SHAPE

# AmazingFit
## COLLECTION

We've done the fitting for you—
with customized pattern pieces
designed to **fit your shape!**

## Princess Seamed Dress

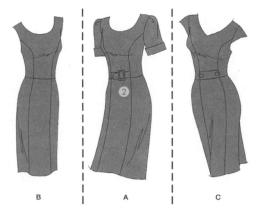

B      A      C

- Separate skirt pattern pieces for each
  figure type – slim, average or curvy
- Separate bodice front pattern pieces
  for A,B,C, D cup sizes
- 1" seam allowances in key areas to
  fine tune your fit
- Professional tips and fit–as–you-sew
  techniques
- Fit-for-Petite

A
CURVY

A
SLIM/AVERAGE

C   B
CURVY

C   B
SLIM/AVERAGE

## 0000   ◼ 🍁 A US $16.95

**Misses' / Miss Petite Dress With
Individual Pattern Pieces For Slim,
Average And Curvy Fit And For A, B, C, D
Cup Sizes**

**Señoritas / Señoritas Pequeñas: Vestido
Con Piezas Individuales Para Tallas
Delgada, Mediana Y Desarollada Y Copas
De Sostén A, B, C, D**

**Jeune Femme / Petite Jeune Femme:
Robe Avec Pièces Separées Pour Tailles
Mince, Moyenne Et Developpée Et
Bonnets De Soutien-gorge A, B, C, D**

Size: H5(6-8-10-12-14) U5(16-18-20-22-24)
Euro: H5(32-34-36-38-40) U5(42-44-46-48-50)
Fr.:   H5(34-36-38-40-42) U5(44-46-48-50-52)

Instrucciones En Español

**Simplicity®**

# THE PATTERN ENVELOPE

The outside of the pattern envelope features much the same information as the catalog page, but in greater detail. The back of the envelope, in particular, serves as a convenient shopping list for the fabric and notions you'll need to make the pattern.

## THE ENVELOPE FRONT

The front of the envelope, right, includes the same sketches and photographs that were featured on the catalog page, as well as the pattern number, the price, the size range, any identifying logos for special pattern categories and the UPC bar code.

RIGHT The envelope front.

OPPOSITE This is an example of a catalog page from the Simplicity Pattern Catalog. For an explanation of the information provided (as indicated by the circled numbers) see page 17.

SIMPLICITY
0000 SIZE H5

0 39363 32604 5

$16 95 USA
price code A code pour prix

SIMPLICITY PATTERN CO. INC., 2 PARK AVENUE, NEW YORK, NY 10016, USA
DOMINION SIMPLICITY PATTERNS LTD., 5240 FINCH AVENUE EAST, UNITS 5 AND 6, SCARBOROUGH, ONTARIO M1S 5A2, CANADA
SIMPLICITY PATTERNS PTY. LTD., 35 VIOLET STREET, REVESBY, NSW 2212, AUSTRALIA
SIMPLICITY LTD., P.O. BOX 387, CORONATION STREET, STOCKPORT, SK3 7WZ, UK
© 2009 BY SIMPLICITY PATTERN CO. INC.   PRINTED IN USA   SIMPLICITY IS A REGISTERED TRADEMARK

0000 SIZE H5 6,8,10,12,14
EUR. 32-40   FR. 34-42

Simplicity®

AmazingFit
COLLECTION

BODICE FRONT
FOLLOWS CONTOURS OF THE BUST SMOOTHLY

NECKLINE
LAYS FLAT AGAINST THE BODY

WAISTLINE SEAM
SITS AT THE NATURAL WAISTLINE

SKIRT SEAMS
FIT SMOOTHLY OVER THE BODY SHAPE

Sign-up for our free newsletter today at simplicity.com

0 39363 32604 5

B     A     C

## THE ENVELOPE BACK

The back of the envelope repeats and expands on some of the information that was on the catalog page, such as the pattern identification number and the back views, as well as supplying some new information such as the finished garment measurements. The sample envelope illustrated includes numbers keyed to the following information.

**The envelope back features important information to help you select the pattern that is right for you.**

> **TIP** Patterns are not returnable, so make sure you've got the pattern you want, in the size and figure type you need, before you pay for it.

### ❶ IDENTIFICATION INFORMATION

This includes the pattern number and the number of pattern pieces, and notes if the pattern includes French or Spanish translations. It also includes basic size category and style information, such as "Misses'/Miss Petite Dress".

### ❷ BACK VIEWS

These help clarify how the garment looks and fits.

### ❸ SUGGESTED FABRIC LIST

This expands on the information that is printed on the catalog page and is your guide to selecting the fabric that will give you the best results. See pages 30–34 for additional information.

### ❹ NOTIONS

This lists all of the extras, such as buttons, zippers, seam bindings and

**0000**

17 PIECES/PIEZAS

**Medidas e Instrucciones de costura en Español en el Interior del Patrón.**

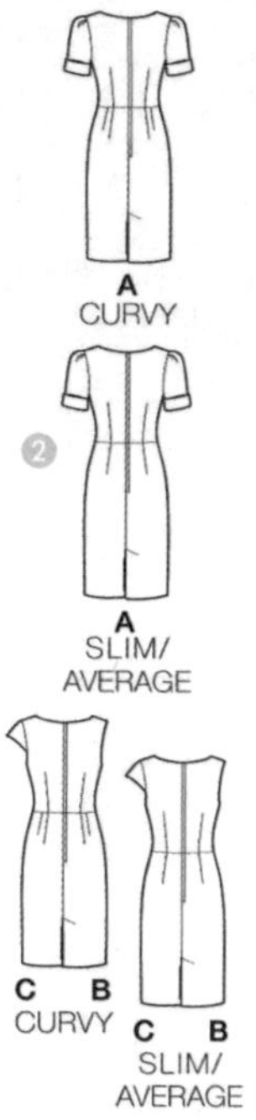


**MISSES' / MISS PETITE DRESS WITH INDIVIDUAL PATTERN PIECES FOR SLIM, AVERAGE AND CURVY FIT AND FOR A,B,C,D CUP SIZES**

**Fabrics**: Lightweight Poplin, Lightweight Sateen, Lightweight Wool and Wool Blends, Sandwashed Silk, Sueded Silks/Rayons, Silk Linen, Lightweight Double Knits, Soft Lightweight Linen and Linen Blends.
Extra fabric needed to match plaids, stripes or one-way design fabrics.

**Notions:** Thread, one 22" zipper, hook and eye. **A:** One 2" buckle. **C:** Two 1" buttons.
Look for Simplicity notions and Wrights® Trims.

| | | | | | | | | | | | |
|---|---|---|---|---|---|---|---|---|---|---|---|
| **BODY MEASUREMENTS (For Sizing Help Visit www.simplicity.com)** | | | | | | | | | | | |
| **Bust** | 30½ | 31½ | 32½ | 34 | 36 | 38 | 40 | 42 | 44 | 46 | In |
| **Waist** | 23 | 24 | 25 | 26½ | 28 | 30 | 32 | 34 | 37 | 39 | " |
| **Hip-9" below waist** | 32½ | 33½ | 34½ | 36 | 38 | 40 | 42 | 44 | 46 | 48 | In |
| **Back-neck to waist** | 15½ | 15¾ | 16 | 16¼ | 16½ | 16¾ | 17 | 17¼ | 17⅜ | 17½ | In |
| **Pattern Size** | 6 | 8 | 10 | 12 | 14 | 16 | 18 | 20 | 22 | 24 | |
| **Sizes-European** | 32 | 34 | 36 | 38 | 40 | 42 | 44 | 46 | 48 | 50 | |
| **A Dress** | | | | | | | | | | | |
| 45"*** | 2¼ | 2⅜ | 2⅜ | 2½ | 2½ | 2½ | 2⅝ | 2⅝ | 2⅝ | 2⅝ | Yd |
| 60"** | 1¾ | 1¾ | 1¾ | 1¾ | 1¾ | 2 | 2 | 2⅛ | 2⅛ | 2⅛ | " |
| **Interfacing** ½ yd. of 20" to 25" lightweight fusible | | | | | | | | | | | |
| **B Dress** | | | | | | | | | | | |
| 45"*** | 2 | 2 | 2 | 2 | 2 | 2⅛ | 2¼ | 2¼ | 2¼ | 2¼ | Yd |
| 60"*** | 1½ | 1½ | 1½ | 1½ | 1⅝ | 1⅝ | 1⅝ | 1⅝ | 1¾ | 1¾ | " |
| **Interfacing** ¾ yd. of 20" to 25" lightweight fusible | | | | | | | | | | | |
| **C Dress** | | | | | | | | | | | |
| 45"*** | 2⅛ | 2⅛ | 2¼ | 2¼ | 2¼ | 2¼ | 2⅜ | 2⅜ | 2⅜ | 2⅜ | Yd |
| 60"** | 1⅝ | 1⅝ | 1⅝ | 1⅝ | 1⅝ | 1⅝ | 1¾ | 1¾ | 1¾ | 1⅞ | " |
| **Interfacing** ⅞ yd. of 20" to 25" lightweight fusible | | | | | | | | | | | |
| **FINISHED GARMENT MEASUREMENTS (Includes Design and Wearing EASE)** | | | | | | | | | | | |
| **All Views Bust for A cup** | 33½ | 34½ | 35½ | 37 | 39 | 41 | 43 | 45 | 47 | 49 | In |
| **All Views Bust for B cup** | 34 | 35 | 36 | 37½ | 39½ | 41½ | 43½ | 45½ | 47½ | 49½ | In |
| **All Views Bust for C cup** | 34½ | 35½ | 36½ | 38 | 40 | 42 | 44 | 46 | 48 | 50 | In |
| **All Views Bust for D cup** | 35 | 36 | 37 | 38½ | 40½ | 42½ | 44½ | 46½ | 48½ | 50½ | In |
| **Hip for Slim Fit** | 35½ | 36½ | 37½ | 39 | 41 | 43 | 45 | 47 | 49 | 51 | " |
| **Hip for Average Fit** | 36 | 37 | 38 | 39½ | 41½ | 43½ | 45½ | 47½ | 49½ | 51½ | " |
| **Hip for Curvy Fit** | 36½ | 37½ | 38½ | 40 | 42 | 44 | 46 | 48 | 50 | 52 | " |
| **Finished back length from base of neck:** | | | | | | | | | | | |
| **All Views** | 37½ | 37¾ | 38 | 38¼ | 38½ | 38¾ | 39 | 39¼ | 39½ | 39¾ | In |
| **All Views Width** | 36½ | 37½ | 38½ | 40 | 42 | 44 | 46 | 48 | 50 | 52 | " |

*without nap **with nap ***with or without nap

**JEUNE FEMME / PETITE JEUNE FEMME: ROBE AVEC PIÈCES SEPARÉES POUR TAILLES MINCE, MOYENNE ET DEVELOPPÉE ET BONNETS DE SOUTIEN-GORGE A,B,C,D:**

**Tissus**: Popeline légère, Satinette légère, Laine et mélanges de laines légers, Soie lavée au sable, Rayonnes/Soies Suédées, Mélanges Soie et lin , Jersey double léger, Lin et mélanges de lin légers.
Prévoyez davantage de tissu pour raccorder les écossais, rayures ou motifs unidirectionnels.

**Mercerie**: Fil, une glissière de 55cm, une agrafe. **A:** Une boucle de 5cm. **C**: Deux boutons de 2.5cm.
Demandez la mercerie de Simplicity et les garnitures de Wrights® Trims.

| | | | | | | | | | | | |
|---|---|---|---|---|---|---|---|---|---|---|---|
| **MESURES NORMALISEES** | | | | | | | | | | | |
| **Poitrine** | 78 | 80 | 83 | 87 | 92 | 97 | 102 | 107 | 112 | 117 | cm |
| **Taille** | 58 | 61 | 64 | 67 | 71 | 76 | 81 | 87 | 94 | 99 | " |
| **Hanches (23cm au-dessous de la taille)** | 83 | 85 | 88 | 92 | 97 | 102 | 107 | 112 | 117 | 122 | cm |
| **Dos (encolure à taille)** | 39.5 | 40 | 40.5 | 41.5 | 42 | 42.5 | 43 | 44 | 44 | 44.5 | cm |
| **Tailles** | 6 | 8 | 10 | 12 | 14 | 16 | 18 | 20 | 22 | 24 | |
| **Tailles-Fr.** | 34 | 36 | 38 | 40 | 42 | 44 | 46 | 48 | 50 | 52 | |
| **A Robe** | | | | | | | | | | | |
| 115cm** | 2.10 | 2.10 | 2.20 | 2.20 | 2.30 | 2.30 | 2.30 | 2.40 | 2.40 | 2.40 | m |
| 150cm** | 1.60 | 1.60 | 1.60 | 1.60 | 1.60 | 1.80 | 1.90 | 1.90 | 1.90 | 2.00 | " |
| **Entoilage** 0.50m de 51cm à 64cm léger thermocollant | | | | | | | | | | | |
| **B Robe** | | | | | | | | | | | |
| 115cm** | 1.80 | 1.80 | 1.90 | 1.90 | 1.90 | 2.00 | 2.00 | 2.00 | 2.00 | 2.10 | m |
| 150cm** | 1.40 | 1.40 | 1.40 | 1.40 | 1.50 | 1.50 | 1.50 | 1.50 | 1.50 | 1.60 | " |
| **Entoilage** 0.60m de 51cm à 64cm léger thermocollant | | | | | | | | | | | |
| **C Robe** | | | | | | | | | | | |
| 115cm** | 2.00 | 2.00 | 2.00 | 2.00 | 2.10 | 2.10 | 2.10 | 2.20 | 2.20 | 2.20 | m |
| 150cm** | 1.50 | 1.50 | 1.50 | 1.50 | 1.50 | 1.50 | 1.50 | 1.60 | 1.60 | 1.70 | " |
| **Entoilage** 0.80m de 51cm à 64cm léger thermocollant | | | | | | | | | | | |
| **MESURES DES VETEMENTS FINIS** | | | | | | | | | | | |
| **Toutes Vues Poitrine pour Bonnet A** | 85 | 87.5 | 90 | 94 | 99 | 104 | 110 | 115 | 120 | 125 | cm |
| **Toutes Vues Poitrine pour Bonnet B** | 86.5 | 89 | 91.5 | 95 | 100.5 | 106 | 111 | 116 | 121 | 126 | cm |
| **Toutes Vues Poitrine pour Bonnet C** | 87.5 | 90 | 92.5 | 96.5 | 102 | 107 | 112 | 117 | 122 | 127 | cm |
| **Toutes Vues Poitrine pour Bonnet D** | 89 | 91.5 | 94 | 98 | 103 | 108 | 113 | 118 | 123 | 128 | cm |
| **Hanches pour Taille Mince** | 90 | 92.5 | 95 | 99 | 104 | 110 | 115 | 120 | 125 | 130 | " |
| **Hanches pour Taille Moyenne** | 91.5 | 94 | 96.5 | 100.5 | 106 | 111 | 116 | 121 | 126 | 131 | " |
| **Hanches pour Taille Développée** | 92.5 | 95 | 98 | 102 | 107 | 112 | 117 | 122 | 127 | 132 | " |
| **Longueur finie du dos depuis la base du cou** | | | | | | | | | | | |
| **Toutes Vues** | 95 | 96 | 96.5 | 97 | 98 | 98.5 | 99 | 100 | 100.5 | 101 | cm |
| **Toutes Vues Largeur** | 92.5 | 95 | 98 | 102 | 107 | 112 | 117 | 122 | 127 | 132 | " |

*sans sens **avec sens ***avec ou sans sens

shoulder pads, that you'll need to complete the garment. To save time and to ensure a close color match, you'll probably want to purchase these at the same time as you buy your fabric.

**❺ STANDARD BODY MEASUREMENTS**
These were in the back of the pattern catalog to help you determine your correct pattern size. They're repeated on the envelope as a convenient reference guide for making pattern adjustments later on. For additional information, see Chapter 4.

**❻ YARDAGE CHART**
This tells you how much fabric to buy for the size and view you want to make. Note that different yardage amounts are listed, depending on the width of the fabric and whether it is with or without nap. If a garment is made from 45in (115cm) wide fabric, it usually requires more yardage than if it is made from 60in (150cm) wide fabric. If the fabric has a texture or design that must go in one direction on the finished garment (a with nap fabric), you'll need more yardage than you would for a fabric without a nap (see note below). The yardage requirements for any lining, interfacing, elastic or trim are also included in this chart.

**NOTE**
---
\*   Indicates yardage for without nap fabrics.
\*\*  Indicates yardage for with nap fabrics.
\*\*\* Means it doesn't matter if the fabric has a nap because the pattern layout will be the same for both types of fabric.

**❼ FINISHED GARMENT MEASUREMENTS**
This information will help you judge the length or fullness of the design. For example, "Skirt width" and "Skirt length" may be included on a dress or skirt pattern. "Finished back length from base of neck" may be included on a dress or top pattern. "Pant leg width" or "Side length" may be included on trousers, shorts or culottes patterns. Depending on the type of garment, circumference measurement at the bust and/or hip will also be included. It will be helpful if you take these measurements on several

garments you already own. Write them down and take them with you when you pick out your pattern to give you a meaningful reference point for comparison.

**❽ METRIC EQUIVALENTS**
These are provided on a separate chart, opposite the Imperial chart for the yardage and notion requirements. Also included above the metric charts are the Spanish or French translations (as appropriate) of the lists of suggested fabrics and required notions.

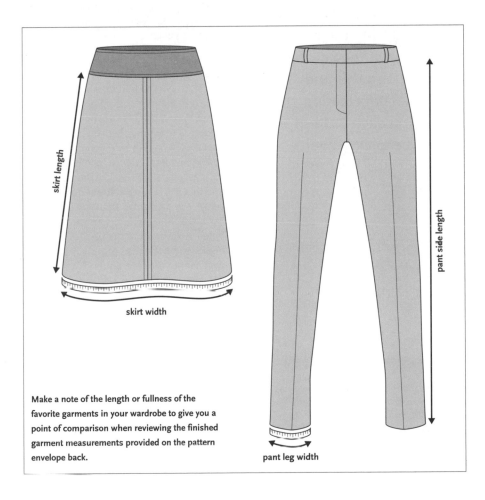

skirt length

skirt width

pant side length

pant leg width

Make a note of the length or fullness of the favorite garments in your wardrobe to give you a point of comparison when reviewing the finished garment measurements provided on the pattern envelope back.

# INSIDE THE ENVELOPE

Inside the pattern envelope are the pattern instruction sheet and all of the pattern pieces you will need to make your garment. The pattern instruction sheet guides your sewing every step of the way, from laying out and cutting the pattern to working at the sewing machine. You will find additional information printed on each pattern piece as explained here.

> **TIP** Although your pattern view may not use every piece, the total number of pattern pieces is one way to evaluate the amount of time or sewing skill a pattern will require. Use it as a guide when you're trying to decide which of two similar designs is the easiest.

## THE PATTERN INSTRUCTION SHEET

Before you purchase the pattern, it can be a good idea to review the pattern instruction sheet. If you're sewing against a deadline, and the pattern has several new techniques, you might want to make another selection. If so, refold the sheet and carefully return it to the pattern envelope.

> **NOTE** Because customers have been careless about the way they treat patterns they decide not to buy, some retailers will not permit their customers to open a pattern until they purchase it. Do ask permission first.

### Read carefully first

Once you get the pattern home, don't do any pinning or cutting until you've carefully read the instruction sheet. If there is more than one instruction sheet, each page is numbered so that you know what order to follow. Make sure you understand all of the notations and that the sewing instructions make sense. Pay particular attention to any sewing technique that is new to you. Refer to the index at the back of this book and review the sections that are pertinent to the technique.

A sample of the instruction sheet is reproduced on pages 23–24 and it includes numbers keyed to the information below.

**❶ LINE DRAWINGS**
These are simplified sketches of all the views or versions that are included in the pattern, clearly showing the design details. In addition, because the layout and the sewing instructions may vary from view to view, these drawings provide you with a convenient way to double-check the view you are following.

**❷ PATTERN PIECES**
This contains simplified diagrams of each pattern piece. Each diagram is identified by a number. Look below the drawings to find out what each number stands for, as well as what view(s) each pattern piece is used for. Put a check mark next to each piece you will need for the view you are making.

**❸ CONTACT INFORMATION**
Details are provided so you can contact Simplicity via phone, e-mail or through our Web site if you have any questions or concerns about the pattern.

**❹ GENERAL DIRECTIONS**
**The Pattern:** Explains the most common pattern symbols and how to make simple lengthen or shorten adjustments.

**Cutting/Marking:** Includes tips to make your cutting and marking easier, along with an explanation of the special cutting notes that may be included in Cutting Layouts, explained below.

**Sewing:** Defines some basic sewing procedures, including pinning, stitching, trimming and pressing a seam. For a more detailed explanation of any of these topics, turn to Chapter 5.

**❺ CUTTING LAYOUTS**
This shows you how to position the pattern pieces properly on your fabric with the least amount of waste. Layouts are given for different pattern sizes and various fabric widths. Find the diagram for your view, pattern size and fabric width, and then draw a circle around it. If you are new to sewing, or if you are using a with nap fabric, or if there is anything you don't understand about the cutting layout, review The Cutting Layout, pages 72–74. Note that the cutting layout may continue on the back of the instruction sheet.

## ❻ SEWING DIRECTIONS

These start on either the front or back of the instruction sheet, and take you step-by-step through the process of constructing the garment. The instructions are organized by garment section so that all of the stitching and pressing is completed in one area, such as the bodice for example, before going on to another. This is the fastest, easiest system for most sewers to follow. However, as you become more experienced, you may find it faster to work on several sections simultaneously, sewing as far as you can on each one until you must stop and press. This method minimizes back-and-forth trips to the ironing board. If you are going to use this faster method, it's absolutely essential that you take the time to read through the sewing directions before you begin. Otherwise, in your enthusiasm, it's all too easy to sew too far or skip a step altogether.

> **TIP** When shopping for patterns and fabrics, it's a very good idea to analyze your wardrobe beforehand, especially the clothing that makes you feel most comfortable and good about yourself. The notes you take about the styles, the types of fabrics, and the colors you like will make a useful buying guide.

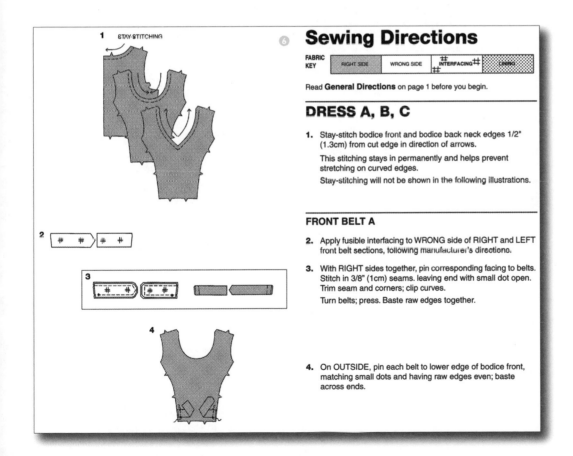

**1** STAY-STITCHING

**2**

**3**

**4**

## ❻ Sewing Directions

| FABRIC KEY | RIGHT SIDE | WRONG SIDE | INTERFACING | LINING |
|---|---|---|---|---|

Read **General Directions** on page 1 before you begin.

### DRESS A, B, C

1. Stay-stitch bodice front and bodice back neck edges 1/2" (1.3cm) from cut edge in direction of arrows.

   This stitching stays in permanently and helps prevent stretching on curved edges.

   Stay-stitching will not be shown in the following illustrations.

### FRONT BELT A

2. Apply fusible interfacing to WRONG side of RIGHT and LEFT front belt sections, following manufacturer's directions.

3. With RIGHT sides together, pin corresponding facing to belts. Stitch in 3/8" (1cm) seams. leaving end with small dot open. Trim seam and corners; clip curves.

   Turn belts; press. Baste raw edges together.

4. On OUTSIDE, pin each belt to lower edge of bodice front, matching small dots and having raw edges even; baste across ends.

# Simplicity® 0000

Thank you for purchasing this Simplicity pattern.
We have made every effort to provide you with a high quality product.
Gracias por haber comprado este patrón de Simplicity.
Hemos hecho todos los esfuerzos para ofrecerle un producto de alta calidad.

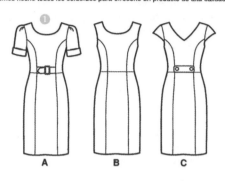

A  B  C

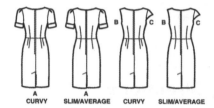

A CURVY A SLIM/AVERAGE CURVY SLIM/AVERAGE

Sign-up for our **free** @ newsletter
today at **simplicity.com**

17 pieces given

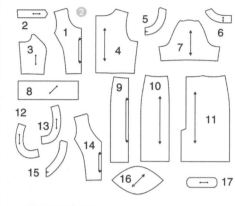

1-BODICE FRONT -A,B
2-FRONT BELT -A
3-BODICE SIDE FRONT
4-BACK
5-FRONT FACING -A,B
6-BACK FACING
7-SLEEVE -A
8-SLEEVE BAND -A
9-SKIRT FRONT
10-SKIRT SIDE FRONT
11-SKIRT BACK
12-FRONT ARMHOLE FACING -B,C
13-BACK ARMHOLE FACING -B,C
14-BODICE FRONT -C
15-FRONT FACING -C
16-FLANGE-C
17-FRONT TAB -C

# 0000
## Cutting Layouts

2/4

☐ pattern printed side down
☐ pattern printed side up

★ ✳ See SPECIAL CUTTING NOTES

POSITION OF PATTERN PIECES MAY VARY SLIGHTLY ACCORDING TO YOUR PATTERN SIZE

MISS PETITE: ADJUST PATTERN BEFORE CUTTING

## A DRESS
USE PIECES 1 2 3 4 5 6 7 8 9 10 11

**1A** 44" 45" (115CM) WITH NAP
ALL SIZES

**1B** 58" 60" (150CM)
WITH NAP
SIZES 6 8 10 12 14

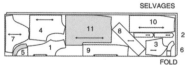

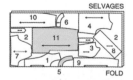

**1C** 58" 60" (150CM)
WITH NAP
SIZES 16 18 20 22 24

## INTERFACING
USE PIECES 2 5 6

**1D** 20" TO 25" (51CM TO 64CM ) FUSIBLE
ALL SIZES

## B DRESS
USE PIECES 1 3 4 5 6 9 10 11 12 13

**2A** 44" 45" (115CM)
WITH NAP
ALL SIZES

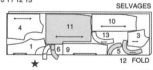

★

**2B** 58" 60" (150CM)
WITH NAP
ALL SIZES

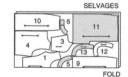

U.S. & Canada Toll-Free
**1-888-588-2700**

**Web Site**
**http://www.simplicity.com**

**E-mail**
**info@simplicity.com**

# ④ General Directions

## The Pattern

### SYMBOLS

 GRAIN LINE Place on straight grain of fabric parallel to selvage.

PLACE SOLID LINE on fold of fabric.

CENTER FRONT OR BACK of garment.

NOTCHES

° ○ DOTS

CUTTING LINE

LENGTHEN OR SHORTEN LINES

SEAM ALLOWANCE: 5/8" (1.5cm) unless otherwise stated is included but not printed on MULTI-SIZE PATTERNS. Mark your size with colored felt tip pen. See chart on tissue for how to use MULTI-SIZE PATTERNS.

### ADJUST IF NEEDED

Make adjustments before placing pattern on fabric.

**TO LENGTHEN:** Cut pattern between lengthen or shorten lines. Spread pattern evenly, the amount needed and tape to paper.

**TO SHORTEN:** At lengthen or shorten lines, make an even pleat taking up amount needed. Tape in place.

When lengthen or shorten lines are not given, make adjustments at lower edge of pattern.

## Cutting/Marking

### BEFORE CUTTING:

PRESS pattern pieces with a warm dry iron. PRE-SHRINK fabric by pre-washing washables or steam-pressing non-washables.

CIRCLE your cutting layout.

PIN pattern to fabric as shown in Cutting Layouts.

• FOR DOUBLE THICKNESS: Fold fabric with RIGHT sides together.

• FOR SINGLE THICKNESS: Place fabric RIGHT side up.

• FOR PILE, SHADED OR ONE WAY DESIGN FABRICS: Use "with nap" layouts

### AFTER CUTTING:

Transfer markings to WRONG side of fabric before removing pattern. Use pin and chalk method or dressmaker's tracing paper and wheel.

**To Quick Mark:**

• Snip edge of fabric to mark notches, ends of fold lines and center lines.

• Pin mark dots.

## Sewing

• SEW garment following **Sewing Directions.**
• PIN or machine-baste seams matching notches.
• STITCH 5/8" (1.5 cm) seams unless otherwise stated.
• PRESS seams open unless otherwise indicated clipping when necessary so seams will lie flat.
• TRIM seams to reduce bulk, as shown below.

Trim enclosed seams into layers

Trim corners

Clip inner curves

Notch outer curves

### SPECIAL CUTTING NOTES

★ If layout shows a piece extending past fold, cut out all pieces except piece that extends.

Open out fabric to single thickness. Cut extending piece on RIGHT side of fabric in position shown.

✳ Mark small arrows along both selvages indicating direction of nap or design. Fold fabric crosswise with RIGHT sides together, and cut along fold (a).

Turn one fabric layer around so arrows on both layers go in the same direction. Place RIGHT sides together (b).

---

## INTERFACING

USE PIECES 5 6 12 13

**2C** 20" TO 25" (51CM TO 64CM ) FUSIBLE ALL SIZES

 13 SELVAGES
6 5 FOLD 12

---

## C DRESS

USE PIECES 3 4 6 9 10 11 12 13 14 15 16 17

**3A** 44" 45" (115CM) WITH NAP ALL SIZES

**3B** 58" 60" (150CM) WITH NAP ALL SIZES

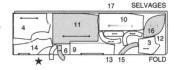

## INTERFACING

USE PIECES 6 12 13 15 17

**3C** 20" TO 25" (51CM TO 64CM ) FUSIBLE ALL SIZES

### Español

SEÑORITA PEQUEÑA: AJUSTE EL PATRÓN ANTES DE CORTAR.

**A VESTIDO** USE LAS PIEZAS 1 2 3 4 5 6 7 8 9 10 11

**1A** 44" 45" (115CM) CON PELUSA / TODAS LAS TALLAS
**1B** 58" 60" (150CM) CON PELUSA / TALLAS 6 8 10 12 14
**1C** 58" 60" (150CM) CON PELUSA / TALLAS 16 18 20 22 24

**ENTRETELA** USE LAS PIEZAS 2 5 6

**1D** 20" A 25" (51CM A 64CM ) ADHESIVA / TODAS LAS TALLAS

**B VESTIDO** USE LAS PIEZAS 1 2 4 5 6 9 10 11 12 13

**2A** 44" 45" (115CM) CON PELUSA / TODAS LAS TALLAS
**2B** 58" 60" (150CM) CON PELUSA / TODAS LAS TALLAS

**ENTRETELA** USE LAS PIEZAS 5 6 12 13

**2C** 20" A 25" (51CM A 64CM ) ADHESIVA / TODAS LAS TALLAS

**C VESTIDO** USE LAS PIEZAS 3 4 6 9 10 11 12 13 14 15 16 17

**3A** 44" 45" (115CM) CON PELUSA / TODAS LAS TALLAS

**3B** 58" 60" (150CM) CON PELUSA / TODAS LAS TALLAS

**ENTRETELA** USE LAS PIEZAS 6 12 13 15 17

**3C** 20" A 25" (51CM A 64CM ) ADHESIVA TODAS LAS TALLAS

SELVAGES = ORILLOS
FOLD = DOBLEZ

## THE PATTERN PIECES

Each pattern piece contains written directions and symbols such as dots and arrows, an easy to learn shorthand that speeds your sewing because it shows you which edges to match and where to position details. Samples of pattern pieces are reproduced below right and opposite and they include numbers keyed to the information below. Although the illustrated pattern pieces only show the information printed in English, this may also be supplied in French and Spanish on the actual patterns.

> **NOTE** The symbols with an asterisk (*) eventually get transferred onto your fabric; you'll learn more about this in Chapter 5.

### ❶ GENERAL INFORMATION
This includes the pattern number, the sizes included on the tissue, the name of the pattern piece and simple cutting directions, such as "Cut 2". An identification number is included so you can quickly tell one piece from the other. The top of the number always points to the top of the pattern piece. These numbers correspond to the ones used on the instruction sheet's diagrams and cutting layout.

### ❷ NOTCHES
These are triangular symbols extending from the cutting line into the seam allowance. To mark notches, cut triangles outward from the seam allowance at each notch position. Cutting the notches inward not only weakens the seam allowance but may also make it impossible to let out the seam later if necessary.

### ❸ SOLID LINES*
These show where buttonholes are positioned, indicate the location of the bustline, waistline and hipline, and show where to fold the fabric.

### ❹ CENTER LINE*
This is a dot-dash line that appears on some pattern pieces.

### ❺ GRAINLINE ARROW
This is used for positioning the pattern piece on the correct fabric grain.

**A straight grainline arrow:** Indicates a pattern piece that must be placed parallel to the selvage edge of your fabric.

**A squared-off grainline arrow:** Indicates a pattern piece that is placed along a folded fabric edge.

### ❻ CUTTING LINES
These are solid lines along the outer edge. Multi-Size patterns have multiple sets of lines, one for each size. Follow the cutting line that corresponds to your desired size when you cut your fabric.

### ❼ FINISHED GARMENT MEASUREMENTS
These are printed at the bustline, waistline and hipline on the appropriate pattern pieces. You'll learn how to use this information as a fitting tool in Chapter 4.

### ❽ DOTS*
These are circles that mark points to be matched before stitching. They also mark the placement of details such as darts, tabs and belt loops.

### ❾ HEM
This tells you how much fabric to turn up for the hem.

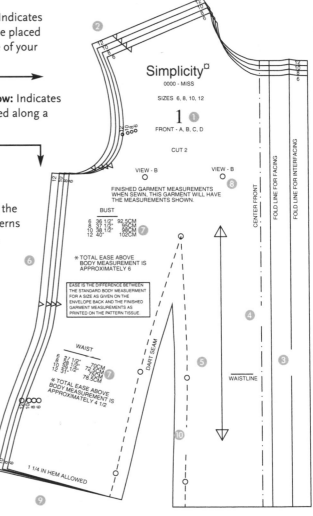

## ⑩ DARTS*

These are shown as V-shaped broken lines with dots. To sew, match the dots, folding fabric with right sides together, and stitch along the broken line. Darts shape fabric to fit over your body curves – bust, hips, shoulders.

## ⑪ LENGTHEN OR SHORTEN LINES

These are two parallel lines that indicate where to make the pattern piece longer or shorter so the finished length will be correct without distorting the garment shape. If the pattern is adjustable for petite sizes, a broken line above the lengthen or shorten line indicates where and how much to shorten the pattern.

## ⑫ TUCKS*

These are shown as broken lines with the word "tuck" in between. To sew, match the broken lines, folding the fabric with right sides together, and stitch along lines.

## ⑬ PLEATS*

These are shown as broken and solid lines with directional arrows in between, at the end of each pleat. To make a pleat, fold your fabric on the solid line and bring the fold to the broken line. Press. Baste across top of pleat.

## Seamlines

Before the advent of Multi-Size patterns, patterns came with one size per envelope and seamlines were marked on the pattern piece with broken lines. As Multi-Size patterns became more popular, pattern companies discontinued marking the seamlines because multiple cutting lines and seamlines were too confusing. Today, it is understood that, for most fashion sewing, seamlines are usually ⅝in (1.5cm) from the cutting line as explained in the General Directions section of the pattern instruction sheet. If a different seam allowance is used, it will

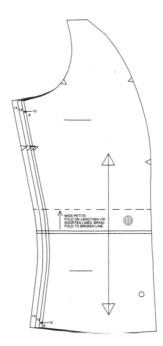

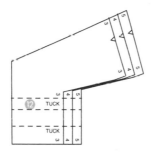

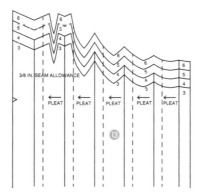

be indicated in the Sewing Directions and is often printed on the pattern piece itself. For example, a tight-fitting bodice might have 1in (2.5cm) seam allowances so there is extra room to adjust the fit; a neckline with a narrow binding might have a ¼in (6mm) seam allowance to match the seam allowance on purchased binding; home decorating and craft projects generally use ½in (1.3cm) and ¼in (6mm) seam allowances.

# A BUYER'S GUIDE

# INTRODUCTION

One of the most exciting things about sewing is being able to put fabric and pattern together to create a garment that is uniquely you – one that expresses your creativity, your wardrobe needs, your color preferences and your fashion style. The information in this chapter will enable you to select fabrics and notions with confidence, and to make informed choices about the tools and equipment you invest in – from scissors to sewing machines – to help you get the most from your sewing.

# FABRIC AND NOTIONS

**Many sewers, especially beginners, are so afraid of making a mistake that they spend hours looking for the exact fabric and notions featured in the pattern catalog. If the fabric suggested is a fabric that suits your needs, that's fine. However, if you always let someone else's taste in fabrics dictate your selection, you're missing out on half the fun of sewing.**

## SELECTING FABRICS – HOW TO BEGIN

Start by studying the fashion photograph and fashion sketches on the catalog page and pattern envelope. Notice how the fabric falls in relation to the model's figure. It might be relaxed and flowing, gently accentuating the curves of the body. It might hug the figure closely, imitating the body's contours. It might be stiff and structured, creating a silhouette that is fuller or more architectural than the body that's underneath.

Next, read the list of fabric suggestions printed on the catalog page and on the back of the pattern envelope. Because there are so many fabric blends on the market today, the suggestion list often starts by indicating the type of fabric to look for, such as "silk and silk types" or "cotton and cotton blends".

Some garments require soft, drapeable fabrics such as jersey, crepe de chine, charmeuse, challis or handkerchief linen. Other garments call for crisper, more structured fabrics such as corduroy, gabardine, suiting weight linens, taffeta, brocade or tweed. Sometimes the list of fabric suggestions may include both fabrics that are crisp, such as taffeta, and fabrics that are soft, such as dotted swiss. Because the silhouette is versatile enough for either type of fabric, the choice depends on the fashion mood you desire.

## WHEN ONLY A KNIT WILL DO

Many patterns are suitable both for wovens and for knits with a small amount of stretch, such as double knit or jersey. However, some patterns are designed exclusively for stretch knit fabrics. Most swimwear, sweatshirts and exercise wear, as well as many body-hugging silhouettes, are knits-only fashions. If you tried to use a woven fabric or a knit that did not have enough stretch, the garment would be much too tight. In fact, since many of these garments are pull-on-over-the-head or pull-up-over-the-hips styles, you probably couldn't even get them on.

On Simplicity® patterns, if it is a knits-only style, a caution under fabric suggestions will say "sized for stretch knits only". Then, printed on the back

---

**FABRIC CHOICES**

✂ When people-watching, notice how your eye is automatically drawn to garments that feature lighter or brighter colors or bold or large-scale prints.

✂ Texture too can make quite an impact, including bulky fabrics, such as tweed, mohair and fake fur; fabrics that cling, such as jersey and any fabric cut on the bias; and fabrics that attract the light, such as satins and metallics.

✂ Use what you learn from observing other people to select fabric for yourself.

✂ Choose fabrics that emphasize your good features, while minimizing your less-than-perfect ones.

✂ If you're large busted, use eye-catching fabrics for a skirt or pants, not for a top or jacket.

✂ If you're small busted, use bold patterned fabrics for your top or jacket and a plain fabric for your bottom half to help balance out your body proportions.

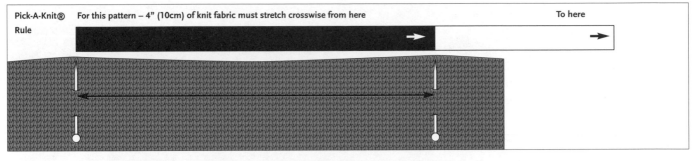

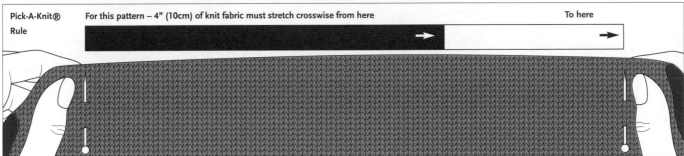

of the pattern envelope, you'll find the Pick-a-Knit® Rule, which is designed to tell you if the knit you want to use has the right amount of stretch.

## Using the Pick-a-Knit® Rule

Fold the knit fabric crosswise and hold it against the left end of the rule. Pull on the knit to see if the indicated amount of fabric (usually 4in or 10cm) will easily stretch to the end of the rule. Now let go of the fabric; it should relax to its original size and shape. If the fabric doesn't have the proper stretch and recovery, it's not the right knit for that pattern.

## FABRIC FACTORS

There's no doubt about it: shopping for fabric is fun and exciting. But before you are dazzled by a particular fabric's color, texture or print – or even its great price – there are some other things you should think about before you part with your money. Examine the information printed on the end of the cardboard bolt or on the attached hangtag. Besides telling you the width and the price per yard/meter, it will also provide you with information about fiber content, special finishes and care requirements.

## Fiber content

Fibers are divided into two categories. Natural fibers, such as cotton, linen, silk and wool, come from plants and animals. Synthetic fibers, such as acrylic, polyester and nylon, are man-made.

Fabrics made from 100 percent natural fibers are generally more comfortable, more durable and more absorbent than those made from 100 percent synthetics. Natural fibers are easier to handle during sewing. Ripples and puckers are less of a problem. When they do occur, they can often be erased with the gentle touch of a steam iron.

On the other hand, synthetic fibers are usually much easier to care for – a particularly important factor for active sportswear and children's play clothes. Most can be either hand or machine washed. Usually, they are wrinkle resistant. Once sewn, the garment rarely has to be pressed between cleanings. However, during sewing, this same characteristic sometimes makes it difficult to get synthetics to hold a crease or retain a sharp edge. You can't rely on a steam iron to do all of the work. Instead, you must use topstitching or edgestitching to hold the edges flat.

Blends combine the best features of naturals and synthetics. As a rule, the fiber that is present in the highest percentage dominates the characteristics of the fabric. The chart on page 32 tells you what performance characteristics to expect from various types of fibers.

> **TIP** Examine the labels in your favorite ready-to-wear garments. Note their fiber content and care requirements. Which ones seem to dominate your wardrobe? These are the ones to keep in mind as you select your fabric.

# FIBER FACTS

| | FIBER AND TRADENAMES | COMMON FABRIC TYPES | SPECIAL PROPERTIES | | TYPICAL CARE |
|---|---|---|---|---|---|
| | | | ADVANTAGES | DISADVANTAGES | |
| **NATURALS** | **COTTON** | Batiste, broadcloth, corduroy, denim, flannel, seersucker, sheeting, terry, velveteen | Absorbent, cool, strong | Wrinkles and shrinks (unless treated, it is weakened by mildew) | Machine wash, tumble dry; can be bleached; iron while damp |
| | **LINEN** | Damask, handkerchief, lawn, fabrics with nubby textures | Absorbent, cool, strong | Wrinkles, shrinks; weakened by mildew | Dry clean to retain crispness, or wash to soften; iron while damp |
| | **SILK** | Broadcloth, charmeuse, chiffon, crepe de chine, linen, organza, raw silk, satin | Absorbent, warm, lustrous; drapes beautifully | Weakened by sunlight and perspiration | Dry clean, although some can be hand washed; iron on wrong side at low temperature |
| | **WOOL** | Challis, crepe, flannel, gabardine, jersey, melton, tweed | Absorbent, warm; flame and wrinkle resistant; good insulation | Shrinks; attracts moths; knits tend to stretch during wear | Dry clean, although some can be machine washed; press with steam iron and press cloth on right side |
| **SYNTHETICS** | **ACETATE** Celebrate® Estron® | Satin, silk-like fabrics, taffeta, twill | Silk-like luster; drapes well; dries quickly; low cost | Fades; relatively weak; exhibits static cling; wrinkles | Dry clean or gently machine wash, tumble dry (low); iron low temperature |
| | **ACRYLIC** Acrilan®, Biokryl® Creslan®, MicroSupreme®, Orlon® | Double knits, fleece, pile fabrics, wool-like fabrics | Warm; resists wrinkles, mildew, moths and oily stains | Sensitive to heat; pills; has static cling | Machine wash, tumble dry; needs no ironing |
| | **NYLON** Anso IV®, Antron® Caprolan®, Softglow®, Tactel® | Illusion, net, tricot, two-way stretch knits (swimwear) wet-look ciré | Strong, warm, lightweight; resists moths, wrinkles and mildew | Has static cling; pills; holds body heat | Hand or machine wash, tumble dry; iron at low temperature |
| | **POLYESTER** Dacron®, EcoSpun®, Encron®, Fortrel®, Hollofil®, Kodel®, Micromattique®, Trevira® | Cotton-, silk- and wool-like fabrics, crepe, double and single knits, fleece, georgette, jersey, panne velvet, satin, taffeta | Strong, warm; very wrinkle-resistant; holds shape and a pressed crease; resists moths and mildew | Has static cling; pills; stains are hard to remove; holds body heat | Machine wash, tumble dry; needs little or no ironing |
| | **RAYON** Avril®, Modal®, Polynosic®, Zantrel® | Challis, crepe, faille, linen-like fabrics, matte jersey, velvet | Absorbent | Relatively fragile; holds body heat; wrinkles; shrinks | Dry clean or gently machine wash; iron at moderate temperature; can be bleached |
| | **SPANDEX** Cleerspan®, Glospan® Lycra®, Spandelle® | Stretch wovens; two-way stretch knits (swimwear, activewear fabrics) | Excellent stretch properties; good durability; no pilling or static cling | White fabrics may become yellow from prolonged exposure to air | Wash or dry clean; iron quickly on low temperature setting |
| | **BLENDS** | Combination of two or more fibers | Meant to bring out the best properties of each fiber included | | Care determined by most sensitive fiber |

## Permanent fabric finishes

Fabrics are often treated with special finishes that improve or alter their basic characteristics. The following are some of the most common fabric finishes. If the fabric is treated with one of these, it will be mentioned on the hangtag.

**Flame-retardant:** Resists spread of flames, required by law on children's sleepwear and home furnishings fabrics.

**Permanent press:** Sheds wrinkles after wearing or washing; needs little pressing. Cottons treated with a permanent press finish retain the look and feel of cotton without the wrinkling. However, when you sew a permanent press cotton, it will handle like a synthetic. You won't be able to use your iron to steam out any puckers. Instead, you can keep the puckers away by carefully holding the fabric taut, with one hand in front and one hand behind the presser foot as you stitch.

**Preshrunk or shrink-resistant:** Keeps later (residual) shrinkage to a minimum. However, have you ever noticed how some ready-to-wear garments labeled preshrunk develop small puckers along the stitching lines after the first washing? Even a small amount of residual shrinkage can cause this. To keep it from happening to the garments you sew, make it a practice to pretreat your fabrics according to their care labels, regardless of the finish, before cutting out your pattern. Pages 70–71 include more information on pretreating your fabric.

**Wash and wear:** Requires little or no ironing after laundering.

**Waterproof:** Fabric treated so no moisture or air can penetrate it. Garments made of waterproof fabric may keep you dry but can make you feel clammy.

---

**Water-repellent/water-resistant:** Resists absorption of liquids; they will bead on the surface. However, because air can penetrate the spaces between the yarns, fabrics with this type of finish make comfortable rainwear and running suits.

## Temporary fabric finishes

The most common temporary fabric finish is "sizing", a starch or resin added to the fabric for extra body. As it is not a permanent finish, you will not find it mentioned on the fabric label. Unbranded, bargain fabrics may be sized to make them look and feel like their more costly counterparts; but the first time these fabrics are washed, the sizing disappears, leaving you with a limp piece of goods. As it is better to discover this before you make up your garment, always pretreat your fabric. You may be able to tell by eye if the fabric has been sized. Examine the fabric carefully: if the weave is loose, but the fabric feels firm and crisp, it is a result of sizing.

## Rating a fabric's sewability

When it comes to easy sewing, not all fabrics are equal. If you are just learning to sew, or speed sewing is your goal, listed overleaf are some fabrics you may want to avoid.

✂ Don't buy a dry-clean-only trim for a garment that you intend to wash.

✂ If you're buying elastic for a swimsuit, make sure it is labeled safe for swimwear. Some elastics lose their stretch when wet; others lose their stretch or turn yellow when they come in contact with chlorine.

✂ Check buttons for care requirements. Some are dry-clean only. A few very special ones may be too fragile to risk even dry cleaning. Are you willing to remove them every time the garment is cleaned?

✂ Don't buy a trim that's too heavy for your fabric. For example, if you tried to trim a delicate chiffon with a heavy beaded trim, puckers and a sagging hemline would result.

✂ Select an interfacing that's compatible in weight and care with your fashion fabric. For a review of interfacing types and techniques, see pages 131–133.

✂ If your pattern calls for lining, make sure you're purchasing a fabric that's suitable. Since a lining is designed to protect the inside of a garment and make it easier to get the garment on and off, the lining fabric should have a smooth, slippery surface. Silk types and satins are good choices, but 100 percent silk may not be practical because, though luxurious, it is weakened by perspiration.

## NOTIONS

At the same time that you're shopping for fabric, purchase the other supplies necessary to complete your project. Review the information on the back of the pattern envelope. Look at the yardage requirements for your particular view. Note how many yards of interfacing, lining and/or trim you need to buy. Look at the Notions section. Note if, and how much, you'll need of items such as seam tape, elastic, shoulder pads, buttons, hooks and eyes, snaps, zippers, etc. As you purchase these extras, keep your fashion fabric selection in mind, and check the labels for care requirements.

**Slippery fabrics:** These are hard to handle as you cut and stitch. For best results, cut them out in a single thickness and baste whenever necessary before machine stitching.

**Loosely woven fabrics:** Because these fray easily, special seam finishes are required. However, if you own a serger, finishing the raw edges is easy.

**Sheer fabrics:** Because you can see through these, the inside of the garment must look as nice as the outside. This requires extra time and care, unless you own a serger so you can stitch narrow, finished seams in one operation.

**Thick, bulky fabrics:** These are hard to pin, sew and press.

**Fabrics with a one-way design:** The design can be difficult to match up perfectly, unless, of course, your pattern features a with nap layout.

**Pile fabrics:** Corduroy, velvet and velveteen for example. In addition to a with nap layout, these fabrics also call for special techniques to keep the layers from shifting as you pin and stitch, and – in the case of velvet – to keep the pile from being flattened as you press.

**Stripes and plaids:** It takes extra time and thought to lay out the pattern pieces so that the color bars are attractively placed and accurately matched on the finished garment. For more information on matching plaids and stripes, see Special Layouts, pages 75–76. For more information on sewing special fabrics, see Chapter 7.

**TIP** If you cannot find the fabric you are looking for at your local store, consider mail order. For names, addresses, Web sites and specific details, consult the advertising pages of your favorite sewing magazine.

**TIP** If you can't find the right color lining to exactly match your garment, don't despair. For a vivid effect, use a contrasting color; for a subtle effect, choose a neutral (gray, black, beige, white, navy) to complement the fabric.

# SEWER'S TOOLS

To get the most from your sewing, you need to invest in quality equipment for stitching, cutting and marking. This section gives you some essential tips for buying the tools for the job, whether that be pins, needles, thread, scissors or measuring aids.

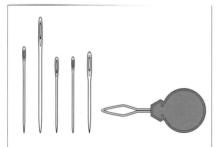

**NEEDLES FOR HAND SEWING**
Illustrated above are, from left to right:
**Sharps:** These ordinary sewing needles are available in several sizes.
**Darner:** A long needle used for darning and basting.
**Large-eye embroidery:** For thicker embroidery yarn.
**Small-eye embroidery:** For fine embroidery yarn.
**Tapestry:** This has a large eye for canvas embroidery and is useful for threading thin elastic or ribbon.
**Needle threader:** For threading even the smallest needle easily.

## STITCHING ESSENTIALS

The time to stock up on the everyday essentials is when you're in the store buying your fabric.

### Straight pins
All-purpose or dressmaker pins, in rust-proof stainless steel or brass, are good for all general pinning. Pins come with regular (flat) or round heads. Many sewers prefer round heads because they are easier to see and handle. If you have a choice between glass-headed and plastic-headed pins, choose the glass ones as they won't melt under the heat of your iron.

You can keep your pins in a plastic box – a tin may make them go rusty – but a pincushion saves having to open a box when you need a pin in a hurry. A magnetic pin dispenser is ideal.

A magnetic pin dispenser.

### Needles
Refer to your sewing machine manual to see what brands/types of needle are recommended, then keep an assortment of sizes on hand. Use the notes on the needle package as a guide to matching needle size to fabric. If you've made the wrong choice, you'll find out quickly. If the needle breaks (and you didn't sew over a pin), it's too small. If the seam draws up, or if your machine skips stitches, the needle is too large. Always

change to a new needle at the start of a new project. While you may not be able to spot a worn or bent needle, your machine will. All too often, we blame the thread or the sewing machine for our difficulties, when the real culprit is the needle. Problems such as skipped stitches, puckered seams, poor tension and thread breakage may all be the result of a damaged needle.

> **TIP** Check with your sewing machine dealer to see what needle brands he or she recommends. If a certain type of needle isn't compatible with your machine, this knowledge will save you hours of frustration.

### Thread
The most important thing to remember when purchasing thread is to buy quality thread. How do you recognize quality thread? The next time you're shopping, pick up a spool of promotional thread (the type that's offered at a price too good to be true) and compare it to a spool of more expensive, branded thread. Notice the "fuzzies" on the cheaper thread. They're a sure sign that the thread is made inexpensively from short fibers. This type of thread will fray and break as you try to stitch with it. It will also deposit little bits of lint that will eventually clog up your sewing machine.

Make sure you choose the thread that matches the job and the fabric you are working with.

### Polyester or cotton-covered polyester
**thread:** The universal recommendation for all fabrics. It's a must if you're sewing on synthetics. Use regular for general sewing, and extrafine for lightweight fabrics, such as chiffon, organdy, organza and tricot knit, as well as for machine embroidery.

**Mercerized cotton thread:** Used on fabrics with little or no stretch.

**Silk thread:** Used on silk, wool and silk-like synthetic fabrics, but, because it is expensive, sometimes hard to find and only available in a limited color range, many sewers prefer to use polyester or cotton-covered polyester.

**Special purpose or decorative threads:** Elastic, metallic and wooly nylon threads, for example, can have an important place in your sewing. In Chapter 6, you'll learn how to use these, as well as thicker "threads" such as yarn, crochet cotton or narrow knitting ribbon, to achieve special effects with both your serger and conventional machine.

**TIP** If you can't find the right color thread to match your fabric, choose one that is a shade darker. Thread usually looks lighter when sewn.

## CUTTING TOOLS

These are the basic cutting tools to get you started. As your sewing skills develop, you may want to invest in other specialty scissors and cutting tools.

**Dressmaking shears:** These have 7in or 8in(18cm or 20.5cm) blades and varied handle shapes to accommodate the configuration of your fingers for better control. On bent-handled dressmaking shears, one handle is bent at right angles so that the fabric stays flat on the table as you cut out your pattern.

**Seam ripper:** Even the most experienced seamstress makes mistakes. This pencil-thin tool with a curved blade makes it easy to remove stitches without harming the fabric.

**Embroidery scissors:** A pair of small fine-pointed scissors is very useful for those detail cutting jobs and for clipping off threads.

## MEASURING TOOLS

Accurate measuring is very important for most projects, so  the golden rule is take each measurement at least twice.

**Tape measure:** A flexible 60in (150cm) synthetic or fiberglass tape measure is your essential sewing companion.

**Yardstick or meter stick:** This 36in (1m) wooden ruler is particularly handy during pattern layout to check the grainline position (see page 74).

**Seam gauge:** A small metal ruler with sliding marker, useful for marking or checking measurements in construction (or use a 6in/15cm plastic ruler).

**NOTE** For information on fitting tools, see page 56. For information on marking tools and pressing tools, see Marking Tools, page 79, and Types of Pressing Equipment, page 118.

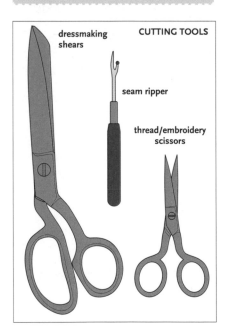

dressmaking shears

CUTTING TOOLS

seam ripper

thread/embroidery scissors

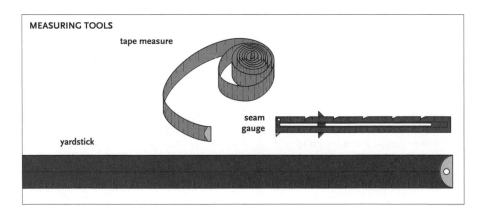

MEASURING TOOLS

tape measure

seam gauge

yardstick

# SEWING MACHINES

Although there is no one "perfect" machine, factors such as your skill level, sewing style and sewing interests will affect your final decision. If you are a beginning sewer, you may be in the market for a new or used machine. If you already have a sewing machine, it may be time to trade in your old one for a newer model, or you might consider investing in a serger to complement your conventional machine.

## BUYING A CONVENTIONAL SEWING MACHINE

Before you start seriously shopping for a sewing machine you need to ask yourself some questions.

### What is my sewing expertise?

If you are just getting started, you may only need an inexpensive machine with a range of basic stitches such as straight stitch, a few different zigzags and a buttonhole function. However, if you plan to develop your skills you will soon want a wider range of stitches, functions and accessories, and you will benefit from a machine that makes repetitive tasks, such as stitching a buttonhole and finishing off seam allowances, as simple as possible. Extra stitches and functions cannot be added later to the more basic machines, so think ahead. An already experienced sewer will probably require many more features to begin with and maybe some special functions such as dual feed, adjustable bobbin tension or the ability to compose and store embroidery patterns, so a computerized model may be worth the extra investment. Take a look at the flow chart on page 38 to determine what type of machine matches your sewing skill. The key is to be realistic so that you do not end up with more machine than you need.

### How do I rate my current machine?

Have you been pleased with its performance? Is it easy to use? What features do you wish it had? Do you want to replace it with a newer machine, one with similar features but with state-of-the-art electronics? If you have friends who sew, ask them about their machines.

### What are my sewing interests?

If everyday sewing and mending are all you expect to do, a basic mechanical machine that does a simple buttonhole and comes with a few basic attachments, such as an all-purpose presser foot, a zipper foot, a buttonhole foot and a button sewing foot, will serve you well. But if you are interested in garment construction, home decor sewing and quilting (even if these are on your

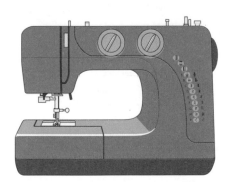

A budget electric machine has no fancy extras so it is very simple to operate. It will only have a small range of preset stitches and may not have some functions, such as the option to adjust the stitch width; however, it will be fine for basic sewing.

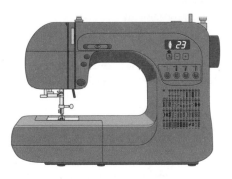

A basic computerized machine will have a wide range of preset stitches, including several buttonhole designs, and stitch width and length can be used as preset or adjusted to create special effects.

A top-of-the-range multifunctional embroidery machine will offer extra functions, such as being able to plan out large stitch sequences and the ability to embroider or quilt across a large area in sections without a visible join.

"someday" list), you'll want a machine with a greater variety of features, such as a free arm, more stitch options and more specialized presser feet.

## What are my customer service expectations?

Although today's machines are far superior to the ones our grandmothers used, there is always a possibility that your sewing machine, like any other household appliance, could break down. Conventional wisdom says to shop for a sewing machine dealer as carefully as you shop for the machine itself so that you will have a place to go for questions and lessons, as well as for repairs. Although this is still the ideal situation, our society is increasingly mobile. The best buy may not be the one closest to home and "home" may change anyhow.

There are so many other ways to buy a machine than going to a store, such as mail order, and the television shopping

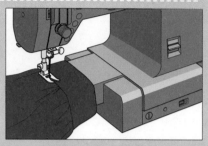

### THE DRESSMAKER'S SEWING MACHINE

The more complex the garments you want to make, the more likely it is you will need a machine with a wide range of features. Look for the following.

✂ **Free arm:** For easier sewing of sleeves and pant legs. Some flat bed machines can be converted to free arm when required by removing a section of the bed.

✂ **Serger stitch:** Used to neaten seams and hems for a professional look, but if this stitch takes the machine out of your budget range you can use a close-set zigzag stitch instead.

The free arm makes stitching narrow cylindrical items easier, and the removable section of the flat bed often doubles up as a storage box

✂ **Automatic buttonholes:** Choose a machine with a one-step buttonhole function; the ability to stitch more than one design of buttonhole will be useful.

✂ **Presser feet:** A zigzag foot, blind hem foot, concealed zipper foot and rolled hem foot should come as standard or be available as extras.

✂ **Adjustable foot pressure:** This allows you to reduce the pressure of the foot against the feed dog when sewing delicate or stretchy fabrics.

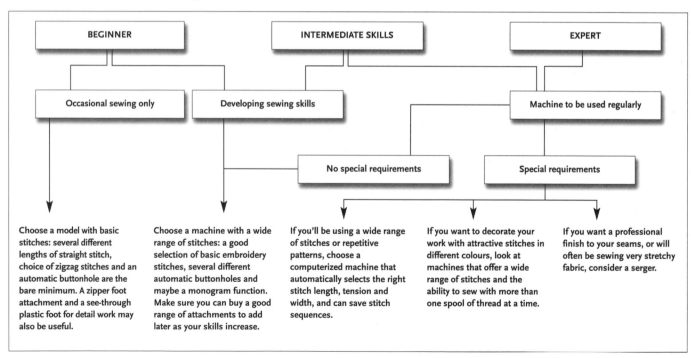

| BEGINNER | | INTERMEDIATE SKILLS | | EXPERT |
|---|---|---|---|---|

Occasional sewing only | Developing sewing skills | | Machine to be used regularly |

No special requirements | Special requirements

Choose a model with basic stitches: several different lengths of straight stitch, choice of zigzag stitches and an automatic buttonhole are the bare minimum. A zipper foot attachment and a see-through plastic foot for detail work may also be useful.

Choose a machine with a wide range of stitches: a good selection of basic embroidery stitches, several different automatic buttonholes and maybe a monogram function. Make sure you can buy a good range of attachments to add later as your skills increase.

If you'll be using a wide range of stitches or repetitive patterns, choose a computerized machine that automatically selects the right stitch length, tension and width, and can save stitch sequences.

If you want to decorate your work with attractive stitches in different colours, look at machines that offer a wide range of stitches and the ability to sew with more than one spool of thread at a time.

If you want a professional finish to your seams, or will often be sewing very stretchy fabric, consider a serger.

networks. So do check with the manufacturer if this will affect aftercare before you make a final decision. Some sewing machine manufacturers will refer you to a local dealer for service regardless of where you bought the machine; others will make arrangements for you to return the machine directly to their service center. In the case of the latter, it is important that you hold on to the machine's original carton and packing materials. If you no longer have them, ask the manufacturer about proper packing materials before sending off your machine. Never return a machine directly to the manufacturer without checking first.

**TIP** It's easy to locate a manufacturer's address and phone number. Most advertise regularly in the sewing magazines, or you can surf the Internet

## What is my price range?

Whatever your budget, there is a machine that will give you hours of sewing satisfaction. You can always start out with a modest machine and trade up as your sewing skills improve. If you have your heart set on a particular machine but can't afford the newest version, check out the classified ads, garage sales, and the online auction sites for bargains on a used machine. Be familiar with the machine before you shop so you will know if there are missing parts or feet.

## Where can I find out how to get the best from my machine?

Your sewing machine's manual is key to getting the best performance from your machine. In fact, sewing machine manufacturers estimate that 80 percent of all expensive repairs could be avoided if owners would read and follow the guidelines in the manual. If your manual

is missing, contact the manufacturer for a new one. To ensure that you get the right manual, include the model number of your machine with your request. The number is usually stamped on a small metal plate secured to the machine. On a free arm machine, the plate is located to the back of the machine; on a flat bed machine, it is located on the front.

**TIP** Visit a specialist retailer for advice on buying a sewing machine and take the chance to try out as many different models as possible. Testing the machine's buttonhole function is a good way to check that it makes even, balanced stitches in all directions. Take a variety of fabric swatches with you when you test-sew.

### TYPES OF PRESSER FEET

**Buttonhole foot:** This is useful for machine-stitched buttonholes. Most machines have an automatic program enabling you to stitch buttonholes using the general presser foot, but an automatic buttonhole foot has a special attachment that holds the button and sizes the buttonhole automatically to fit.

**Rolled or narrow hem foot:** This has a special curled piece of metal at the front, which turns the edge of light and medium-weight fabrics under and so creates a double folded hem as you stitch.

**Concealed zipper foot:** With a concealed zipper the closed opening looks like a continuous seam, giving a clean finish for special-occasion garments. Some sewing machines have a rolling zipper foot for inserting concealed zippers.

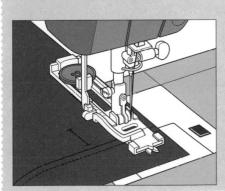

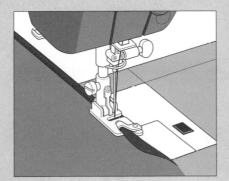

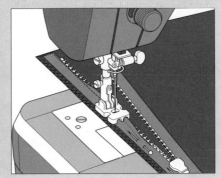

# BUYING A SERGER

A serger or overlock sewing machine can stitch a seam, trim, and finish the edge all in one step, giving a professional finish to garments and other projects. A serger is so much faster than a conventional sewing machine for such work, but it is unable to offer the full range of sewing functions such as buttonholes and topstitching for instance. However, if you are a regular sewer, the serger may be worth investing in. They can do narrow rolled hems on anything from linen napkins and tablecloths to lightweight silks and chiffons. They can clean-finish the edge of a garment, eliminating the need for facings, with a stitch that is both functional and decorative. And they perform all of these feats at a speed that's twice as fast as the fastest conventional machine. Chapters 5 and 6 are full of examples of how the serger can enhance your conventional sewing.

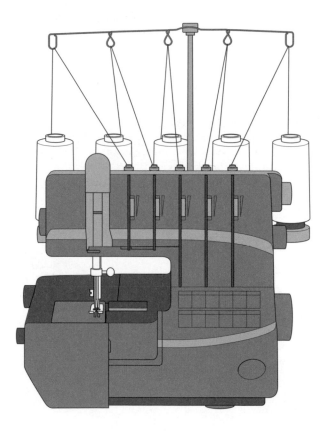

A serger stitches in a different way to a conventional sewing machine. Stitches are formed by needle threads combining with looper threads that take the place of the bobbins. Sergers can stitch with two, three, four or five threads, using different combinations of needles and loopers. A machine with the capability to handle more threads can be set up to use less, so will be more versatile.

## SERGER STITCHING

✂ Generally a serger will not replace a conventional sewing machine. However it will save you the time that you would otherwise spend finishing off raw edges and is useful for creating special effects, so it is worth investing in if you plan to do a lot of sewing.

✂ With some of the less expensive sergers, the fabric may stretch and pucker as you stitch. This is quite a common problem so be sure to try out several models before you buy.

✂ Some sergers use standard sewing machine needles, but many models use special needles, so make sure these are easy to purchase.

✂ For more sewing options, choose a machine with differential feed. This will enable you, for example, to adjust the feed when working with knits to obtain a good flat seam, to speed up the feed to create a ruffle on a single layer of woven fabric, or to create a waved edge effect.

✂ There are now several lightweight inexpensive sergers on the market, but be very wary of these. A serger is designed to sew at quite a rate, so it needs some weight to keep it firm and steady on the table. A very light machine may start to jump around as you speed up, which can be dangerous.

# A PLACE TO SEW

Everyone needs a place to sew. However, your workspace need not be as fancy or elaborate as sometimes suggested. While it is nice to dream about having a whole room devoted to sewing projects, where you can leave everything in progress and just close the door, it shouldn't hold you back from sewing if you don't have that kind of space available to you.

## MINIMUM REQUIREMENTS

All you really need to get started is a cleared-off surface for your sewing machine and a good light (an adjustable lamp is best). If possible, set up your iron and ironing board nearby to cut down on tedious trips back and forth between the sewing machine and the ironing board.

Store your sewing notions within easy reach. Put them in a sewing box, a wicker basket, a rolling cart with wire baskets, or a set of plastic organizers. If your sewing area is permanent, hang the notions you use most often from a pegboard above your sewing machine.

You'll also need a place to store all of the pieces of your project between sewing sessions. Consider an empty drawer, a large wicker basket, a large dress box, or an empty suitcase.

One final piece of equipment is a full-length mirror. If you can, put it in the same room as your sewing machine. You'll need it for the fit-as-you-go techniques you'll learn in Chapter 4.

For good sewing posture, your forearms should be at right angles to your body and the sewing bed should be at the same level as the bottom of your elbows. To achieve this you might need a higher chair or a lower table than normal. Your wrists should be resting approximately midway between your waist and chest.

## SEWING SPACE

✂ Find a convenient corner where you can keep out your equipment and work in progress without disrupting the rest of the household.

✂ The unused space under the stairs or in the eaves can often be transformed into a perfect working area – folding doors or screens can hide away all your sewing clutter.

✂ Ideally your working area should be chosen so you have the benefit of as much natural light as possible.

✂ If you work in a spare bedroom or dining room, install suitable storage so sewing projects and equipment can be stored away tidily when you need the room for other purposes.

✂ Convenient electrical outlets for sewing machine and iron, and adequate task lighting are essential.

✂ Make sure you have all the equipment you will need close at hand before you begin work. Ensure an iron and ironing board are accessible nearby for pressing.

✂ For a temporary cutting table, use a folding decorator's table or balance a board on two trestles. When not in use, dismantle and store away out of sight – behind a cupboard or under a bed, for instance.

✂ Do hang up garments under construction between work sessions so that they do not crease, and use padded hangers to prevent marking.

# A PERFECT FIT

# INTRODUCTION

Once upon a sewing time, making a muslin fitting shell was the recommended – and extremely time-consuming – way to determine if you needed to make any pattern adjustments to ensure a finished garment with a perfect fit for your body shape. Thankfully, today's sewer can say goodbye to that tedious method and turn to her tape measure instead. Getting the perfect fit begins with something so basic that you might think it's obvious – selecting the right size pattern. Too many people purchase a pattern by their ready-to-wear size, without ever looking at, or analyzing, the measurements provided in the pattern catalog.

# MEASURING YOUR BODY

**Getting the correct body measurements is key to selecting the pattern size that is right for you. As ready-to-wear sizes can alter substantially from one brand manufacturer to another, your ready-to-wear dress size cannot dictate the pattern size you require. Take your body measurements carefully, but get a friend to help.**

Few of us wear the same size pattern above and below the waistline, so all Simplicity patterns are Multi-Sized to help you get a custom fit.

## FINDING YOUR PATTERN SIZE

Most people think that they know what size they are. You may "know" that you are a size 12. But think honestly about the last time you went shopping for clothes. Did every size 12 dress, skirt or pair of pants fit you? The chances are that they did not. Each ready-to-wear manufacturer has its own set of standard measurements. That's why you might be a size 12 in some clothes, but a size smaller or larger in others.

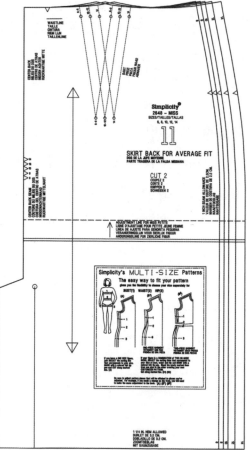

To choose the right size pattern for your body, you'll need to clear your head of any preconceived notions about what size you wear. Now follow these three simple steps.

✂ **Step 1:** Take your measurements.

✂ **Step 2:** Determine your figure type.

✂ **Step 3:** Select the pattern size within your figure type.

You may end up with a pattern size that corresponds to your ready-to-wear size, but this won't necessarily be the case; and you may even end up with a different size pattern for tops and bottoms. It is for this reason that Multi-Size patterns are so popular. A Multi-Size pattern is marked with lines to cut several different sizes of garment.

## TAKE YOUR MEASUREMENTS

You won't know where to begin to choose figure type and pattern size unless you have taken some body measurements to guide you. Using the Personal Measurement Chart opposite, record your body measurements in the column headed "Yours".

Height and back waist length will be used to determine your correct figure type. Bust, waist and hips will be used to determine your correct pattern size. The other measurements will help you fine-tune the fit of your pattern.

The procedures for determining figure type and pattern size are the same for everyone, male or female, adult or child. Basically, the same measurements are needed. The exceptions are the high bust and the shoulder-to-bust measurements (for females only) and the neck measurement (for males only). If you're sewing for a child, these measurements are not necessary.

## PERSONAL MEASUREMENT CHART

| WHAT TO MEASURE | BODY MEASUREMENTS | | ADJUSTMENT |
|---|---|---|---|
| | YOURS | SIMPLICITY STANDARDS (See charts pages 51–54) | (+ or –) |
| 1  HEIGHT (without shoes) | | | |
| 2  BACK WAIST LENGTH from prominent bone at back neck base to waist | | | |
| 3  NECK (males only) at the Adam's apple. Add ½in (1.3cm) to neck body measurement. This measurement is now the same as the ready-to-wear collar size | | | |
| 4  HIGH BUST (females only) directly under the arms, above the bust and around the back | | | |
| 5  BUST/CHEST around the fullest part | | | |
| 6  WAIST over the string (see page 47) | | | |
| 7  HIPS/SEAT* around the fullest part. See note (*) below for information pertinent to the various figure types | | | |
| 8  FRONT WAIST LENGTH from shoulder at neck base to waist (over bust point on females) | | | |
| 9  SHOULDER TO BUST (females only) from shoulder at neck base to bust point | | | |
| 10  SHOULDER LENGTH from neck base to shoulder bone | | | |
| 11  BACK WIDTH** across the midback. See note (**) below for information pertinent to the various figure types | | | |
| 12  ARM LENGTH from shoulder bone to wristbone over a slightly bent elbow | | | |
| 13  SHOULDER TO ELBOW (females only) from end of shoulder to middle of a slightly bent elbow | | | |
| 14  UPPER ARM around arm at fullest part between shoulder and elbow | | | |
| 15  CROTCH DEPTH Sit on a hard, flat chair and use a straightedge ruler. Measure from side waist to chair | | See page 56 | |
| 16  CROTCH LENGTH Measure from center back waist, between legs, to center front waist | | See page 56 | |
| 17  BACK SKIRT LENGTH (females only) Measure from center back at waist to desired length | | Measure pattern piece | |
| 18  PANTS SIDE LENGTH Measure from side waistline to desired length along outside of leg | | Measure pattern piece | |

NOTES

\*   To determine the HIP measurement, measure around the body at these distances below waist:
    MISSES' & WOMEN'S–9in (23cm)
    MISS PETITE, WOMEN'S PETITE, JUNIORS' & TEEN-BOYS–7in (18cm)
    GIRLS' & GIRLS' PLUS–5in to 7in (12.5cm to 18cm)
    BOYS'–6in (15cm)
    CHILD'S–4in to 5⅝in (10cm to 14.3cm)
    TODDLERS'–3in to 4in (7.5cm to 10cm)

\*\*   To determine the BACK WIDTH measurement, measure across the back at these distances below the neck base:
    MISSES', MISS PETITE, WOMEN'S, WOMEN'S PETITE & JUNIORS'–5in (12.5cm)
    MEN–6in (15cm)
    TEEN-BOYS'–4in (10cm)
    GIRLS', GIRLS' PLUS & BOYS'–4in (10cm)
    CHILDS'–3in (7.5cm)
    TODDLERS'–2in (5cm)

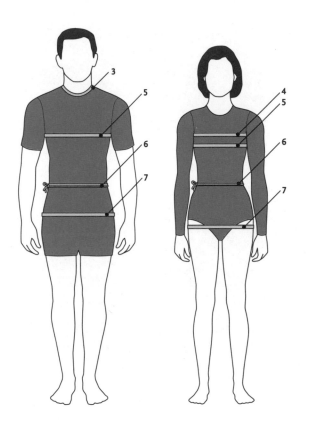

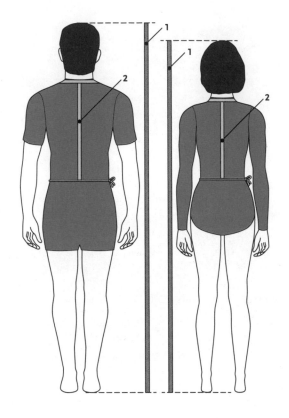

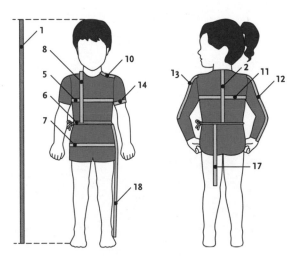

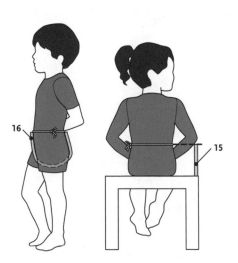

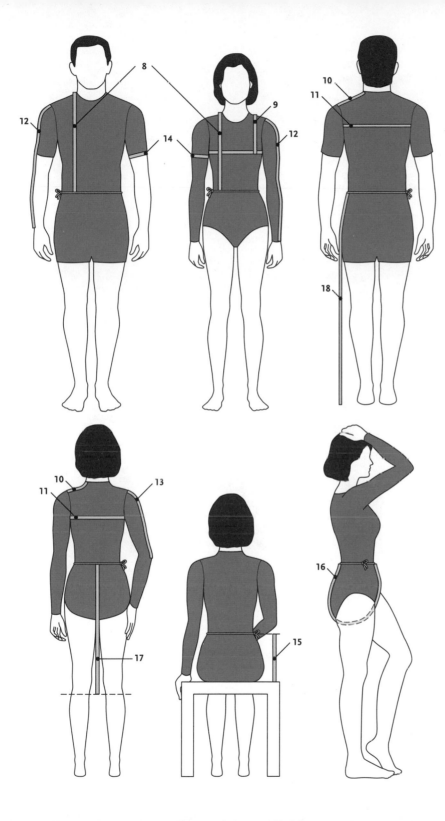

## How to measure

Don't try to take your measurements by yourself. Get a friend to help. For women and girls, take the measurements over undergarments or a leotard. For men and boys, take them over a T-shirt and shorts or unbelted, lightweight slacks. Stand in a relaxed, normal position and look straight ahead. Retake all these measurements every six months (with rapidly growing children, you will probably need to remeasure more often).

The illustrations featured left show the measurements you need to take to fill in the corresponding sections of the Personal Measurement Chart on page 45.

**To find the natural waistline:** Tie a string snugly around the waist. If the waist is hard to find (a common problem on men and children), have the person bend sideways. The crease that forms is at the natural waistline.

**To find the shoulder point:** Raise the arm to shoulder level; a dimple will form at the shoulder bone, and is the shoulder point.

**To find the back neck bone:** Bend the head forward so you can feel the first neck bone, or vertebra.

**To find the base of the neck in front:** Shrug your shoulders so that a hollow forms at the neck base.

**For the "around" measurements:** Keep the tape measure parallel to the floor; the tape should be snug, but not tight, against the body.

> **TIP** Use your flexible tape measure, and hold it at each body point so that it's comfortably snug. If the tape is cutting into your flesh, it's too tight; if you have room in between the tape and your body, it's too loose.

## DETERMINE YOUR FIGURE TYPE

Your height and back waist length (measurements 1 and 2), along with your body proportions, are the keys to determining your figure type.

To find your figure type, examine the Figure Types and the Pattern Body Measurements charts on pages 51–54. Read the figure type descriptions, study the sketches and locate the back waist length measurements. If you find two figures with similar bust, waist and hip measurements, choose the one with the back waist length measurement that is closest to your own.

**TIPS FOR ENSURING A PERFECT FIT**

✂ To select your pattern size, use your body measurements, not your ready-to-wear size.

✂ To achieve the best results, measure over the undergarments you normally wear.

✂ When taking measurements, hold the tape measure comfortably snug, but not tight.

✂ Never try to take your own measurements; always ask a friend to help.

✂ Periodically check your measurements for changes just in case your figure has changed enough to require another size pattern or different adjustments.

✂ For more help on finding your correct pattern size, download your free fit brochure – the Simplicity Fit Guide (visit Fit Help at www.simplicity.com)

✂ This brochure is also available in printed form for free in your favorite fabric and craft store. Be sure to ask for it by name if you don't see it at the check out counter or in the pattern department.

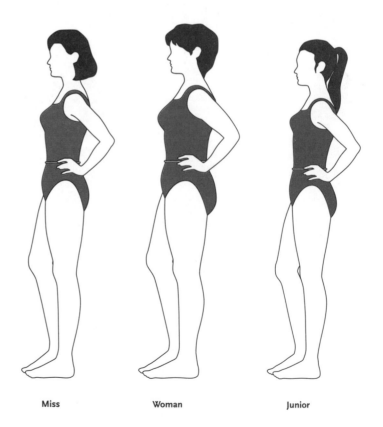

Miss          Woman          Junior

## SELECTING THE PATTERN SIZE

Compare your bust, waist and hip measurements to the ones listed for your figure type. If you're a perfect match, lucky you! You can always buy the same size pattern, regardless of what you're making. However, if like most people you are not an exact match, when selecting your pattern size, consider the type of garment being made. By varying the size according to the type of garment, you'll be able to achieve the best possible fit with the fewest adjustments or alterations (see box, right). For some of the common questions we receive about pattern size, see page 50.

### KEY MEASUREMENTS FOR PATTERN SELECTION

| TYPE OF GARMENT | KEY MEASUREMENT TO USE FOR PATTERN SELECTIONS |
|---|---|
| 1 Dress, blouse, shirt, jumpsuit, coordinated separates pattern | **Bust** for adult females. However, if there is a 2¹/₂ in (6.3cm) or more difference between your bust and your high bust, use your **high bust** measurement.<br>**Bust** for young females.<br>**Chest** or ready-to-wear **neck band** (collar) size for males. |
| 2 Suits, coats and jackets | Use same guidelines as for dress, blouse, shirt and jumpsuit. These patterns are designed with enough ease to fit over other garments. |
| 3 Pants and slim skirts | Use your hip measurement. |
| 4 Fuller skirts | Use your waist measurement. |

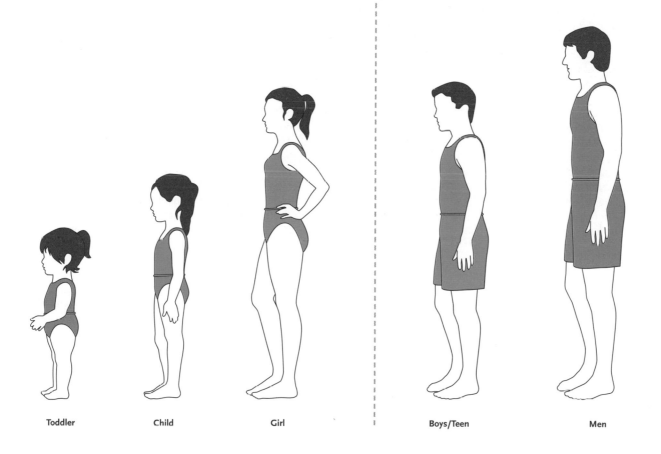

Toddler    Child    Girl    Boys/Teen    Men

## Why is my pattern size not the same as my ready-to-wear size?

This is the question we are asked most often. One of the reasons that people sew is to get a garment that fits perfectly. People come in all shapes, heights and sizes. Like ready-to-wear clothes, sewing patterns come in several different sizes to fit all of these different bodies. Patterns can come in numbered (10-12-14, etc.) or lettered (S-M-L, etc.) sizes, just like ready-to-wear garments. But the similarities in sizing end there, so it's very important to remember that pattern sizes are not the same as retail clothing sizes.

No doubt you have tried on similar skirts from two different brands, both marked with the same size, only to find that they fit differently. That's because each brand or manufacturer decides for itself what a size 8 is, what a size 10 is, and so on. Since each brand makes its own decision about sizing, there is no across-the-board standardized sizing at retail for pattern companies to match up to. This is why you can't just buy a pattern in the same size that you normally buy garments when shopping in a department store or boutique.

Unlike ready-to-wear clothes, patterns have consistent, standardized sizing from pattern brand to pattern brand. This sizing is based on the body measurements that all pattern companies have agreed to.

**TIP** Pattern sizes have not changed over the years. So a pattern size 10 from thirty years ago is based on the same body measurements as a pattern size 10 today.

## How do I know what size maternity pattern to buy?

Purchase the same size as before pregnancy or use your bust measurement. Don't buy a larger size as maternity patterns already include the required additional ease.

## What if I fall between sizes?

Choose the smaller size if you're small boned, want a closer fit or are using a knit. Choose the larger size if you're large boned, want a looser fit or are using a woven fabric.

## Why do you recommend buying most patterns by the bust size?

Sewing should be easy – and pattern adjustments are much easier to make in the waist and hip areas.

## Are there any shortcuts to adjusting a pattern if I'm a different size on top and on the bottom?

Multi-Size patterns are printed with several sizes on the same pattern tissue, which means you can use one set of cutting lines for the upper portion of your garment and another set for the lower portion.

## What size bra cup are patterns designed for ... and why do I need to take my high bust measurement?

Patterns are drafted for the B-cup figure. If your bra cup size is larger than a B, it will affect the way the pattern fits. To determine your cup size, subtract your high bust measurement from your bust measurement. If the difference is less than $2^1/2$ in (6.3cm), you're an A or B cup. If the difference is $2^1/2$ in to 3in (6.3cm to 7.5cm), you're a C cup. If it's $3^1/2$ in to 4in (9cm to 10cm), you're a D cup. If you are a B cup or smaller, purchase your pattern according to your bust measurement. If you are a C cup or larger, determine your pattern size by matching your high bust measurement to the bust measurement on the Standard Body Measurement Chart. This will ensure good fit in those hard-to-adjust areas – shoulders, neckline, chest and upper back. Follow the directions starting on page 60 to adjust the cup size.

## I'm confused about the difference between Toddlers' and Child's sizes. How do I know what figure type to look at when sewing for little ones?

Toddlers' patterns include a built-in "diaper allowance"; Child's patterns do not. The Child's figure type is also slightly taller than the Toddlers'.

## If I'm a Petite, why can't I just shorten the pattern at the hemline?

The Miss Petite and Women's Petite figures all have shorter back waist lengths and a shorter distance between waistline and hipline than the Misses' or Women's figures. Patterns with the FIT *for* PETITE™ logo have special, easy-to-follow instructions for adjusting the lengthwise proportions of the pattern to suit the Petite figure.

## How do I determine my size in Small, Medium, Large Size patterns? What about Unisex patterns?

Patterns sized small, medium and large are cut for the largest size in each designation. Unisex patterns, because they are designed to fit both men and women, use the man's chest measurement to determine the size range. For these patterns, match your bust measurement to the chest measurement.

## FEMALES: FIGURE TYPES AND PATTERN BODY MEASUREMENTS

Misses'/Miss Petite–For well-proportioned, developed figures.
Misses' about 5ft 5in (1.65m) to 5ft 6in (1.68m) tall without shoes. Miss Petite under 5ft 4in (1.63m) tall without shoes.

| INCHES | | | | | | | | | | | | Sizes | CENTIMETERS | | | | | | | | | | | |
|---|---|---|---|---|---|---|---|---|---|---|---|---|---|---|---|---|---|---|---|---|---|---|---|---|
| 4 | 6 | 8 | 10 | 12 | 14 | 16 | 18 | 20 | 22 | 24 | 26 | Sizes | 4 | 6 | 8 | 10 | 12 | 14 | 16 | 18 | 20 | 22 | 24 | 26 |
| 30 | 32 | 34 | 36 | 38 | 40 | 42 | 44 | 46 | 48 | 50 | 52 | European | 30 | 32 | 34 | 36 | 38 | 40 | 42 | 44 | 46 | 48 | 50 | 52 |
| 29½ | 30½ | 31½ | 32½ | 34 | 36 | 38 | 40 | 42 | 44 | 46 | 48 | Bust | 75 | 78 | 80 | 83 | 87 | 92 | 97 | 102 | 107 | 112 | 117 | 122 |
| 22 | 23 | 24 | 25 | 26½ | 28 | 30 | 32 | 34 | 37 | 39 | 41½ | Waist | 56 | 58 | 61 | 64 | 67 | 71 | 76 | 81 | 87 | 94 | 99 | 106 |
| 31½ | 32½ | 33½ | 34½ | 36 | 38 | 40 | 42 | 44 | 46 | 48 | 50 | Hip-9in (23cm) Below Waist | 80 | 83 | 85 | 88 | 92 | 97 | 102 | 107 | 112 | 117 | 122 | 127 |
| 15¼ | 15½ | 15¾ | 16 | 16¼ | 16½ | 16¾ | 17 | 17¼ | 17⅜ | 17½ | 17¾ | Back Waist Length | 38.5 | 39.5 | 40 | 40.5 | 41.5 | 42 | 42.5 | 43 | 44 | 44 | 44.5 | 45 |
| 14¼ | 14½ | 14¾ | 15 | 15¼ | 15½ | 15¾ | 16 | 16¼ | 16⅜ | 16½ | 16⅝ | Petite-Back Waist Length | 36 | 37 | 37.5 | 38 | 38.5 | 39.5 | 40 | 40.5 | 41.5 | 41.5 | 42 | 42 |
| 16⅜ | 16¾ | 17 | 17⅜ | 17¾ | 18 | 18⅜ | 18⅝ | 19 | 19¼ | 19⅞ | 20⅜ | Front Waist Length | 41.5 | 42.5 | 43 | 44 | 45 | 45.5 | 46.5 | 47.5 | 48.5 | 49 | 50 | 51.5 |
| 15⅜ | 15⅞ | 16⅛ | 16½ | 16¾ | 17⅛ | 17¼ | 17¾ | 18⅛ | 18⅜ | 18¾ | 19⅛ | Petite-Front Waist Length | 38.5 | 40 | 40.5 | 42 | 42.5 | 43 | 44 | 45 | 45.5 | 46.5 | 47.5 | 48.5 |
| 8⅞ | 9⅛ | 9⅜ | 9⅝ | 9⅞ | 10⅛ | 10⅜ | 10⅝ | 10⅞ | 11⅛ | 11⅜ | 11⅝ | Shoulder to Bust | 22 | 23 | 23.5 | 24.5 | 25 | 25.5 | 26 | 26.5 | 27.5 | 28 | 28.5 | 29.5 |
| 4½ | 4⅝ | 4¾ | 4⅞ | 5 | 5⅛ | 5¼ | 5⅜ | 5½ | 5⅝ | 5¾ | 5⅞ | Shoulder Length | 11.5 | 11.5 | 12 | 12 | 12.5 | 12.5 | 13.5 | 13.5 | 14 | 14 | 14.5 | 15 |
| 13½ | 13¾ | 14 | 14¼ | 14⅝ | 15¼ | 15¾ | 16 | 16½ | 16⅞ | 17⅛ | 17⅝ | Back Width | 34.5 | 35 | 35.5 | 36 | 37 | 38 | 39.5 | 40.5 | 42 | 42.5 | 43.5 | 44.5 |
| 22 | 22¾ | 23 | 23¼ | 23½ | 23¾ | 24 | 24¼ | 24½ | 24¾ | 25 | 25¼ | Arm Length | 56 | 58 | 58.5 | 59 | 59.5 | 60.5 | 61 | 61.5 | 62 | 63 | 63.5 | 64 |
| 13⅜ | 13½ | 13⅝ | 13¾ | 13⅞ | 14 | 14¼ | 14¼ | 14⅜ | 14½ | 14⅝ | 14¾ | Shoulder to Elbow | 34 | 34.5 | 34.5 | 35 | 35.5 | 35.5 | 36 | 36 | 36.5 | 36.5 | 37 | 37 |
| 8¾ | 9¼ | 9¾ | 10⅛ | 10¾ | 11¼ | 11⅜ | 12¼ | 12¾ | 13¼ | 13¾ | 14¼ | Upper Arm | 22 | 23.5 | 25 | 26 | 27.5 | 28.5 | 30 | 31 | 32.5 | 33.5 | 35 | 36 |

Women's/Women's Petite–For the larger, more fully mature figures.
Women's about 5ft 5in (1.65m) to 5ft 6in (1.68m) tall without shoes. Women's Petite under 5ft 4in (1.63m) tall without shoes.

| INCHES | | | | | | | | Sizes | CENTIMETERS | | | | | | | |
|---|---|---|---|---|---|---|---|---|---|---|---|---|---|---|---|---|
| 18W | 20W | 22W | 24W | 26W | 28W | 30W | 32W | Sizes | 18W | 20W | 22W | 24W | 26W | 28W | 30W | 32W |
| 44 | 46 | 48 | 50 | 52 | 54 | 56 | 58 | European | 44 | 46 | 48 | 50 | 52 | 54 | 56 | 58 |
| 40 | 42 | 44 | 46 | 48 | 50 | 52 | 54 | Bust | 102 | 107 | 112 | 117 | 122 | 127 | 132 | 137 |
| 33 | 35 | 37 | 39 | 41½ | 44 | 46½ | 49 | Waist | 84 | 89 | 94 | 99 | 105 | 112 | 118 | 124 |
| 42 | 44 | 46 | 48 | 50 | 52 | 54 | 56 | Hip-9in (23cm) Below Waist | 107 | 112 | 117 | 122 | 127 | 132 | 137 | 142 |
| 17⅛ | 17¼ | 17⅜ | 17½ | 17⅝ | 17¾ | 17⅞ | 18 | Back Waist Length | 43 | 44 | 44 | 44.5 | 45 | 45 | 45.5 | 46 |
| 16⅛ | 16¼ | 16⅜ | 16½ | 16⅝ | 16¾ | 16⅞ | 17 | Petite-Back Waist Length | 40.5 | 41.5 | 41.5 | 42 | 42 | 42.5 | 42.5 | 43 |
| 19⅜ | 19⅝ | 19⅞ | 20⅛ | 20⅜ | 20⅝ | 20⅞ | 21⅜ | Front Waist Length | 49 | 49.5 | 51 | 51.5 | 52 | 52.5 | 53 | 54 |
| 18⅝ | 18¾ | 19 | 19¼ | 19½ | 19¾ | 20 | 20½ | Petite-Front Waist Length | 47 | 47.5 | 48.5 | 49 | 49.5 | 50 | 51 | 52 |
| 11¾ | 12 | 12¼ | 12½ | 12¾ | 13 | 13¼ | 13½ | Shoulder to Bust | 30 | 30.5 | 31 | 32 | 32.5 | 33 | 33.5 | 34.5 |
| 4⅞ | 5 | 5 | 5⅛ | 5⅛ | 5⅛ | 5¼ | 5⅜ | Shoulder Length | 12 | 12.5 | 12.5 | 13 | 13 | 13.5 | 13.5 | 14 |
| 15¾ | 16¼ | 16¾ | 17¼ | 17¾ | 18¼ | 18¾ | 19¼ | Back Width | 40 | 41.5 | 42.5 | 44 | 45 | 46.5 | 47.5 | 49 |
| 23½ | 23¾ | 24 | 24¼ | 24½ | 24¾ | 25 | 25¼ | Arm Length | 59.5 | 60.5 | 61 | 61.5 | 62 | 63 | 63.5 | 64 |
| 14¼ | 14⅜ | 14½ | 14⅝ | 14¾ | 14⅞ | 15 | 15⅛ | Shoulder to Elbow | 36 | 36.5 | 37 | 37 | 37.5 | 37.5 | 38 | 38 |
| 13 | 13½ | 14 | 14¼ | 15 | 15½ | 16 | 16½ | Upper Arm | 33 | 34.5 | 35.5 | 37 | 38 | 39.5 | 40.5 | 42 |

# FEMALES: FIGURE TYPES AND PATTERN BODY MEASUREMENTS

JUNIORS'–A developing figure, slightly shorter than a Miss, about 5ft 3in (1.60m) to 5ft 5in (1.65m) tall, with a shorter waist length than the Miss.

| | | | | INCHES | | | | | | | | | | | | | | CENTIMETERS | | | | | | |
|---|---|---|---|---|---|---|---|---|---|---|---|---|---|---|---|---|---|---|---|---|---|---|---|
| 3/4 | 5/6 | 7/8 | 9/10 | 11/12 | 13/14 | 15/16 | 17/18 | 19/20 | 21/22 | 23/24 | Sizes | 3/4 | 5/6 | 7/8 | 9/10 | 11/12 | 13/14 | 15/16 | 17/18 | 19/20 | 21/22 | 23/24 |
| 28 | 29 | 30½ | 32 | 33½ | 35 | 36½ | 38½ | 40½ | 42½ | 44½ | Bust | 71 | 73.5 | 77.5 | 81.5 | 85 | 89 | 92.5 | 98 | 103 | 108 | 113 |
| 22 | 23 | 24 | 25 | 26 | 27 | 28 | 29½ | 31 | 33½ | 35½ | Waist | 56 | 58.5 | 61 | 63.5 | 66 | 68.5 | 71 | 75 | 78.5 | 85 | 90 |
| 31 | 32 | 33½ | 35 | 36½ | 38 | 39½ | 41½ | 43½ | 45½ | 47½ | Hip-7in (18cm) Below Waist | 78.5 | 81.5 | 85 | 89 | 92.5 | 96.5 | 100.5 | 106 | 111 | 116 | 121 |
| 13½ | 14 | 14½ | 15 | 15⅜ | 15¾ | 16⅛ | 16⅜ | 16⅝ | 16⅞ | 17⅛ | Back Waist Length | 34.5 | 35.5 | 37 | 38 | 39 | 40 | 41 | 42 | 42.5 | 43 | 43.5 |
| 14¾ | 15¼ | 15⅞ | 16⅜ | 17 | 17½ | 18⅛ | 18⅝ | 19⅛ | 19⅝ | 20⅛ | Front Waist Length | 37.5 | 38.5 | 40 | 42 | 43 | 44.5 | 45.5 | 47 | 48.5 | 49.5 | 51 |
| 8½ | 8¾ | 9⅛ | 9½ | 9¾ | 10 | 10¼ | 10½ | 10¾ | 11 | 11⅛ | Shoulder to Bust | 21.5 | 22 | 23 | 24 | 25 | 25.5 | 26 | 26.5 | 27.5 | 28 | 28.5 |
| 4 | 4⅛ | 4¼ | 4⅜ | 4½ | 4⅝ | 4¾ | 4⅞ | 5 | 5⅛ | 5¼ | Shoulder Length | 10.5 | 10.5 | 11 | 11.5 | 11.5 | 12 | 12 | 12.5 | 12.5 | 13 | 13.5 |
| 12½ | 12¾ | 13⅛ | 13½ | 13⅞ | 14¼ | 14⅞ | 15⅛ | 15⅝ | 16⅛ | 16⅜ | Back Width | 32 | 32.5 | 33 | 34.5 | 35 | 36 | 37.5 | 38.5 | 40 | 41.5 | 42.5 |
| 21¼ | 21¾ | 22⅛ | 22⅝ | 23 | 23⅜ | 23¾ | 24⅛ | 24½ | 24⅞ | 25¼ | Arm Length | 54 | 55 | 56 | 57 | 58.5 | 59.5 | 60.5 | 61 | 62 | 63 | 63.5 |
| 11¾ | 12 | 12⅜ | 12¾ | 13 | 13⅜ | 13¾ | 14⅛ | 14½ | 14⅞ | 15¼ | Shoulder to Elbow | 30 | 30.5 | 32 | 32.5 | 33 | 33.5 | 35 | 36 | 37 | 38 | 38.5 |
| 8⅞ | 9⅜ | 9⅞ | 10⅜ | 10⅞ | 11⅜ | 11¾ | 12⅛ | 12⅝ | 13 | 13⅜ | Upper Arm | 22.5 | 23.5 | 25 | 26 | 27.5 | 28.5 | 30 | 30.5 | 32 | 33 | 34 |

# CHILDREN: FIGURE TYPES AND PATTERN BODY MEASUREMENTS

TODDLERS'–For figures that are taller than Babies but shorter than Children.
Pants have a diaper allowance and often apply to both boys and girls; dresses are shorter than Children's sizes.

| | | INCHES | | | | | | CENTIMETERS | | | |
|---|---|---|---|---|---|---|---|---|---|---|---|
| ½ | 1 | 2 | 3 | 4 | Sizes | ½ | 1 | 2 | 3 | 4 |
| 19 | 20 | 21 | 22 | 23 | Chest | 48 | 51 | 53 | 56 | 58 |
| 19 | 19½ | 20 | 20½ | 21 | Waist | 48 | 50 | 51 | 52 | 53 |
| 20 | 21 | 22 | 23 | 24 | Hip | 51 | 53.5 | 56 | 58.5 | 61 |
| 7½ | 8 | 8½ | 9 | 9½ | Back Waist Length | 19 | 20.5 | 21.5 | 23 | 24 |
| 8⅜ | 8⅞ | 9⅜ | 9⅞ | 10⅜ | Front Waist Length | 21.5 | 22.5 | 24 | 25 | 26.5 |
| 2⅜ | 2½ | 2⅝ | 2¾ | 2⅞ | Shoulder Length | 6 | 6.5 | 6.5 | 7 | 7.5 |
| 7¾ | 8 | 8¼ | 8½ | 8¾ | Back Width | 19.5 | 20.5 | 21 | 21.5 | 22.5 |
| 10 | 10¾ | 11½ | 12¼ | 13 | Arm Length | 25.5 | 27.5 | 29.5 | 31 | 33 |
| 6½ | 6⅞ | 7¼ | 7⅝ | 8 | Shoulder to Elbow | 16.5 | 17.5 | 18.5 | 19.5 | 20.5 |
| 6¼ | 6½ | 6¾ | 7 | 7¼ | Upper Arm | 16 | 16.5 | 17 | 18 | 18.5 |
| 28 | 31 | 34 | 37 | 40 | Approx. Height | 71 | 79 | 87 | 94 | 102 |

# CHILDREN: FIGURE TYPES AND PATTERN BODY MEASUREMENTS (CON'T)

CHILD'S—The younger child has the same chest and waist measurements as Toddlers' but is taller with wider shoulders and back. In many instances, designs are suitable for both boys and girls.

| | INCHES | | | | | | | | | CENTIMETERS | | | | | | | |
|---|---|---|---|---|---|---|---|---|---|---|---|---|---|---|---|---|---|
| 2 | 3 | 4 | 5 | 6 | 6X | 7 | 8 | Sizes | 2 | 3 | 4 | 5 | 6 | 6X | 7 | 8 |
| 21 | 22 | 23 | 24 | 25 | 25½ | 26 | 27 | Chest | 53 | 56 | 58 | 61 | 64 | 65 | 66 | 69 |
| 20 | 20½ | 21 | 21½ | 22 | 22½ | 23 | 23½ | Waist | 51 | 52 | 53 | 55 | 56 | 57 | 58 | 60 |
| – | – | 24 | 25 | 26 | 26½ | 27 | 28 | Hip | – | – | 61 | 64 | 66 | 67 | 69 | 71 |
| 8½ | 9 | 9½ | 10 | 10½ | 10¾ | 11½ | 12 | Back Waist Length | 22 | 23 | 24 | 25.5 | 27 | 27.5 | 29.5 | 31 |
| 9⅜ | 9⅞ | 10⅜ | 10⅞ | 11⅜ | 11⅝ | 12⅝ | 13⅛ | Front Waist Length | 23.5 | 25 | 26.5 | 27.5 | 29 | 29.5 | 32 | 33 |
| 2⅞ | 3 | 3⅛ | 3¼ | 3⅜ | 3½ | 3⅝ | 3¾ | Shoulder Length | 7.5 | 7.5 | 8 | 8.5 | 8.5 | 9 | 9.5 | 10 |
| 9½ | 9¾ | 10 | 10¼ | 10½ | 10⅝ | 11½ | 11⅞ | Back Width | 24 | 24.5 | 25.5 | 26 | 26.5 | 27 | 29 | 30.5 |
| 12¾ | 13½ | 14¼ | 15 | 15¾ | 16⅛ | 17½ | 18¼ | Arm Length | 32.5 | 34.5 | 36 | 38 | 40 | 41 | 44.5 | 46.5 |
| 7¾ | 8⅛ | 8⅝ | 9 | 9½ | 9⅞ | 10⅜ | 10⅞ | Shoulder to Elbow | 20 | 21 | 22 | 23 | 24 | 25 | 26.5 | 28 |
| 6¾ | 7 | 7¼ | 7½ | 7¾ | 7⅞ | 8¼ | 8½ | Upper Arm | 17 | 18 | 18.5 | 19 | 19.5 | 20 | 21 | 21.5 |
| 35 | 38 | 41 | 44 | 47 | 48 | 50 | 52 | Approx. Height | 89 | 97 | 104 | 112 | 119 | 122 | 127 | 132 |

GIRLS'/GIRLS' PLUS—For the growing girl who has not yet begun to mature.
Girls' Plus are designed for girls over the average weight for their age and height.

| GIRLS INCHES | | | | | | GIRLS' PLUS INCHES | | | | | | GIRLS CENTIMETERS | | | | | | GIRLS' PLUS CENTIMETERS | | | | |
|---|---|---|---|---|---|---|---|---|---|---|---|---|---|---|---|---|---|---|---|---|---|---|
| 7 | 8 | 10 | 12 | 14 | 16 | 8½ | 10½ | 12½ | 14½ | 16½ | Sizes | 7 | 8 | 10 | 12 | 14 | 16 | 8½ | 10½ | 12½ | 14½ | 16½ |
| 26 | 27 | 28½ | 30 | 32 | 34 | 30 | 31½ | 33 | 34½ | 36 | Chest | 66 | 69 | 73 | 76 | 81 | 87 | 76 | 80 | 84 | 88 | 92 |
| 23 | 23½ | 24½ | 25½ | 26½ | 27½ | 28 | 29 | 30 | 31 | 32 | Waist | 58 | 60 | 62 | 65 | 67 | 70 | 71 | 74 | 76 | 79 | 81 |
| 27 | 28 | 30 | 32 | 34 | 36 | 33 | 34½ | 36 | 37½ | 39 | Hip | 69 | 71 | 76 | 81 | 87 | 92 | 84 | 88 | 92 | 96 | 96 |
| 11½ | 12 | 12¾ | 13½ | 14¼ | 15 | 12½ | 13¼ | 14 | 14¾ | 15½ | Back Waist Length | 29.5 | 31 | 32.5 | 34.5 | 36 | 38 | 32 | 34 | 35.5 | 37.5 | 39.5 |
| 12⅜ | 13 | 13⅞ | 14¾ | 15⅝ | 16½ | 12½ | 13¼ | 14 | 14¾ | 15½ | Front Waist Length | 31.5 | 33 | 35.5 | 37.5 | 39.5 | 42 | 32 | 33.5 | 35.5 | 37.5 | 39.5 |
| 6¾ | 6⅞ | 7¼ | 7⅝ | 8 | 8⅜ | 7⅜ | 7¾ | 8⅛ | 8½ | 8⅞ | Shoulder to Chest | 17 | 17.5 | 18.5 | 19.5 | 20.5 | 21.5 | 18.5 | 19 | 20.5 | 21.5 | 22.5 |
| 3⅝ | 3¾ | 4 | 4¼ | 4⅜ | 4½ | 4⅛ | 4¼ | 4½ | 4¾ | 5 | Shoulder Length | 9.5 | 9.5 | 10.5 | 10.5 | 11 | 11.5 | 10.5 | 11 | 11.5 | 12 | 12.5 |
| 11¾ | 12 | 12½ | 13 | 13½ | 14 | 12⅜ | 13 | 13⅝ | 14¼ | 14⅞ | Back Width | 30 | 30.5 | 31.5 | 33 | 34.5 | 35.5 | 32 | 33 | 34 | 36 | 37.5 |
| 17⅞ | 18½ | 19¾ | 21 | 21½ | 22 | 19 | 20½ | 22 | 23½ | 24 | Arm Length | 45.5 | 47 | 50.5 | 53.5 | 54.5 | 56 | 48.5 | 52 | 56 | 59.5 | 61 |
| 10⅝ | 11 | 11⅝ | 12¼ | 12⅜ | 12⅝ | 10¾ | 11⅛ | 12¼ | 13 | 13¼ | Shoulder to Elbow | 27 | 28 | 29.5 | 31 | 31.5 | 32 | 27.5 | 28 | 31 | 33 | 33.5 |
| 8¼ | 8½ | 9 | 9½ | 10 | 10½ | 9½ | 10 | 10½ | 11 | 11½ | Upper Arm | 21 | 21.5 | 23 | 24 | 25.5 | 26.5 | 24 | 25.5 | 26.5 | 28 | 29 |
| 50 | 52 | 56 | 58½ | 61 | 61½ | 52 | 56 | 58½ | 61 | 63½ | Approx. Height | 127 | 132 | 142 | 149 | 155 | 156 | 132 | 142 | 149 | 155 | 161 |

## MALES: FIGURE TYPES AND PATTERN BODY MEASUREMENTS

**BOYS' & TEEN BOYS'**—For growing boys and young men who have not reached full adult stature.

| INCHES | | | | | | | | | CENTIMETERS | | | | | | | |
|---|---|---|---|---|---|---|---|---|---|---|---|---|---|---|---|---|
| 7 | 8 | 10 | 12 | 14 | 16 | 18 | 20 | Sizes | 7 | 8 | 10 | 12 | 14 | 16 | 18 | 20 |
| 26 | 27 | 28 | 30 | 32 | 33½ | 35 | 36½ | Chest | 66 | 69 | 71 | 76 | 81 | 85 | 89 | 93 |
| 23 | 24 | 25 | 26 | 27 | 28 | 29 | 30 | Waist | 58 | 61 | 64 | 66 | 69 | 71 | 74 | 75 |
| 27 | 28 | 29½ | 31 | 32½ | 34¼ | 35½ | 37 | Hip | 69 | 71 | 75 | 79 | 83 | 87 | 90 | 94 |
| 11⅜ | 11¾ | 12½ | 13¼ | 14 | 14¾ | 15½ | 16¼ | Back Waist Length | 29 | 30 | 32 | 33.5 | 35.5 | 37.5 | 39 | 41 |
| 12⅜ | 12¾ | 13½ | 14¼ | 14⅝ | 15⅜ | 16⅛ | 16⅞ | Front Waist Length | 31 | 32 | 34.5 | 36 | 37 | 39 | 41 | 43 |
| 4 | 4⅛ | 4¼ | 4½ | 4¾ | 5 | 5¼ | 5½ | Shoulder Length | 10 | 10.5 | 11 | 11.5 | 12 | 12.5 | 13 | 14 |
| 11½ | 11¾ | 12½ | 12¾ | 13⅞ | 14½ | 15⅛ | 15¾ | Back Width | 29 | 30 | 31 | 32 | 35 | 37 | 38.5 | 41 |
| 16⅝ | 17¼ | 18½ | 19¼ | 21⅞ | 22½ | 23⅛ | 23¾ | Arm Length | 42 | 44 | 47 | 50 | 55.5 | 57 | 59 | 60.5 |
| 8 | 8¼ | 8¾ | 9¼ | 9¾ | 10¼ | 10¾ | 11¼ | Upper Arm | 20.5 | 21 | 22 | 23.5 | 25 | 26 | 27.5 | 28.5 |
| 11¼ | 11½ | 12 | 12½ | 13 | 13½ | 14 | 14½ | Neck | 28.5 | 29.5 | 30.5 | 32 | 33 | 34.5 | 35.5 | 36.5 |
| 11¾ | 12 | 12½ | 13 | 13½ | 14 | 14½ | 15 | Neck Band | 30 | 31 | 32 | 33 | 34.5 | 35.5 | 37 | 38 |
| 22⅜ | 23¼ | 25 | 26¾ | 29 | 30 | 31 | 32 | Shirtsleeve | 57 | 59 | 64 | 68 | 74 | 76 | 79 | 81 |
| 48 | 50 | 54 | 58 | 61 | 64 | 66 | 68 | Approx. Height | 122 | 127 | 137 | 147 | 155 | 163 | 168 | 173 |

**MEN'S**—For men of average build about 5ft 10in (1.78m) tall without shoes.

| INCHES | | | | | | | | | | | | CENTIMETERS | | | | | | | | | | |
|---|---|---|---|---|---|---|---|---|---|---|---|---|---|---|---|---|---|---|---|---|---|---|
| 32 | 34 | 36 | 38 | 40 | 42 | 44 | 46 | 48 | 50 | 52 | Sizes | 32 | 34 | 36 | 38 | 40 | 42 | 44 | 46 | 48 | 50 | 52 |
| 42 | 44 | 46 | 48 | 50 | 52 | 54 | 56 | 58 | 60 | 62 | Sizes-Eur/Fr | 42 | 44 | 46 | 48 | 50 | 52 | 54 | 56 | 58 | 60 | 62 |
| 32 | 34 | 36 | 38 | 40 | 42 | 44 | 46 | 48 | 50 | 52 | Chest | 82 | 87 | 92 | 97 | 102 | 107 | 112 | 117 | 122 | 127 | 132 |
| 27 | 28 | 30 | 32 | 34 | 36 | 39 | 42 | 44 | 46 | 48 | Waist | 66 | 71 | 76 | 81 | 87 | 92 | 99 | 107 | 112 | 117 | 122 |
| 34 | 35 | 37 | 39 | 41 | 43 | 45 | 47 | 49 | 51 | 53 | Hip | 84 | 89 | 94 | 99 | 104 | 109 | 114 | 119 | 124 | 130 | 135 |
| 17¼ | 17½ | 17¾ | 18 | 18¼ | 18½ | 18¾ | 19 | 19¼ | 19½ | 19¾ | Back Waist Length | 44 | 44.5 | 45 | 45.5 | 46.5 | 47 | 47.5 | 48.5 | 49 | 49.5 | 50.5 |
| 17½ | 17¾ | 18 | 18¼ | 18½ | 18¾ | 19 | 19¼ | 19½ | 19¾ | 20 | Front Waist Length | 44.5 | 45 | 45.5 | 46.5 | 47 | 47.5 | 48.5 | 49 | 49.5 | 50.5 | 51 |
| 6 | 6⅛ | 6¼ | 6⅜ | 6½ | 6⅝ | 6¾ | 6⅞ | 7 | 7⅛ | 7¼ | Shoulder Length | 15 | 15.5 | 15.5 | 16 | 16.5 | 16.5 | 17 | 17.5 | 17.5 | 18 | 18.5 |
| 15½ | 16 | 16½ | 17 | 17½ | 18 | 18½ | 19 | 19½ | 20 | 20½ | Back Width | 39.5 | 40.5 | 42 | 43.5 | 44.5 | 45.5 | 47 | 48.5 | 49.5 | 50.5 | 52 |
| 23⅜ | 23⅝ | 23⅞ | 24⅛ | 24⅜ | 24⅝ | 24⅞ | 25⅛ | 25⅜ | 25⅝ | 25⅞ | Arm Length | 59 | 60 | 60.5 | 61.5 | 62 | 62.5 | 63.5 | 64 | 64.5 | 65 | 65.5 |
| 10 | 10½ | 11 | 11½ | 12 | 12½ | 13 | 13½ | 14 | 14½ | 15 | Upper Arm | 25.5 | 26.5 | 28 | 29 | 30.5 | 32 | 33 | 34.5 | 35.5 | 37 | 38 |
| 13 | 13½ | 14 | 14½ | 15 | 15½ | 16 | 16½ | 17 | 17½ | 18 | Neck | 33 | 34 | 35.5 | 36.5 | 38 | 39.5 | 40.5 | 42 | 43.5 | 44.5 | 46 |
| 13½ | 14 | 14½ | 15 | 15½ | 16 | 16½ | 17 | 17½ | 18 | 18½ | Neck Band | 34.5 | 35.5 | 37 | 38 | 39.5 | 40.5 | 42 | 43 | 44.5 | 45.5 | 47 |
| 31 | 32 | 32 | 33 | 33 | 34 | 34 | 35 | 35 | 36 | 36 | Shirtsleeve | 78.5 | 81 | 81 | 84 | 84 | 87 | 87 | 89 | 89 | 91.5 | 91.5 |

## UNISEX: FIGURE TYPES AND PATTERN BODY MEASUREMENTS

**UNISEX**—For figures within Misses', Men's, Teen-Boys', Boys' and Girls' size ranges.

| INCHES | | | | | | | | CENTIMETERS | | | | | | |
|---|---|---|---|---|---|---|---|---|---|---|---|---|---|---|
| XXS | XS | S | M | L | XL | XXL | Sizes | XXS | XS | S | M | L | XL | XXL |
| 28-29 | 30-32 | 34-36 | 38-40 | 42-44 | 46-48 | 50-52 | Chest/Bust | 71-74 | 76-81 | 87-92 | 97-102 | 107-112 | 117-122 | 127-132 |
| 29-30 | 31-32½ | 35-37 | 39-41 | 43-45 | 47-49 | 51-53 | Hip | 74-76 | 79-83 | 89-94 | 99-104 | 109-114 | 119-124 | 130-135 |

# PATTERN ADJUSTMENTS

The "basic five" measurements – bust, waist, hip, height and back waist length – are those used to determine your figure type and pattern size. The Figure Types and Pattern Body Measurements charts that feature on pages 51–54, include additional measurements for pattern fitting to help you to fine-tune your garment fit.

The finished garment measurement on the pattern envelope includes the wearing ease and body ease that is built into the pattern. If you can't visualize what these measurements mean, measure and compare them with the garments you already have in your wardrobe.

## DO YOU NEED TO FINE-TUNE THE FIT?

Using the Figure Types and Pattern Body Measurements charts on pages 51–54, locate the Simplicity® standard measurements for your pattern size. Record these standards in the column headed "Simplicity Standards" of the Personal Measurement Chart on page 45. To determine if you will need any adjustments, compare your personal measurements with the Simplicity® standard. Record any differences in the column headed "Adjustment".

### Pattern ease

Don't make the mistake of thinking it's easier and more efficient to determine adjustments by comparing your measurements with the actual pattern piece measurements. Sewers who do that may find themselves in big trouble because of something called ease.

Ease, or the fullness included in a pattern design, determines how the fashion will fit and look. Patterns are designed with two types of ease – wearing ease and design ease.

The finished garment measurements that appear on the pattern tissue and the back of the pattern envelope are the sum total of three elements:

Standard Body Measurements
+
Wearing Ease
+
Design Ease
=
Finished Garment Measurements

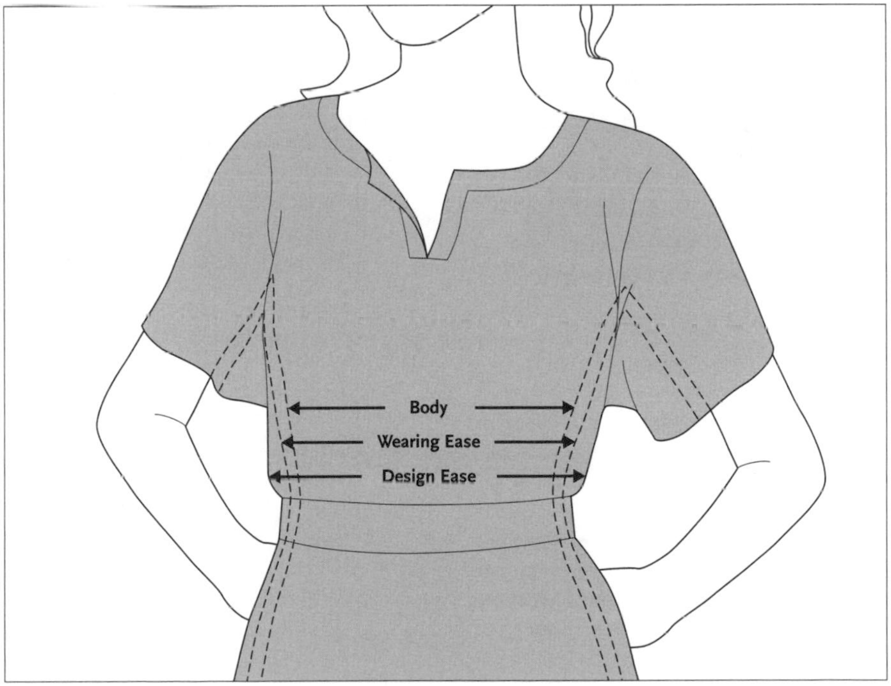

Wearing ease is the amount of "wiggle room" built into a garment. Without it, your garment would be skintight. Because this extra fullness is added to the standard body measurements when the pattern is designed, the actual pattern pieces will measure more than the standard body measurements. All garments, except swimwear and some exercise wear, contain some wearing ease. Patterns designed for knits only include less wearing ease because the fabric itself stretches to provide the necessary fit, comfort and mobility; some of these patterns will measure a bit less than the standard body measurement to accommodate for the stretch factor of the recommended knit fabric.

Design ease is fashion ease; it's the extra fullness, over and above wearing ease, that determines the garment's silhouette. In today's fashion world, there is no one contemporary silhouette. Garments that hug the body closely are just as fashionable as those that are loose and billowy.

## Stop and think: Is this adjustment really necessary?

As you review the entries you made in the Adjustments column of the Personal Measurement Chart (page 45), don't get discouraged if it looks like everything needs to be adjusted. This is not usually the case: in fact, many people have a tendency to overfit. To analyze whether or not the adjustment is necessary, keep three things in mind.

✂ The amount of the adjustment.

✂ Its location on the garment.

✂ The style of the garment

LENGTHWISE MEASUREMENTS
These are critical to the fit and proportion of a garment.

**Crotch depth and crotch length:** If either of these varies ¹/₈ in (3mm) or more from the pattern tissue measurement, you should always make the adjustment (see pages 65–67).

**Back waist length and front waist length:** Examine the silhouette and analyze the amount of the adjustment. If it's ¹/₈ in (3mm) or less, and the garment has no waistline seam and no design features below the waist, you can omit the adjustment and simply cut the hem a little bit longer. However, if the garment has any type of defined waistline, and the difference in the back waist length measurement is more than ¹/₈ in (3mm), it will be necessary to make adjustments to the pattern following the guidance on pages 57–58.

### FITTING TOOLS

In addition to your ever-present tape measure, these fitting tools will come in handy.

✂ **Gridded ruler:** A wide, clear plastic, straightedge ruler with vertical and horizontal markings is particularly helpful when you need to keep the cut edges of the pattern parallel. It can also do double duty as a T-square. Choose one that is at least 4in (10cm) wide and 14in (35cm) long.

✂ **French curve:** Sometimes called a styling curve, this is used to re-draw shaped or curved areas, such as armholes, necklines and princess seams.

✂ **Tape:** Clear cellophane tape will work just fine. Some sewers like to use a special pattern tape because it can be lifted and repositioned easily without tearing the pattern.

✂ **Paper:** Tissue paper (the type used for gift wrapping) is probably the most common paper for pattern adjustments.

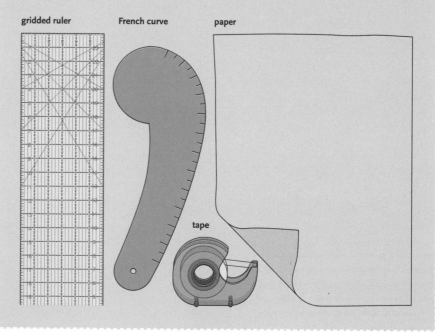

gridded ruler     French curve     paper

tape

## WIDTHWISE MEASUREMENTS

**Bust, waist and hip:** These basic circumference adjustments may or may not be necessary, depending on the amount of the difference and the silhouette of the garment. Loose-fitting silhouettes will require fewer adjustments than close-fitting ones. For adjustments of ¹/₂ in (1.3cm) or less, you can usually accommodate these by simply stitching narrower seam allowances.

**Arms and shoulders:** On long-sleeved garments, arm length is critical. On fitted garments with set-in sleeves, shoulder length is also important. If your shoulders are narrow, an alternative to pattern adjustment is to add, or use thicker, shoulder pads. If you have broad shoulders, you might want to avoid the issue altogether by choosing patterns with dropped or extended shoulders, or raglan or kimono-style sleeves.

## ADJUSTING FOR LENGTH

Special lines printed on the pattern piece indicate where to shorten or lengthen it. Sometimes you can also change the length at the lower edge.

### To shorten

**ALONG THE SHORTEN/LENGTHEN LINE**
**A1** Measure up from the printed shorten/lengthen line the amount needed; draw a new line straight across the pattern at that point.

**TIP** Don't be confused by the terms adjustment and alteration. Adjustment refers to a change made on the pattern tissue before the garment is cut out; alteration refers to a change made on the actual garment.

**A2** Fold the pattern along the printed line, bring the fold to the drawn line and pin or tape the fold in place.
**A3** Re-draw the affected cutting and stitching lines, including any darts.

**AT THE LOWER EDGE**
Measure and mark the change; then cut off the excess pattern tissue.

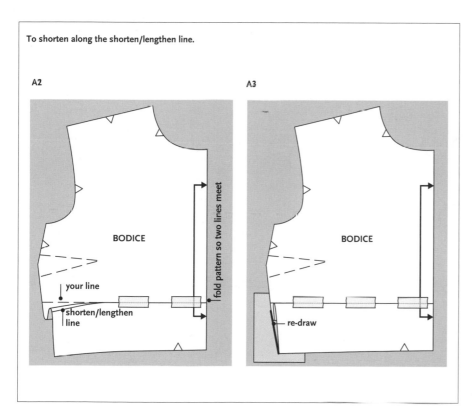

To shorten along the shorten/lengthen line.

A2

A3

BODICE

BODICE

your line

shorten/lengthen line

fold pattern so two lines meet

re-draw

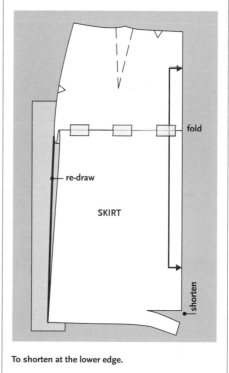

SKIRT

fold

re-draw

shorten

To shorten at the lower edge.

## To lengthen

### ALONG THE SHORTEN/LENGTHEN LINE

**B1**  Cut the pattern piece apart on the printed shorten/lengthen line. Place one portion of the pattern piece on top of a piece of paper and pin or tape in place along the printed line.

**B2**  Measure down from the printed line the amount needed; draw a line straight across the paper at that point.

**B3**  Using a ruler to keep the grainline or fold line aligned, position the printed line of the remaining pattern piece along the drawn line; pin or tape in place to the paper.

**B4**  Connect the affected cutting and stitching lines, including any darts.

### AT THE LOWER EDGE

**C1**  Pin or tape paper in place underneath the pattern.

**C2**  Extend the cutting lines evenly and re-draw the lower edge.

> **TIP**  Remember to make adjustments on all corresponding pattern pieces. For example, if you adjusted the waistline on a skirt, you must also adjust the waistband a corresponding amount.

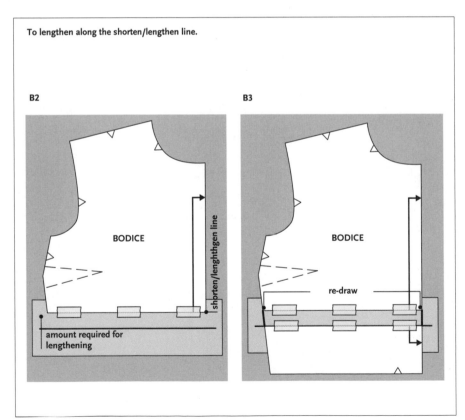

To lengthen along the shorten/lengthen line.

**B2**

BODICE

shorten/lengthten line

amount required for lengthening

**B3**

BODICE

re-draw

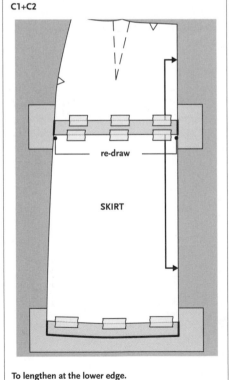

**C1+C2**

re-draw

SKIRT

To lengthen at the lower edge.

## ADJUSTING FOR WIDTH

When you're adding to the pattern, you may need to pin or tape extra paper underneath the pieces.

### Waist and hip adjustments

**TO ADJUST LESS THAN 2IN (5CM)**
Add or subtract one-quarter of the total amount at the side waist (for a waist adjustment) or the side seam (for a hip adjustment). Do this on both the front and back pattern pieces. Taper the new cutting line back to meet the original cutting line.

**TO ADJUST MORE THAN 2IN (5CM)**
First check your pattern size again – you may need a larger or smaller size. If you do need to make an adjustment, analyze the style of the garment. Adding more than 2in (5cm) at the sides may distort the design lines. If this is the case, you will be better off adjusting the pattern by slashing and spreading the front and back pattern pieces one-quarter of the total amount.

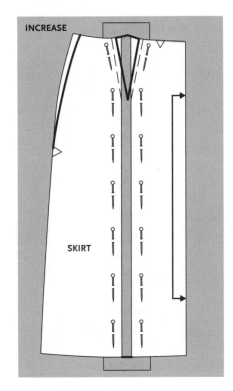

Hip adjustment (more than 2in/5cm).

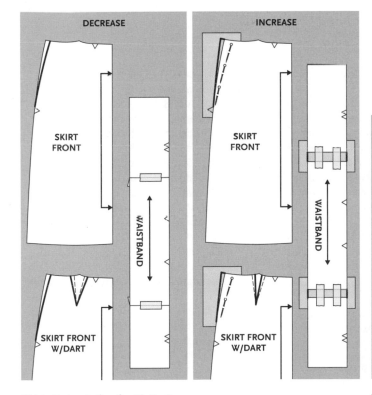

Waist adjustments (less than 2in/5cm).

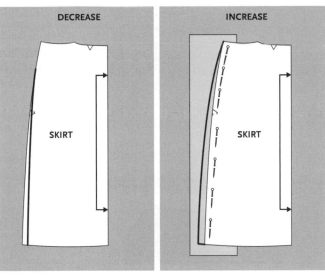

Hip adjustments (less than 2in/5cm).

## Bust adjustments

Decrease bust area if fabric puckers.

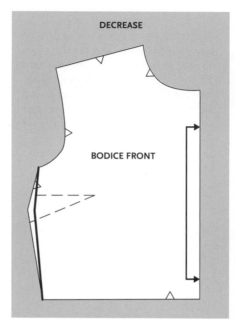

DECREASE

BODICE FRONT

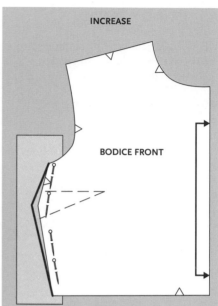

INCREASE

BODICE FRONT

Bust adjustements (up to 1in/2.5cm).

Increase bust area if fabric pulls.

**TO INCREASE OR DECREASE
UP TO 1IN (2.5CM)**
Small adjustments (up to 1in/2.5cm) may be required if you are an A cup or if you are a B-cup figure with a bust measurement that is up to 1in (2.5cm) larger than the one listed for your pattern size.
**A1** Mark half of the amount of increase or decrease at the side seam along the bustline. (For an increase place paper under the side edges.)
**A2** Draw a new cutting line, tapering up to the original line at the armhole and down to the original line at the waistline.

> **TIP** If you have narrow or uneven shoulders, or a large bust, adding shoulder pads to your garment may eliminate the need for any pattern adjustments. See Shoulder Pads, pages 169–171.

**TO INCREASE MORE THAN 1IN (2.5CM)**
If you require a larger cup (C or D), your clothes may pull across the front and perhaps across the back too. They may ride up at the front waistline where more length is needed. Since adding 1in (2.5cm) or more at the side seams will distort the fit of the garment, a different remedy is required. The first step is to create the adjustment lines on your pattern (B1–B3). Then, increase the cup size (B4–B7).
**B1** The bust point is located approximately ½in (1.3cm) from the end of the bust dart. The bust point may already be marked on your pattern or you may need to do this yourself. Once it is marked, reinforce the bust point with a piece of transparent tape.
**B2** Draw a line parallel to the center front, from the lower edge (a) through the bust point. Extend the line diagonally up to the armhole notch (b).

**B3** Draw a line from the bust point through the center of the existing underarm dart (c).

**B4** Cut along lines (a) and (b) from the bottom edge of the pattern, stopping just short of the armhole seamline. Now cut along line (c) from the side, stopping just short of the bust point.

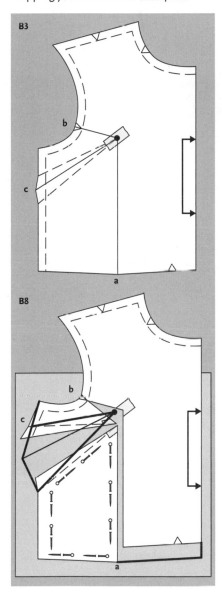

**B5** Place tissue paper under the cut edges of the pattern tissue and pin between the center front and the cut edge. Spread the pattern at the bust point, keeping the cut edges parallel below the bust point.

**For a C cup:** Spread $\frac{1}{2}$ in (1.3cm).

**For a D cup:** Spread $\frac{3}{4}$ in (2cm).

**For larger than a D cup:** Spread $1\frac{1}{4}$ in (3.2cm).

**B6** Pin or tape all the cut edges in place. Re-draw the center front edge.

**B7** Mark a new bust point at the same level as the original one, but 1in to $1\frac{1}{4}$ in (2.5cm to 3.2cm) closer to the side seam. Draw new dart lines from the side seam to the new bust point.

**B8** To re-draw the side cutting lines, pin the new dart together and fold it down. Draw over the dart, connecting the original cutting lines and, if necessary, tapering up to the armhole. Unpin the dart and re-draw the remaining cutting lines.

## Bust dart position

If your shoulder-to-bust measurement is longer or shorter than the measurement indicated for your pattern size, you may need to change the position of the pattern's bust darts.

**C1** Subtract your shoulder-to-bust measurement from the pattern's standard measurement. This will tell you how much you need to raise or lower the dart.

**C2** Trace the original dart area, including the bust point, from the pattern tissue onto another piece of tissue.

**C3** Tape the traced dart in place on the pattern tissue at the appropriate level, keeping the old and new bust points aligned vertically. Re-draw the side cutting lines, as appropriate.

**TIP** Before changing the bust dart position do make sure that it is necessary – it may only appear to be wrong simply because of poorly fitting or unsupportive underwear.

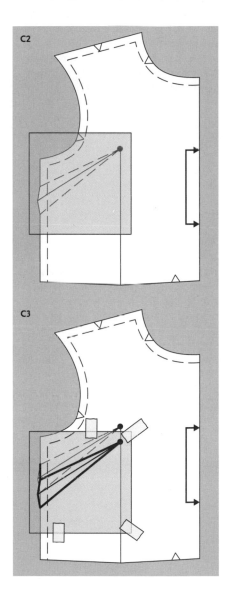

## Shoulder length

To adjust up to ¼in (6mm), mark the amount inside (to shorten) or outside (to lengthen) the shoulder seam at the armhole. Draw a new cutting line, tapering to the original line at the armhole notch. Do this on both the front and back pattern pieces.

Because this adjustment may affect the way the sleeve hangs on the finished garment, baste the sleeve in place first and try on the garment. If necessary, pull out the basting stitches and reposition the sleeve until it hangs properly; then permanently stitch it in place.

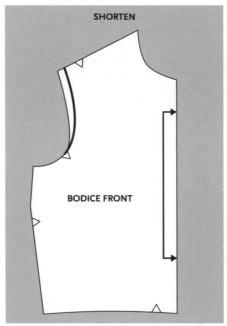
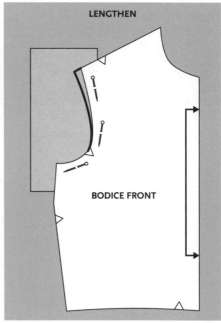

Shoulder length.

## Back width

To adjust up to 1in (2.5cm), mark half of the amount needed inside (to decrease) or outside (to increase) the armhole cutting line. Do this above the notch on the back pattern piece only. Do not adjust the front. Draw a new cutting line, starting at the mark and tapering up to the shoulder and down to the underarm.

This adjustment may affect the hang of the sleeve. Be sure to baste in the sleeve and try on the garment before permanently stitching the sleeve in place.

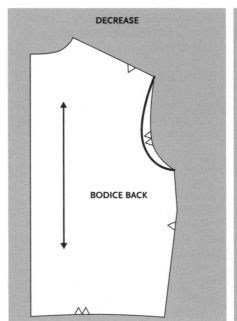
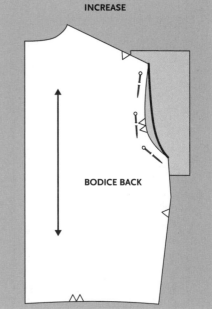

Back width up to 1in/2.5cm.

## Rounded back

Whether the cause is poor posture or body changes that occur over time, a rounded back can cause your garment to wrinkle across the back shoulders and ride up at the back waistline. If the problem is severe, you may also have a noticeable bump at the back of your neck, which is called a dowager's hump. If this is the case, the garment's neckline will stand away from the body. The adjustment is similar for both, although instructions are given separately for the dowager's hump, below.

**D1** Begin by drawing in the seamlines on the bodice back pattern piece. At the point where your back curve is most prominent, draw a horizontal line that extends from the center back just to the armhole seam and is at right angles to the grainline. Mark the midpoint on this line.

**D2** Draw a diagonal line from the middle of the shoulder to the midpoint mark. (If there is a shoulder dart, draw the line through the dart.)

**D3** Slash along the horizontal line just to, but not through, the armhole seamline. Slash along the diagonal line just to, but again not through, the horizontal line.

**D4** Place paper under the pattern, and keeping the center back aligned, spread along the horizontal slash until you have added the indicated amount. The pattern will automatically open along the diagonal slash to create a new or deeper dart. Pin or tape the cut edges in place. Clip the armhole seam allowance, if necessary, to make the pattern lie flat. Draw new stitching lines in the dart area and new cutting lines.

## Dowager's hump

**E1** At the point where your back curve is most prominent, draw a horizontal line that extends from the center back just to the armhole seam and is at right angles to the grainline. Mark the midpoint on this line.

**E2** Draw a diagonal line from the middle of the neckline to the midpoint.

**E3** Slash along the horizontal line just to, but not through, the armhole seamline. Slash along the diagonal line just to, but not through, the horizontal line.

**E4** Place paper under the pattern and keeping the center back aligned, spread along the horizontal slash until you have added the indicated amount. The

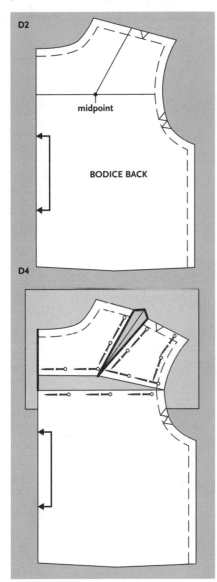

**Rounded back.**

**Dowager's hump.**

pattern will automatically open along the diagonal slash to create a new or deeper dart. Pin or tape the cut edges in place. Clip the armhole seam allowance, if necessary, to make the pattern lie flat. Draw new stitching lines in the dart area and new cutting lines.

## Full upper arm

Make this adjustment if you need more width in the upper sleeve.

**F1**   Draw in the seamlines and hemline on the sleeve pattern piece.

**F2**   Now draw a horizontal line that extends across the bottom of the sleeve cap, between the seamlines, and is at right angles to the grainline. Draw a vertical line that extends from the black dot at the top of the sleeve to the hemline and is parallel to the grainline.

**F3**   Place the sleeve pattern on top of a large sheet of tissue paper and trace around the sleeve cap cutting line.

**F4**   Slash along both lines just to, but not through, the seamlines and hemline.

**F5**   At the point where the slashes intersect, spread the pattern until the bicep area is at least equal to your upper arm measurement plus 2in (5cm) for wearing ease. Clip the seam allowances at the cap and underarm seams, as necessary, to make the cap lie flat as the horizontal slashed lines overlap. Pin or tape the cut edges in place.

**F6**   Draw a vertical line from the dot at the top of the sleeve cap to the slash line at the hemline. Draw a new grainline parallel to this line.

**F7**   Use the traced sleeve cap as the new cutting line.

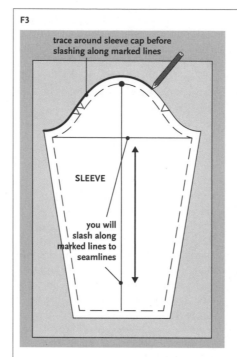

F3

trace around sleeve cap before slashing along marked lines

SLEEVE

you will slash along marked lines to seamlines

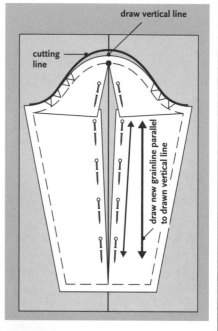

F6

draw vertical line

cutting line

draw new grainline parallel to drawn vertical line

## SOME PANTS ADJUSTMENTS

Pants should fit smoothly and comfortably with enough room to move, bend and sit easily. The crotch depth and crotch length must be the correct ones for your body or else the pants will bind or sag.

The way your ready-to-wear pants fit provides clues to the type of adjustments you may have to make. If yours "smile" when you're standing, that is if there are wrinkles that point up from the crotch area, then they are too tight in the crotch area. If they "frown", they are too loose. Smiles or frowns can occur in the front or the back, depending on your figure.

Take another look at the Figure Types and the Pattern Body Measurements charts (pages 51–54). Note that the standards for crotch depth and length are not included. Now, remember the earlier rule about never measuring the actual pattern pieces? Well, here's the exception to that rule. For an accurate fit, you must compare your body measurements with the actual pattern pieces.

### Crotch depth

**NOTE** Check and adjust the crotch depth first, before checking and adjusting the crotch length. This is important otherwise your pants won't fit properly.

To check the crotch depth on your pattern, measure from the crotch line up to the waistline seam. Your measurement line should be close to the side seam, but parallel to the grainline. This measurement should be equal to your crotch depth, plus ¹/₂ in or 1.3cm of ease for hips up to 36in (91.5cm) wide. Larger sizes may need to include up to 1¹/₄ in (3.2cm) of ease.

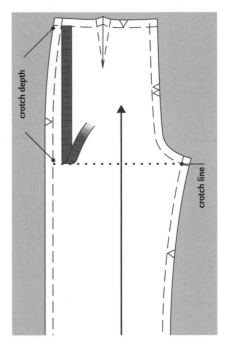

**Crotch depth measurement**

**When wrinkles point down the crotch is too loose.**

**When wrinkles point up the crotch is too tight.**

To lengthen or shorten the crotch depth, use the shorten/lengthen line on the pattern piece. Follow the procedures described for Adjusting for Length, pages 57–58, slashing and spreading the pattern pieces to lengthen, or lapping them to shorten.

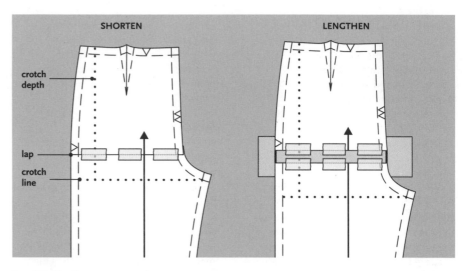

Crotch depth adjustment.

## Crotch length

Once you've checked and made any changes in the crotch depth, stand a tape measure or flexible ruler on end and measure along the stitching line of the center front and center back seams of your pants pattern. Measure from the waistline seam to the inner leg seam on both the front and back pattern pieces. Add these two measurements together to get the pattern's crotch length.

The pattern's crotch length should be equal to your crotch length measurement plus 1½in to 2in (3.8cm to 5cm). This extra amount is the ease you need to be able to sit down.

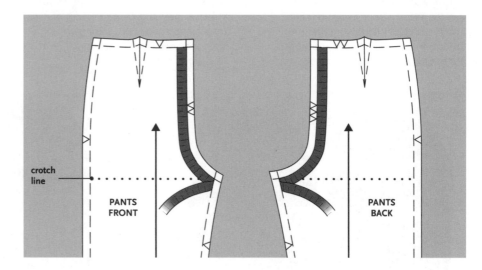

Crotch length measurement.

**TIP** Remember that stitching lines are not marked on Multi-Size patterns. In order to make accurate adjustments, you may need the stitching lines as a reference point. To create stitching lines on your pattern, measure and mark ⅝in (1.5cm) in from the appropriate cutting lines, as indicated in the illustrations for each adjustment.

Before you make any adjustments on the pattern tissue, stand sideways and take a look in the mirror. You can divide the difference in half and make an equal adjustment on the front and the back of the pants. However, depending on your shape, you can also divide it unevenly between the front and back. In fact, if you're round in the front and flat in the back, you might want to add the entire amount to the front; if you're "normal" in front but have a very flat bottom, you could subtract the entire amount from the back. Experience and your own good judgment are your best guides.

Lengthen or shorten the crotch by adding or subtracting half the adjustment amount at the inner leg seam.

## FITTING AS YOU SEW

Because fabric is not the same as tissue paper, you can't be guaranteed a good fit simply by making the indicated adjustments on your pattern tissue. As you sew, stop at least twice to try on the garment, and allow for the first fitting once the main garment seams are sewn.

Be sure to wear the undergarments that you plan to wear with the finished outfit (it is amazing how a change of bra can alter the fit of a garment, for example). If the pattern calls for shoulder pads, be sure to have a set available for your fittings. In fact, have several sets in different thicknesses. The right thickness of shoulder pad can solve many a fitting dilemma.

If the garment is a fitted or semi-fitted style, it might be a good idea to try it on with the major garment seams only basted together. Then, if alterations are required, you won't have to rip out any permanent stitching.

If you anticipate fitting problems in the sleeve area, baste them in first. Try the garment on a second time before permanently setting in the sleeves.

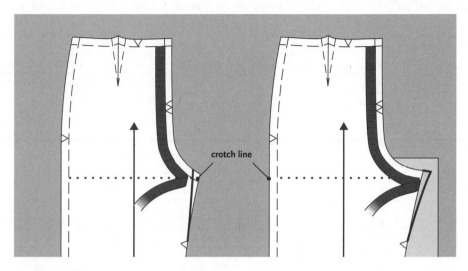

Crotch length adjustment.

**If the sleeve cap twists toward the back:** Reset the sleeve, moving the center forward of the shoulder seam and redistributing the ease until the sleeve cap hangs smoothly.

**If the sleeve cap twists toward the front:** Reset the sleeve, moving the center behind the shoulder seam and redistributing the ease until the sleeve cap hangs smoothly.

**If there is excess fullness in the sleeve cap:** Reset the sleeve, taking a deeper seam allowance in the sleeve cap.

The final fitting should be to check the length before the garment is hemmed. Be sure to wear the same height heel, if not the same shoes, as you plan to wear with the finished garment. It's the smartest way to ensure pleasing lengthwise proportions.

# UNIVERSAL
# BASICS

# INTRODUCTION

No matter what style pattern you choose, what fabric catches your eye, or what your level of sewing skill, there are certain "universal basics" that are common to almost any project you make. Much of what you'll learn in this and the two chapters that follow will challenge some of traditional sewing's hard-and-fast rules. Fortunately, today's sewer can have it both ways – easy techniques and professional results – by combining serger sewing with conventional sewing.

# PATTERN CUTTING

The first step, before you can even think about cutting out your garment, is preparing your fabric. This includes preshrinking, straightening, and folding of the fabric prior to pinning out the project pattern. Only then are you ready to cut out. From outlining standard pattern layouts to exploring special layouts, this section covers all you need to know.

## FABRIC PREPARATION

Have you ever purchased a ready-to-wear garment that turned into a total disaster after its first laundering or dry cleaning? When you make your own clothes, it's easy to prevent these unpleasant (and expensive) surprises .

### Preshrinking the fabric

Your first task is to preshrink the fabric. The simplest preshrinking method is to put washable fabrics in the washing machine and take dry-clean-only fabrics to the dry cleaner. Pay attention to each manufacturer's recommendations for water temperature, drying cycle or dry-cleaning solvents.

If the fabric is marked "sponged" or "preshrunk", or if the label says it will shrink less than 1 percent, you may be tempted to omit this step. However, shrinkage control is not the only reason you should pretreat your fabric. By preshrinking, you can discover a fabric's true character. For example, some fabrics contain special finishes or sizings that dissolve the first time the fabric is cleaned. If you skip the preshrinking step, you won't discover this until your once-crisp garment comes out soft and limp after its first wash. If you're a fabric collector, make it a habit to preshrink your yardage before you put it away. Then it's always "needle ready".

Notions such as tapes, braids, zippers, linings and interfacings may require preshrinking too. Read the labels and check the fiber content. Trims, braids and zipper tape made from 100 percent polyester do not need to be preshrunk. Although most interfacings should be preshrunk, many fusibles do not require it. Always check each manufacturer's information.

> **TIP** Some knits contain sizings that will cause your sewing machine to skip stitches. Preshrinking removes these sizings and eliminates the problem.

## A GLOSSARY OF FABRIC TERMS

✂ **Selvage:** One of two finished lengthwise edges on a piece of fabric. These edges, which will not fray, are usually a little stiffer and firmer than the crosswise, cut edges of the fabric.

✂ **Straight, or lengthwise, grain:** Refers to the threads (in a woven) or the ribs (in a knit) that are parallel to the selvages. Pattern pieces are usually laid out along the lengthwise grain because it has the least stretch and is the most stable.

✂ **Crosswise grain:** Refers to the threads that run across the fabric between the two selvages, perpendicular to the lengthwise threads or ribs. Fabric stretches more on the crosswise than on the lengthwise grain.

✂ **Bias:** Any diagonal direction.

✂ **True bias:** The diagonal edge formed when fabric is folded so that the lengthwise and crosswise grains match. Fabric has the greatest amount of stretch along the true bias.

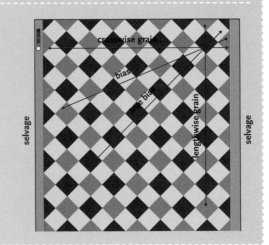

## Straightening the fabric

The ideal fabric is "on-grain" with lengthwise and crosswise yarns that are exactly perpendicular to one another.

One of the recurring myths of sewing is that every fabric should be straightened so that it is perfectly on-grain before the pattern pieces are cut out. Otherwise, the theory goes, the finished garment will have out-of-kilter seams and a drooping hem – the result of yarn's natural tendency to hang perpendicular to the floor. This was true before the advent of knits, modern synthetics and wonder finishes. When many of these newest fabrics are pulled off-grain during the manufacturing process, the fabric acquires a permanent memory that can't be altered, no matter how hard you try to straighten it.

### TRUING THE FABRIC

Truing the fabric is today's smart substitute for straightening.

**If the fabric has a crosswise design:** Fold it so that the design matches across the width of the fabric (see above right).

**If the fabric does not have a crosswise design:** Draw a line at one end of the fabric that is at right angles to a selvage edge as illustrated below. This crosswise line will function as your crosswise grainline. Fold the fabric so that this crosswise line matches at the selvage.

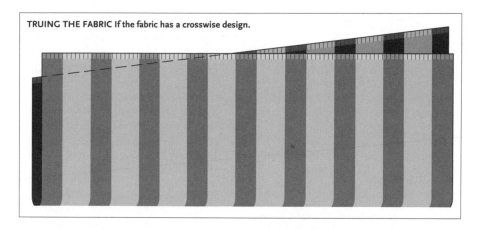

TRUING THE FABRIC If the fabric has a crosswise design.

It's possible that the selvages won't match along the length of the fabric. If this is the case, use the lengthwise fold, not the selvage edge, as your reference point when you lay out the pattern pieces.

### STRAIGHTENING WITH STEAM

A few fabrics, particularly those made of 100 percent natural fibers such as cotton, wool or linen, do not have a permanent memory. These fabrics usually can, and should, be straightened.

**A1** Begin by unraveling a few crosswise threads until you can pull one thread off across the entire width of the fabric. Trim off the resulting fringe. Repeat at the other end of the fabric.

**NOTE** If the fabric is a woven plaid, check or crosswise stripe, pulling threads is unnecessary. Instead, cut along one of the crosswise bars.

**A2** Spread the fabric out on a large, flat surface and fold it in half lengthwise, matching the selvages and the cut, crosswise ends. If the fabric bubbles, or if it ripples along the lengthwise fold, it is off-grain.

**A3** To straighten, steam-press until the bubbles or ripples disappear. As you press, move the iron in the lengthwise and crosswise direction only. Never move it diagonally, as this will further distort the fabric.

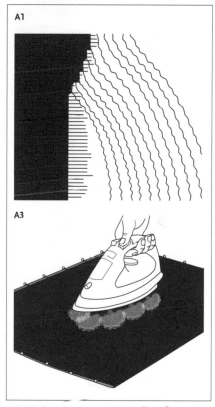

**NOTE** Don't attempt to pull or force any fabric into shape. Fabrics that require more than a gentle steam treatment are probably permanently and forever off-grain. If this is the case, use the Truing the Fabric method.

## THE CUTTING LAYOUT

Open up your pattern envelope and pull out the instruction sheet. On the first page, you'll find a variety of cutting diagrams, or layouts. To locate the one you need, look for these three things.

✂ The pattern view you're making.

✂ The fabric width that is the same as yours.

✂ Your pattern size.

Once you've found the right layout, circle it so it's easy to locate as you refer back and forth from instruction sheet to fabric.

### Fold the fabric

Make careful note of how the fabric is folded in your chosen layout. The most common way of folding fabric for cutting is the lengthwise fold but, as pattern layouts are designed to make the most efficient use of the fabric, this is not the only way. For a detailed explanation of all the layouts you may encounter, see Types of Cutting Layout opposite.

Although fabric can be folded with either the right or the wrong sides together, most sewers prefer to fold it right sides together because it makes it easier to transfer the pattern markings to the fabric and center seams are automatically matched and ready to sew once the pattern tissue is removed. For more information on folding fabric, see Special Layouts, page 75 and also refer to Chapter 7, Sewing on Special Fabrics.

> **TIP** If your fabric has a bold design or one that requires matching, it's easier to fold it wrong sides together so you can readily see the design as you pin and cut.

### Lay out the pattern pieces

To make sure you don't miss any important information as you lay out and cut your pattern pieces, look over the pattern instruction sheet before you begin. Start at the upper left-hand corner and, reading each section completely, work your way from left to right. This may sound too obvious to have to mention, but you'd be surprised at how many people just let their eyes wander over the instruction sheet reading sections at random.

Check to make sure you have all of the pattern pieces you need for the view you are making. You'll find them listed at the beginning of each view's cutting layout. If you have followed the guidelines in Chapter 4, A Perfect Fit, you will have already identified the cutting lines for your size and adjusted these pattern pieces to give you the best possible fit.

Before laying out your pattern, it's a good idea to press the pieces with a warm, dry iron to remove any creases. This will ensure that your garment sections are accurate in size and shape.

The cutting layout not only shows you how to fold your fabric, but also shows you where to place the pattern pieces. Examine your cutting layout carefully for any special notations and be aware of the shading key that tells you how to place the pattern (see Cutting Layout Shading Key, page 74). If your pattern includes interfacings or linings, these cutting layouts are usually grouped with the fabric layouts for each view.

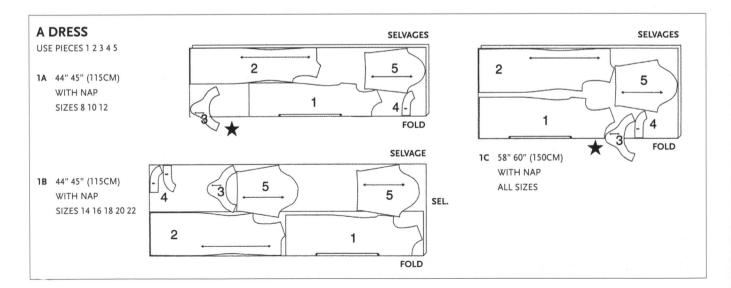

**A DRESS**

USE PIECES 1 2 3 4 5

**1A** 44" 45" (115CM)
WITH NAP
SIZES 8 10 12

**1B** 44" 45" (115CM)
WITH NAP
SIZES 14 16 18 20 22

**1C** 58" 60" (150CM)
WITH NAP
ALL SIZES

# TYPES OF CUTTING LAYOUT

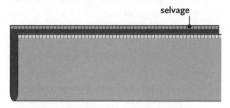

**LENGTHWISE FOLD** The most common way of folding fabric for cutting is in half lengthwise, with the selvage edges matching.

**CROSSWISE FOLD** This is used only for fabrics that do not have a nap or one-way design.

**NOTE** Your pattern layout will be more accurate if you pin the selvages in place. This will keep the fabric from shifting as you pin and cut. Depending on how your fabric is folded, pin the two selvages together or pin one selvage in place along the length of the fabric.

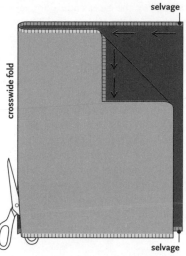

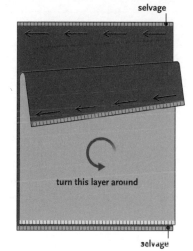

turn this layer around

**CROSSWISE CUT** This type of "fold" is used for fabrics that have a nap, such as velvet or corduroy, and for fabrics that have a one-way design. The fabric is folded in half along the crosswise grain, and then cut along the fold (above). Next, the top layer is turned around so that the nap is running in the same direction on both layers (below).

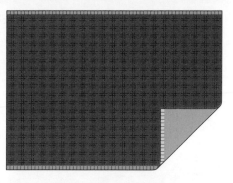

**SINGLE THICKNESS** Fabric is placed right side up; often used for thick nap fabrics as layers might shift as you pin and cut.

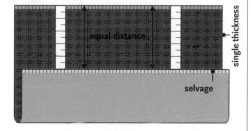

equal distance

**COMBINATION OF LENGTHWISE FOLD AND SINGLE THICKNESS** The fabric is folded along a lengthwise grain so that the selvages are parallel to each other but not matching.

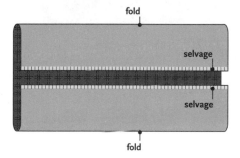

**TWO LENGTHWISE FOLDS** The fabric is folded so that the selvages meet in the center.

**STEP 1**
Position the larger pieces first, beginning with those that should be placed on the fabric fold.

**STEP 2**
Position all other pattern pieces so that the grainline arrow is parallel to the selvages or to the lengthwise fold. To be sure each piece is parallel, measure from each tip of the grainline marking to the selvage or the fold. Both measurements should be the same. If they don't match, shift the pattern piece a bit until the measurements are equal.

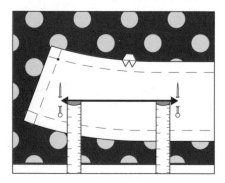

**STEP 3**
Once a pattern piece is properly positioned, pin it in place at each end of the arrow so it won't shift off-grain.

**NOTE** As you work, don't let the fabric hang over the edge of the table or it might stretch out of shape. Instead, loosely roll up the excess fabric and leave it on the end of the table. Unroll it as you work your way along the cutting layout.

## Using a cutting board
As your sewing skills progress, you may want to invest in a cutting board. This heavy-duty cardboard surface opens up to 36in × 68in (91.5cm × 173cm) and accordion folds for easy storage. It's marked with a 1in (2.5cm) grid, as well as special markings to aid you in cutting circles, scallops and bias strips. Align the selvage edges with one of the lines on the board. Use pushpins to hold the selvages in place.

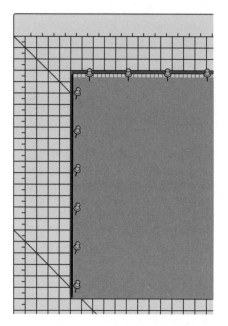

## Pinning
Pin through all of the layers of pattern and fabric. First, position the pattern piece on-grain, anchoring it with pins at both ends of the grainline arrow. Next,

pin diagonally at the corners, smoothing the pattern out from the grainline arrow as you go. Then add pins around the edge of the pattern. These pins should be placed parallel to the cutting line, at 2in–3in (5cm–7.5cm) intervals. Don't let the pins extend beyond the cutting line.

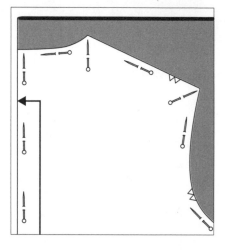

Depending on the size of your cutting surface, you may want to position all of the pattern pieces on-grain first. Once they are all positioned, you can go back and finish pinning each piece. If your cutting surface is small, you may have to work in sections. As you pin, check to make sure none of your cutting lines overlap. And unless you're following a special layout or your layout requires several different folds, don't do any cutting until all of your pattern pieces are in place. Cutting as you go means any miscalculations in your layout will be permanent.

## SPECIAL LAYOUTS

With most fabrics, you can confidently follow the layouts printed on the pattern instruction sheet. However, there are a few fabrics that require some special planning. Some need to be laid out so that all of the pattern pieces run in the same direction; others must be laid out so that the design either matches at the seamline or is attractively spaced on the body. As well as the information provided here, you should also review Chapter 7, Sewing on Special Fabrics.

If your fabric requires a special layout, it will be easier to plan if you choose a simple pattern with a limited number of seams.

### With nap layout

Some fabrics will change the way they look depending on which way you hold them. Sometimes the difference is very obvious, as in the case of one-way designs. At other times, the difference might be a very subtle variation in color. For layout purposes, these are called "with nap" fabrics and include the list below. Take another look at your pattern instruction sheet and at the example on pages 24–25. Note that the words "with nap" or "without nap" are printed next to each cutting layout. If your fabric falls into one of the categories listed below or if you are unsure about whether it has a nap, follow the "with nap" layout.

**Pile fabrics:** Such as velvet, velveteen, velour and corduroy. If you hold the fabric with the nap going down, it feels smoother and the color is lighter. If the nap runs up, the color is darker. For deeper color, the nap should go up; for better wear, the nap should go down.

**Fuzzy-surfaced fabrics:** Such as brushed flannel and fake fur. Cut with the nap running down.

**Knits and shiny fabrics:** Such as satin and damask. These reflect the light differently depending on which way you hold them. You can choose either direction, but make sure all the pattern pieces run in the same direction.

**Plaids and stripes:** For those with an uneven repeat you'll need to plan the placement of the pattern pieces so that the color bars match.

**Printed or woven motifs:** With a "this end up" look. For example, all of the flowers should "grow" in the same direction on every part of your garment.

Sometimes, because of space limitations on the instruction sheet, the pattern doesn't include a "with nap" layout. If this is the case, you'll need to develop your own. Use the "without nap" layout as a guide, reversing the position of the pattern pieces as necessary so that the tops of all of the pattern pieces are pointed in the same direction. To accommodate this new layout, it is likely that you will need to purchase more fabric than the pattern envelope recommends.

### Designs that must be matched

Garments made from plaids, bold stripes, big and medium-size checks, border prints and large design motifs must match at the seams. To accomplish this, you must first mark the seamlines on your pattern tissue. Unless otherwise indicated on the pattern tissue or instruction sheet, seamlines are 5/8 in (1.5cm) in from the cutting line. Next, you'll have to make some adjustments to the cutting layout provided on your instruction sheet. In general, you'll find it easier to work with the fabric folded right side out or on a single thickness with the right side facing up.

Extra yardage is required to allow for this pattern matching. How much extra will depend on the size of the motif and the frequency of the repeat. Small, even plaids and stripes require 1/4yd –1/2yd (25cm–50cm) extra; large, even designs require 1/2yd –1yd (0.5m–1m) extra.

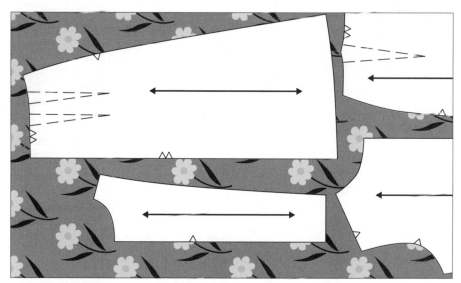

Printed or woven motifs have a pattern, often floral, that must run the same way on all pattern pieces.

For fabrics with designs that must be matched you need to think about where you want the most prominent bar or motif to fall on your body.

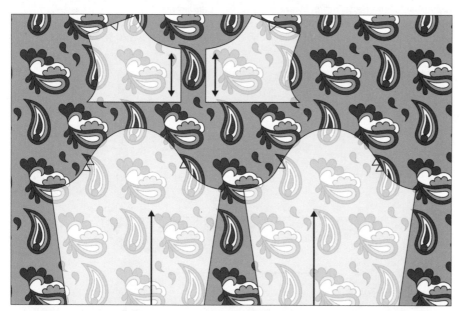

For fabrics with designs that must be matched at the seamlines, it is best to lay out your pattern on the right side of the fabric working on a single thickness. For advice on positioning motifs (or bars) see Positioning Bars or Motifs, right.

## LAYING OUT THE PATTERN

As you lay out the first piece, be sure that the grainline arrow is parallel to the selvages or to the bars of the design. Then position the remaining pattern pieces so that the adjoining pieces match at the seams.

**NOTE** Some details can't be matched, no matter how hard you try. These include raglan seams, shoulder seams, darts, the area above a bust dart on princess seams, the back of the armhole seam, gathered or eased seams, and circle skirts. Half-circle skirts will chevron at the seams.

### POSITIONING BARS OR MOTIFS

Beginning with the main front section, position the pattern pieces on the fabric so that:

✂ Prominent vertical bars and large squares or motifs fall at the center front and back of the garment, and at the center of sleeves, yokes and collars.

✂ Dominant horizontal bars fall at straight or slightly curved hemlines. As you do this, observe what will happen on the rest of the garment – you may not want a repeat of the dominant bar or motif to fall at the fullest part of the bust, abdomen or hips.

✂ In the case of a border print or large motif, the hemline falls just below the lower edge of the design.

✂ Where possible, motifs should not be chopped off at the seamlines, creating an unattractive effect.

✂ The design matches vertically as well as horizontally – i.e., center back of collar to center back of garment.

**A1** Trace the design of the fabric onto the pattern at the notch and indicate colors.

**A2** Place the pattern piece to be joined on top of the first piece, lapping seamlines and matching notches. Trace the design onto the second piece.

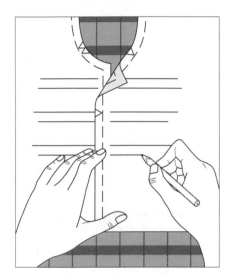

**A3** Place the second pattern piece on the fabric so that the traced design matches the fabric.

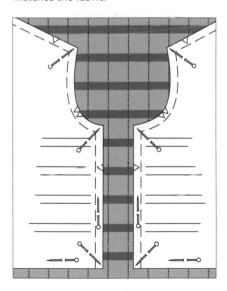

**TIP** For more about working with special fabrics and plaids and stripes in particular, see Chapter 7, Sewing on Special Fabrics.

## CUTTING

Use a pair of sharp dressmaking shears. The ones with the 7in or 8in (18cm or 20.5cm) blades are the most popular. Do not use pinking shears to cut out your garment – they won't give you the sharp, straight cutting line that is the necessary guideline for accurate stitching. Keep pinking shears for finishing seams (see page 97). Use your free hand to hold the edge of the pattern flat as you cut.

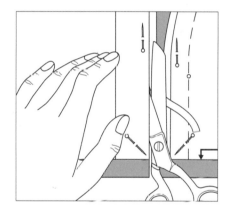

The notches are printed on the pattern tissue as triangles within the seam allowances. Do not cut into these triangles. This will weaken your seam allowances. Instead, using the tip of your scissors, cut outward triangles at the notch locations.

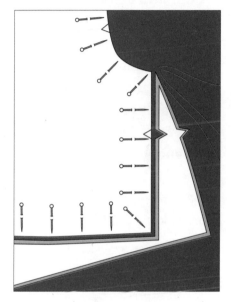

If you prefer, you can ignore the notches completely until you transfer the other pattern markings (see page 78). Then, using the tip of your scissors, make a very small clip in the seam allowance at the center of each notch.

**TIP** Keep a magnetic pincushion close by as you pin and cut. It's a fast tool for "sweeping up" all those loose pins from the floor and the cutting surface.

# PREPARING TO SEW

Once the fabric has been cut out and before you begin to sew the pieces together, you need to transfer all the markings that are on the pattern to the fabric and to temporarily join the fabric pieces together before permanent sewing. There are several ways to do this depending on the fabric you are working with.

## MARKING

In addition to the notches, which you may have already marked as you cut out your pattern (see page 77), always mark the following notations and symbols.

**Dots:** Including those that indicate dart stitching lines.

**Solid lines:** Those that indicate foldlines, as well as position lines for details such as pockets and buttonholes. Do not mark the solid line that indicates the grainline arrow.

**Center front and center back:** As indicated by a broken line or a foldline, unless these are located on seamlines.

**Stitching lines:** Those that occur within the body of the garment section, such as pleats, tucks or fly-front zipper openings.

## Marking methods

When transferring symbols there are many choices available to you. Your aim is to make an unobtrusive but visible mark on the fabric that will not show on the finished project. Use the method, or combination of methods, that suits your needs and your fabric.

### FABRIC MARKING PENS

These are one of the fastest and easiest ways to mark. They contain disappearing ink that makes it possible to mark on either the right or wrong side of the fabric. With a lightweight fabric, you can mark directly on the pattern tissue. Using a fabric-marking pen, press hard so that the ink will bleed through the tissue paper and both layers of fabric. There are two types of disappearing ink pens.

**Water-soluble marking pens:** These contain blue ink that disappears when the marks are treated with plain water.

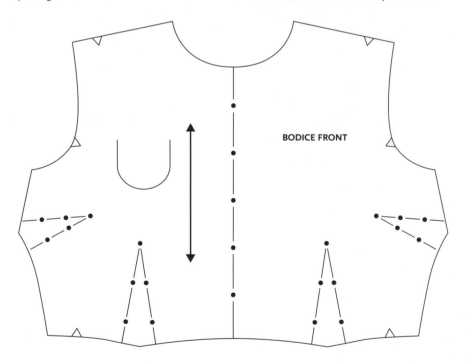

BODICE FRONT

As you learned in Chapter 2, pages 26–27, a variety of notations, or symbols, are printed on the pattern tissue. Many of these symbols serve as guidelines for matching up garment sections and for sewing details, such as darts and pockets for example.

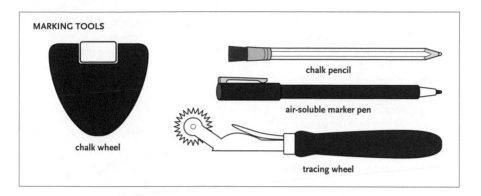

**MARKING TOOLS**

chalk wheel

chalk pencil

air-soluble marker pen

tracing wheel

**Evaporating, or air-soluble, marking pens:**
These contain purple ink that simply evaporates from the fabric, usually in less than 48 hours. To guarantee your markings will still be visible when you need them, don't use these pens until just before you're ready to sew.

Whichever type of marking pen you choose, be sure to test for removability on a scrap of your fashion fabric. If your fabric water-spots or is dry-clean-only, then the water-soluble pen is not a good choice. If the evaporating ink leaves an oily residue on the fabric, it's not a good choice, either.

To mark with either of these pens, stick pins straight through the pattern tissue and both fabric layers at all marking points.

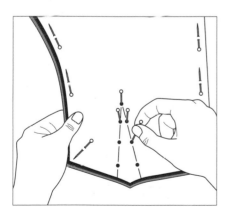

Starting from the outside edges of the pattern piece, carefully separate the layers of tissue and fabric just enough to place an ink dot where the pin is inserted. Mark both layers of fabric; then remove the pin. As you work your way from the outer cut edges of the pattern to the center or center fold, continue separating and marking the layers.

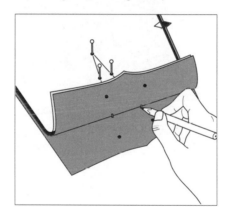

**TIP** If you've used an evaporating marking pen and your sewing gets interrupted, put your work in a large self-sealing bag, squeeze out the air and seal it. The markings will remain until you reopen the bag.

**DRESSMAKER'S MARKING PENCILS**
These are available in two styles. The first contains a lead-like substance that can be washed out of the garment. The second contains a soft, chalk-like substance. Chalk pencils have a stiff brush on one end to "erase" markings once the garment is completed. Test first on a scrap of your fabric to determine if you can use the chalk on the right side of the fabric. Mark as for the disappearing pens, using straight pins to locate the position of the symbols. Mark on the right or wrong side of the fashion fabric, as appropriate.

**TRACING PAPER AND TRACING WHEEL**
Tracing paper (sometimes referred to as dressmaker's carbon) and a tracing wheel are a good choice for marking smooth, flat-surfaced fabrics. On textured or bulky fabrics, the markings may be hard to see.

Traditionally, tracing paper markings were permanent. This meant that you couldn't use this method for sheers or for marking on the right side of the fabric. The introduction of "disappearing" tracing paper has changed all that since the markings can be sponged off with water. Read the manufacturer's directions carefully and test first on a scrap of your fashion fabric. The heat of your iron may permanently set some of these formulas, and, if this is the case, sponge off the markings before you press that area of the garment.

You can usually save time by marking two layers at once. However, heavyweight fabrics must be marked one layer at a time so the markings are clearly visible.

There are three types of tracing wheels to choose from: smooth edge, blunt edge teeth or sharp (pinpoint) teeth. If you are using one with sharp teeth, mark on a protected surface, such as a cutting board, or slip a piece of cardboard underneath.

To mark, remove any pins that are in your way and position the tracing paper between the layers of fabric and pattern. For standard tracing paper, the carbon side should face the wrong sides of the fabric; for disappearing tracing paper, the carbon can face either the right or the wrong sides of the fabric.

Roll the tracing wheel over any symbols to be marked. Use a ruler as a guide when tracing straight lines.

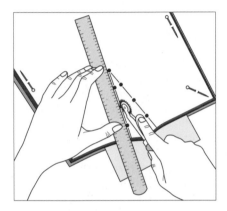

Mark dots with an 'X' so that one of the bars of the 'X' is on the stitching line.

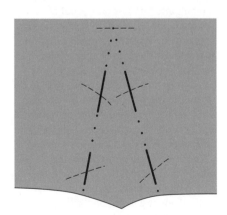

## HAND OR MACHINE BASTING

This is a way to transfer markings from the wrong side to the right side of the fabric. It's particularly useful for indicating placement lines, such as those for pockets or buttonholes, for marking center front and center back along the full length of the pattern piece, and for marking pleat foldlines and placement lines.

Use any appropriate method to mark on the wrong side of the fabric. Then separate the layers of fabric and hand- or machine-baste along the marking points. The markings will be visible now on the inside and outside of the garment.

## SNIP MARKING

This is a fast way to mark the ends of darts, foldlines, pleats and tucks, as well as center fronts and center backs. It's also an alternative way to mark notches. But think carefully before you snip-mark; this is not a suitable technique to use if there's any possibility that you'll need to let out the seams later on.

To snip mark, just make a small clip (1/8 in or 3mm deep) in the seam allowance at the marking point.

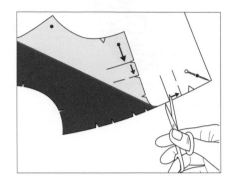

## PRESS MARKING

This is used in conjunction with snip marking to mark foldlines for details such as extended facings, folded casings, pleats and tucks.

**A1** Make a tiny clip in the seam allowance at each end of the foldline. If pleats or tucks do not extend the length of the pattern piece, use one of the methods described earlier to mark the end of the foldline.

**A2** Unpin and remove the pattern to press-mark each fabric layer separately.

**A3** Fold the fabric wrong sides together, using the clip marks as guides, and press the fold.

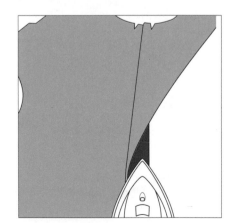

## BASTING

Basting refers to any of several methods that can be used to temporarily join layers of fabric until they're permanently stitched on the machine.

### Pin basting

Pin basting is the most common method. Place pins perpendicular to the seamline, 1in–3in (2.5cm–7.5cm) apart. Insert the pins so you take small bites of fabric right at the seamline. The pin heads should be to the right of the presser foot so they can be efficiently removed as you stitch.

If your machine has a hinged presser foot, it is possible to sew right over the pins – but only if your manual describes this feature. Otherwise it is best not to experiment as the result could be a damaged sewing machine needle, which can cause all sorts of stitching problems.

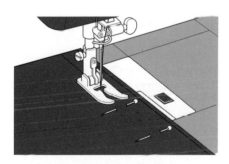

**TIP** If you're doing a lot of machine basting, use different color threads in the bobbin and the needle. Later on, it will be easy to see which thread to clip and which one to pull.

### Paper clip basting

Paper clips are a quick substitute for pins on bulky, hard-to-pin fabrics, such as fake fur. They're also useful for fabrics where pins would leave permanent holes, such as leather and vinyl. *Never* try to stitch over a paper clip.

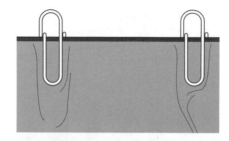

### Fuse basting

This is a fast way to hold fabric layers in place for hand finishing or topstitching. Cut a strip of fusible web the desired length. Sandwich it between the two fabric layers and fuse, holding the iron in place for only a few seconds. Follow the manufacturer's recommendations for heat and steam.

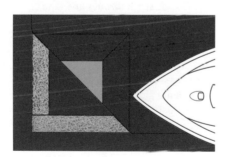

### Machine basting

This is most often used to temporarily sew a garment together in order to check the fit.

**A1** Pin baste the fabric layers together, matching the markings.

**A2** Loosen the needle thread tension, adjust the stitch setting to the longest length and stitch. Do not secure the stitching at the ends of the seams.

**A3** To remove the basting easily, clip the needle thread every 1in (2.5cm) or so; then pull out the bobbin thread.

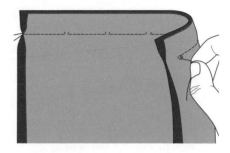

### Hand basting

This is a very secure method of basting. It is frequently used in detail areas where pin basting would not be accurate or secure enough and where machine basting would be difficult to do. It can also be used on sheer or very slippery fabrics, such as satin.

**TIP** Fasten a strip of magnetic tape to the bed of your sewing machine or keep a magnetic pincushion close by. Use it to catch the pins as you remove them.

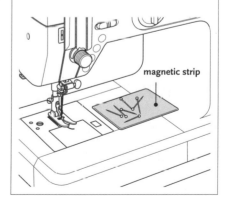

magnetic strip

**For the firmest holding power:** Weave the needle in and out of the fabric so that the stitches and the spaces between them are the same size, approximately ¼ in (6mm) long.

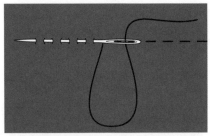

**For areas that don't need to be as secure:** Make the stitches ¼ in (6mm) long and the spaces between them ½ in–¾ in (1.3cm–2cm) long.

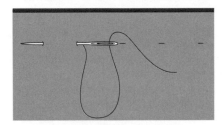

### Double-faced basting tape

This is a valuable aid when you need to be sure that stripes or plaids match at the seamline, or for positioning detail areas such as zippers and pockets. The water-soluble version will disappear when your garment is washed.

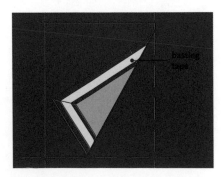

basting tape

**TO MATCH A STRIPE OR PLAID ALONG A SEAMLINE**

**B1**   Press one seam allowance under at the seamline.

**B2**   Position the basting tape so that the sticky side is against the right side of the seam allowance, about ⅛ in (3mm) from the fold.

**B3**   Remove the protective covering from the tape. Lap the pressed seam allowance over the unpressed one, matching both the seamline and fabric design.

**B4**   Turn the garment sections to the wrong side, open out the folded seam allowance and stitch along the crease line. Do not stitch through the tape, as it will gum up your needle.

### Glue stick

This can be used instead of basting tape. Unlike basting tape, you can stitch right through the glue without harming your needle. Just be sure you've allowed a few minutes for the glue to dry thoroughly before stitching.

### Liquid basting glue

This comes in a squeeze bottle with a nozzle applicator. It is particularly useful to hold small details, such as appliqués and trims, in place for permanent stitching. Be sure the glue is dry before stitching through it.

# MACHINE SEWING

**Your conventional sewing machine is the most useful and valuable piece of sewing equipment you own. As features and capabilities will vary among models and manufacturers, you should study the manual that comes with your sewing machine. It will tell you all you need to know to get the best from your machine.**

## SEWING MACHINE ANATOMY

Knowing the names of the parts of your sewing machine will help you maximize its performance. The actual location and configuration of some of these features will vary, depending on the make and model of your machine.

**THINGS YOUR MACHINE MANUAL WILL TELL YOU**

✂   How to keep it clean and lint-free.

✂   Whether or not it requires oiling and lubricating – and how often this should be done.

✂   Recommended types and sizes of needles.

✂   Instructions for adjusting tension, pressure and stitch length.

# FRONT

**1 Foot pressure dial:** To adjust foot pressure when sewing lightweight or heavyweight fabrics or bulky layers; however, a machine with automatic foot pressure will be adequate for the average sewing project.

**2 Thread take-up lever:** Moves up and down with the needle and controls the amount of thread needed for stitching.

**3 Bobbin thread guide with tension disc:** To take the thread from the spool to the bobbin winding spindle. This guide has a tension disc so the bobbin thread is wound tightly.

**4 Speed control:** This enables you to limit the maximum stitching speed for more even stitching.

**5 Thread guides:** There are several of these along the threading run to take the thread in the right direction.

**6 Bobbin winder spindle:** Used when filling up the bobbin with thread.

**7 Stitch width dial:** Controls the distance the needle moves from side to side when sewing zigzag or other decorative stitches.

**8 Stitch length dial:** For adjusting the length of your stitches – a machine that allows a good range of stitch lengths will be more versatile in the long run.

**9 Stitch selector dial:** Used to select the machine's built-in stitches.

**10 Reverse stitch lever:** Allows you to sew in reverse. On some models reverse stitch is selected by turning the stitch length dial (8) to a minus number.

**11 Drop feed lever:** Lowers the feed dog below the needle plate to put it out of action when free-motion sewing. Alternatively, it may be possible to temporarily fix a plate over the feed dog.

**12 Knee lifter socket:** Where the knee lifter (if one is provided) plugs in.

**13 Hook cover release button:** Releases the hook cover plate to access the bobbin (top-loading machines only).

**14 Flat bed:** A large flat sewing area. On some machines part of this may detach to reveal the free arm. Narrow cylindrical items, such as sleeves and pant legs, can then be threaded onto the arm for easier stitching.

**15 Hook cover plate:** Covers the bobbin in its casing (only found on a top-loading bobbin machine).

**16 Needle plate:** Also known as the throat plate, this is marked with common seam allowances as a guide to accurate sewing. It can be removed by unfastening tiny screws to clean the bobbin casing, feed dog and hook race.

**17 Thread cutter:** For cutting the needle thread.

**18 Tension dial:** Used to adjust the tension of the needle thread for a perfectly balanced stitch.

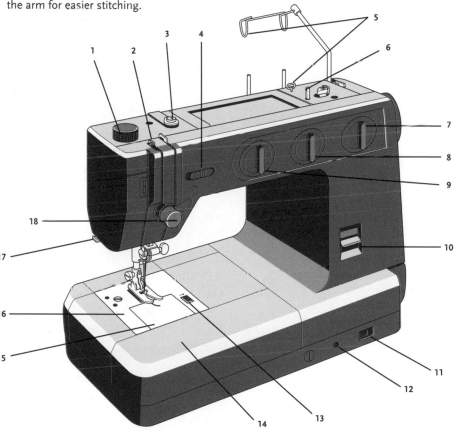

## BACK

**19 Foot control socket:** Connect the plug here for the foot pedal that controls the stitching speed.

**20 Power switch:** Turns the power and the machine's built-in sewing light on or off.

**21 Hand wheel:** Turning the hand wheel raises and lowers the needle. Always turn the hand wheel counter-clockwise.

**22 Thread cutter:** Used to cut the thread when the bobbin is fully wound.

**23 Bobbin winder stopper:** This is pushed against the bobbin when winding begins. When the bobbin is full it pops back and stops the bobbin winding mechanism.

**24 Carrying handle:** Always carry the machine by its handle.

**25 Thread spool pins:** These hold the thread for the needle and can be set vertically or horizontally.

**26 Presser foot lifting lever:** Lift it to raise the presser foot and release the thread tension; lower it to lower the presser foot and engage the thread tension.

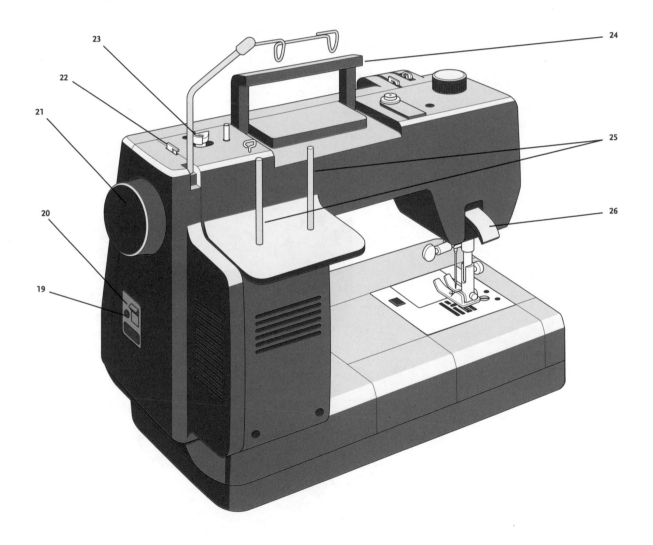

## PRESSER FOOT DETAIL

**27 Thread guides:** Take the needle thread towards the eye of the needle.

**28 Presser bar:** The foot holder clips around this, held in place by the thumbscrew.

**29 Presser foot thumbscrew:** Releases the entire presser foot holder.

**30 Presser foot holder:** Clips onto the presser bar – on some machines the foot and the foot holder are all one piece.

**31 Presser foot:** Holds the fabric firmly against the needle plate and feed dog so that the stitches form properly.

**32 Needle:** The needle takes the upper thread through the fabric and down through the needle plate.

**33 Needle clamp screw:** Loosen to remove a needle; tighten to secure a needle in position.

**34 Feed teeth:** The metal teeth under the needle plate, which push or feed the fabric through the machine. This area is sometimes referred to as the feed dog.

### LOWER THREAD DETAIL

**Bobbin:** A metal or clear plastic spool that holds the lower thread. Bobbins can be top-loading (the bobbin is dropped into the bobbin case through a sliding or hinged panel in the needle plate) or front/side loading (the bobbin is placed into the bobbin case outside the machine, and the filled bobbin case is then inserted into the machine at the front or side through an opening door).

> **TIP** The feed dog automatically feeds the fabric under the presser foot as you stitch. It needs to be put out of action – either by dropping it or by covering it with a special plate – for some tasks such as free-motion stitching and sewing on buttons.

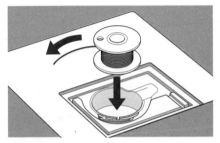

Top-loading bobbin.

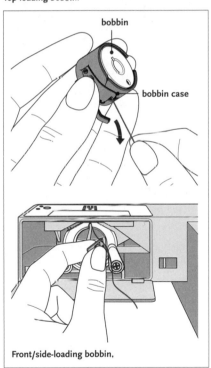

Front/side-loading bobbin.

**Shuttle area:** Where the mechanisms that move the bobbin are housed. Dust and loose threads can build up here so check regularly and brush clean following your machine's manual.

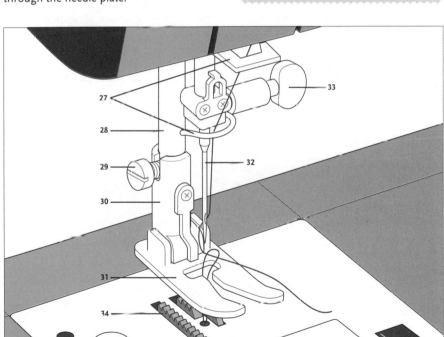

# PERFCT STITCHING

If you follow the recommendations in the manual and keep your sewing machine in good working order, you can expect it to reward you with good-quality stitching. Then you'll be able to make the simple adjustments that fine-tune the stitch quality to match your fabric.

Before you sew even one seam on your garment, test-stitch on scraps of your fashion fabric.

> **TIP** If you don't understand how to operate some of the attachments or special features on your machine, stop in at a local dealer and ask about a few lessons. For excellent background information, refer to the *Simplicity How to Use a Sewing Machine* book.

## Thread tension

Tension refers to the amount of drag, or tautness, exerted on both the needle thread and the bobbin thread as they move through the sewing machine. When the tension is correctly set, the stitches should be perfectly balanced; the two threads interlock in the center of the fabric so that the stitches look the same on both sides of the fabric.

If the tension is not balanced, your manual will tell you how to correct it by adjusting the dial or button that controls the needle tension. Adjusting the needle tension to match the bobbin tension can solve most tension problems. Although some machines have a screw on the bobbin case that controls the bobbin tension, most manufacturers do not recommend adjusting this screw, and advise referral to a skilled repairperson.

## Presser foot pressure

Pressure refers to the force the presser foot exerts on the fabric as it moves between the presser foot and the feed dog. The amount of pressure needed can be affected by the fabric's weight, bulk, texture or finishes. If the pressure is correctly set for the fabric, both layers will move through the machine at the same rate.

On most machines, the amount of pressure is regulated by a knob or dial. Check your manual to be sure. Your manual will also suggest suitable settings for various fabrics and sewing situations.

## Stitch length

Depending on the make and model of your machine, you will be able to adjust the stitch length by pushing a button or moving a lever or dial. These will all have numbers that correspond to various stitch lengths. On some machines, these numbers represent the number of stitches per inch; on other machines, they indicate, in millimeters, the length of each individual stitch. Consult your manual for information.

### STITCH LENGTH GUIDE
The following is a guide to the most commonly used stitch lengths.

---

**TO TEST FOR BALANCED TENSION**

Take a scrap of the fashion fabric and fold it along the bias. Put a row of stitching about $1/2$ in (1.3cm) from the fold. Then pull the fabric until a thread breaks.

✓ If both the bobbin and the needle thread break, the tension is fine.

✗ If only the bobbin thread breaks, the bobbin tension is tighter than the needle tension.
**Solution:** Tighten the needle tension to match the bobbin.

✗ If only the needle thread breaks, the needle tension is tighter than the bobbin tension.
**Solution:** Loosen the needle tension to match the bobbin.

**Regulation:** 10–15 stitches per inch (per 2.5cm), or 2mm–2.5mm long, is the length used for most general sewing, including stitching seams.

**Basting:** The longest stitch on your machine, usually 6–8 stitches per inch (per 2.5cm) or 3mm–4mm long. Since this is temporary stitching, the longer stitch is easier to remove.

**Reinforcing:** The shortest stitch length, usually 18–20 stitches per inch (per 2.5cm) or 1mm–1.5mm long.

**Easing or gathering:** 8–10 stitches per inch (per 2.5cm) or 2.5mm–3mm long.

> **TIP** If you have trouble remembering which number is for the shortest stitch and which is for the longest, write them down on a small piece of masking tape and tape it to the machine. With more sewing experience, this information will become automatic, and you'll be able to throw the tape away.

## MACHINE STITCHING TECHNIQUES

The guidelines for good stitching outlined here are so easy to follow that they soon become automatic.

> **QUICK STITCH SOLUTIONS**
>
> ✂ Don't confuse tension problems with stitch length problems.
>
> ✂ If the fabric puckers, use a shorter stitch length.
>
> ✂ If the fabric "waves" out of shape, the stitches are too dense for the fabric. To correct, lengthen the stitch.

### Get a good start
This technique guarantees that your beginning stitches will be smooth and that the thread won't get jammed up in the needle plate hole.

**A1** Grasp the needle and bobbin threads with one hand and pull them under, and then behind, or to the side of, the presser foot.

**A2** Place the fabric under the presser foot so that the right edge is aligned with the desired marking on the needle plate. The bulk of the fabric should be to the left of the presser foot.

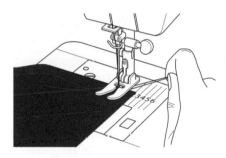

**A3** Turn the wheel to lower the needle into the fabric near the beginning of the seamline.

**A4** While still holding the thread tails, lower the presser foot and begin stitching with a slow, even speed. Continue to hold on to the thread tails until you have stitched for approximately 1in (2.5cm).

**A5** Release the thread tails and continue stitching.

> **TIP** If your fabric is being swallowed up into the needle plate opening at the beginning of each seam, try using a smaller size needle. If the problem persists, use a scrap of nonwoven, tear-away stabilizer, such as Stitch-n-Tear® or Trace Erase® as a seam starter.

### Guide the fabric
Rest one hand on the fabric in front of the presser foot and the other hand behind the presser foot. Use both hands to gently guide the fabric through the machine as you stitch. At the same time, keep your eye on the cut edge of the fabric rather than on the needle. This helps you keep the stitching straight.

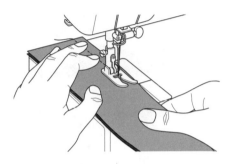

### Keep it accurate
The easiest way to maintain accurate stitching is to align the right edge of the fabric with one of the following five stitching guides.

**Seam allowance guidelines:** The lines permanently etched on the needle plate of many sewing machines. These are placed at 1/8in (3mm) intervals.

**Masking tape guide:** A piece of tape placed on the needle plate at the desired distance from the needle hole.

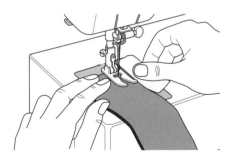

**A screw-on or magnetic seam guide:**
This can be placed the desired distance
from the needle hole. Place it parallel to
the presser foot for straight edges or at
an angle for curves.

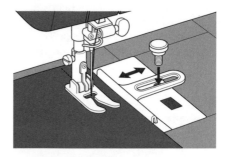

**A quilting foot attachment:** One with an
edge guide will help you to keep the
fabric aligned with the edge of the foot to
ensure a perfect ¼in (6mm) seam.

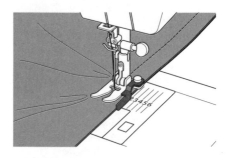

**The toe of the presser foot:** This is
particularly useful when stitching close
to an edge or ¼in (6mm) away from it.

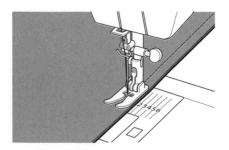

## Prevent slipping and shifting

If you're working with two or more layers
of fabric, you'll want to pin or baste them
together to keep them from slipping as
you sew. Match raw edges, markings
and notches; then baste them together
using one of the techniques described
on pages 81–82. As you become more
proficient, you may find that simple,
straight seams will require only one or
two pins unless the fabric is very slippery.

## Secure the thread ends

To prevent the stitching from coming
undone at the beginning and end of the
seam, use one of these techniques.

### BACKSTITCH

Insert the needle about ½in (1.3cm)
from the beginning of the seam, set the
machine to stitch in reverse and backstitch to the edge. Set the machine to
stitch forward and complete the seam,
slowing down near the end. Finish by
reversing back along the stitching line
for around ½in (1.3cm).

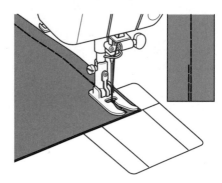

### TIE THE THREADS

This technique is useful if the line of
stitching ends before you reach the edge
of the fabric, such as on a patch pocket,
or if your machine doesn't stitch in
reverse. Leave thread tails at least 4in
(10cm) long at the beginning and end of
the stitching.

Before tying the threads, it may be
necessary to bring both tails of thread to
the same side of the fabric. To do this,
tug gently on one thread until the loop of
the other thread appears; then insert a
pin through the loop and draw it up.

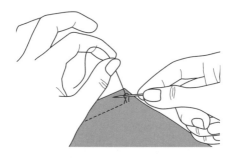

To tie the threads, hold the threads in
the left hand and form a loop. With the
right hand, bring the tails through the
loop. Then insert a pin into the loop so
that the tip of the pin is at the end of the
line of stitching. Pull the thread ends
until the loop forms a knot at the tip of
the pin. Remove the pin and clip the
thread tails.

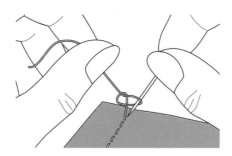

**TIP** If the seamline or stitching line
will ultimately be intersected by another
row of stitching, there is no need to
secure the ends as the second row
of stitching will "lock" the first row
in place.

## SEWING MACHINE TROUBLESHOOTING

If something looks wrong with your stitching, the problem is often very easy and simple to put right. For causes of, and solutions to, many of the problems you may encounter, see the chart below which continues on page 90.

### Servicing

To get the best from your sewing machine have it regularly serviced. If the machine is still within its guarantee period, servicing should be carried out by an approved technician in accordance with the manufacturer's warranty terms. After the guarantee has lapsed, the choice of service engineer is more flexible, but it is important to make sure that whoever you choose is a qualified technician, especially in the case of computerized machines. If you use your machine very heavily – at least five times a week – then it should be serviced once a year. For moderate to light usage – on average less than once a week – service your machine every two years. Even if you don't use your machine very often, it should be serviced occasionally. Always send the machine for a service if it has been dropped or damaged, has become wet, or has jammed up completely.

| PROBLEM | POSSIBLE CAUSE | SOLUTION |
|---|---|---|
| irregular stitches | The top thread tension is too loose. | Tighten the top thread tension. |
| | The fabric is being pulled manually through the machine faster than it can stitch. | Do not pull on the fabric – just guide it gently in the right direction, allowing the feed dog to do the work. |
| | The presser foot pressure is set too light. | Increase the pressure on the presser foot . |
| | The presser foot is too loose. | Tighten or reset the presser foot. |
| Skipped stitches | The needle is bent, blunt or incorrectly inserted. | Change the needle. Make sure the needle is the correct way round and that it is fully inserted into the needle clamp. |
| | The needle and thread are not the correct type for the fabric being sewn. | Change the needle to the correct size and type for the fabric and use the correct thread, consulting your manual. |
| | The top thread tension is too tight. | Reset the thread tension. |
| | The thread take-up lever has not been threaded. | Rethread the machine correctly, making sure that the thread goes through the take-up lever |
| Stitches not formed properly | The thread has not been pulled into the thread tension unit. | Rethread the top thread correctly, making sure that the presser foot is up, which opens up the tension mechanism to allow the thread to locate correctly, and also ensuring that the thread is kept taut while threading. |
| | The bobbin case is incorrectly threaded. | Rethread the bobbin case correctly. |
| | The spool cap is the wrong size for the thread spool. | Replace the spool cap with the correct size. |

| PROBLEM | POSSIBLE CAUSE | SOLUTION |
| --- | --- | --- |
| Seams puckering | The top thread tension is too tight. | Reset the thread tension. |
| | The top thread is not threaded correctly. | Rethread the top thread correctly, making sure that the presser foot is up and that the thread is kept taut while threading. |
| | The point of the needle is blunt or it is too heavy for the fabric being sewn. | Change the needle, making sure it is the correct size and type for the fabric being sewn . |
| | The stitch length is too long for the fabric being sewn. | Decrease the stitch length. |
| | The wrong presser foot is fitted. | Change the presser foot to the correct type. |
| | The fabric is too sheer or soft. | Layer the fabric with material backing or tissue paper before stitching the seam. |
| | There are two different sizes or kinds of thread in the machine. | Make sure the top thread and the bobbin thread are the same weight and type. |
| Thread looping/bunching under the fabric | The top thread tension is too loose. | Reset the thread tension. |
| | The machine is not correctly threaded. | Rethread the top thread correctly, making sure that the presser foot is up and that the thread is kept taut while threading. |
| | The needle is not the correct type for the thread being used. | Change the needle to the correct size and type for the thread and fabric, and use the correct thread. |
| Fabric not feeding smoothly through type of stitching | The stitch length is set to 0. | Select the correct stitch length for the the machine |
| | The feed dog is lowered. | Raise the feed dog. |
| | Lint is caught under the needle plate. | Clean the machine, particularly between the feed dog teeth. |
| | The stitch length is too short for the fabric being sewn. | Increase the stitch length. |
| | The presser foot pressure is too low. | Set the presser foot pressure adjustment lever to normal. |
| | The machine is set in buttonhole mode. | Select the correct stitch type and length. |

# MACHINE STITCH GLOSSARY

Apart from straight stitching there are several other basic machine stitches that you will use time and again when making clothes.

## Easestitching

This technique is used when you are joining a longer garment edge to a slightly shorter one. Although the technique is similar to one used for gathering, there shouldn't be any folds or gathers visible on the outside of the garment once the seam is stitched.

**A1** Loosen the needle tension slightly and adjust the machine to sew with a longer stitch (3mm or 8–10 stitches per inch).

**A2** Stitch just next to the seamline, within the seam allowance. Stitch slightly beyond the markings on your pattern tissue that indicate the area to be eased. If desired, add a second row of stitches ¼in (6mm) inside the seam allowance.

**A3** Pin the eased section to the longer edge, matching any markings. Draw the fabric up along the bobbin thread and distribute the fullness evenly.

## EASE-PLUS STITCHING

If only a small amount of easing is required, try ease-plus stitching – a quick method that crowds the fabric, distributing the fullness. Using a regulation stitch length, stitch between the ease markings. As you do this, press your index finger against the back of the presser foot. Stitch for several inches (centimeters), letting the fabric pile up between your finger and the presser foot. Release the fabric and repeat.

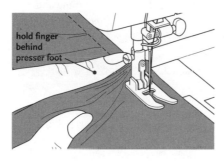

**TIP** When easestitching and ease-plus stitching, stitch the seam with the eased edge on top and the flat edge below.

## Edgestitching

This extra row of regulation-length stitches appears on the outside of a garment. It's placed approximately ⅛in (3mm) or less away from a seamline or foldline, or close to a finished edge. Although it is similar to topstitching, edgestitching is less noticeable because it is closer to the edge and is always done in matching thread.

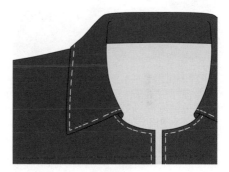

## Reinforcement stitching

This technique strengthens the stitching in areas that will be closely trimmed, at corners for example, or along deep curves that will be clipped or notched at frequent intervals. The basic premise is simple – just sew that section of the seam with a shorter stitch length.

**At inside and outside corners:** Reduce the stitch length for about 1in (2.5cm) on either side of the corner.

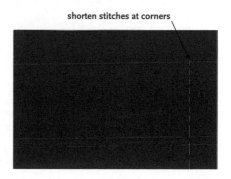

shorten stitches at corners

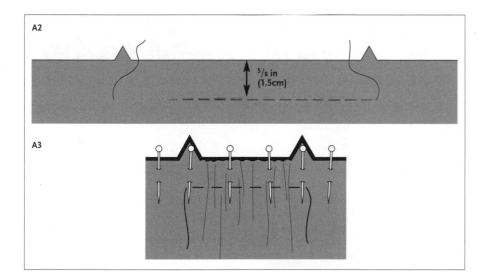

A2

⅝in (1.5cm)

A3

**When joining an inside corner to an outside corner:** First reinforce the inside corner with small stitches, and then clip just to the stitching.

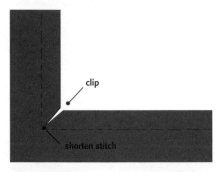

## Staystitching

This line of regulation-length stitching prevents curved or bias edges, such as necklines, shoulders and waistlines, from stretching out of shape as they are handled. If your garment section requires it – the pattern instructions will tell you where it is necessary – staystitching should be the very first type of stitching you do.

To staystitch, stitch with a regulation-length stitch ¹⁄₈ in (3mm) inside of the seam allowance, between the seamline and the cut edge. On a standard ⁵⁄₈ in (1.5cm) seam allowance, this distance is ¹⁄₂ in (1.3cm) from the cut edge of the

fabric. On deep curves, shorten the stitch length so the staystitching doubles as reinforcement stitching.

To keep the edge of the fabric from stretching as you staystitch, stitch in the same direction as the fabric grain. As a guideline, you may find arrows printed on the instruction sheet illustrations to indicate stitching direction.

Staystitching remains in the garment as a permanent aid to prevent stretching and buckling. Because it is in the seam allowance between the seamline and the cut edge, it will be invisible on the finished garment.

> **TIP** If there are no arrows to direct you, you can determine which way to stitch by "stroking the cat". Run your finger along the cut edge of the fabric. The yarns will curl smoothly in one direction, just the way a cat's fur does. This is the direction to stitch in.

## Stitch-in-the-ditch

This technique is a quick way to hold layers of fabric in place at the seams. It's an effective way to secure neckline, armhole or waistband facings, as well as fold-up cuffs. On the outside of the garment, stitch in the groove formed by

the seam. Be sure to catch all of the underneath layers in your stitching.

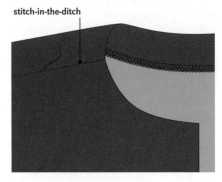

## Topstitching

This is an extra row of stitching on the outside of the garment along or near a finished edge. Although topstitching is usually added as decoration, it can also be functional. For example, it can be used to attach a patch pocket or to help keep seam allowances flat on hard-to-press fabrics. Stitch with a slightly longer stitch (3mm, or 8–10 stitches per inch).To keep your stitching straight, use one of the stitching guides as described on pages 87–88.

Use a matching or contrasting color thread, depending on how noticeable you want the stitching to be.

Staystitching.

Before topstitching on your garment, test-stitch using the same number of layers (fashion fabric, interfacing, facing, lining, seam allowances, etc.) as your garment has. To make each stitch more pronounced, you may want to slightly loosen the needle thread tension. You may also need to adjust the presser foot pressure to accommodate the extra layers.

## Understitching

This row of stitching prevents an inside layer of fabric, usually a facing, from rolling to the outside of the garment. Understitching is done after the seam allowances are trimmed, graded and clipped or notched (see Sewing with Your Scissors, pages 98–99).

**B1** Press the seam allowances toward the facing.

**B2** On the right side of the garment, stitch $^1/_8$ in (3mm) from the seamline, through the facing and the seam allowances only.

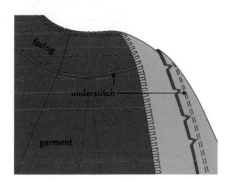

# SEAMS AND SEAM FINISHES

**A seam is basically a line of stitching that joins two or more layers of fabric. Seams are the backbone of your sewing. Happily, there's nothing to learn about seams that's difficult to grasp. Once you know the techniques, you're on your way to achieving wonderful sewing results.**

## SEAM TECHNIQUES

Seams are stitched on the seamline. The seam allowance is the distance between the seamline and the cut edge. Unless your pattern instructions tell you otherwise, the standard seam allowance is $^5/_8$ in (1.5cm) wide. Some seams require special handling. In this section we outline some terms and techniques you should be familiar with.

## Directional stitching

This means to stitch in the direction of the fabric grain. Directional stitching helps keep fabrics, especially knits and napped fabrics, from stretching out of shape or curling. Always use directional stitching when you staystitch. For more information, see Staystitching, page 92.

Many sewing books will tell you to use directional stitching throughout your garment. In theory, this is a great idea,

but in reality it isn't always practical when stitching seams. With some techniques and situations, you may not be able to clearly see what you're doing, or you may end up with too much fabric in the smaller working space that's to the right of the machine needle. So, use directional stitching wherever it is practical to do so.

## Intersecting seams

When one seam or dart will be crossed by another – for example, side seams crossed by a waist seam or the inside corners of a waistband – diagonally trim the ends of the first seam allowance or dart to reduce bulk.

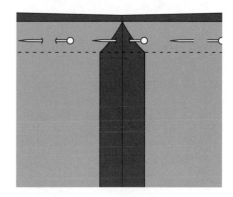

## Trimming and grading

Enclosed seams – those that end up sandwiched in between two layers of fabric – must be trimmed and graded to reduce bulk, or thickness. Enclosed seams are frequently found at the outer edges of collars and cuffs, as well as along any faced edges. See Sewing with Your Scissors, page 98, for more detailed information about trimming and grading techniques.

## Gathered or eased seams

Always stitch with the gathered side up (this is a good example of where directional stitching may not be possible). Guide the fabric with your hands to prevent unwanted tucks or puckers from forming.

## Bias seams

To join two bias edges, such as the side seam of a bias-cut skirt, hold the fabric in front and in back of the presser foot and stretch it gently as you stitch. Although this allows the seam to "give" as you stitch, it will also relax into a smooth seam when you are finished.

---

### PERFECT CORNERS

✂ The trick to perfect corners is knowing just where to pivot the fabric. The easiest way to do this is to make a mark, using chalk or a disappearing marking pencil, at the intersection point of the two seamlines.

✂ Stop machine stitching when you come within a few stitches of the mark. Then use the hand wheel to form the next few stitches until the needle is exactly at the mark.

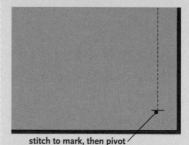

stitch to mark, then pivot

✂ With the needle still in the fabric, raise the presser foot. Pivot the fabric to bring it into the correct position for stitching the seam on the second side of the corner, lower the presser foot and continue stitching.

---

## Corners

To strengthen seams at corners, shorten the stitch length for about 1in (2.5cm) on either side of the corner. This reinforcement stitching helps prevent the corner from fraying after it is trimmed and turned right side out. Cutting away excess fabric in the seam allowance before you turn corners and points right side out will eliminate bulk and help you to achieve a neat finish.

### FOR OUTWARD CORNERS

Trim diagonally. If your fabric frays a lot, seal the corner with a dot of liquid seam sealant after you've trimmed it.

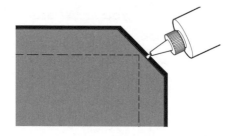

### FOR SHARP OUTWARD CORNERS

For example, on a collar point, take one or two diagonal stitches across it instead of stitching right up to the point. Trim across the point first and then trim diagonally on either side.

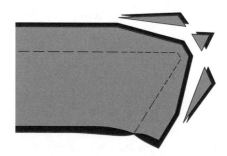

### FOR INWARD CORNERS

Clip almost to the stitching.

---

### TO JOIN AN INWARD CORNER TO AN OUTWARD CORNER

For example, on a yoke, work as follows.

**A1** Reinforce the inward corner with small stitches and clip just to the stitching.

**A2** Pin the two sections together, matching seamlines and markings, with the clipped section on top.

**A3** Stitch to the corner, leave the needle in the fabric, raise the presser foot and pivot the fabric so that the clipped edge spreads apart and the cut edges of the fabric match.

**A4** Lower the presser foot and continue stitching.

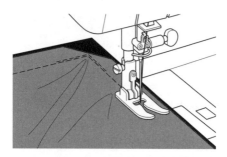

## TYPES OF SEAMS

The plain seam is the one that you'll use most often. However there are other choices if you want to achieve a specific decorative look or if you are using a fabric that requires some special handling. The plain seam usually requires a seam finish. However, many of the other seams highlighted here incorporate the seam finish into the seam technique.

**NOTE** Your pattern instructions will probably utilize a plain seam but you have the option of changing that. Chapter 7, Sewing on Special Fabrics, has some seam suggestions for special fabrics. Always be sure to make a sample seam in some scraps of your fabric before you begin.

## Plain seam

This is the simplest form of seam, designed to hold two or more layers of fabric securely together.

**A1**  With right sides together, stitch along the seamline, which is usually ⅝ in (1.5cm) from the cut edge, with a regulation-length stitch. For knits, stretch the fabric slightly as you sew.

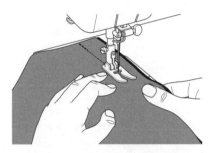

**A2**  Press the seam flat and then open.

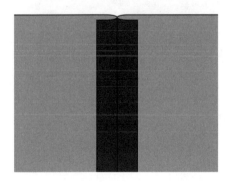

**A3**  Finish the seam allowances with an appropriate finish (see Seam Finishes, page 97).

> **TIP**  If you're using a machine zigzag, overcast or overlock stitch to finish your plain seams, plan ahead. Finish all the seam allowances at one time, before stitching the seams.

## Double-stitched seam

This is a combination seam-and-edge finish that creates a narrow seam especially good for sheers and knits. To prevent the fabric from unraveling, it's stitched twice.

**B1**  Stitch a plain seam.

**B2**  Stitch again, ⅛ in (3mm) away, within the seam allowance, using a straight or zigzag stitch.

**B3**  Trim close to the second row of stitching.

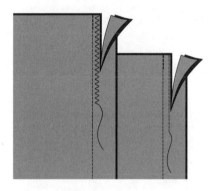

**B4**  Press the seam flat to set the stitches, and then press to one side.

## Stretch knit seams

Stretch knits need seams that are supple enough to "give" with the fabric. You can sew them with straight stitches, zigzag stitches or one of the stretch stitches built in to many conventional machines, or on your serger. Here are some variations utilizing the straight stitch and the zigzag stitch.

**Method 1:** Stitch a plain seam, and stretch the fabric slightly as you sew.

**Method 2:** For extra strength, stitch a double-stitched seam.

**Method 3:** For even greater strength, straight-stitch along the seamline or use a narrow, medium-length zigzag stitch. Then zigzag ¼ in (6mm) away, within the seam allowance, and trim close to the last line of stitching.

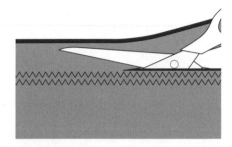

**NOTE**  If your machine has a built-in stretch stitch, consult your owner's manual for instructions. Usually, it is unnecessary to trim the seam allowance before stitching.

## Stabilizing knit seams

Seams at the neckline, shoulders and waistlines should not stretch. If they do, the knit garment will lose its shape. Stabilize these seams by stitching seam binding or twill tape into the seams, or use Stay-Tape™, a lightweight stabilized nylon tape that works well on lightweight knits and curved edges.

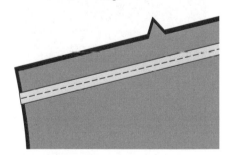

## Flat-fell seam

The flat-fell seam is frequently used on sportswear, menswear and reversible garments. It is designed to give a strong join on heavy-duty fabric subject to wear and tear and is traditionally used for jeans.

**C1** With the wrong sides of the fabric together, stitch a plain seam.

**C2** Trim the seam allowance on one side only to ⅛in (3mm).

**C3** Press the seam flat. Turn under ¼in (6mm) of the untrimmed seam allowance and fold it over to cover the trimmed edge. Pin or baste in place.

**C4** Edgestitch close to the fold.

## French seam

This seam adds a couture look to the inside of garments made from sheers and lightweight silks. The finished seam, which should be very narrow, completely encloses the raw edges of the seam allowances.

**D1** With the wrong sides together, stitch a ⅜in (1cm) seam.

**D2** Trim the seam allowances to a scant ⅛in (3mm) and then press them open.

**D3** Fold the fabric right sides together along the stitching line; then press. Stitch ¼in (6mm) from the fold.

**D4** Press the seam allowances flat and then to one side.

## Lapped seam

This type of seam is frequently used on nonwoven fabrics, such as synthetic suede and leather, and on real suede and leather, as their edges do not fray. It is used to join pieces with minimum bulk.

**E1** Trim away the seam allowance on the upper (overlap) section.

**E2** Lap the edge over the underneath section, placing the trimmed edge along the seamline; hold it in place with double-faced basting tape, glue stick or fuse basting.

**E3** Edgestitch along the trimmed edge. Topstitch on the overlap ¼in (6mm) away from the first line of stitching.

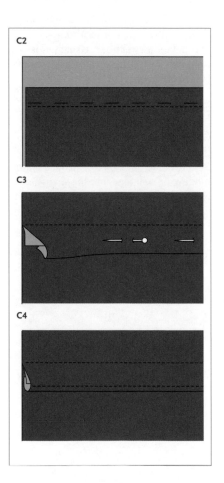

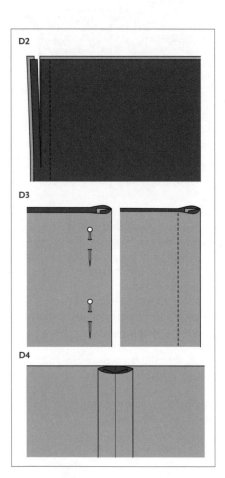

seamline

**TIP** As a timesaving reference, keep your sample seams in a notebook along with a record of stitch length, thread tension, needle size, etc.

### Topstitched seam, method 1

This treatment accents the seamlines. It also helps keep the seam allowances flat – a great benefit when you're working with crease-resistant fabrics.

**F1**  Stitch a plain seam (page 95) and press it open.

**F2**  Working on the outside of the garment, topstitch on both sides of the seam ¹⁄₈ in–¹⁄₄ in (3mm–6mm) from the seamline.

### Topstitched seam, method 2

As an alternative, stitch a plain seam, press the seam allowances to one side and topstitch ¹⁄₈ in–¹⁄₄ in (3mm–6mm) from the seam, through all of the layers.

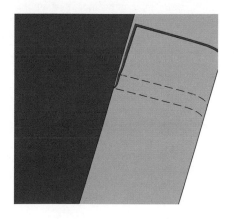

### Welt seam

This type of seam is a good way to reduce bulk and hold seam allowances flat on heavyweight fabrics. From the outside, it looks like a topstitched seam.

**G1**  With the fabric right sides together, stitch a plain seam. Finish the seam allowance on one side with an overcast or zigzag stitch. Trim the seam allowance on the other side to a scant ¹⁄₄ in (6mm). Press both seam allowances to one side, so the finished edge covers the trimmed edge.

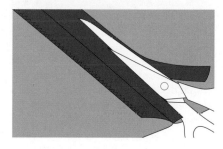

**G2**  Working from the right side, topstitch ³⁄₈ in (9mm) away and parallel to the original seamline to hold the seam allowances in place.

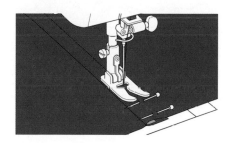

### Double-welt seam

From the right side, this looks like a flat-fell seam. Work as the welt seam, but also work a line of edgestitching close to the seamline.

## SEAM FINISHES

To prevent unraveling and add durability, plain seams usually require some type of seam finish. However, if the garment is going to be lined, or if the fabric is very tightly woven, no seam finish is required.

Here are some easy-to-do seam finishes. They can also be used as an edge finish on facings and hems.

### Stitch and pink

This is the quickest method for finishing fabrics that do not fray easily. Stitch ¹⁄₄ in (6mm) from each seam allowance edge. Trim close to the stitching with a pair of pinking shears.

**TIP**  Don't use pinking shears on knit fabrics. It's unnecessary work and may cause the fabric to curl.

### Zigzag

This is a good choice for most fabrics, including heavyweight ones that unravel. Zigzag over, or as close as possible to, each raw edge. Experiment with the stitch width, using a smaller stitch width for lightweight fabrics and a larger one for heavyweights.

> **TIP** If your machine has an overcast stitch, you can use it in place of the zigzag stitch.

### Overlock stitch

Use the two-thread or three-thread overlock stitch as close as possible to each raw edge.

### Straight stitch

Use this finish on knits that curl, including swimwear fabrics, jersey and stretch terry. To minimize curling, finish the seams before stitching them. Stitch 1/4 in (6mm) from the raw edges.

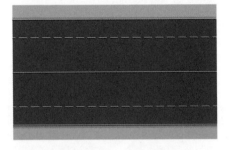

### Tricot bound

This is a custom finish that's suitable for any fabric. However, if the fabric frays a great deal, bind the seam allowances before stitching the seams. Use Seams Great®, a sheer, lightweight tricot seam binding. To make sure you are applying it so the binding automatically curls around the seam allowance, hold the tricot up and tug on the ends.

Position the binding so it curls around the seam allowance and secure it at the beginning with a pin. Take one or two machine stitches, remove the pin and continue to stitch, gently stretching the tape so it encases the fabric. As you stitch, you'll be sewing through both edges of tape at once. You can use a straight stitch, but for best results, particularly on fabrics that fray, use a narrow zigzag stitch.

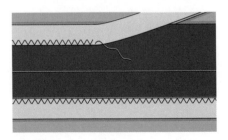

# SEWING WITH YOUR SCISSORS

**Not all good sewing techniques are centered on the sewing machine. Your scissors are an invaluable aid to professional results. Thanks to scissors, your garments can have crisper corners and flatter edges, as well as smoother curves and seams. There are three key techniques you need to master – trimming, grading, and clipping and notching.**

## TRIMMING

Trimming simply means to cut away some of the seam allowance. See When Should You Trim?, opposite.

## GRADING

Grading refers to the process of trimming each seam allowance to a different width so that the layers won't create ridges on the outside of the garment. This technique is most commonly used on enclosed seams, such as those sometimes found along collar, cuff, pocket and faced edges. If the fabric is lightweight, grading is usually not necessary – trimming is enough. However, if the fabric is medium- to heavyweight, all enclosed seams must be trimmed and graded. Corners require special treatment as is described in detail on page 94.

To grade, trim the seam allowance that will end up closest to the inside of the garment to ⅛ in (3mm); trim the seam allowance that will be closest to the outside of the garment to ¼ in (6mm). The wider seam allowance acts as a cushion for the narrower one.

## CLIPPING AND NOTCHING

Clipping and notching are techniques used to reduce bulk in the seam allowances to make curved seams lie flat.

**On inside, or concave, curves:** Make little slits, or snips, in the seam allowance just to, but not through, the stitching.

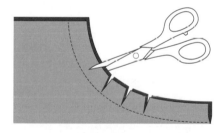

**On outward, or convex, curves:** Cut wedge shaped notches from the seam allowance to eliminate excess fullness when the seam is pressed open.

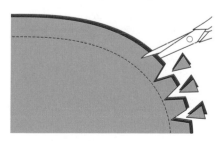

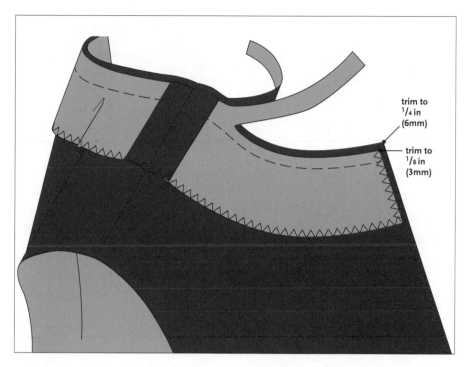

trim to ¼ in (6mm)

trim to ⅛ in (3mm)

Grading is the process of trimming each seam allowance to a different width to avoid visible ridges on the right side.

**When joining an inward curve to an outward curve:** For a stronger seam, staystitch each curve a scant ¼ in (3mm) inside the seamline. Pin or baste the garment sections together and stitch the seam. Then, being careful not to cut through the staystitching, clip one seam allowance to release the fabric and notch the other to eliminate excess fullness.

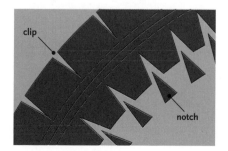

clip

notch

### WHEN SHOULD YOU TRIM?

✂ In areas such as the underarm section of an armhole seam, where the wider seam allowance would interfere with the fit.

✂ When a special seam technique, such as a French seam or a welt seam, requires it.

✂ On enclosed seams as a preliminary step to grading.

✂ To eliminate excess fabric at the seam allowances of corners and points, so that they will lie smooth and flat once they're turned right side out.

# SEWING WITH A SERGER

**No matter what type of serger you choose, the best advice anyone can give you is read your machine's manual to familiarize yourself with its capabilities. Sergers are extremely easy to operate. Once you've learned how to thread the machine, and which tension dials control which thread, you're ready to get serging.**

## SERGER ANATOMY

A serger stitches in a different way than a conventional sewing machine: it often has more than one needle and uses several loopers instead of one bobbin. The illustrations on these pages cover the basic parts common to most sergers.

## FRONT

**1  Foot pressure dial:** Adjustable foot pressure allows you to sew very lightweight or heavyweight fabrics more successfully. This function may not be available on all models.

**2  Differential feed dial:** This can be adjusted to prevent waving seams on stretch fabrics and to ensure pucker-free seams on lightweight fabrics. This function may not be available on all models (see Differential Feed Function, page 104 for more detail).

**3  Flat bed:** With some sergers it is possible to remove part of the bed to create a free-arm facility just as it is on some conventional sewing machines.

**4  Needle plate:** Some sergers come with a second needle plate for stitching rolled hems; others have a special plate already built in – you need to pull a lever or press a button to bring it into play.

**5  Stitch or cutting width dial:** To regulate the width of the serged seam.

**6  Presser foot:** Holds the fabric against the needle plate and feed dog. Like a sewing machine, the serger has different types of foot for different tasks, but serger and sewing machine feet are not interchangeable.

**7  Needle:** Sergers may have one, two or three needles; use the recommended needle for your machine. Serger and sewing machine needles are not generally interchangeable.

**8  Hinged case:** The lower section of the body opens up to access the threading areas for the loopers. There is often a color-coded threading diagram inside for your guidance.

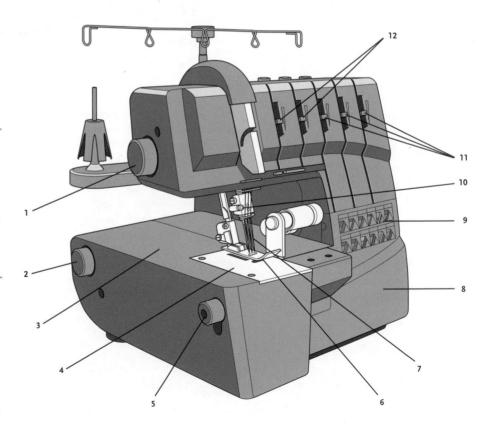

**9 Stitch patterns:** Illustrated reference for the types of stitch that can be sewn, with reference numbers that match those on the stitch selector.

**10 Needle clamp screws:** To release the needles when they require changing.

**11 Looper thread tension levers:** Used to adjust the tension of the looper threads; there may be two or three, depending on the model. The loopers are located in the interior of the serger, accessed by a hinged door – they create the knitted look of the serger seam.

**12 Needle thread tension levers:** Used to adjust the tension of the upper needle threads; there may be one, two or three, depending on the model.

## BACK

**13 Thread guide:** Each separate thread has its own guide. The threading runs are color-coded for ease of threading.

**14 Stitch selector dial:** For selecting the type of serger stitch to be sewn.

**15 Stitch length dial:** For regulating the length of the stitches.

**16 Hand wheel:** Turn the hand wheel towards you (counterclockwise) to move the needle up and down slowly or to take the new thread through when rethreading using the knot method.

**17 Power switch:** To turn the machine on and off.

**18 Power socket:** Socket for the power cable and the foot pedal; on some models there may be a separate socket for the foot pedal.

**19 Telescopic rod:** Can be extended to take the thread guide hanger up to its full height or telescoped down for easier storage.

**20 Presser foot lifting lever:** This is behind the thread spool and is used to lift the presser foot to slide the fabric beneath, or when changing the foot.

**21 Thread spool pins:** These hold the thread for the needles and the loopers, one for each threading run. Sergers use a great deal of thread, so larger spools or cones are a better option.

**22 Thread guide hanger:** Each thread guide should be positioned above a corresponding cone beneath. Make sure the thread guide hanger is pulled up to its full height on its telescopic rod when using the serger to ensure that the thread flows smoothly off the spool.

**Cutting blades (not shown):** A serger has a lower blade and an upper blade, which can be retracted if you want to stitch without trimming the fabric edge. The cutting blades are positioned to the right of the presser foot.

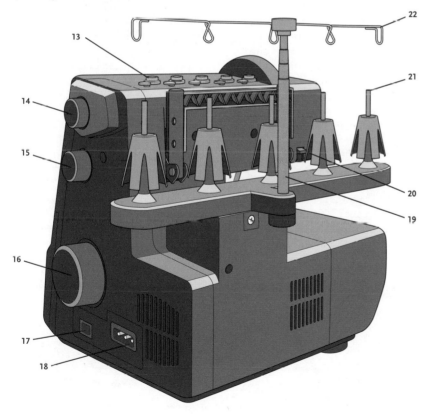

**TIP** There will be variations depending on make and model, and on how many threads the serger accommodates. Different models may have different controls in alternative positions, so take time to study your machine's manual.

## SERGER FUNCTIONS

Not all sergers can create every type of overlock stitch. Some machines perform only one or two functions or stitch configurations, while others can perform several. You'll hear them described as two-thread, three-thread, three/four-thread, four-thread, four-thread mock safety and even five- or eight-thread machines. While no serger uses all eight threads at the same time, more thread paths offer the flexibility to perform more thread functions. The key to choosing a serger is to understand what each stitch function can do, then select the serger model that offers the functions that are most important to you.

### Two-thread functions

There are two basic types of two-thread stitch functions.

#### TWO-THREAD SERGER OR OVERLOCK STITCH

This stitch uses one needle and one looper. The two threads interlock at the fabric edge. On the underside of the fabric, the needle thread forms a V. Because the two-thread stitch uses only two threads, the result is a flat, economical stitch that's ideal for a seam finish (see page 98).

It can also be used to create a flatlock stitch used for decorative outside seaming and to reduce bulk in speciality fabrics such as fake fur and sweater knits, and to create a blind hem (see opposite).

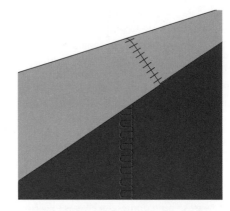

The flatlock stitch can be done so that the "ladders" appear on the inside or outside of the garment.

### CHAIN STITCH

The two-thread chain stitch (or double chain stitch as it is sometimes known) uses one needle and one looper to create a single line of stitches. This stitch is occasionally used alone as a replacement for the straight stitch on the conventional machine. Use it only for wovens; it is not flexible enough for knits. With the blade disengaged, the chain stitch can be used to create interesting decorative topstitching. Most often, however, it is used in conjunction with the two-thread or three-thread serger stitch, particularly where extra stretch or security is desired. Five-thread sergers, like the one shown on pages 100 and 106, can create the chain stitch and the three-thread serger stitch simultaneously.

### Three-thread functions

As well as the stitch described below, see also the Narrow Rolled Edge Function described opposite.

#### THREE-THREAD SERGER OR OVERLOCK STITCH

This stitch uses one needle and two loopers. All three threads interlock at the fabric edge. It is a very versatile stitch and can be used by itself to join and overcast a seam or as an edge finish for a seam stitched on a conventional machine (see page 98).

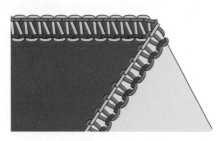

It can also be used or to create a mock flatlock seam. It is a useful stitch for hemming; use for a narrow hem (see page 195) and for a blind hem, although the resulting hem is not quite as nice as the two-thread version (see opposite). In addition, the three-thread stitch is the most popular choice for decorative work.

Three-thread mock flatlock.

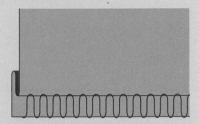

Stitching the two-thread blind hem.

Finished two-thread blind hem.

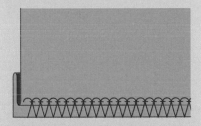

Stitching the three-thread blind hem.

Finished three-thread blind hem.

## Four-thread functions

There are three types of four-thread serger stitches.

### FOUR-THREAD SAFETY STITCH

This stitch is a combination of chain stitch and two-thread serger stitch. It uses two needles and two loopers. One needle and one looper create a two-thread safety chain stitch; the remaining needle and looper create a two-thread serger stitch.

This stitch is suitable for stable or woven fabrics. Because the chain isn't a flexible, stretchable stitch, this stitch is not recommended for knits. The chain will "pop" when the fabric is stretched.

On machines that have this function, you can use the serger and chain stitches together or separately, as described in Two-thread Functions, opposite.

### FOUR-THREAD SERGER OR OVERLOCK STITCH AND THE FOUR-THREAD MOCK SAFETY STITCH

These stitches use two needles and two loopers. The looper threads interlock with the needle threads at the left and with one another at the fabric edges. Although these functions were designed specifically with knits in mind, they can also be used on wovens. The extra row of straight stitching that runs down the middle of the overlock stitch configuration adds stability.

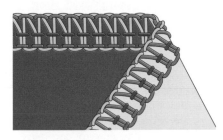

Four-thread serger or overlock stitch.

Four-thread mock safety stitch.

## Narrow rolled edge function

This is a variation of the three-thread overlock stitch. It's used to create a fine edge finish on a wide variety of items such as ruffles, scarves, napkins, tablecloths and garment hems.

The narrow rolled hem uses one needle and two loopers. The lower looper tension is tightened so that the upper looper thread rolls the fabric edge and encases it.

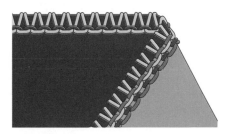

### Coverstitch function

This stitch is created with two or three needles and one looper thread. The result is two or three parallel rows of stitching on one side of the fabric depending on whether two or three needles are used. The other side has one set of loops that interlock between the needle threads. Because this stitch is done away from the edge of the fabric, the upper blade must be disengaged.

This stitch can be used for decorative hemming or topstitching, with either the looper threads or the needle threads on the outside of the garment. Because the coverstitch has some "give" it is a good choice for stretch fabrics.

**TIP** Here's a quick way to learn which thread forms which part of the stitch. Use a different color thread for each looper and needle. Make some practice seams, changing the tensions. Observe what happens to the stitch formation.

### Differential feed function

Sergers equipped with a differential feed have two independent sets of feed dog, one in the front and one in the back. When the differential feed is set at "N" (normal), the front feed dog will move the fabric along at the same rate as the back feed dog. By changing their relative motions, these sets of feed dog can be used to stretch or compress the material near the needle.

When the differential feed is set at 1.3 to 2, the front feed dog will move the fabric at a faster rate than the back feed dog. As a result, the fabric will be gathered. Differential feed settings from 1.3 to 2 are used for gathering and easing, as well as to compensate for stretch distortion on knit fabrics.

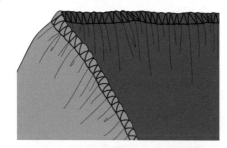

When the differential feed is set at 0.6 to 0.8, the front feed dog moves the fabric at a slower rate than the back feed dog. This feature is useful for eliminating puckering on woven fabrics and for stretching knit fabrics for a decorative waved (lettuce-edge) effect.

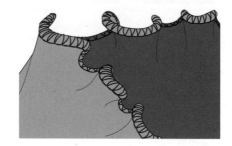

## THREADING THE SERGER

When it comes to choosing thread for your serger, the same basic rule applies as for your conventional sewing machine: good-quality thread equals better stitch quality and results in fewer problems with thread breakage. This means you should select a thread that is made from long, continuous fibers. Take some time to review the thread options below and then practice threading up your machine.

**TIP** One way to tell if the thread you are selecting is a quality thread is to examine it carefully for the "fuzzies". These indicate that the thread is made up of lots of short fibers, resulting in a weaker thread that will break easily. The fuzzier the thread, the poorer the quality.

### Types of serger thread

Because the serger sews fast – from 1,200 to 1,800 stitches per minute – the thread should be strong enough to withstand the speed, yet fine enough to create a soft, supple seam finish. One of the best all-purpose threads for conventional sewing is cotton thread with a polyester core, and, although it is possible to use this same thread in your serger, you'll be happier with the results if you use one especially designed for the serger. There are many to choose from.

**Cotton-wrapped or 100 percent polyester serger threads:** These threads are similar to, but finer than, conventional sewing threads. They're available on large (1,000 yards or more) cones.

**Nylon serger thread:** This is very strong and is recommended for knit swimwear, lingerie and active sportswear, including leotards or other clothing made with Lycra® or elasticized fabric. It also works well for rolled hems when threaded through the upper looper. (see page 193.)

**Wooly nylon thread:** This is a texturized (unspun) thread with a slightly kinked surface. As with nylon serger thread, it is recommended for knit swimwear, lingerie and leotards, as well as Lycra®

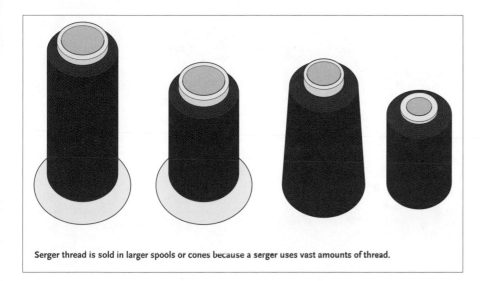

Serger thread is sold in larger spools or cones because a serger uses vast amounts of thread.

**TIP** If you're using conventional thread in your serger needle(s), place it on the spool pin with the notched end down and use a spool cap. This will prevent the thread from getting caught in the spool's rough edges as it rapidly unwinds.

spool cap

notch

or elasticized fabric. Because these garments have seams that come in direct contact with the body, you may prefer wooly nylon to 100 percent nylon serger thread because it's softer. It also lies flatter than many other threads. For a narrow rolled hem, this thread is a great choice for the upper looper. It will roll smoothly over the edge of the fabric and, because of its texturized surface, it will fill the edge with color.

**100 percent silk thread:** This is the same silk thread used in a conventional sewing machine. It has a luster, shine and color range difficult to find in other threads. However, it is expensive and may not be readily available. Save your silk thread and use it where it has the greatest value – for rolled hems. Because silk is very resilient and lustrous, it will create a tighter, richer-looking edge.

**100 percent cotton serger thread:** This type of thread isn't quite as strong as other threads. It is fine for woven fabrics, but if you intend to use it for other fabrics, use it in the loopers, with polyester or nylon thread in the needle(s).

**Conventional sewing thread:** Sometimes this is the only thread you can find in the color you want. If that is the case, use the matching conventional thread in the needle(s) and use serger thread in the loopers. The serger thread should be in a color that "blends" with your fashion fabric. For example, try gray for medium to dark fabrics, white or ecru on pastels, brown on rust, navy on purple, etc.
**NOTE** Black threads can sometimes cause static, leading to skipped stitches, so if possible use a dark gray instead.

**Decorative threads:** Because a serger's loopers have large eyes that can accommodate heavier threads, you can use a wider range of decorative threads on it than on the conventional sewing machine so have fun experimenting. If you are just starting out, it is probably a good idea to use decorative threads in the loopers only. Try baby yarn, metallic or silk thread, No. 8 pearl cotton, $1/16$ in (2mm) wide silk or rayon ribbon, machine embroidery thread, shiny rayon thread, candlewicking thread, crochet cotton or even embroidery floss (two, three or six strands).

---

**DECORATIVE THREAD IDEAS**

✂ Thread the upper looper with baby yarn and serge the edges of a placemat, coat or jacket. It's a great substitute for fold-over braid or bias tape.

✂ Use metallic or silk thread in the upper looper for a beautiful rolled hem (see page 193).

✂ Use variegated No.8 pearl cotton in the looper and flatlock your seams, using the two-thread stitch configuration.

✂ With a three-thread stitch configuration, try a mock flatlock seam, with the pearl cotton in the upper looper.

## Threading with the knot method

Threading your serger in the proper sequence is key to achieving a balanced stitch. This may vary depending on the brand and model of your serger. Do make sure you follow the exact order of threading given in your machine's manual or you may find the thread keeps breaking when you try to stitch.

The easiest way to thread a serger with existing threads in place is to knot the new thread to an existing thread and pull the new thread through, either by winding the hand wheel or pulling through by hand. Tie the new thread to the end of the old using a flat reef knot. Take the ends of thread, one in each hand. Take the left end over the right end and under, so the left end is now on the right and vice versa. Take the end now on the right over the one on the left and under. You should now have a symmetrical flat knot. Trim the thread ends, but not too close to the knot as it may pull undone.

Make sure the presser foot lever is up and loosen the tension dials to 0, then wind the new threads through the serger using the hand wheel, or pull each through gently one at a time from above the needle or looper eye. Ease the knot gently at key points – such as through the tension plates. On the needle threads, stop the knot before the eye of the needle, snip it off and thread the needle by hand. If not done automatically, reset the tension when the machine is correctly rethreaded.

> **TIP** A new machine may have threads in place running through the machine with the ends hanging from the loops on the thread guide hanger towards the spool pins. Do not remove, as they are there to help you to thread the machine the first time.

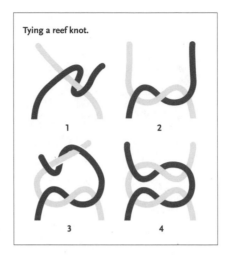

Tying a reef knot.

1  2  3  4

BELOW **The two needles are threaded in red and blue, the upper looper in yellow, the lower looper in orange and the chain-stitch looper in green.**

### AVOIDING THREADING PROBLEMS

✂ Never set the machine stitching to work the knots through, as they can easily damage the mechanism.

✂ If threading from scratch, the loopers should always be threaded before the needles. Some sergers are best threaded in the following order: lower looper; upper looper; right needle; left needle. On others the order is: upper looper; lower looper; right needle; left needle. Check your machine's manual.

✂ If the looper thread breaks, you will have to unthread the needle threads from the eye of the needle before trying to rethread the looper.

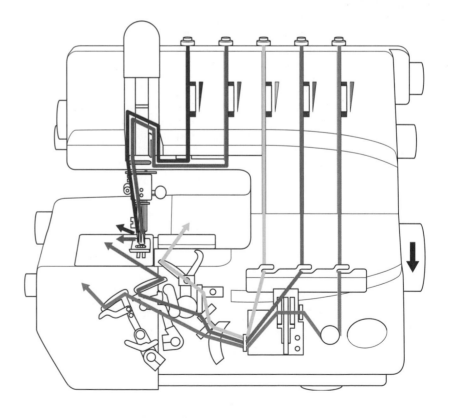

## TECHNIQUES FOR SERGING

The serger is designed to stitch very fast and to cut the fabric as it stitches, so it has sharp, moving cutters or blades. You need to be very aware of safety when you are using it, particularly when you are guiding the fabric towards the needle. Covered here are a few of the techniques that will help you to get the best from your serger.

### Pinning and basting

Although it is possible to sew over pins on some conventional sewing machines, you must never do so on a serger! Sergers have both stationary and movable cutters, or blades. As you serge, they are constantly moving, cutting off the excess seam allowances or ragged fabric edges. If a pin happens to be in the way, it will be cut off, dulling the blades and sending pin fragments through the air. Flying pins can cut your face or damage your eyes, or get into the inner workings of your machine with expensive consequences.

This doesn't mean you have to forgo pin basting altogether and the illustrations below show two safe ways for you to pin and serge, so saving you time as you stitch.

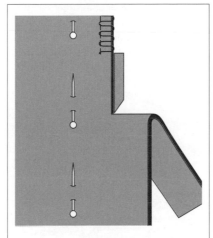

Place the pins at least 1in (2.5cm) from the cut edge, parallel to the seamline. This method is good for long seams but not for detail areas.

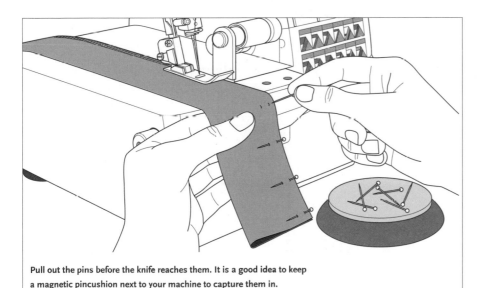

Pull out the pins before the knife reaches them. It is a good idea to keep a magnetic pincushion next to your machine to capture them in.

### DOUBLE-FACED BASTING TAPE

As a substitute for pin basting, place double-faced basting tape as close to the cut edge of the fabric as you can (to avoid stitching or cutting through it).

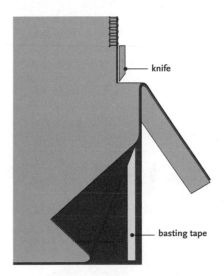

knife

basting tape

### Where to position your hands

As you stitch, it is important to keep your hands safely away from the cutting blade. Place your left hand forward to move the fabric, and to guide and steady it so it doesn't twist as it is stitched, while keeping your right hand further back away from the blade.

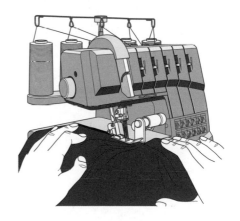

## Starting serging

With a conventional sewing machine, you must always remember to lower the presser foot before stitching and raise it again when you've finished or else your machine won't form the stitches properly. With a serger, you can leave the presser foot in the "down" position all the time. For a smooth start, serge a 2in–3in (5cm–7.5cm) thread chain; then gently feed the fabric under the foot. If you're sewing on very thick fabric, or through many layers, you may want to serge a chain and use your thumb to lift the front of the foot onto the fabric.

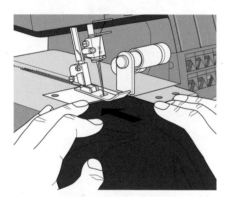

**Starting serging for an unseen seam.**

If you're using your serger to finish the seams, or if other seams will intersect the seams, you don't need to bother securing the thread ends. To simply end your stitching, serge off the fabric for about 5in–6in (12.5cm–15cm). Without raising the presser foot, bring the chain and fabric around so the chain crosses in front of the blade. Stitch for a few more seconds so that the blades automatically cut the thread chain off.

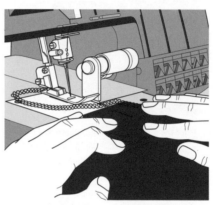

**Finishing serging when securing threads ends is unnecessary.**

## Backstitching

Your conventional machine usually has a backstitch button or knob that allows you to sew two or three stitches back over themselves to secure thread ends as necessary. Although this isn't possible with a serger, it is possible to stitch back over a serged seam or thread chain for a neat finish where the beginning or end of a seam will be seen.

### AT THE BEGINNING OF THE SEAM
**A1** Serge a 2in (5cm) thread chain.
**A2** Lift the tip of the presser foot with your thumb, place the garment underneath and take four or five stitches, leaving the needle in the fabric.
**A3** Raise the presser foot. Swinging the chain around to the front from the left of the needle, place it in the seam allowance, between needle and knife.
**A4** Lower the presser foot and serge, encasing the thread chain in the seam allowance.

**TIP** Remember – if the serged seam is crossed by another seam, there is no need to backstitch.

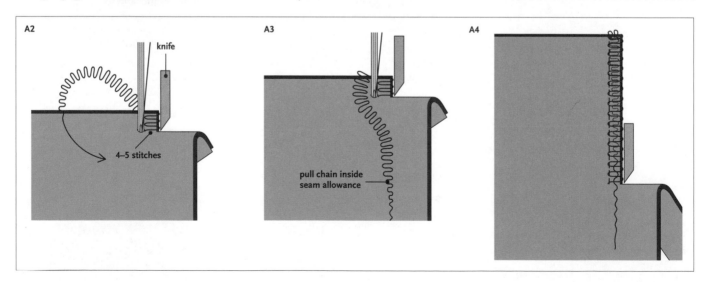

A2
knife
4–5 stitches

A3
pull chain inside seam allowance

A4

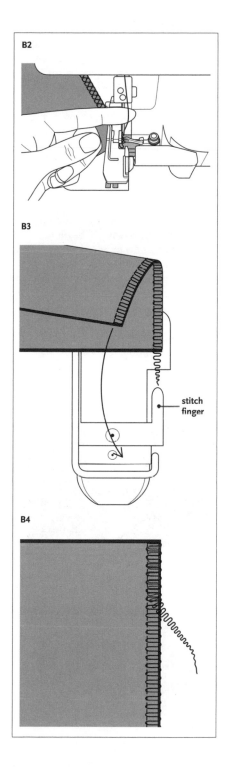

**B2**

**B3**

stitch finger

**B4**

## AT THE END OF A SEAM

**B1**  Serge to the end of the seam, one stitch past the edge of the fabric. Stop with the needle up, out of the fabric.

**B2**  Raise the presser foot. Then gently pull on the needle thread just above the needle to create slack.

**B3**  Pull the last stitch off the stitch fingers. Flip the fabric over and bring it around to the front of the needle.

**B4**  Lower the presser foot and eliminate the slack by pulling on the needle thread just above the tension dial. Serge over the previous stitching for about 1in (2.5cm); then serge off the edge.

## Tying off

Another way to neaten and secure the ends is to tie off the threads. There are two ways to do this. The first method is quick but a little bulky. The second method takes a little more time but will result in an almost invisible knot.

### METHOD 1

Gently run your fingertips along the thread chain to smooth it out. Then tie the threads as described for securing conventional machine stitching (see Secure the Thread Ends, page 88).

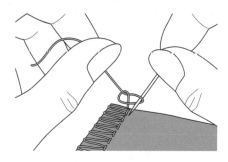

### METHOD 2

Hold the project and thread chain in one hand. With the other hand, use a pin (an extra-long quilting pin works very well) to loosen the needle thread(s).

Pull the needle thread(s) out of the chain. Once the threads are free they can be tied in a small knot.

## Burying the threads

Thread the chain onto a large-eyed craft needle and then tunnel it back along the seam allowance, between the fabric and the stitches.

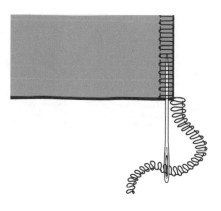

## Liquid seam sealant

Apply a drop of liquid seam sealant, such as Fray Check™, to the last stitches. Let it dry and then clip off the threads. For extra security, tie off the thread ends first.

## SERGING SEAMS

Your serger can be used as a finishing machine for seams that will eventually be sewn on a conventional sewing machine or it can be used to simultaneously finish and stitch a seam.

When sewing on a conventional machine, the top layer of fabric always feeds slightly faster than the bottom layer. As a result, the rule is to stitch with the grain whenever possible and practical. With your serger, this is a rule that you can happily break. Because the presser foot has a firmer pressure and the loopers "knit" the threads across the fabric, as well as along its length, shifting is virtually eliminated. As a result, you can stitch your seams in any direction.

### Continuous overcasting

If you plan to stitch your seams on a conventional machine, you can use your serger and the continuous overcasting technique to speed up the mundane task of finishing the raw edges.

Use a two-thread or three-thread stitch to overcast, or serge, the edges. As you serge, the blade should skim the edge of the fabric so nothing is trimmed off the seam allowance except a few loose threads.

For continuous overcasting, you will need to line up all the garment sections so that the stitching is not broken as you move from the edge of one section to the edge of another. Once the overcasting is finished, the thread chains are clipped and the garment sections are separated.

For example, suppose you are making a simple top and matching pair of shorts, here's how you would line up the pattern pieces and feed them into the serger.

**A1** Begin by overcasting all of the hem edges. Once completed, cut the threads in between.

**A2** Starting with the bodice front, begin at the hemline and overcast one side seam (A), the two shoulder seams (B and C) and then the other side seam (D).

**A3** Without snipping the thread, and without raising the presser foot, move on to the bodice back. Overcast in the same sequence as for the bodice front (E, F, G and H).

**A4** Without snipping the threads, overcast the outside legs of the shorts front and shorts back (I, J, K and L). Your work-in-progress will begin to resemble an oddly shaped kite tail.

**A5** When you are finished with the outside legs, turn everything around and overcast the inside legs (M, N, O, P, Q, R, S and T). Once all are complete, serge off.

**A6** To separate the garment sections, simply snip through the connecting thread chains.

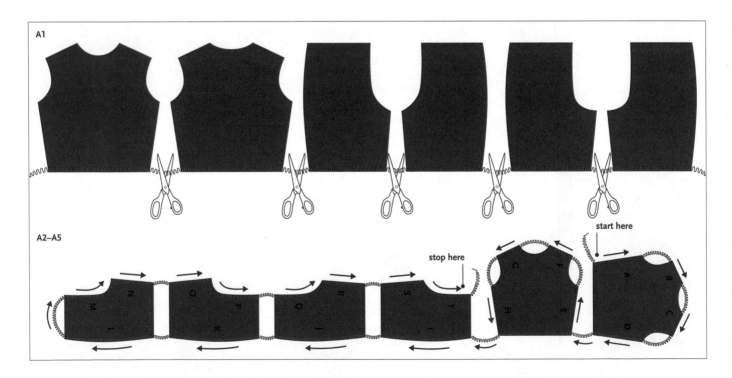

## Speed seaming

This technique for joining the seams of a garment is similar to the sequence for continuous overcasting. Suppose, for example, you are making a simple top and want to join and finish the seams using only the serger.

**B1** Overcast the bottom hem edges; then cut the threads in between.

**B2** Pin the garment together at the side and shoulder seams.

**B3** Starting at the hemline, serge up one side seam (A). Chain off but do not cut the threads.

**B4** Serge the first shoulder seam (B), from armhole to neck edge, and chain off. Again, do not cut the threads.

**B5** Serge the second shoulder seam from neck edge to armhole and then chain off (C).

**B6** Serge the remaining side seam (D) from armhole to hemline.

**B7** Snip the threads between the seams. Press the seams, and you're ready to go on to the finishing details, such as facing, bands and hems.

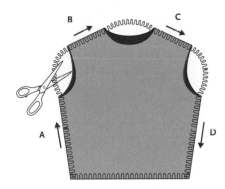

## Staystitching

Fabrics that require special handling on a conventional machine are easy to sew on the serger. Stretchy sweater knits, stretch terrycloth and velour, slippery crepe de chine, jersey and nylon tricot are a few of the difficult fabrics that your serger will handle just like a piece of crisply woven cotton.

One of the reasons that many sewers have avoided these "special" fabrics is their tendency to stretch out of shape, during both handling and sewing. Staystitching is the way to prevent fabric distortion and on a serger it's really easy to do.

Place a strand of ¼in (6mm) twill tape, knitting ribbon or baby yarn so that it goes under the presser foot and over the finger guard, and serge slightly to the right of the seamline. If your machine has a presser foot with a hole for inserting cording, thread the tape, ribbon or yarn through the hole first; then pull it under the back of the foot and serge.

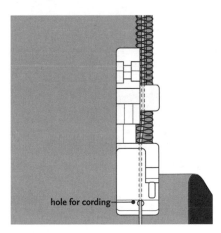

hole for cording

When you are ready to serge your garment together, remember that the blade on your serger has trimmed away the excess seam allowance. Sections that are staystitched will now have ¼in (6mm) seam allowances.

## Staystitch and seam

Some garment sections may not require any handling between the time you staystitch and the time you serge the seams. If this is the case, staystitch and join the seams at the same time. Pin the garment together along the seamline, position the twill tape and serge the seam. Remember to remove the pins as they approach the blade.

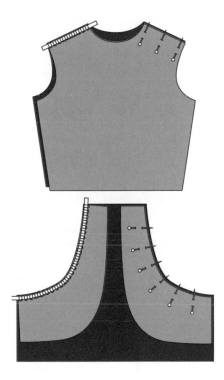

**TIP** On very stretchy knits or loosely woven fabrics, staystitch over elastic thread. In its relaxed position, elastic thread is strong enough to hold a shape. However, it will also stretch and give when you pull the garment on and off.

## SERGER SPECIAL TECHNIQUES

### Serging outside corners

Because of the way a serger creates the stitches, going around an outside corner calls for some special treatment. If you don't use the following procedure, one of two things will happen: either a small, untidy cloverleaf of thread will form at the corner, or you won't be able to pivot the fabric to get a sharp point. But don't worry; the technique is very easy to do.

**A1**  Starting at one edge of the outside corner, make a 2in (5cm) long slash, parallel to and $^3/_8$ in (9mm) in from the edge of the fabric.

**A2**  Beginning on side A, serge to the corner, going just one stitch past the edge of the fabric.

**A3**  Lift the presser foot and gently pull on the needle thread to create a little bit of slack.

**A4**  Carefully pull the last stitch off the stitch finger(s) and pivot the fabric, positioning it so that the new stitches will butt up against the previous stitches.

**A5**  Pull the needle thread back up above the tension control to remove the slack.

**A6**  Serge side B. The result is a neat, clean corner.

> **TIP**  To prevent any "bumps" or distortion that might occur when serging over bulky, intersecting seams, press the seam allowances so that they will face in opposite directions when you serge.

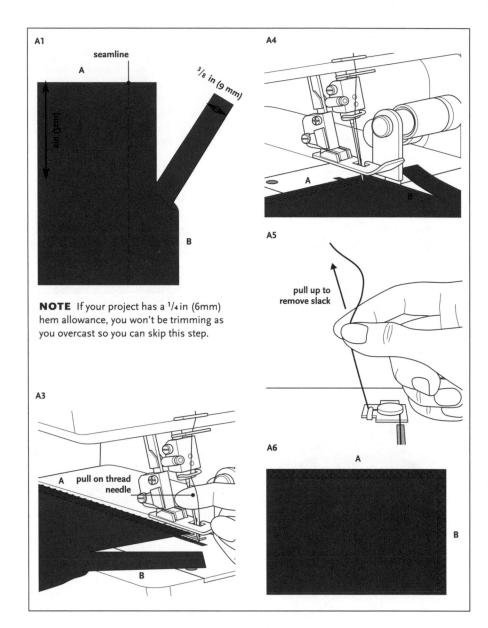

**NOTE**  If your project has a $^1/_4$ in (6mm) hem allowance, you won't be trimming as you overcast so you can skip this step.

## Serging inside corners

On rare occasions, you may want to serge an edge that includes an inside corner. This technique takes practice, so try it out first on some scraps of fabric until you are happy with the results.

**B1** Using a disappearing marking pen, mark the corner at the intersection of the ⅝in (1.5cm) seamlines. If your fabric is soft, staystitch the inside corner on your conventional sewing machine.

**B2** Clip the corner, ending the clip ⅛in (3mm) from the corner mark.

**B3** Starting at the clip, and working on side B of the corner, trim the seam allowance down to ⅛in (3mm) for approximately 1in (2.5cm).

**B4** Beginning at side A, serge until side B is just in front of the knife. Spread the fabric open so that the cut edge of side B is even with the edge of the blade. (A small pleat will appear in the fabric as you do this.) Continue serging side B.

## Serging in a circle

As serger stitches must always begin and end at the edge of the fabric, and because a serger cannot backstitch, sewing in a circle requires some special – but simple – techniques. Suppose, for example, you want to attach a circular band to a neckline, or a circular cuff to the edge of a sleeve, or finish the edges of an oval placemat or round tablecloth. To help you to do these tasks, you can choose from either the Serge On/Serge Off technique described right, or the Clip Method outlined on page 114.

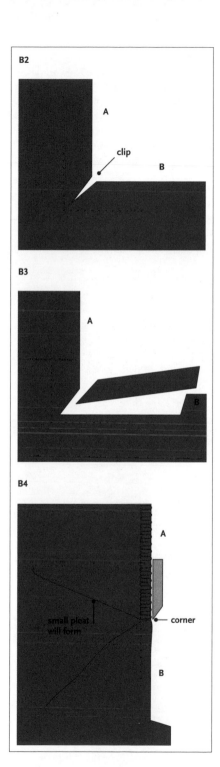

Since this is the fastest – but not the neatest – method, it is usually used when the seam will be hidden inside the garment. All of the intersecting seams are serged before the circular seam is stitched.

**C1** With right sides together, pin the two garment sections together.

**C2** At some point along the seamline (usually the center back), make a 2in (5cm) long mark along the ⅝in (1.5cm) seam allowance with a disappearing marking pen.

**C3** Serge, starting just before the mark and angling the fabric until you are stitching along the mark.

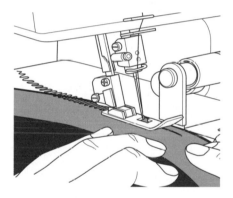

**C4** Serge around the circular area until the stitches meet at the mark. Serge off the fabric.

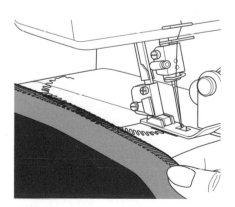

### CLIP METHOD

Use this method when you are finishing a continuous edge, such as the neckline or hemline of a garment, or hemming an item such as an oval placemat or round tablecloth.

**D1** If you have a seam or hem allowance that is deeper than ¼ in (6mm), make two parallel clips in the seam allowance 2in (5cm) apart. Trim the seam allowance away between the clips.

**NOTE** If the project has a ¼ in (6mm) seam allowance, skip this step.

**D2** Raise the presser foot and place the fabric so that the trimmed edge is next to the knife and the needle is at the top of the clipped area. Carefully lower the presser foot onto the fabric.

**D3** Serge around the edge until the stitches meet and overlap for two or three stitches.

**D4** Pull the thread through the needles by hand to create about 3in (7.5cm) of slack. Lift the presser foot and pull the fabric toward the back so the stitches come off the stitch fingers. Separate the thread chain and tie off the threads (see page 109).

## Removing stitches

Even the most experienced sewer makes mistakes now and then, and believe it or not, ripping out serger stitching is often easier than ripping out conventional stitching. However, when you restitch, remember that the blade has already trimmed the seam allowance.

### FOR TWO-, THREE- OR FOUR-THREAD SERGER OR OVERLOCK STITCHES

Simply run a seam ripper along the edge of the fabric, under the upper looper threads, cutting them as you go.

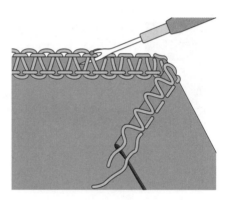

### FOR A FOUR-THREAD SAFETY STITCH

To remove the "chain" part of the stitch, work from the underneath side of the serged stitches and start ripping at the end of the chain. If you can locate the looper thread, pull it. The chain will come undone like ready-to-wear stitches often do. To remove the overedge stitches, turn the fabric to the wrong side and cut along the V created by the needle threads.

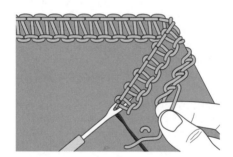

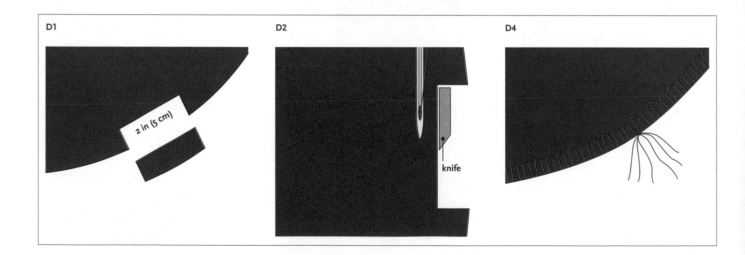

D1

2 in (5 cm)

D2

knife

D4

# SERGER TROUBLESHOOTING

Your serger manual will provide information on how to adjust your tension settings to achieve a well-balanced stitch. Sometimes, however, you may have stitching problems that no amount of fiddling with the tension will correct. For causes of, and solutions to, many of these problems see the chart below which continues on page 116.

which continues on page 116.

> **TIP** Always make sure you turn off the power and unplug the machine before undertaking any maintenance.

## Care and maintenance

A serger often uses far more thread over a shorter period than a conventional sewing machine and the cutting action can create a great deal of lint to build up inside; this can cause stitching problems as well as excess wear on the machine. You should make it your practice to clean out the lint every time you sit down to sew. Open the front and side covers to expose the loopers. Using the small brush that is supplied with your machine, get rid of all of the lint that has accumulated. To keep the mechanism super-clean, you can apply a few squirts of compressed air.

The cutting blades should last for several years before becoming blunt, but if they are not cutting cleanly, wipe them with a little alcohol on a soft cloth and tighten the screws. If either of the blades is still not cutting properly you will need to replace it. If the blade is not cutting at all, check if you have the upper blade disengaged.

| PROBLEM | POSSIBLE CAUSE | SOLUTION |
|---|---|---|
| Skipped stitches | The needle is too heavy for the fabric being stitched. | Change to a finer needle. |
| | The upper looper tension is too tight. | Loosen the upper looper tension. |
| | The needle is damaged or blunt. | Replace the needle. |
| | The needle tension is too loose. | Tighten the needle tension. |
| | The needle is not the correct type. | Always use the type of needle recommended for your serger. |
| | The serger is not threaded correctly. | Rethread the serger, making sure you are going through all the threading guides correctly. |
| Stitches pulling through to the right side | The needle plate being used is the wrong one. | Change to the correct needle plate. |
| | The stitch width is set too narrow for the weight of fabric. | Increase the stitch width. |
| | The thread is not correctly placed into the tension mechanism. | Holding the thread above the tension mechanism, pull it firmly below to slide it into the tension mechanism correctly. |
| | The needle is damaged or blunt. | Replace the needle. |
| | The blade is not correctly set. | Check the manual for instructions on resetting the blade. |

| PROBLEM | POSSIBLE CAUSE | SOLUTION |
|---|---|---|
| **Loops are forming at the seam edge** | The thread is not correctly placed into the tension mechanism. | Holding the thread above the tension mechanism, pull it firmly below to slide it into the tension mechanism correctly. |
| | The looper tension is too loose. | Tighten the looper tension. |
| | The thread has slipped out of the thread guides. | Rethread the serger, making sure you are going through all the threading guides correctly. |
| | The blade is cutting off too much fabric. | Check that the blade is aligned with the edge of the needle plate. Consult the manual if the blade needs realigning. |
| **Serger is jamming** | Presser foot pressure is too heavy for the fabric being sewn. | Reduce the presser foot pressure. |
| | Fabric has been inserted behind the blade. | The blade is in front of the needle, so always insert the fabric from the front so the edge can be trimmed before it reaches the needle. |
| | Thread is caught under the presser foot. | Clean out around the presser foot. Make sure you continue stitching a chain of around 2in (5cm) after completing a row of stitching. |
| **The threads keep breaking** | The serger is not threaded correctly. | Rethread the serger, making sure you are going through all the threading guides correctly and threading the loopers before the needles in the correct order. |
| | The thread guide hanger is not in the right position. | Make sure the telescopic rod is fully extended and that each thread guide is aligned over its corresponding spool pin. |
| | The tension on the thread that is breaking is too tight. | Loosen the tension on that thread. |
| | The thread is caught on the spool or spool pin. | Check the spool is not damaged and that the thread is flowing smoothly. |
| | The thread is old or not strong enough. | Change the thread. Always use good-quality thread. |
| | The needle is damaged or blunt. | Replace the needle. |

# SEWING WITH YOUR IRON

To ensure professional results, careful pressing is just as important as accurate stitching. Sewers press rather than iron. What is the difference? To press means to move the iron across the fabric by lifting it up and putting it back down in an overlapping pattern. To iron means to slide the iron across the fabric with a back-and-forth motion. Ironing may distort the shape of the garment; pressing won't.

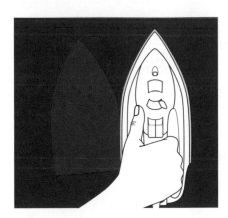

When pressing, the iron is used with an up-and-down action, and not the sliding action used when ironing clothes. The iron is moved across the fabric in an overlapping pattern.

## PRESS AS YOU GO

Pressing seams as you work is an essential part of any sewing project and will give it a much crisper, more professional look. The cardinal rule in sewing is press as you go. This means that you should never cross one seam with another without first pressing the original seam. However, this doesn't mean that you must constantly be hopping back and forth from ironing board to sewing machine. Organize your sewing so that you are working on several different sections of the garment at the same time. Sew as far as you can on each section; then take them all to the ironing board and press everything that needs it. Alternatively, keep your iron and a tabletop ironing board, or a sturdy sleeve board, within arm's reach of your sewing machine. That way, you can do small detail pressing without getting up.

### For perfect results

Although some sewing procedures require special pressing techniques, as you will see in Chapter 6, Sewing Techniques, there are three universal steps for achieving good results.

### RULE 1
Press flat along the stitching line to blend the stitches.

### RULE 2
Press the seam allowances open or to one side, as indicated in the pattern instructions, or to one side if the seam is serged.

> **TIP** If speed sewing is your goal, learn to "batch press". This means sewing as far as you can on different sections of your garment, then taking everything to the ironing board at once.

### RULE 3
Press the seam or detail area from the right side. If necessary, protect the fabric with a press cloth.

Generally, it's best to use light pressure, without resting the full weight of the iron on the fabric. Some delicate fabrics or fabrics with a texture that could be flattened, such as velvet or fake furs, can be finger pressed. To do this, hold the iron above the fabric and apply a generous amount of steam. Then use your fingers, not the iron, to press seams, darts and edges.

The chart on the page 119 is a useful guide to pressing today's common fibers and textures.

> **TIP** To avoid seam allowance imprints on the outside of your garment, slip recycled paper strips underneath the seam allowances as the seams are pressed open.

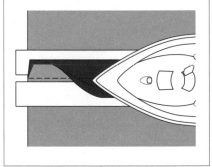

## PRESSING EQUIPMENT

In addition to your iron and ironing board, there's a wide range of pressing equipment available. Pressing aids are designed to provide a shaped pressing surface that simulates the curves of the body, and allow you to press detail areas without putting creases into the rest of the garment.

There is no need to buy all of the equipment listed below. Start with a seam roll (or the no-cost substitute described) and some press cloths; you can add to your collection as your sewing skills develop.

### TYPES OF PRESSING EQUIPMENT

**Seam roll:** Useful for pressing seams open on long, cylindrical garment sections, such as sleeves and pant legs. If you press the seams open using the tip of your iron, the curved surface prevents the seam allowances from creating imprints on the outside of the garment. As a quick no-cost substitute , place a magazine on top of a piece of muslin, roll it up tightly and secure with a few rubber bands.

**Tailor's ham:** Useful for pressing curved areas such as darts, Princess seams and sleeve caps.

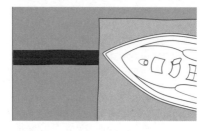

**Press cloths:** Used between your iron and your fashion fabric to prevent scorch marks and iron shine. Use any of the following: specially treated press cloths; muslin in several different weights; a piece of your fashion fabric; a man's handkerchief.

**Needle board:** This is a good investment if you plan to sew with lots of velvets, velveteens or corduroys. Place the fabric facedown on the board and press. The short, dense needles keep the pile from being flattened by the weight of the iron. A fluffy terry cloth towel or a scrap of self-fabric provides a cushioned surface that can substitute for a needle board.

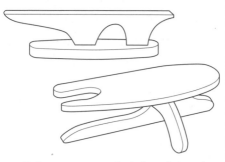

**Point presser or tailor's board:** A multi-edged surface that makes it possible to press seams open on detail areas such as collars, cuffs and facings.

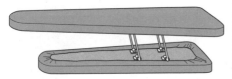

**Sleeve board:** Great for pressing narrow garment sections that won't fit over the regular ironing board.

## PRESS-AS-YOU-SEW GUIDE

| FIBER | PRESSURE | HEAT | MOISTURE | SPECIAL INSTRUCTIONS |
|---|---|---|---|---|
| Acetate | Light | Very low | Dry iron | Use press cloth on right side. |
| Acrylic | Light | Moderate | Dry iron | Same as acetate. |
| Cotton | Light to moderate | Moderate to high | Dry or steam iron | Press with steam iron. For more moisture, dampen fabric and press with dry iron. To avoid shine on dark colors, press from wrong side or use press cloth on right side. |
| Linen | Light to heavy | High | Dry or steam iron | Same as cotton. |
| Nylon | Light | Low to moderate | Dry or steam iron | Little or no ironing required. |
| Polyester | Moderate | Low to moderate | Dry or steam iron | May need press cloth on right side; test first. |
| Rayon | Light | Low to moderate | Dry or steam iron | Use press cloth to prevent shine and water spots. |
| Silk | Light | Low to moderate | Dry or steam iron | Press light to medium-weights with dry iron. For heavy-weights, use steam iron and dry press cloth to avoid water spots. |
| Wool | Light to moderate | Moderate | Dry or steam iron | Press with steam iron. For more moisture, press with dry iron and slightly damp press cloth. Use press cloth on right side to prevent shine. Press crepe with dry iron. |
| Blends | Press according to requirements of the most delicate fiber. | | | |

| TEXTURE | PRESSURE | HEAT | MOISTURE | SPECIAL INSTRUCTIONS |
|---|---|---|---|---|
| Crepe | Light | Low to moderate | Dry iron | Use press cloth on right side. |
| Deep Pile | Finger press | Moderate | Steam iron | Experiment on scraps to determine amount of pressure. |
| Glossy | Light | Low | Dry iron | Same as crepe. |
| Nap, Pile | Light or finger press | Low to moderate | Dry or steam iron | Press fabric over needle board, using light pressure or finger press. |

## IRON-ONS AND FUSIBLES

There are certain areas of sewing where you can put your sewing machine aside and "sew" with a wide range of heat-sensitive, iron-on sewing aids. Time-saving and easy to use, these iron-ons and fusibles are a fundamental part of today's sewing – provided you know how to use them. You'll find techniques for using these products throughout Chapter 6, Sewing Techniques. But first, the basics.

**Iron-on:** Generally applied using heat and pressure only – no steam. Mending tape, mending patches and some hem tapes are today's most common iron-ons. Other iron-on products available include embroidered appliqués and sequin trims.

**Fusible:** Applied using a combination of heat, steam and pressure. Fusible products include fusible interfacings and fusible web. Fusible interfacings are used to shape, support or reinforce your fabric. Fusible web can be applied to adhere two layers of fabric, for easier appliqué for example, or for hemming.

Both iron-on and fusible products come with instructions. Be sure to follow them carefully. To be on the safe side, always use a press cloth to protect your fabric.

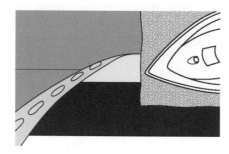

Iron-on hem tape provides a quick and easy no-sew method for hemming casual clothes and children's garments. Alternatively, use fusible web.

### Using fusible web

Fusible web is an adhesive web that "glues" two layers of fabric together. If you examine fusible web carefully, you'll see that it's a network of fibers. When the prescribed combination of heat, steam and pressure is applied, these fibers melt and "disappear" causing the two layers of fabric to adhere securely to one another.

Some fusible webs, such as Wonder-Under® from Pellon®, come with a paper backing that provides the stability needed to cut the web into any shape, no matter how small or detailed. With a light touch of your iron, and following the manufacturer's directions, you can transfer the web to fabric, peel away the paper and then fuse.

fusible web strip

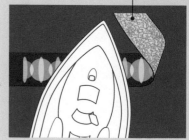

# HAND SEWING

**Although most of your sewing will be done at the machine, there are times when only a hand stitch will do. Indeed, good-quality professional items are almost always finished by hand. So take the time to make sure your hand-stitching techniques are up to scratch.**

## HAND SEWN STITCHES

You have already been introduced to hand basting, a useful technique for transferring marking to the right side of the garment and for temporarily holding the garment together (see page 81). In addition, the following stitches are the ones you'll use most frequently.

### Backstitch
Backstitch (see diagram above right) creates a row of stitches set end-to-end and looking from the right side like machine stitching; on the reverse, the end of each stitch overlaps the next. It is ideal for mending and to hand stitch short seams securely. To work backstitch, bring the needle through the fabric, insert it a short distance behind where it came out and bring it up through the fabric again the same distance ahead. Each subsequent stitch begins at the end of the previous stitch; all stitches should be the same size.

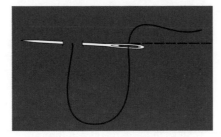

### Pickstitch
This stitch is also referred to as a half-backstitch. It can be useful when inserting a zipper in a fragile or hard-to-handle fabric, such as those used in bridal or evening wear, and is used in place of the final topstitching. To ensure a straight line of pickstitches, add a row of hand basting stitches as a guideline. Starting from the bottom of the zipper, fasten the thread on the underside of the zipper and bring the needle up through the zipper tape and garment layers. Insert the needle back down through all of the layers a thread or two behind the point where it first emerged. Bring the needle up again about ¼in (6mm) ahead of the first stitch. Continue along the length of the zipper.

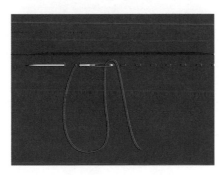

### Hemming stitch
Use this stitch if the hem allowance is finished with seam binding. Begin at a seam, fastening the thread in the seam allowance. Take a tiny stitch through the garment, picking up a single thread.

Insert the needle between the seam binding and the garment, and bring it out through the seam binding, about ¼in (6mm) to the left of the first stitch. Take another stitch in the garment, ¼in (6mm) to the left of the second stitch. Continue, alternating from seam binding to garment, and taking several stitches on the needle before drawing the thread through the fabric.

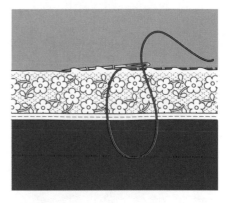

### Slipstitch
This is a good choice for securing turned-under edges because the stitches are invisible on both the inside and outside of the garment. Bring the needle up through the folded edge of one side, take a tiny stitch through just one or two threads in the opposite layer or fold, then insert the needle back into the fold of the first layer. Slide the needle along inside the fold and bring it out ¼in (6mm) away. Repeat the sequence.

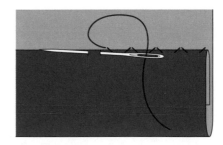

### Blindstitch

This stitch is useful for hemming knits and bulky fabrics. It will help prevent a ridge from forming at the hemline on the outside of the garment. Fold back the garment slightly below the hem edge and hold it with your thumb. Fasten the thread in the hem edge and, working from right to left, take a tiny stitch about ¼in (6mm) to the left in the garment. Take the next stitch ¼in (6mm) away in the hem edge. Continue, alternating from garment to hem and keeping the stitches evenly spaced.

### Catchstitch

This stitch has some built-in stretch, which makes it an especially good choice for hemming knits and for holding edges, such as facings, in place. Fasten the thread to the wrong side of the hem or facing. Work from left to right, with the needle pointing to the left. Take a tiny stitch in the garment ¼in (6mm) to the right, close to the hem or facing edge. Take the next stitch ¼in (6mm) to the right in the hem or facing, so that the stitches form an 'X'. Continue, alternating from garment to hem or facing, keeping the stitches fairly loose.

### Tacking

This stitch helps keep facings in place at the seams and is useful for permanently attaching snaps or hooks and eyes (see page 204). Holding the edge of the facing and the seam allowance together, take three or four short stitches in one place through both layers. Do not sew through the garment fabric. Repeat on the other seam allowance.

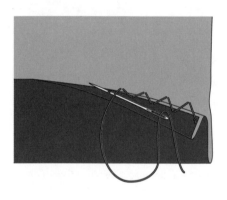

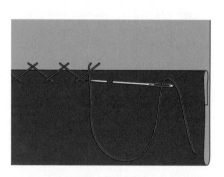

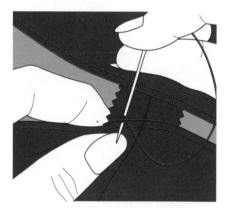

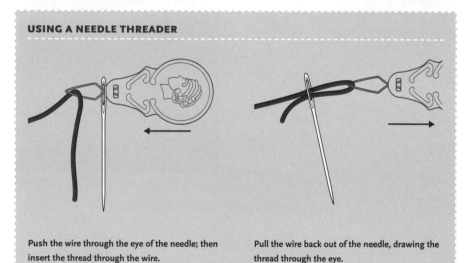

**TIP** Stitch-in-the-ditch (see page 92) is the quick machine alternative to hand tacking a facing in place.

**USING A NEEDLE THREADER**

Push the wire through the eye of the needle; then insert the thread through the wire.

Pull the wire back out of the needle, drawing the thread through the eye.

# HAND SEWING TIPS

## For tangle-free sewing
**A1** Cut the thread in lengths no longer than18in (45.5cm).
**A2** Draw the thread through beeswax. This will also make the thread stronger.

## For easy needle threading
**B1** Cut the thread diagonally by holding your scissors at a slant.
**B2** Hold the needle up against a white background to see the eye clearly.
**B3** Use a calyx-eyed needle. These are designed with a tiny opening at the top for easy threading. Alternatively, use a needle threader (see opposite).

## To knot the thread
**C1** Insert the thread through the eye of the needle and then cut it off at the desired length.
**C2** Working with the end you just cut off the spool, hold the thread between your thumb and index finger, and then wrap the thread around your index finger.
**C3** While holding the thread taut, slide your index finger back along your thumb until the thread ends twist into a loop.
**C4** Continue sliding your index finger back until the loop slides off your finger.
**C5** Bring your middle finger down to hold the open loop; then pull on the thread to form a knot.

## To secure the stitching
**D1** Form a thread loop by taking a very small backstitch at the point where the needle last emerged.

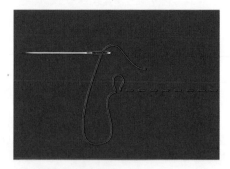

**D2** Take a second small backstitch on top of the first. As you complete the stitch, bring the needle and thread through the loop.

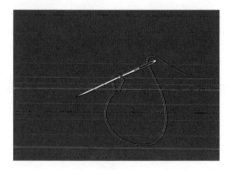

**D3** Pull on the thread, drawing up the loop and making both stitches taut.
**D4** If the stitching is subject to a great deal of strain, repeat to form a second "knot". Cut the thread.

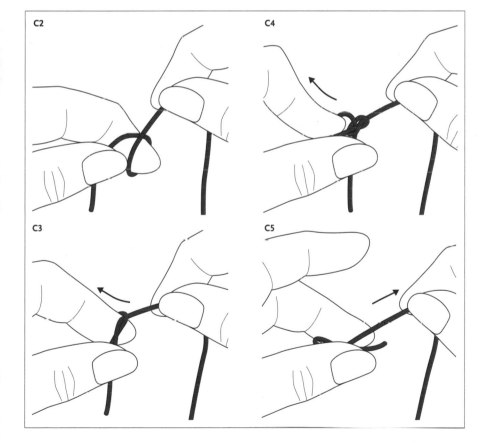

# SEWING
# TECHNIQUES

# INTRODUCTION

This chapter is designed to support the techniques included on your pattern's instruction sheet, providing you with more detailed information on the key elements used in garment construction and the variations on them. With this information at your fingertips, you will have the confidence to adapt any pattern to your own personal preferences, to alter style details, fabric choice or add decorative finishes, enabling you to create a wardrobe that is as individual as you are.

# USING A SERGER

Although many patterns are identified as containing special serger instructions, almost every pattern can benefit from blending serger and conventional sewing techniques. For ease of reference, featured serger techniques are identified with a special logo Ⓢ.
It may surprise you just how often a serger can provide you with an alternative to a conventional method.

| TECHNIQUE | | | | |
|---|---|---|---|---|
| TYPE OF SERGER STITCH: | | 3 | 4 | MINE |
| Stitch length: | | 4mm–5mm | 4mm–5mm | |
| Stitch width: | | Widest | Widest | |
| Tensions | Needle: | Tight | Tight | |
| | Right Needle: | N/A | Normal | |
| | Upper Looper: | Normal | Normal | |
| | Lower Looper: | Normal | Normal | |

This is an example of the serger charts you will find in this chapter. The information they provide will help you to get the most from your serger.

## HOW TO USE THE SERGER CHARTS

Many of the serger techniques in this section include a chart with recommended settings for two-, three-, or four-thread serger stitch settings, as appropriate. Because every serger, like every conventional machine, has its own personality, there's also a space for you to record the appropriate settings for your machine. An example of a serger chart appears above. In each chart you will find the following pieces of information.

### Type of serger stitch
This identifies the serger settings for a two-, three- or four-thread stitch. If you don't know what type(s) your serger can make, check your owner's manual. The spaces under the final column headed "Mine" have been left blank for you to record the settings that are appropriate for your machine.

### Stitch length
When serging seams on a woven fabric, a shorter stitch length provides greater durability. You might also want to shorten your stitch for some decorative effects or when making a narrow rolled hem. Where durability is not an issue, such as when overcasting the raw edges of a conventional seam, lengthen the stitch to save thread.

The stitch-length adjustment is usually located on the bottom left of the serger. It's turned either by hand or by using a screwdriver and a lock screw. The stitch length is calibrated on the metric system and ranges from slightly shorter than 1mm to about 5mm.

### Stitch width
When serging on a woven fabric, you might want to widen your stitch so that your seam allowances will be deeper, resulting in seams that are more durable. When serging on knits, where unraveling of the fabric is not a problem, a narrower width will give you a daintier seam. On sheer fabrics that do not unravel excessively, a narrow width creates a neater look, both inside and out.

Stitch width is generally determined by the needle plate and presser foot, or by whether you use the right or left needle. However, instead of changing needle plates, some machines use a dial-type width adjustment for both three-thread and four-thread serging.

### ON A THREE-THREAD SERGER

✄ Use a needle plate with a narrow stitch finger for a narrow width (approximately 1mm–2mm).

✄ Use a needle plate with a wider stitch finger for the widest setting (usually 4mm–5mm, although some machines go as wide as 7.5mm).

### ON A FOUR-THREAD SERGER

✄ Use the right needle to create a three-thread stitch with a narrow width (approximately 1mm– 2mm). To fine-tune the width, use a needle plate with a narrow stitch finger.

✄ Use the left needle for the widest stitch (approximately 4mm– 5mm). To fine-tune the width, use a needle plate with a wide stitch finger.

**NOTE** Some sergers have adjustable stitch fingers that move in and out so you don't have to change the needle plate. Check your owner's manual for specific information.

## Tensions – thread paths

### NEEDLE AND RIGHT NEEDLE

✄ The three-thread serger stitch uses only one needle, so follow the guidelines for Needle tensions.

✄ The four-thread serger has a left and a right needle. Follow the Needle guidelines for the left needle and the Right Needle guidelines for the right needle.

✄ When N/A (not applicable) appears next to Right Needle, it means that you do not use the right needle for this type of stitch.

### UPPER LOOPER

This identifies how to set the tension on the upper looper. Thread suggestions may also be included.

### LOWER LOOPER

This identifies how to set the tensions on the lower looper.

## Tensions – settings

Thread tension dials are usually numbered or calibrated to indicate the tension settings.

### NORMAL

When the tension is normal, the looper threads are smooth on both sides of the fabric and lock together evenly along the fabric edge. When a seam with normal tension is pressed to one side, you won't see any puckering or threads pulled to the surface on the right side of the fabric.

> **TIP** Once you have established what the normal setting is for your serger, write it on a small piece of masking tape and stick it to your machine for future reference.

### VERY LOOSE

Set the appropriate tension dial approximately one-third of the way between 0, or no tension, and your normal setting.

### TIGHT

Set the appropriate tension dial approximately one-third to half of the way between your normal setting and the tightest possible tension setting for your serger.

### VERY TIGHT

Set the appropriate tension dial almost as tight as it can be adjusted.

# FACINGS AND INTERFACINGS

A facing is a second layer of the main fabric that finishes a garment at necklines, armholes, front and back openings and, occasionally, at the waistline or the lower edge of a sleeve. An interfacing is a specially designed fabric, often sandwiched between a facing and the garment, to provide shape and support in detail areas such as collars, cuffs, lapels, necklines, pockets, waistbands and along opening edges.

## FACINGS

Most facings are created by attaching a separate piece of fabric to the garment edge. However, a garment that opens at the center front or back often has a special facing, called a self-facing, that is cut in one piece with the garment. When this extension is folded back, it serves as the facing for both the opening edges and part of the neckline. To finish off the rest of the neckline, the garment will also have a back neck facing and/or a collar.

### Facing basics

Although the shape and the location can vary, the basics for creating a facing that lies flat and looks professional remain the same.

#### STAYSTITCH

If the facing is located at the neckline or the waistline, staystitch the neck/waist edges on both the garment and the facing. For armhole facings and front and back edges, staystitching will not be necessary.

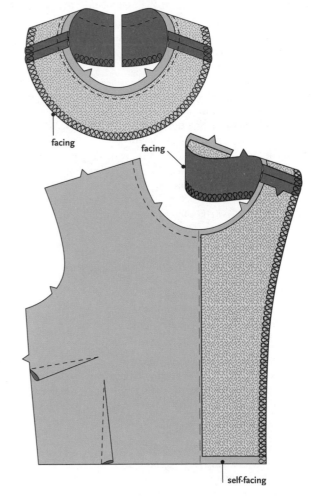

A facing is cut from a separate pattern piece; a self-facing is cut in one with the garment rather than being a separate piece. Both are frequently interfaced.

facing

facing

self-facing

### INTERFACE

Apply interfacing to either the facing section or the garment section, as recommended in your pattern instructions. Fusible interfacing is generally applied to the facing section.

### FINISH THE EDGE

Stitch the facing sections together at the shoulder or side seams; then finish the outer edge. If appropriate, the stitch and pink or the zigzag/overcast finish will add the least amount of bulk (see pages 97 and 98). If your fabric is very bulky and/or unravels a great deal, use the tricot-bound finish (see page 98).

### ATTACH THE FACING

Stitch the facing to the garment, as indicated on your pattern instructions. If there are any corners, remember to shorten your stitch length for about 1in (2.5cm) on either side of each corner.

### TRIM AND GRADE

To prevent ridges from showing on the outside, remove bulk from the seams by trimming the seam allowances to ¼in (6mm). On thick fabrics, also trim the facing seam allowance to ⅛in (3mm) so that the layers are graded. To ensure a smooth edge when the facing is turned to the inside, clip or notch all curved seam allowances.

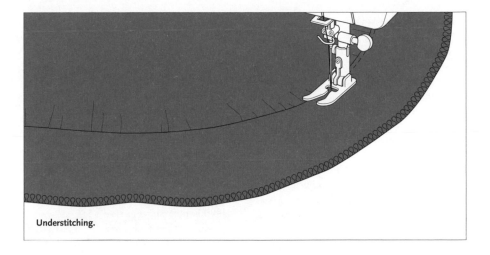

Understitching.

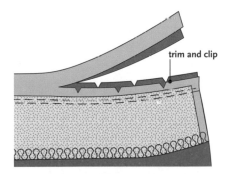

trim and clip

Trim and grade to avoid bulky seams; curved seams may also need clipping or notching.

### PRESS

Press the seam allowances flat to blend the stitches. Next, press open; then press toward the facing.

### UNDERSTITCH

Open the facing out. With the facing on top, stitch through the facing and both seam allowances very close to the seam.

> **TIP** If you have clipped the curves, understitch carefully, checking frequently to make sure those small wedges of seam allowance don't get caught in the stitching.

### PRESS AGAIN

Fold the facing to the inside of the garment along the seamline and press.

### SECURE IN PLACE

To keep the facing from rolling to the outside, secure it at the seam allowances by basting it by hand, stitching in the ditch, or applying a small piece of fusible web.

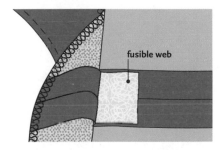

fusible web

Unless the garment is being topstitched, the facing should be secured to the seam allowances to prevent it from being seen. Use fusible web as shown, or hand-baste or stitch in the ditch.

> **TIP** If your fabric is loosely woven or tends to fray, apply fusible interfacing to the facing. It will reinforce the fabric and seal the yarns, making it possible for you to use the easy stitch and pink finish (see page 97).

## ⑤ The serger method

When it comes to facings, your serger can save you a lot of time. Use it first to finish the edges of the facing. Then, if the edge to be faced is a straight edge or a gradual curve, you can use your serger to attach the facing to the garment. Because the serger automatically gives you very narrow seam allowances, trimming, grading, notching and clipping won't be necessary.

**A1**  Serge the facing pieces together. Press the seams to one side.

**A2**  Finish the facing by serging around the outside edges.

**A3**  Pin the facing to the garment edge. If the faced edge has an opening, fold the garment and facing to the inside along the opening edge and pin.

**A4**  Serge along the ⁵/₈ in (1.5cm) seamline, through all of the layers.

**A5**  Press the seam allowances toward the facing; then understitch on your conventional machine.

## Bias tape facing

As an alternative to a regular facing, you can substitute single-fold bias tape. It's a quick and easy technique that's particularly popular for children's clothes. Because the tape is made from bias strips of fabric, it will fit smoothly around curves of neckline and armhole edges. Use either ¹/₂ in (1.3cm) or ⁷/₈ in (2.2cm) wide single-fold bias tape.

**B1**  Trim the garment seam allowance to ¹/₄ in (6mm).

**B2**  Open out one fold of the tape. If you are facing a curved edge, steam-press the tape and pre-shape it to match the garment curve.

**B3**  With right sides together and raw edges even, pin the tape to the garment. To join the ends of the tape, turn under ¹/₂ in (1.3cm) on the first end; lap the other end over it. Straight-stitch or serge a ¹/₄ in (6mm) seam.

**B4**  Turn the tape to the inside and press. As you press, roll the tape slightly to the inside of the garment so it will not show on the outside.

**B5**  On the outside, edgestitch close to the garment edge and then top-stitch about ³/₈ in–³/₄ in (1cm–2cm) from the edge.

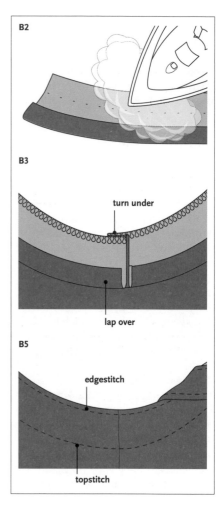

B2

B3

turn under

lap over

B5

edgestitch

topstitch

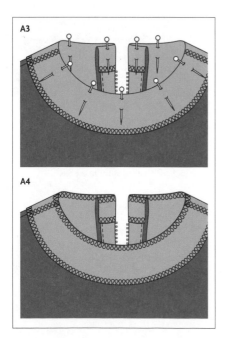

A3

A4

> ⑤ **TIP**  To reduce bulk, make sure the facing seam allowances and the corresponding garment seam allowances are pressed in opposite directions before serging the facing to the garment.

> **TIP**  If the fabric you have chosen is sheer, eliminate the facings and finish the edge with a bias binding cut from your fashion fabric. For more information, see page 144.

### ⓢ Serged neckline

Instead of facing a collarless neckline, try serging it. The serger stitches create a decorative, finished edge. This is a great technique for firmly woven fabrics and knits that don't curl.

Always test first to be sure you like the results before serging your garment's neckline. To test stitching and thread tension, cut the test fabric swatch so that it duplicates the curve of the garment's neckline.

**C1** Adjust your serger to the appropriate setting (see Serged Neckline chart).
**C2** Serge one shoulder seam; serge around the neckline along the ⅝in (1.5cm) seamline.
**C3** Serge the remaining shoulder seam, beginning at the armhole and chaining off 3in–4in (7.5cm–10cm) at the neckline edge. To secure the stitches, thread the chain onto a tapestry needle and weave it back through the shoulder seam stitches.

> ⓢ **TIP** The serged neckline technique can also be used to replace the facing in other parts of a garment, such as an armhole, a hemline or the opening edges of a jacket.

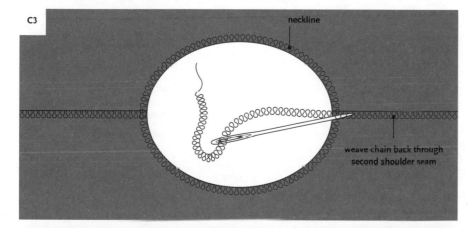

C3

neckline

weave chain back through second shoulder seam

### SERGED NECKLINE

| TYPE OF SERGER STITCH: | | 3 | 4 | MINE |
|---|---|---|---|---|
| Stitch length: | | 3mm | 3mm | |
| Stitch width: | | Widest | Widest | |
| Tensions | Needle: | Tight | Tight | |
| | Right Needle: | N/A | N/A | |
| | Upper Looper: | Normal | Normal | |
| | Lower Looper: | Normal | Normal | |

## INTERFACING

The two basic types of interfacings are sew-in and fusible. Both are available in woven, knitted and nonwoven versions, and in a variety of weights, ranging from heavy to sheer weight. In addition to these specially developed interfacing fabrics, batiste, organza and organdy can be used as interfacings on sheer to lightweight fabrics. As a general rule of thumb, the interfacing should always be slightly lighter in weight than the fashion fabric.

Choosing between a fusible and a sew-in interfacing is really a matter of personal preference. In general, fusibles provide slightly crisper results. Because fusibles "set" the yarns, they're an excellent choice for fabrics that fray. However, some fabrics do not react well to fusibles. These include metallic, beaded, sequined or re-embroidered fabrics, rayon and acetate velvets, most brocades, fake furs, leather, and vinyl, as well as openwork fabrics, such as lace and mesh. Always test fusible interfacing on a scrap of the fashion fabric before you begin. Use the chart on page 132 to match fabric type with suggested interfacings.

Most people think of fusibles as easier to use and they are – as long as you take the time to follow the manufacturer's fusing directions carefully. The key to successful results is the prescribed combination of heat, steam and pressure. In addition, even if the directions do not suggest it, take the time to go through the entire fusing process twice, first on the wrong side and then on the right side of the garment section. This extra step will ensure a strong, even bond.

Be sure to store any interfacing leftovers neatly in self-sealing plastic bags, and, for fusibles, be sure to keep a copy of the fusing directions with the interfacing.

| FABRIC AND USE | INTERFACING | |
|---|---|---|
| | FOR A SOFT EFFECT | FOR A CRISP EFFECT |
| **VERY LIGHT TO LIGHTWEIGHT FABRICS** (voile, gauze, crepe, challis, calico, chambray, interlock knit, jersey, single knit, batiste)<br><br>**USE:** Blouses, shirts and dresses<br><br>NOTE Do not use fusibles on chiffon or seersucker | Batiste; organza; sew-in sheer, regular or stretch very lightweight nonwoven; self-fabric | Organdy; sew-in or fusible lightweight or sheer (nonwoven or woven); fusible knit |
| **MEDIUM-WEIGHT FABRICS** (linen, denim, poplin, flannel, gabardine, satin, duck, chino, velour, stretch terry, double knit, sweater knit)<br><br>**USE:** Dresses, lightweight suits, active sportswear<br><br>NOTE Do not use fusibles on rainwear fabrics | Sew-in or fusible medium-weight woven; regular or stretch light- to medium-weight nonwoven; fusible knit | Sew-in or fusible lightweight hair canvas; sew-in or fusible medium-weight (woven or nonwoven) |
| **HEAVYWEIGHT FABRICS** (corduroy, tweed, worsted, camel hair, melton, sailcloth, canvas, gabardine, coatings)<br><br>**USE:** Jackets, suits, coats | Soft, lightweight canvas; sew-in or fusible medium-weight nonwoven | Sew-in or fusible medium- or heavyweight woven; crisp medium- or heavyweight hair canvas; fusible heavyweight nonwoven |
| **LEATHER TYPES** (suede, suede cloth)<br><br>NOTE Do not use fusibles on real leather | Crisp or soft canvas; fusible or sew-in medium-weight nonwoven or woven | |
| **WAISTBANDS** | Fusible nonwoven precut strips; woven stiffener sold by the width; sew-in or fusible medium- to heavyweight (woven or nonwoven) | |
| **CRAFTS**<br><br>**USE:** Belts, hats, bags, camping gear, home decorations | Sew-in nonwovens in all weights; fusible medium- to heavyweight (woven or nonwoven) | |

## When to interface

Your pattern will tell you which pieces require interfacing and the back of your pattern envelope will tell you how much to buy. But you can add interfacing to certain areas of your garment, even if the pattern doesn't suggest it; for example, you might want to add a little bit of crispness to a patch pocket. And you do not have to use the same weight interfacing throughout the garment. For example, you might decide that the collar should have softer shaping than the cuffs.

To help you decide when to interface, take a look at some of the better ready-to-wear garments and note how some detail areas in the same garment feel crisper than others. Aim to replicate this in the garments that you sew.

## Cutting and marking

Woven and knitted interfacings have lengthwise, crosswise and bias grains. The interfacing pieces should be cut out so that the pieces are on-grain as indicated in the pattern layouts.

Technically, nonwoven interfacings do not have a grain. However, this doesn't mean that you can cut out your pieces anyhow. Some of these interfacings are stable in all directions, others stretch in the crosswise direction, and still others are all bias. Read the interfacing instructions and follow the advice for how to position the pattern pieces.

Transfer the pattern markings to the interfacing sections rather than to the fabric. Buttonhole markings are the exception to this rule as you must be able to see them on the outside of your almost-finished garment.

> **TIP** For small detail areas, such as pockets, pocket flaps, collars or cuffs, fuse the interfacing to the fashion fabric before cutting out the garment section.

## Application

Interfacing is usually applied to the wrong side of what will ultimately be the outermost layer of fabric. For example, apply to the upper collar rather than the undercollar, to the cuff rather than to the cuff facing. Since there are exceptions, be sure to follow your pattern instructions.

### SEW-IN INTERFACING

To minimize bulk, trim the outside corners of the interfacing diagonally, just inside the point where the seamlines meet. Pin- or glue-baste the interfacing to the wrong side of the garment section, and machine-baste ½ in (1.3cm) from the edges. Trim the interfacing seam allowances close to the stitching and trim off any hem allowances.

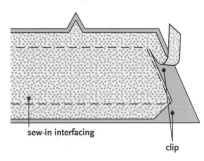

sew-in interfacing

clip

### FUSIBLE INTERFACING

Trim the corners diagonally, the same way as for sew-in interfacings and trim off any hem allowances. However, for all but the heaviest fabrics, there is no need to trim the interfacing seam allowances. It's just too difficult to get the interfacing

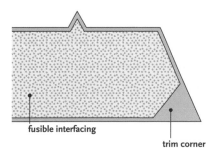

fusible interfacing

trim corner

positioned correctly on the garment section once it's trimmed. Besides that, the amount of bulk it adds is minimal. Fuse the interfacing in place, following the manufacturer's directions.

> **TIP** Sometimes one edge of the interfacing does not extend all the way to a seamline, for example, on a collarless neckline or on the front of a jacket. With a fusible interfacing, a ridge may be visible on the outside of the garment. Test-fuse a piece of the interfacing to the fashion fabric. If a ridge forms, cut the edge of the interfacing with pinking shears. If this doesn't help, apply the interfacing to the facing rather than to the garment body.

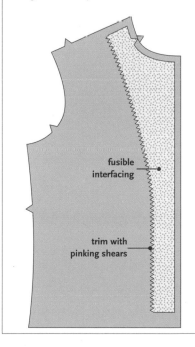

fusible interfacing

trim with pinking shears

# DARTS, TUCKS, PLEATS AND GATHERS

These essential techniques will help you to add shape and structure to garments. Darts are used to mold fabric so that it conforms to the curves of the body. Tucks, pleats and gathers are also ways of controlling fabric fullness, and they can often have the advantage of being very decorative.

## DARTS

Darts can be straight (for an easy fit) or curved (for a closer-to-the-body fit). A dart usually starts at a seamline, tapering to nothing at its tip. However, a double-pointed dart, found on one-piece dresses and closely fitted shirts, blouses and jackets, is actually two darts combined into one. The result is a long dart with the widest part occurring at the waist. It tapers to nothing near the bust (or shoulder blade on the back of a garment) and near the hip.

### Marking

Examine the shape of your dart. If the stitching line is straight, all you need to do is mark the dots. If the stitching line is curved, however, mark the entire stitching line to ensure that you stitch the curve exactly right.

### Stitching

**NOTE** It is not possible to achieve the "tapered-to-nothing" look of a professional dart on a serger so it will be necessary to turn to your conventional sewing machine.

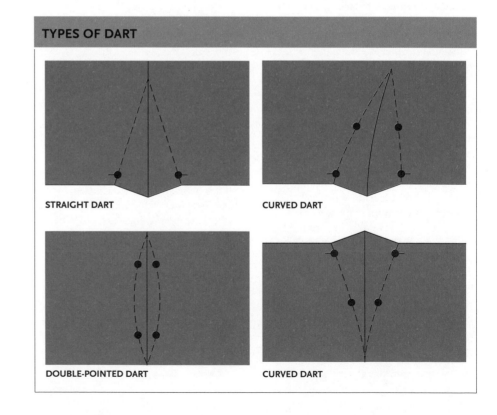

**TYPES OF DART**

STRAIGHT DART

CURVED DART

DOUBLE-POINTED DART

CURVED DART

## A SINGLE DART

With right sides together, fold the fabric through the center of the dart, matching the markings and the stitching lines. Place pins at right angles to the stitching lines. Stitch the dart from the wide end to the point. To prevent a bubble at the point, make the last few stitches right at the fold and leave the thread ends long enough to tie a knot. Do not backstitch at the point.

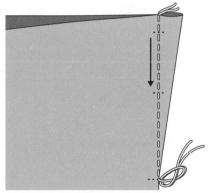

Stitching a single dart.

## A DOUBLE-POINTED DART

Pin and stitch as for a single dart, working from the middle to one end; then, overlapping several stitches, work from the middle to the other end. Carefully clip the dart at its widest point so that it will lie flat.

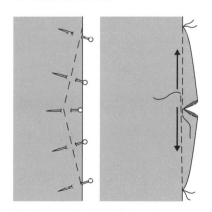

Stitching a double-pointed dart.

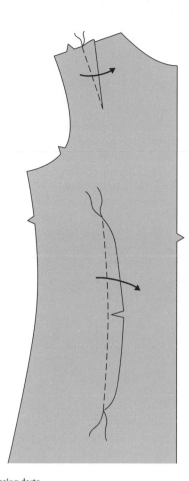

Pressing darts.

## Pressing

Press the darts flat and then open or to one side, as indicated on your pattern instructions. As a rule, vertical darts are pressed toward the center of the garment and horizontal ones are pressed downward as illustrated above.

Occasionally, your pattern instructions will tell you to slash the dart along the foldline and press it open as shown right.

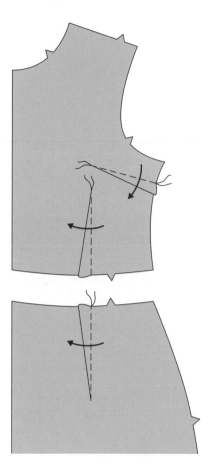

## TUCKS

Alone or in groups, tucks can be found just about any place – at shoulders, waistline or hipline, or adorning a yoke, pocket, cuff or hemline. A special type of tuck, called a growth tuck, can be incorporated into children's garments so that they can be quickly and easily lengthened (see page 138).

### Marking and stitching

Depending on the design of your pattern, tucks can appear on the outside or be hidden on the inside of your garment. If the tucks will be folded and stitched on the inside of the garment, transfer the markings to the wrong side of the fabric. If the tucks will be folded and stitched on the outside, transfer the markings to the right side of the fabric. Choose a method that won't leave permanent marks on the fabric.

If the tucks are straight and parallel to each other, they'll be easier to stitch if you press in the foldlines first as indicated in the pattern instructions: vertical tucks are usually pressed away from the center front or center back; horizontal tucks are usually pressed down. Stitch all tucks in the same direction. (For adding tucks to a pattern, see the tip on page 138).

### NARROW OR PIN TUCKS

These are usually indicated on the pattern tissue by a series of solid lines. Because pin tucks are narrow, the stitching lines are not indicated.

Fold the fabric along the solid line and stitch the specified distance from the fold.

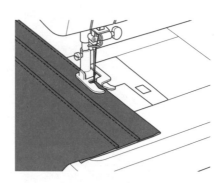

Using an edgestitch foot can help you to keep the line of stitching very near and parallel to the fold.

### WIDE TUCKS

Wide tucks are indicated on the pattern tissue by a series of solid and broken lines. To create the tuck, fold the fabric on the solid line, matching the broken lines to each other. Then stitch along the broken lines as illustrated below.

To save time, transfer only the solid lines to the fabric, fold, then use a stitching guide, such as the needle plate markings for example, to evenly stitch the specified distance from the fold.

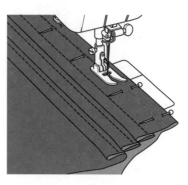

### Decorative pin tucks

#### THE CONVENTIONAL METHOD

If your sewing machine does decorative stitching with regular thread, you can add pretty shell tucks or tucks with fancy stitches to lingerie, dainty blouses or children's dress-up clothes. On lightweight knits or sheers, create a shell tuck by using a machine blindstitch along the folded edge.

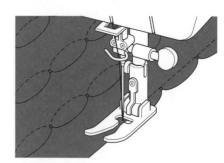

Pattern pieces showing how narrow pin tucks (left) or wide tucks (right) are marked.

On crisper fabrics, choose an appropriate machine embroidery stitch. Position the stitching so that the design falls within the tuck.

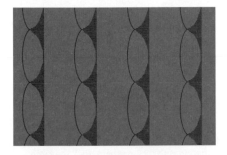

**TIP** If thread build-up is a problem with a decorative stitch, put a strip of water-soluble or heat-disintegrating stabilizer underneath your stitching.

**S THE SERGER METHOD, STANDARD**
For colorful, decorative tucks, thread the upper looper with pearl cotton, embroidery floss, variegated crochet yarn, knitting ribbon or metallic thread.
**A1** Adjust your serger to the appropriate setting (see Pin Tucks chart).
**A2** Mark and press on the tuck foldline as for conventional tucks.
**A3** Serge, keeping the fold slightly to the left of the blade so that the fabric isn't cut. Repeat for as many tucks as desired.
**A4** Press the tucks to one side.

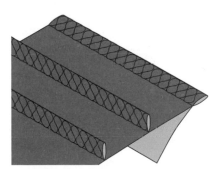

**S TIP** The narrow rolled hemstitch can also be used to make lovely pin tucks. Adjust your machine for its three-thread narrow rolled hem function. Fold the fabric wrong sides together along the tuck line and then serge over the fold. For a satiny appearance, try using a silk or 100 percent rayon thread in the upper looper.

**S THE SERGER METHOD, DECORATIVE**
To add another interesting dimension to your serger tucks, use decorative thread in the upper and lower loopers. Then use your conventional machine to straight stitch horizontally across the serged tucks. Stitch the rows ³/₄in–1in (2cm–2.5cm) apart, alternating the stitching direction. This makes the tucks appear wavy.

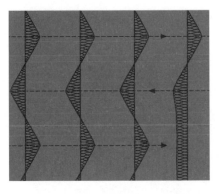

MOCK PIN TUCKS
On light- and medium-weight fabrics, you can create a tucked effect without actually making tucks. Use a twin needle and two matching spools of thread in the top of your machine. The two needle threads combine with one bobbin thread to create raised rows that look like narrow pin tucks.

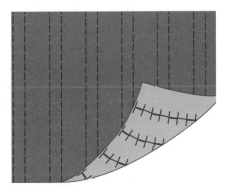

**TIP** If your sewing machine doesn't have an extra spool holder, put the second spool of thread in a glass placed behind, and to the right of, the machine. It will unwind smoothly without rolling away.

| PIN TUCKS | | | |
|---|---|---|---|
| TYPE OF SERGER STITCH: | | 3 | MINE |
| Stitch length: | | 3mm–5mm | |
| Stitch width: | | Widest | |
| Tensions | Needle: | Normal | |
| | Upper Looper: | Loose* | |
| | Lower Looper: | Normal | |
| *Use decorative thread in the upper looper. | | | |

## Growth tucks

Children often grow taller faster than they grow wider. As a result, garments may be too short long before they're too tight. To solve this problem, you can incorporate a growth tuck into the garment. Plan on doing this before the pattern is cut out so you can alter the pattern pieces to allow for extra length.

### HEMLINE GROWTH TUCK

Growth tucks can be incorporated into any straight hemline. The most obvious place to allow for growth is in the skirt hem. However, this technique can also be used on long- or short-sleeve shirts, blouses and pants for both boys and girls.

**B1** Before you cut out the garment, add 3in (7.5cm) to the hem allowance.

**B2** Construct the garment and finish the hem allowance edge.

**B3** Using a machine basting stitch, form a 1½in (3.8cm) tuck on the right side of the fabric, within the hem allowance. Press the tuck toward the hemline.

### WAISTLINE GROWTH TUCK

On a dress with a waistline seam, you can incorporate the growth tuck in the bodice area.

**C1** Before you cut out the garment, lengthen the front and back bodice 1in–3in (2.5cm–7.5cm).

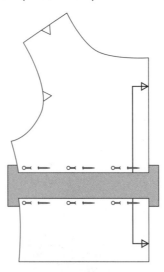

**C2** Sew the bodice together at the side seams.

**C3** On the inside of the bodice, baste a tuck half as wide as the amount you lengthened the bodice. Position the tuck so it is about ¼in (6mm) above the waistline seam.

**C4** Press the tuck up; then join bodice to skirt and complete the garment.

**TIP** If you're adding tucks to a pattern that doesn't include them, tuck the fabric first and then cut out the garment. Be sure to purchase extra fabric to accommodate the tucks.

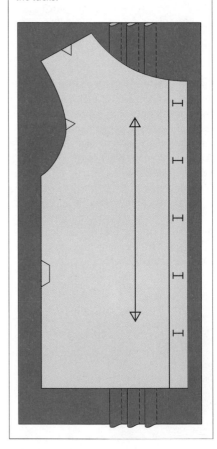

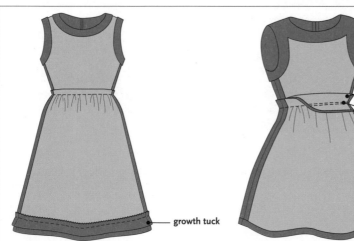

growth tuck

waistline seam

growth tuck

**HEMLINE GROWTH TUCK** When you need to lengthen the garment, remove the basting and press, creating a new hemline. If necessary, you can stitch ribbon or trim over the old hemline crease to disguise it.

**WAISTLINE GROWTH TUCK** To lengthen the garment, release the tuck. If there is a zipper, rip out the lower part, release the tuck and re-stitch the zipper and the seam. If necessary, cover fade marks with a contrasting ribbon or sash.

## PLEATS

Pleats are multiple folds of fabric that control fullness. They can be soft or crisp, depending on the fabric you choose and whether they're pressed or unpressed.

If you're new to sewing, or your sewing skills are rusty, wait until you've got a little more experience at your machine before you attempt pleats. It's not that pleats are difficult to sew, but they do require accurate cutting, marking and stitching. If, for example, you were making a pleated skirt with eight box pleats, and you were "off" $1/8$ in (3mm) on each pleat, the skirt would be 1in (2.5mm) too large or too small at the waistline.

Pleats can be formed by working on either the right or the wrong side of a garment. Your pattern instructions will tell you what to do. Mark the pleats on the wrong side of the fabric; then transfer the markings to the right side, if necessary. Mark both the foldlines and the placement lines. If you're using tracing paper or thread basting, use a different color paper or thread so you can quickly distinguish between the two types of lines.

### Basic pleat formations

#### KNIFE OR STRAIGHT PLEATS
These pleats all face in the same direction. To make them, fold the fabric on the solid line and bring the fold to the broken line, following the arrows printed on the pattern piece. Hand-baste or pin the pleats along the folded edges; then baste across the top of all of the pleats.

If the pleats are to be pressed, do it before the pleated section is attached to the rest of the garment.

**SHORTCUT METHOD FOR STRAIGHT PLEATS**

✂ Snip-mark the pleat lines within the seam allowance.

✂ Use pins to mark the rest of each pleat line using regular, flat head pins to mark the solid lines and round head pins to mark the broken lines.

✂ Crease the fabric along the solid line, press gently and remove the pins. Bring the pressed edge to meet the broken line and pin in place.

✂ Continue until all of the pleats are formed. Machine-baste across the top of the pleats; then press the inside folds.

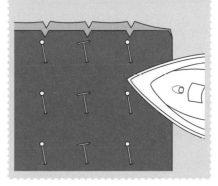

### KNIFE PLEATS

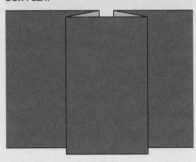

### BOX PLEAT

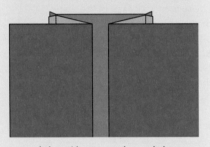

### INVERTED PLEAT

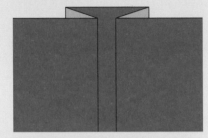

Inverted pleat with integrated pleat underlay.

Inverted pleat with separate pleat underlay.

### BOX PLEATS

Each pleat consists of two straight pleats facing in opposite directions. Following your pattern instructions, fold, baste and press as for straight pleats.

### INVERTED PLEATS

Often used at center front or back, an inverted pleat looks like two straight pleats that face each other, with their folds meeting at the center. An inverted pleat has a pleat underlay. It can be a separate underlay section that is seamed to the garment, or it can be formed by basting and then folding and pressing the garment section itself. Your pattern instructions will tell you how to do this.

## Pressing

The best looking pleats are those that have been carefully – and properly – pressed. Once the pleats are formed,

you'll be pressing over several thicknesses of fabric. To prevent these layers from creating ridges on the outside of your garment, always use a press cloth (or a scrap of your fashion fabric instead). Put strips of brown paper between the garment and the unbasted fold of each pleat as you press.

### SOFT (UNPRESSED) PLEATS

Use a dry press cloth. Hold the iron 2in–3in (5cm–7.5cm) above the fabric and apply just a little bit of steam. Do not rest the iron directly on the fabric.

### CRISP (PRESSED) PLEATS

Use a damp press cloth, lots of steam and the full pressure of your iron. Since the garment still has to be hemmed, press lightly when you get to within 8in (20.5cm) of the hemline. Once the hem is put in, thoroughly re-press this area.

**NOTE** Once you have pressed the pleats, be sure your garment is thoroughly dry before handling it.

## Topstitching and edgestitching

Pleats are often topstitched and/or edgestitched to hold them in place. The topstitching, which starts at the waistline and extends into the hip area, is done through all of the layers.

If the fabric does not hold a crease well, it's also a good idea to edgestitch below the hip, catching only the fold of the pleat in your stitching. Do this, too, if you're going to wash your garment rather than have it dry-cleaned. The pleats will be much easier to re-press if they're edgestitched.

To make the topstitching above and the edgestitching below the hip look like one continuous line, edgestitch the pleat fold below the hipline first. Edgestitch to within about 8in (20.5cm) of the hemline. Starting at the waistline edge, topstitch between the waist and the hip, overlapping the stitches at the hipline. Once the garment is hemmed, go back and complete the edgestitching.

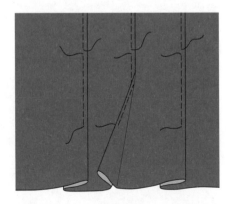

Edgestitching along just the fold of the pleat below the hipline will help to keep it well defined.

## Hemming

If a seam falls at the inside fold of a pleat, you'll need to perform a little magic with your scissors to make sure everything lies flat.

**A1** Clip the seam allowance to the line of stitching at the top of the hem allowance.

**A2** Press the seams open below the clip and trim them to ¼ in (6mm).

**A3** Finish the raw edge of the hem allowance and hem the garment.

**A4** Working on the inside of the garment, edgestitch the pleat folds within the hem allowance to keep it flat.

**A5** Once the garment is hemmed, go back and re-press the lower edges of the pleats.

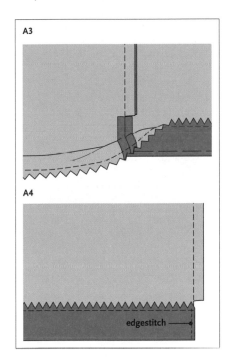

# GATHERS

Gathers are used to control fullness in just about any part of the garment. You'll find them at the waistline, at a yoke seam, at the cuff of a full sleeve or on the cap of a puffed sleeve. Gathers are also used to create ruffles (see Ruffles, page 213). The fabric you choose will affect the appearance of your gathers. The softer the fabric, the more the gathers will drape and cling to the body. Crisper fabrics create billowy, stand-away-from-the-body gathers.

## The conventional method

The most common way to create gathers is to use a long, straight machine stitch.

**A1** Loosen the needle thread tension slightly. This will make it easier to pull up the bobbin thread later.

**A2** Set the stitch length for a long stitch; the heavier the fabric, the longer the stitch.

**A3** Working on the right side of the fabric, stitch along the seamline of the area to be gathered. Stitch again, ¼ in (6mm) away, within the seam allowance. Be sure to leave long thread tails and do not backstitch. (See the illustrated tip above right for more guidance.)

**A4** With right sides together, pin the section to be gathered to the shorter one, matching notches, seams and markings.

**A5** Gently pull the bobbin threads at each end, sliding the fabric along until it fits the shorter section. At both ends, wrap the excess bobbin thread around the pins in a figure of eight. Distribute the gathers evenly and pin.

**A6** Before stitching the seam, make sure you have readjusted the needle thread tension on your machine. Working with the gathered side up, stitch on the seamline, just next to the first row of gathers. To keep tucks from forming along the seamline, use the tips of your fingers to hold the fabric on either side of the presser foot.

**WHEN GATHERS INTERSECT A PREVIOUS SEAM**

**On light- and medium-weight fabrics:** Trim the ends of the seam allowances diagonally before stitching gathers.

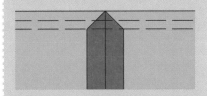

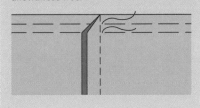

**On bulky fabrics:** Trim seam ends; stitch up to the seams, keeping the seam allowances free.

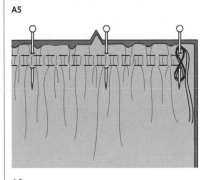

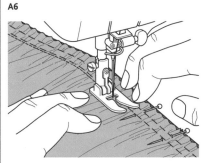

### GATHERING LONG SECTIONS

The longer the area you're working on, the greater the chances of having a thread break while you are forming the gathers. To avoid this, work as follows, or alternatively see Gathering Over a Cord, right.

**B1** Divide the edges of both the short and long sections into four or eight equal parts and mark with safety pins or straight pins.

**B2** On the edge to be gathered, make separate rows of gathering stitches for each section.

**B3** Pin the edges together, distribute the fullness and stitch as for straight stitch gathering.

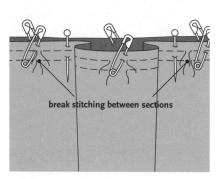

break stitching between sections

### GATHERING OVER A CORD

This fast method for gathering a long section eliminates any worries about threads breaking.

**C1** Cut a piece of strong, thin cord (such as pearl cotton or lightweight packing string) that is slightly longer than the edge to be gathered. Set your machine for a zigzag stitch wide enough to stitch over the cord without catching it in the stitches. Position the cord within the seam allowance so that the left swing of the needle falls just short of the seamline and stitch.

**C2** Hold the cord taut and slide the fabric along it. Even out the gathers. Wrap one end of the cord around a pin in a figure of eight to secure it.

**C3** Pin the gathered and flat sections together, matching notches, seamlines and markings.

**C4** Set the machine stitch back to normal. Working with the gathered side up, stitch along the seamline, being

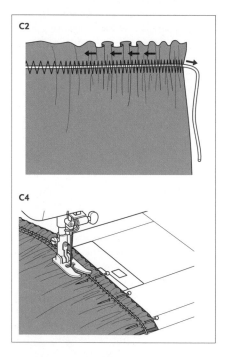

C2

C4

careful not to catch the cord. Depending on the weight of your fabric and the thickness of your cord, you may find it easier to use your machine's zipper foot.

**C5** When the seam is completely stitched, gently pull out the cord.

### ⓢ The serger method

One of the most frustrating things about gathering is that just when you think you have everything adjusted, you give one last yank, the gathering stitches break, and you have to start all over again. When using a conventional machine, gathering over a cord will make the gathering more secure; alternatively you can put your serger to work. However, remember that the serger will trim your seam allowances to ¼ in (6mm) which isn't always an advantage on a gathered edge.

**D1** Adjust your serger to the appropriate setting (see Basic Gathering chart, opposite).

**D2** Make a test sample. Light- to medium-weight fabrics will gather automatically. For more gathers, tighten the needle thread tension(s). For fewer gathers, loosen the needle thread tension(s).

**D3** Place the garment edge wrong side up and serge along the ⅝ in (1.5cm) seamline.

**D4** Remove the fabric from the machine and adjust the density of the gathers by pulling the needle thread(s) along gently.

**S** GATHERING OVER A CORD

For heavier fabrics, you may want to gather over a cord for extra reinforcement.

**E1**  Adjust your serger to the appropriate setting (see Gathering Over a Cord chart).

**E2**  On some sergers, the foot has a hole in front. If so, thread a strand of cord, pearl cotton, crochet cotton or topstitching thread through the hole. Work from the front, bringing the thread under the foot toward the back.

**E3**  Place the fabric wrong side up and serge along the ⁵/₈ in (1.5cm) seamline. The stitches will form over the cord.

**E4**  To create the gathers, hold the cord taut while sliding the fabric along it.

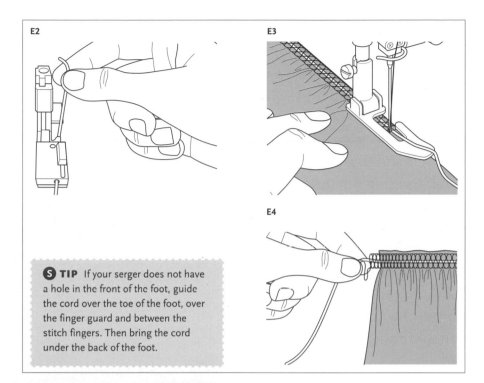

E2

E3

E4

**S** **TIP**  If your serger does not have a hole in the front of the foot, guide the cord over the toe of the foot, over the finger guard and between the stitch fingers. Then bring the cord under the back of the foot.

## BASIC GATHERING

| TYPE OF SERGER STITCH: | | 3 | 4 | MINE |
|---|---|---|---|---|
| Stitch length: | | 3mm–5mm | 3mm–5mm | |
| Stitch width: | | Widest | Widest | |
| Tensions | Needle: | Very Tight | Very Tight | |
| | Right Needle: | N/A | Tight | |
| | Upper Looper: | Normal | Normal | |
| | Lower Looper: | Normal | Normal | |

## GATHERING OVER A CORD

| TYPE OF SERGER STITCH: | | 3 | 4 | MINE |
|---|---|---|---|---|
| Stitch length: | | 2mm–3mm | 2mm–3mm | |
| Stitch width: | | Widest | Normal | |
| Tensions | Needle: | Normal | Normal | |
| | Right Needle: | N/A | Normal | |
| | Upper Looper: | Normal | Normal | |
| | Lower Looper: | Normal | Normal | |

# EDGINGS

In this section we cover some of the techniques you will need to know to finish off the edges of your garments to a professional level. Binding finishes a raw edge by enclosing it in a narrow strip of fabric, while banding uses wider fabric "bands". Where fabric edges meet at a corner they need to be mitered for tailored results.

## BINDINGS

Bindings are a clever way to decorate and finish a raw edge at the same time. Some patterns already include bindings as a design detail. But you are not limited to putting binding on only those patterns that call for it (see To Bind or Not to Bind, opposite). Check the back of the pattern envelope to determine the recommended binding width. Most patterns are designed for a 1/4 in (6mm) or 1/2 in (1.3cm) finished width. You can make your own bias binding, or purchase double-fold bias tape or foldover braid.

> **TIP** If you're adding binding to a pattern that doesn't call for it, trim off the seam allowances on the garment edge(s) that will be encased in the binding. To determine how much binding you will need, measure the cut edges and then add at least 1/4 yd (23cm) for piecing and seam allowances.

### Making custom binding

To provide give and flexibility, cut binding on the bias. The continuous bias method is an easy way to mark and join make-your-own bias strips and a relatively small amount of fabric can yield a large amount of binding. For example, if your fabric is 45in (115cm) wide, a 5in x 45in (12.5cm x 115cm) rectangle will yield approximately 2 1/2 yd (2.3m) of 1/2 in (1.3cm) finished width binding or 5yd (4.6m) of 1/4 in (6mm) finished width binding.

**A1** Cut a rectangle of fashion fabric. The longer side of the rectangle can follow either the lengthwise or the crosswise grain of your fabric. Trim each side of the rectangle so that it exactly follows a thread of fabric.

**A2** Fold one corner of the rectangle so that the crosswise and the lengthwise edges meet, and press; then open out. (This crease is the true bias.)

**A3** Cut a cardboard template the width required for your bias strips. Each strip should be four times the width of the finished binding. For example, for 1/4 in (6mm) finished binding width, mark 1in (2.5cm) wide strips; for 1/2 in (1.3cm) binding, mark 2in (5cm) wide strips. Using the crease as your starting point and the cardboard template as your guide, pencil-mark parallel lines across the width of the fabric until you reach a corner.

**A4** Cut off the triangles of unmarked fabric at either end of the rectangle.

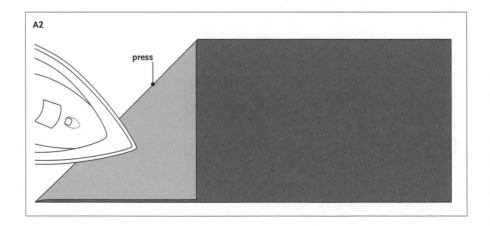

A2

press

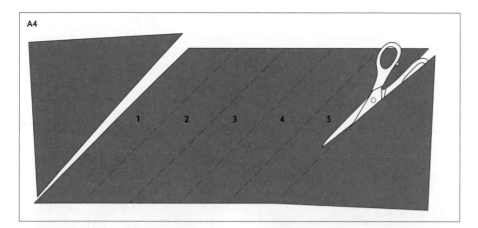

A4

**A5** With right sides together, fold the fabric into a tube. Match the pencil lines so that one width of binding extends beyond the edge on each side. Sew a ¼in (6mm) seam and press open.

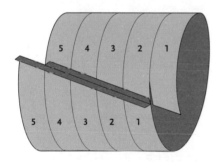

**A6** Starting at one end cut along the pencil line, working your way around the tube until you've separated it into one long, continuous strip.

**TO BIND OR NOT TO BIND**

✂ Use bindings at necklines, armholes, even hemline edges, as an alternative to facings.

✂ Made in a contrasting color, bindings are a great way to liven up a simple garment, and work particularly well on children's clothes.

✂ On sheers, narrow self-fabric bindings eliminate unsightly facing show-through. (Self-fabric facings are cut from your fashion fabric.)

✂ Bindings are an easy way to finish the edges of a reversible garment, such as a jacket or vest.

✂ Bindings add emphasis to home decorating items such as placemats, napkins, tablecloths and curtain edges.

## Piecing individual strips

If you do not have enough fabric leftover after cutting out your project to make a rectangle large enough to construct one long continuous strip, you will need to piece individual strips together. This method can also be used when you need to piece strips of purchased binding together and results in a professional-looking finish.

**B1** Using bias-cut strips of the required width and with right sides together, pin the ends of the strips so that they form a right (90°) angle. Stitch with a ¼in (6mm) seam.

**B2** Press the seam open and trim away the points extending beyond the edge of the binding.

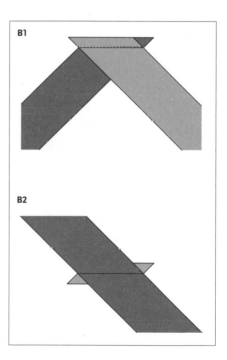

B1

B2

## Two-step application method for custom binding or double-fold bias tape

Because it's the fastest method, most patterns tell you to apply the binding entirely by machine. However, many sewers find it difficult to achieve professional results using this method. The following combination of machine and hand sewing may take you a few minutes longer, but that extra time will pay off in great results. Do review the Notes box below before you begin.

**NOTES**

✂ When applying 1in (2.5cm) bias strips, use ¼in (6mm) seams.

✂ When applying 2in (5cm) bias strips, use ½in (1.3cm) seams.

✂ When applying double-fold bias tape, unfold it and follow the creases for your seam widths.

✂ On binding that you've made yourself, fold and press under one long edge before you begin. The fold should be equal to one-fourth of the width of the binding. This will give you the folded edge you need for Step 2.

✂ Press under one short end of the binding. As you machine-stitch for Step 1, lap the unpressed end over the pressed end. (On the outside, the pressed end will be on top and visible.)

**STEP 1**
With right sides together, machine stitch the binding to the garment edge. Press the seam toward the binding.

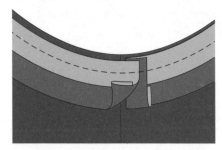

**STEP 2**
Turn the folded edges of the binding to the inside so that it encases the raw edge and just covers the stitching line. Slipstitch in place.

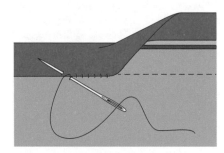

**AT AN OUTSIDE CORNER**
**C1** Use a fabric marking pen or dressmaker's pencil to mark where the seam allowances intersect at the corner.
**C2** Follow Step 1, ending your stitching where the seamlines intersect at the corner. Backstitch a few stitches and cut the thread.
**C3** Fold the binding back on itself to create a diagonal crease at the corner. Now fold the binding back again so that this new fold is even with the edge of the binding on side A and the seamlines of binding and garment match on side B.
**C4** Insert the needle exactly at the corner marking and continue stitching.

**C5** Finish as in Step 2, making a diagonal fold at the corner and slipstitching the binding in place. If desired, slipstitch the corner folds also.

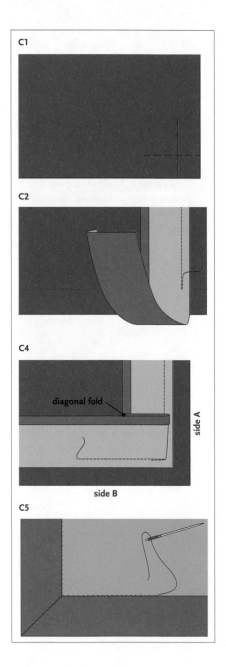

C1

C2

C4

diagonal fold

side A

side B

C5

### AT AN INSIDE CORNER

**D1** Reinforce the corner with small stitches along the seamline. Clip the corner just to the stitches.

**D2** Following Step 1, stitch binding to one fabric edge. Stop stitching when you reach the corner.

**D3** Keeping the needle in the fabric, raise the presser foot and spread the fabric open at the clip so that it lines up with the edge of the binding. Lower the presser foot and continue stitching.

**D4** Press the seam allowances toward the binding. As you do this, a diagonal fold will form at the corner.

**D5** Finish as in Step 2, forming another diagonal fold at the corner. If desired, slipstitch the corner folds.

## Edgestitched application

Use this method with purchased double-fold bias tape or foldover braid. Slip the binding over the raw garment edge and pin or baste in place. Note that these tapes and braids are folded so that one side is slightly wider than the other. Always sandwich your fabric between the folds with the wider side of the tape on the bottom. Then, working on the right side of the fabric, edgestitch the tape in place. To begin and end the binding, press under one short end. As you apply the binding, lap the pressed end over the unpressed end. Do this at an inconspicuous place on the garment, such as the center back or underarm.

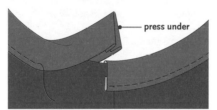
press under

**TIP** To keep the binding from shifting as you sew, apply glue stick to the inside of the binding and then press it into position. Let the glue dry; then edgestitch along the fold.

### AT AN OUTSIDE CORNER

**E1** Edgestitch the binding all the way to the perpendicular edge of the fabric. Remove the fabric from the machine and cut the threads.

**E2** Turn the binding around the corner and down the next side. Pin.

**E3** Make a diagonal fold in the binding on both sides of the corner; press.

**E4** Beginning just below the diagonal fold, backstitch to fold; then edgestitch along the binding. If desired, slipstitch the corner folds.

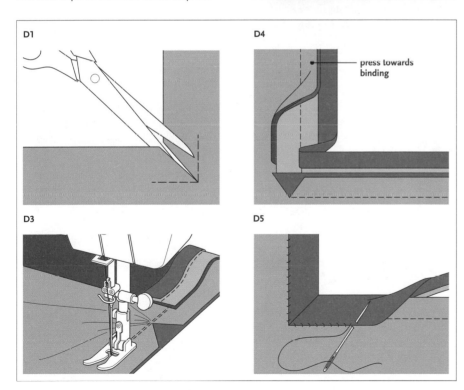

D1

D4
press towards binding

D3

D5

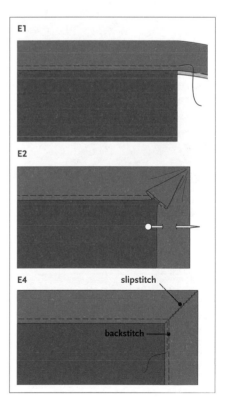

E1

E2

E4
slipstitch
backstitch

### AT AN INSIDE CORNER

**F1**   Reinforce the corner with small machine stitches. Clip the corner just to the stitches.

**F2**   Edgestitch the binding to the garment, stopping at the corner.

**F3**   Keeping the needle in the fabric, raise the presser foot and spread the fabric to transform the corner into a straight edge. Slip the binding back over the fabric, lower the presser foot, and continue edgestitching.

**F4**   Press the binding at the corner so that a diagonal fold forms on both sides of the garment. If desired, slipstitch the corner folds to keep them in place.

## MITERING

Mitering – creating a corner by joining a vertical and a horizontal edge – is one technique that pattern instructions usually assume everyone knows how to do. Doing it is one thing, but doing it so that the corners come out crisp and square is quite another.

Knowing how to make a professional-looking miter comes in useful when you are turning under a corner, whether that is on a patch pocket (a folded miter), or the hem/facing edge of a skirt slit (a stitched miter), or when applying a decorative trim.

### Folded miter

This method works on patch pockets and slit hems.

**A1**   Stitch along the pocket seamlines; then press the seam allowances to the inside along the stitching.

**A2**   Open out the seam allowances at the corners. Fold the corner up diagonally and press; then trim this seam allowance to $1/4$in (6mm).

**A3**   Fold all of the seam allowances back to the inside. The folded edges will just meet forming a neat corner miter.

**A4**   To make sure the corners stay neat as you edgestitch or topstitch the pocket to the garment, slipstitch the edges together; alternatively, secure with glue stick or fusible web.

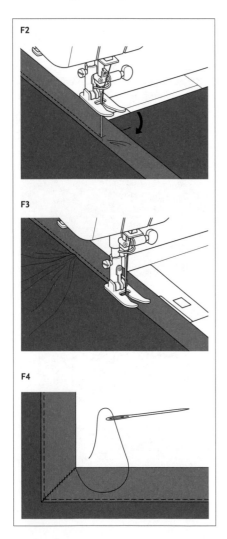

F2

F3

F4

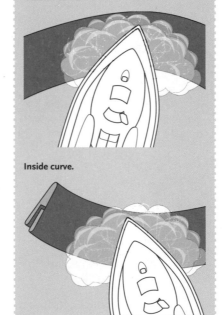

> **TIP**  Be careful not to stretch the binding as you sew, particularly when you are working on a curved edge. You may find it helpful to use steam to preshape the binding before you apply it. Pin the binding to your ironing board in a curve that matches the shape of the garment edge. Using a generous amount of steam, shrink out the excess fullness, let the binding dry, and then attach it to the garment.

Outside curve.

Inside curve.

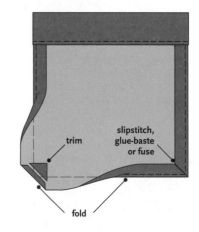

slipstitch, glue-baste or fuse

trim

fold

> **TIP**  If the folded miter is at the corner of a hem, slipstitch for a neater finish.

## Stitched miter

This method is most frequently used at the corner of a turned-up hem.

**B1** Turn the garment edges to the inside along the seamlines or foldlines; press.

**B2** Open out the pressed edges. Fold the corner diagonally across the point so that the pressed lines meet; press.

**B3** Open out the corner and, with right sides together, fold the garment diagonally through the corner so those creases meet (see illustration). Stitch on the diagonal crease line. Trim the corner seam allowance, trimming diagonally at the point.

**B4** Press the corner seam open.

**B5** Turn the seam allowances or the hem facing to the inside and press.

## Mitering flat trims

Flat trims require mitering any time they turn a corner. No matter where the trim is positioned on the garment, the technique is the same. It's the style of the trim – for example, whether it has two straight edges or one straight edge – that determines the mitering technique.

If you're applying the trim any place except along the edge of the garment, mark the trim placement line so that it is visible on the outside of the garment. Use a disappearing marking pen, disappearing tracing paper or a line of machine basting – whichever is appropriate for your fabric.

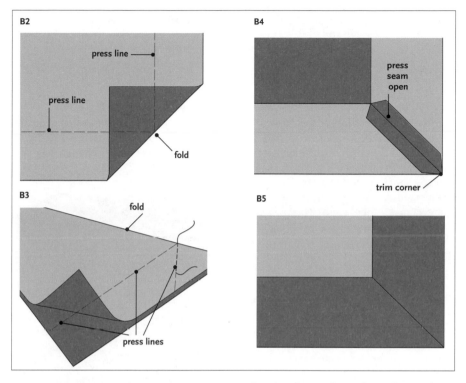

**FOR TRIMS WITH TWO STRAIGHT EDGES**
With this technique, the right edge of the trim is aligned with the garment edge or the placement line.

**C1** Pin the trim to the garment edge or along the placement line. Topstitch both edges, ending the stitching when you reach the corner.

**C2** Working at your ironing board, fold the trim back up on itself and press. Fold the trim diagonally so that it meets the intersecting garment edge or placement line; press again.

**C3** Refold the trim back up on itself and stitch along the diagonal crease through all of the layers.

**C4** Fold the trim back down along the diagonal line of stitching and press. Continue topstitching along both edges of the trim.

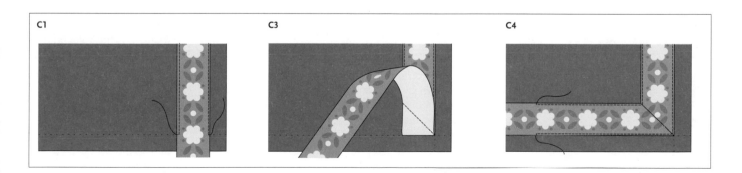

## FOR TRIMS WITH ONE STRAIGHT EDGE AND ONE DECORATIVE EDGE

With this technique, the left (straight) edge of the trim is aligned with the garment edge or placement line.

**D1**  Pin the straight edge of the trim to the garment edge or along the placement line. Topstitch all the way to the corner.

**D2**  Working at the ironing board, fold the trim back up on itself, positioning the fold slightly below the garment edge or placement line. Fold the trim back down diagonally so that it meets the intersecting garment edge or placement line. Secure the trim with a few straight pins; press the corner.

**NOTE**  You may have to refold the trim several times until you get it "just right" before pressing.

**D3**  Fold the trim back up on itself again and stitch along the diagonal crease through all of the layers.

**D4**  Fold the trim back down, press again, and continue stitching the trim to the garment.

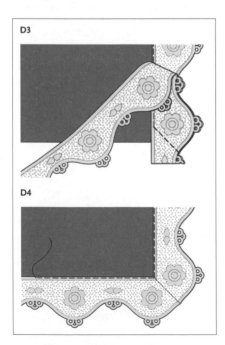

D3

D4

## BANDS AND RIBBING

Bands are a neat, decorative way to finish necklines, armholes and some front closings.

### Lapped V-neck band

This type of band is particularly popular on knit garments that pull on over the head. It can be made from matching or contrasting fabric.

**Lapped V-neck band.**

**A1**  With wrong sides together, fold the band in half lengthwise; pin or baste the raw edges together.

**A2**  On the garment front, reinforce the V at the tip of the neckline with a row of small machine stitches placed just inside the ⅝in (1.5cm) seamline.

**A3**  With right sides together, and beginning on one side of the garment, pin the band to the neck edge. For a smooth, accurate fit, carefully match the band markings. Leave the end of the band free on side B.

**A4**  Begin stitching at the first marking on side A of the band. (This marking should be matched exactly to the top of the V.) Stop stitching when you reach the next-to-the-last marking on side B of the band. Tie the thread ends.

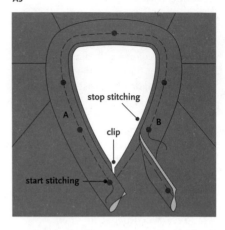

A5

stop stitching

A

clip

B

start stitching

**A5**  Clip the garment seam allowance only at the tip of the V, just to, but not through, the reinforcement stitching. (Be careful that you do not clip the band.) This will make it easier to fold the seam allowances to the inside and finish the band.

**A6**  Turn the band up and tuck the ends inside the garment.

**A7**  On the inside of the garment, lap the free end of the band (side B) over the stitched end (side A), carefully matching all of the markings at the tip of the V. Hand-baste the ends of the bands together at the V (see illustration opposite).

**A8**  Turn the seam allowances up and finish stitching the seam along side B of the neckline. End the stitching at the point of the V and tie off the threads.

**A9**  To secure the loose end of the band, turn the seam allowances up along side A of the neckline V and stitch between the markings, directly on top of the previous stitching.

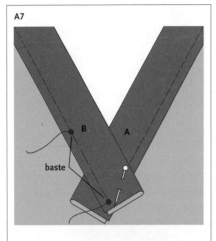

A7

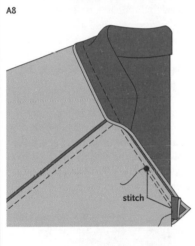

A8

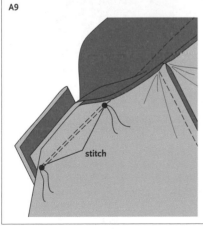

A9

## Placket band

The classic band often used at the necklines of tailored dresses, shirts, tops and blouses. Tailored shirts or shirt jackets may feature a variation of this band as a finishing technique on the sleeve opening. Before you begin, make sure you have transferred all of the markings, including stitching lines and foldlines, to the garment front and band sections.

**NOTE** The following directions will result in a classic women's right-over-left closing. However, your pattern may feature a menswear left-over-right closing.

Placket band at neckline.

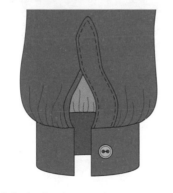

Placket band at sleeve opening.

**B1** On the garment front, machine-stitch along the marked stitching lines. This will reinforce the corners, as well as provide you with a stitching guide when you attach the band sections.

**B2** Slash the garment apart exactly in the middle of the two stitching lines. Make a small flap at the bottom by taking diagonal clips just to the corners of the stitching line. Be very careful not to clip through the stitches. If your fabric has a tendency to fray, treat the edges of the flap with a bit of liquid seam sealant, such as Fray Check™.

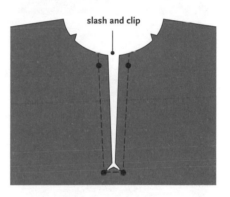

**B3** Interface the band sections according to your pattern instructions.

> **TIP** If you're working with a slippery or stretchy fabric, you may want to interface the entire band. To keep it from becoming too stiff, use a lightweight or sheer weight fusible interfacing.

**B4** Press the seam allowance under on one long edge of the band section and trim to ¼ in (6mm).

**B5** With right sides together, pin the other long edge of the band to the garment front, matching markings.

**B6** Machine-stitch along the stitching line, ending the stitching exactly at the bottom marking.

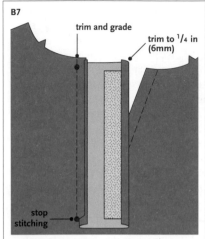

**B7**

trim and grade

trim to ¼ in (6mm)

stop stitching

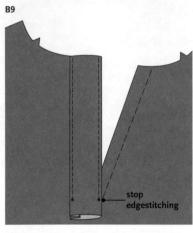

**B9**

stop edgestitching

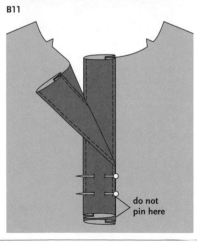

**B11**

do not pin here

**B7** Trim and grade seam allowances, then press them toward the band.

**B8** Fold the band to the outside of the garment, and pin the pressed edge in place along the stitching line.

**B9** Edgestitch close to both long edges of the band, ending the stitching at the lower marking.

**B10** Repeat, attaching the remaining band to the other side of the slashed opening.

**B11** Slip the ends of the bands through to the inside of the garment. On the inside, lap the left band over the right. (For a menswear closing, lap the right over the left.) Pin above the lower markings.

**B12** Working with the wrong side of the garment face down, fold the lower portion of the garment up to expose the flap at the bottom of the opening. Baste the flap and the bands together along the stitching line, then machine-stitch as basted, keeping the garment free. Finish according to the pattern instructions.

**B12**

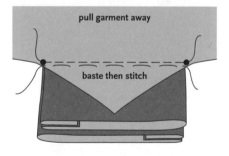

pull garment away

baste then stitch

## Ribbed bands

This type of band can be found at the neckline or the wrists, at the lower edge of a sweater-style top or at the ankles of a pair of sweatpants. Use either rib-knit trim or by-the-yard tubular sweater-knit fabric for the band.

### MEASURING AND CUTTING

Sometimes the hardest part of sewing ribbing is cutting it out. It slides and curls as you try to pin that long, narrow pattern piece to the fabric. This measuring and cutting technique does not require a pattern piece. It works equally well whether you're sewing ribbing on a conventional machine or a serger.

**For the width:** Decide on a finished width. If you have a pattern piece for ribbing, use it as a guide. Double the finished width and then add 1¼ in (3.2cm) for seam allowances. Fold the ribbing lengthwise into two to four thicknesses, mark the width, and cut out the band. Be sure to position the band crosswise with the ribs running up and down so that the greatest amount of stretch goes around the body.

**TIP** If you own a rotary cutter, use it to cut the ribbing. It will do a better job than scissors, especially through several thicknesses. To maintain an even cut, use a straight-edge ruler as a guide.

**For the length:** Using your pattern pieces as a guide, measure the garment opening, eliminating any seam allowances. Before you actually cut the ribbing into what you've determined to be the correct length, check your calculations by pin fitting. To do this, mark off the length, pin the ribbing together, slide it over the appropriate part of the body and analyze the fit. Now add 1¼ in (3.2cm) to the pin-fit length measurement to allow for the two standard seam allowances. Cut the band to the correct length.

## THE FLAT METHOD

Since it's easiest to apply rib-knit trim while the garment is still flat, leave one side seam, shoulder seam, leg seam or the sleeve seam unstitched.

**C1**  With wrong sides together, fold the band in half lengthwise and baste the edges together.

**C2**  Use pin markers to divide the garment into sections. Repeat on the band. Pin the band to the garment, matching the pin markings.

**C3**  With the band side up, machine-stitch the ⅝ in (1.5cm) seam, stretching the ribbing to fit between the markings. Stitch again within the seam allowance, ¼ in (6mm) from the first stitching, using a straight stitch or a zigzag stitch. Trim close to the stitching. Alternatively serge on your serger.

**TIP**  Because heat and steam can distort the ribbing, press it carefully. To press a seam, hold the iron above it and apply steam until any ripples disappear from the seam allowances and the ribbing returns to its unstretched state. Gently press the seam allowances toward the garment by lifting the iron up and putting it back down. Let the ribbing dry thoroughly before you handle it again.

**C4**  Press the seam allowance toward the garment.

**C5**  Stitch the garment seam allowance, beginning at the folded edge of the band. Stitch again within the seam allowance, ¼ in (6mm) from the first line of stitching. Trim the seam allowance close to the stitching. Alternatively, using your serger, chain for 2in (5cm) and then lift the presser foot. Slide the folded edge of the band under it and serge the seam. Press.

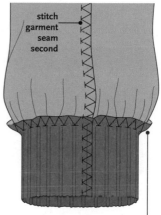

stitch garment seam second

join garment to ribbing first

Many sewers shy away from sewing with sweater knits, stretch terrycloth or stretch velour because they think that the ribbing will be difficult to work with. You'll be delighted at how easy it is to attach it with your serger.

**D1** With right sides together, serge the side seam to form a circle.

**D2** Fold the band in half, wrong sides together, so the raw edges meet, and pin. If the ribbing curls, baste the edges together with a long, wide zigzag stitch on your conventional machine.

**D3** Mark the band into quarters with pins or a marking pen. Do the same for the garment opening.

**D4** With right sides together, pin the band to the garment opening, matching markings. Position the seam in the band so it matches a garment seam. With the band side up, serge, stretching the ribbing to fit the opening. Press the seam allowance toward the garment.

**D5** For the ready-to-wear-look, use your conventional machine and a twin needle to topstitch on both sides of the seamline.

**S ELASTIC THREAD INSERTION**

Incorporating elastic thread into the seam when attaching ribbing to a garment has two main benefits: as you serge, the seam won't stretch out, and when you wear the garment it will maintain its elasticity. You may have a special hole in the presser foot of your serger to assist you in guiding the elastic. If not, guide the elastic by hand over the presser foot so it is caught in the chain as you serge. Do not stretch the elastic as you sew or the seam will pucker. The feed system of your serger will ease the ribbing for you.

Pin the ribbing to the garment edge. Working with the ribbing side up, hold the ribbing up against the toe of your presser foot with your right hand. As you serge, catch the elastic thread in the seam. Serge the remaining garment seam, catching and securing the elastic in the stitching.

**D2**

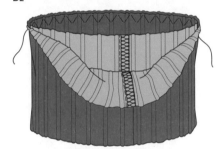

**D5**

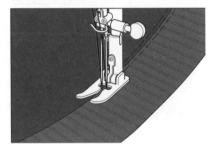

**D4**

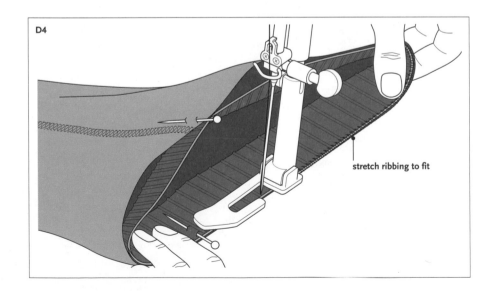

stretch ribbing to fit

# COLLARS

Collars are the finishing touch to the neckline of many garments, and, as they are close to eye level, are most noticeable. Although there are many different fashion terms that describe collars, they fall into three basic categories: flat, rolled and standing. Regardless of the collar style, the techniques for professional results are basically the same.

## COLLAR BASICS

In sewing terminology, a collar has two visible layers: the top layer, called the collar or upper collar; and the bottom layer, called the undercollar or facing. Almost every collar has a third, unseen layer of interfacing. Some collars, called one piece collars, are designed so that the undercollar is an extension of the upper collar. As a result, the outer edge is a fold rather than a seam.

### Interfacing

Most collars have a layer of interfacing sandwiched between the collar and undercollar. Your pattern instructions will tell you what pattern piece(s) to use and where to apply the interfacing. In most cases, the interfacing is fused or machine-basted to the upper collar. This way it acts as a cushion against all of the seam allowances.

To reduce bulk, it is a good idea to trim off $1/2$ in (1.3cm) from the interfacing's seam allowances. For sew-in interfacings, trim the seam allowances after the interfacing has been machine-basted in place. For fusibles, trim the seam allowances first, and then fuse the interfacing. To reduce bulk at the corners, trim the interfacing diagonally, and just inside the seamline.

### Stitching it together

Instead of starting at one edge of the collar and stitching all of the way around to the other edge, you'll get a more symmetrical collar if you stitch in two steps. Step 1, begin at the center back and stitch to one edge of the collar. Step 2, begin again at the center back, overlapping several stitches, and stitch to the other edge of the collar. If your collar has corners or sharp curves, use a smaller stitch for about 1in (2.5cm) on either side. For a sharper corner, take one stitch across the point.

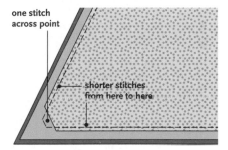

one stitch across point

shorter stitches from here to here

### Trimming and grading

Trim the seam allowances and the corners. On medium and heavy-weight fabrics, grade the seam allowances so that the undercollar seam allowance is narrower than the upper collar seam allowance. Notch your curved collars.

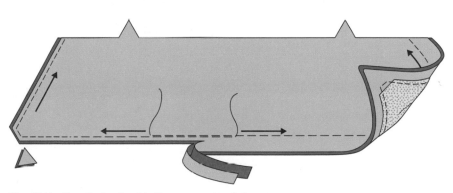

After stitching the collar together, trim the corners and grade the seams.

## TYPES OF COLLAR

**FLAT COLLAR:** Lies flat against the neck edge of the garment. If you compared the neckline seam of the collar with the neckline seam of the garment, you would find that the curves are almost identical.

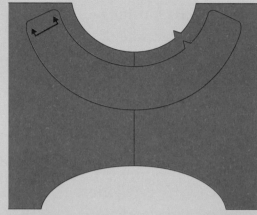

**ROLLED COLLAR:** Rises straight up from the neck edge for a short distance and then rolls down to rest on the garment. The part that rolls down is called the fall. On a rolled collar, the collar neckline seam has a shallower curve than the garment neckline seam.

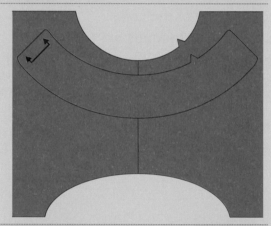

**STANDING COLLAR:** A band that rises straight up from the neckline seam. It can be a narrow, single-layer band or a double-layer band that folds back onto itself. On a standing collar, the collar neckline seam is very straight in comparison to the garment neckline seam.

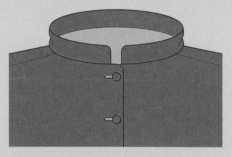

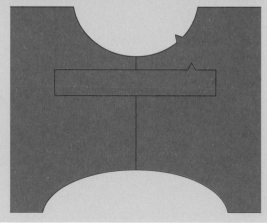

## Pressing

Before turning the collar right side out, press it flat on both the collar side and the undercollar side. This will blend the stitches.

To ensure a sharp edge once the collar is turned, either press the seam allowance open over a point presser or place the collar flat on the ironing board with the undercollar side facing up. Press the undercollar seam allowance toward the collar as shown right.

Turn the collar right side out. If the collar has points, gently coax them out from the inside with the eraser end of a pencil or the tip of a point turner as shown below. Resist the temptation to use the tip of your scissors as it's all too easy to poke them right through the fabric.

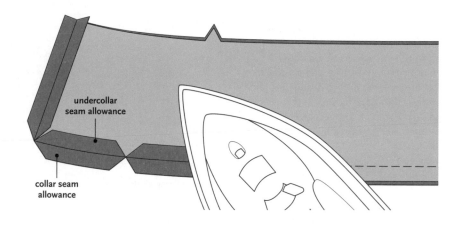

undercollar seam allowance

collar seam allowance

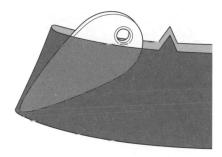

Press the collar. As you press, roll the seamline slightly underneath to the undercollar side.

## Underststitching

Understitching is necessary to ensure that the undercollar is prevented from rolling to the outside. Turn the collar inside out again and slip it under your presser foot so that the right side of the undercollar is facing you. Stitch on the undercollar, next to the seamline, catching all of the seam allowances in your stitching.

If your collar is curved, you'll be able to understitch along the entire length of the collar. If your collar is pointed, understitch along the back edge, between, and almost to, the points. Turn the collar right side out and press again.

## Preparing the garment

The finished collar won't look smooth and neat unless you've done some preliminary work on your garment.

Staystitch the garment's neckline edge to keep it from stretching out of shape as you sew.

Clip the neckline seam allowance at regular intervals, just to, but not through, the staystitching. This releases the fabric and helps it to lie flat as you pin and stitch the collar. The greater the difference between the neckline curves of the garment and the collar, the more clipping you'll have to do. For flat collars, very little clipping is necessary. For standing collars, you may need to clip every 1/2 in (1.3cm) or more.

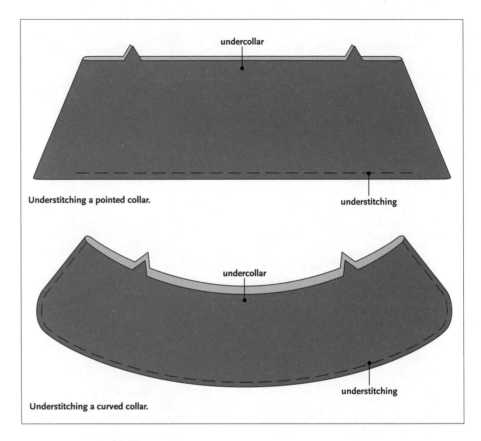

Understitching a pointed collar.

Understitching a curved collar.

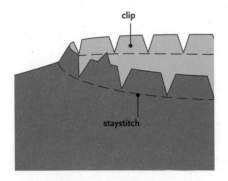

## Attaching the collar

There are many different methods of attaching the collar. Sometimes it is attached at the same time as the neckline facing, so that the facing hides the neckline seam allowances. Sometimes there is no facing. Instead, the collar is attached so that the garment neckline seam allowance is sandwiched between the collar and the undercollar. Follow your pattern directions, making sure that you trim, grade and clip the neckline seam; then press the seam allowances as indicated.

# SLEEVES AND CUFFS

Of the three basic styles of sleeves, kimono and raglan are the best choices for beginner sewers as they are easy to sew and easy to fit. Moving on to set-in sleeves, we'll show you how to create a smooth-fitting sleeve. Buttoned and snug, or turned up and loose, cuffs are a popular finishing detail on sleeves, although the same techniques can be used for cuffs on pants.

**TYPES OF SLEEVE**

SET-IN SLEEVES

KIMONO SLEEVES

RAGLAN SLEEVES

## KIMONO SLEEVES

Kimono sleeves are cut as part of the garment front and garment back. Since there's nothing to deal with but an underarm seam, they're the easiest style to sew.

**A1**  Pin the garment front and back together at the side/underarm seams, matching all the raw edges, notches and markings.

**A2**  Beginning at the lower edge of the garment, stitch along the ⅝in (1.5cm) seamline to the end of the sleeve.

**A3**  Reinforce the underarm area by stitching at the curve. Alternatively center a 4in–5in (10cm–12.5cm) piece of seam binding or twill tape over the curved area before the seam is stitched and baste it in place. When you stitch the seam, shorten the stitch slightly along the length of the tape.

**A4**  Clip the curves and press the seam open. Do not clip the seam binding.

## RAGLAN SLEEVES

Raglan sleeves are joined to the garment front and garment back by diagonal seams that run from the underarm to the neckline. In addition, there may be a shoulder dart or a shoulder seam. To insert the sleeve on your conventional machine, follow your pattern instructions, reinforcing the diagonal seams by stitching again over the first stitching.

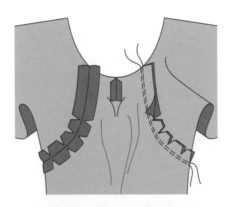

## Ⓢ The serger method

The flatlock or trellis seam is an easy technique that lends a decorative, ready-to-wear look to any item. Because it's a strong seam that can withstand many washings, it's a good choice for raglan sleeve sweatshirts and children's garments. You should also consider it if you want to make your raglan sleeve garment reversible.

Ⓢ **THE TWO-THREAD TRUE FLATLOCK SEAM**

Adjust your serger to the appropriate settings (see True Flatlock Seam chart). With wrong sides together, serge the seams; then, working from the right side of the fabric, pull the two layers apart until the seam lies flat.

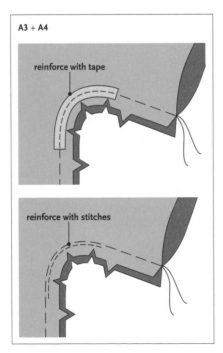

**A3 + A4**

reinforce with tape

reinforce with stitches

### TRUE FLATLOCK SEAM

| TYPE OF SERGER STITCH: | | 2 | MINE |
|---|---|---|---|
| Stitch length: | | 2mm–3mm | |
| Stitch width: | | Widest | |
| Tensions | Needle: | Very Loose | |
| | Right Needle | N/A | |
| | Upper Looper: | N/A | |
| | Lower Looper: | Normal | |

### MOCK FLATLOCK SEAM

| TYPE OF SERGER STITCH: | | 3 | MINE |
|---|---|---|---|
| Stitch length: | | 2mm–3mm | |
| Stitch width: | | Widest | |
| Tensions | Needle: | Very Loose | |
| | Upper Looper: | Normal to loose | |
| | Lower Looper: | Very tight | |

### ⓢ THE THREE-THREAD MOCK FLATLOCK SEAM

If your serger does not have two-thread capabilities, here's how to create the same effect with a three-thread stitch. Don't limit its use to raglan sleeves – it's great anyplace else you want a flatlock effect.

**A1** Adjust your serger to the appropriate settings (see Mock Flatlock Seam chart opposite).

**A2** Trim the seam allowances to ¼in (6mm).

**A3** With the wrong sides together, place the seam under the presser foot so that the raw edge will not be trimmed and the fabric fills up only half of the stitch. (Filling up only half of the stitch width ensures that the flatlock seam will lie perfectly flat.) Serge a test seam to determine exactly where the raw edge needs to be positioned on your serger.

**A4** Serge the seam; then, working from the right side of the fabric, pull the two layers apart until the seam lies flat.

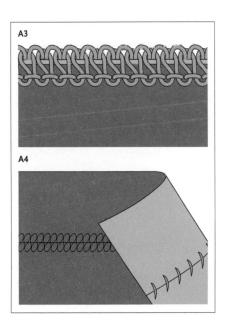

A3

A4

## SET-IN SLEEVES

Unlike a kimono or raglan style sleeve, a set-in sleeve is slightly larger than the armhole of the garment. The excess fabric occurs in the area between the notches, called the sleeve cap. If the sleeve didn't have this extra fabric, there wouldn't be enough "play" for you to raise your arm. The mark of a professional-looking garment is a set-in sleeve that's properly eased into the armhole, creating a smooth seam and a rounded shape for your shoulder. There should be no dimples or tucks along the seam of the sleeve cap.

> **TIP** For your first set-in sleeve, consider one with a tucked or gathered sleeve cap to avoid easing in the fullness.

### Easing the sleeve cap – three methods

For best results, ease the sleeve cap before stitching the sleeve underarm seam. Choose from one of the following alternative methods.

#### THE TRADITIONAL EASING METHOD
Working on the right side of the fabric, easestitch the sleeve cap twice. Easestitch first along the seamline between the notches; then stitch ¼in (6mm) away, within the seam allowance. Be sure to leave the threads long enough to pull them up to create the sleeve cap.

#### THE EASESTITCH-PLUS METHOD
This method is best when working with a pliable, woven fabric. Stitch along the seamline between the notches with a regular stitch. As you stitch, place one forefinger on each side of the seamline just in front of the needle and pull the fabric horizontally so it's stretched off-grain. While you're doing this, push the fabric back and under the presser foot for four or five stitches.

Stop stitching, relax the fabric and then repeat, pulling and pushing the fabric back as you sew. The sleeve will automatically shape itself into a cap.

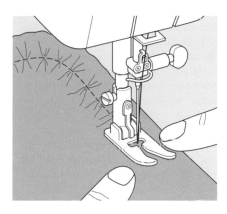

#### ⓢ THE SERGER EASING METHOD
Easing a sleeve cap on the serger is simply a matter of tightening the needle tension until the fabric starts to pull up behind the foot. However, once stitched, these gathers can be adjusted only slightly. There are two techniques to serge your easing stitches (see page 162), but you may want to save these until you know your serger quite well; always test on a scrap of fabric first.

**NOTE** Because the serger easing method will cut off the notches, do make sure that you mark their location with a fabric marking pen or dress-maker's carbon.

**Technique 1:** Adjust your serger to the appropriate setting (see Serger Easing Method chart). Working on the wrong side, serge the easing stitches on the ⁵⁄₈ in (1.5cm) seamline. This leaves you with a ¹⁄₄ in (6mm) seam allowance when you sew the sleeve to the garment.

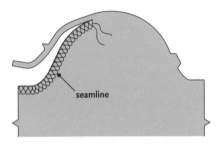

seamline

**Technique 2:** Working on the wrong side, serge the easing stitches, keeping the raw edge of the sleeve cap even with the blade so you don't trim off any of the seam allowance. Later on, when you stitch the sleeve to the garment on your conventional machine, place one forefinger on either side of the presser foot and pull the fabric horizontally so that the sleeve cap is stretched off grain. It's just like easestitch-plus (see page 161), but without pushing the fabric.

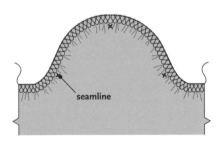

seamline

### Preparing the sleeve

Stitch the sleeve seam and press it open. Finish the lower edge of the sleeve according to the pattern instructions and/or the information provided on the following pages. Now you're ready to pin baste the sleeve to the garment.

| SERGER EASING METHOD | | | | |
|---|---|---|---|---|
| **TYPE OF SERGER STITCH:** | | **3** | **4** | **MINE** |
| Stitch length: | | Normal | Normal | |
| Stitch width: | | Normal | Normal | |
| Tensions | Needle: | Tight | Tight | |
| | Right Needle: | N/A | Very Tight | |
| | Upper Looper: | Normal | Normal | |
| | Lower Looper: | Normal | Normal | |

*If the fabric is heavy or more easing is required, tighten the needle tension(s) even more. If you need to remove the stitches and start again, see page 114 for the fastest way to rip.*

**A1** Turn the sleeve right side out; turn the garment inside out. Slip the sleeve inside the armhole and pin together at the sleeve and garment underarm seams, the shoulder markings and notches.
**A2** Now match and pin the remaining markings.
**A3** Draw up the easestitching at each end, sliding the fabric along to distribute the fullness evenly in the area between the notches. Your goal is to get the sleeve to fit smoothly in the armhole. Pin closely all around the eased area and then pin the underarm area between the notches. If you prefer you can hand-baste in place close to the seamline. This will enable you to try on to check for fit before stitching.

A3

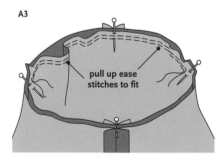

pull up ease stitches to fit

**TIP** If you're working with a knit that stretches, there is no need to easestitch. Working with the garment side up, pin the sleeve to the armhole edge, matching markings. As you stitch, ease in the fullness by stretching the armhole to fit the sleeve.

**TIP** The shallower the curve of the sleeve cap, the less ease the sleeve has. If your sleeve has very little ease, you may find it easier to attach it to the garment before the underarm seam is stitched. Once the sleeve is attached, sew the garment side seam and the underarm sleeve seam in one continuous stitching operation.

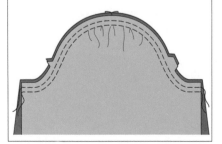

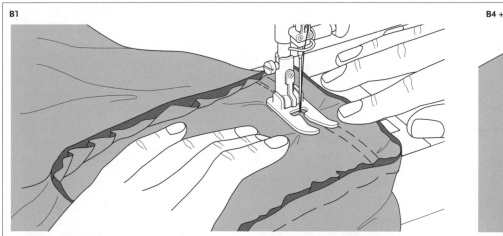

B1

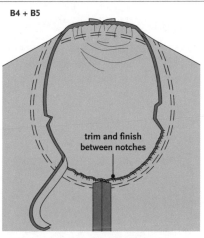

B4 + B5

trim and finish
between notches

## Stitching the sleeve

**B1**  With the sleeve side up, begin at the underarm seam and stitch along the seamline, just to the left of the first row of easestitch. As you stitch, place your forefingers on either side of the presser foot to keep the eased area from puckering under the needle.

**B2**  When you reach the underarm seam, overlap the stitches.

**B3**  Stitch a second row ⅛ in (3mm) away from the first, within the seam allowance.

**B4**  Trim the seam allowance close to the stitching in the underarm area between the notches.

**B5**  To strengthen and reinforce the underarm area, it's wise to finish the seam allowances between the notches by machine zigzagging, overcasting or serging the edges. If your fabric unravels, finish the entire armhole.

## Pressing the sleeve

**C1**  With the sleeve side up, place the upper portion of the armhole seam (the area between the notches) over the end of a sleeve board, tailor's ham or an ironing board.

**C2**  With the point of the iron, press only the seam allowances. Use steam if

appropriate for your fabrics. This blends the stitching and shrinks out some of the fullness. No further pressing is needed because the seam allowances will naturally turn toward the sleeve.

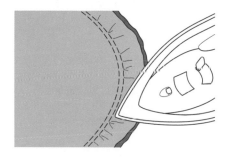

## THE ATTACHED CUFF

Buttoned and snug, or turned up and loose, cuffs are a popular detail on sleeves and pants.

As you read your pattern instructions, keep in mind that most cuffs, like most collars, are made up of three layers. The top layer is called the cuff; the underneath layer is called the facing. In between is the interfacing.

Sewing an attached cuff is very similar to sewing a collar. In fact, the basics of assembling – interfacing, stitching,

trimming and grading, and pressing – are exactly the same. Before you make a cuff, read Collars, pages 155–158.

An attached cuff can be a continuous band cuff or it can have a cuff opening. If the cuff opens, there is a corresponding sleeve opening, or placket, that can be finished in a variety of ways (see Types of Cuff Opening, page 164).

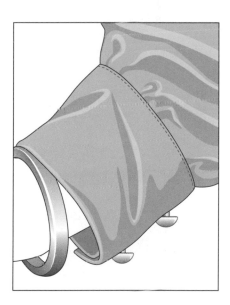

## TYPES OF CUFF OPENING

**SEAM OPENING:** To create this easiest placket style, stitch the seam to the mark and backstitch; then press the entire seam open.

**HEMMED OPENING:** Some patterns have a small sleeve opening that's formed by turning up part of the seam allowance and the method is explained in this chapter.

**THE TAILORED PLACKET:** This is similar to the conventional neckline placket band. If you're making this type of placket, review the information on the placket band (see pages 151–152).

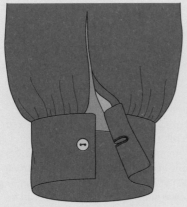

**FACED OPENING:** If your pattern calls for this type of placket opening, it will include a pattern piece for the facing and complete instructions.

**CONTINUOUS LAP OPENING:** This type of opening is bound with a strip of fabric and is often seen on a tailored shirt cuff. Instructions for working on a conventional sewing machine or a serger are explained in this chapter.

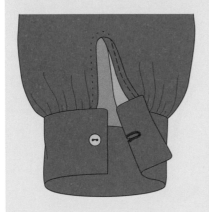

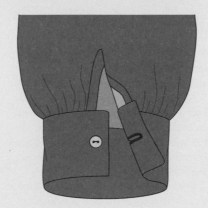

## Hemmed opening

**A1**  Reinforce along the seamline, as indicated on your pattern, extending the stitching ¹/₂ in (1.3cm) beyond the mark.
**A2**  Clip to the stitching at the mark.
**A3**  Fold the flap up and press. Turn the raw edge of the flap in to meet the stitching line and press again.
**A4**  To secure the flap to the sleeve, use fusible web or slipstitch it in place across the top of the fold.

## Continuous lap opening

This is done before the underarm seam is stitched. Your pattern either includes a pattern piece for this strip or tells you how to measure and cut it.

### THE CONVENTIONAL METHOD

The following method may be slightly different from the one in your pattern instructions. Continuous laps can be tricky but with this method even your first attempt will be successful.

### Creating the opening at the lower edge of the sleeve:

**B1**  Mark the slash stitching lines.
**B2**  Stitch along these lines, using reinforcement-length stitches for 1 in (2.5cm) on either side of the point and taking one stitch across the point.
**B3**  Cut an opening between the stitching lines, being careful not to slash through the stitch at the point.

### Attaching the lap:

**B4**  Spread the edges of the opening apart to form an almost straight line.
**B5**  With right sides together, pin the fabric strip to the slashed edge so that the stitching line on the opening is ¹/₄ in (6mm) from the edge of the strip.

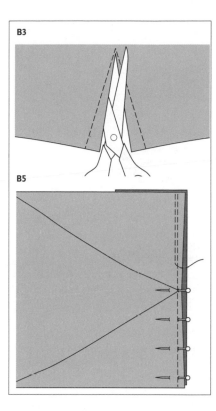

**B6**  Working with the sleeve on top, machine-stitch, stitching just to the left of the previous stitching. As you come to the point of the opening, fold the extra sleeve fabric out of the way.
**B7**  Press the seam allowance toward the strip.
**B8**  Press under ¹/₄ in (6mm) on the remaining long edge of the strip.
**B9**  Pin this edge over the seam on the inside of the sleeve and slipstitch in place.
**B10** Press the front portion of the lap to the inside and baste it in place across the lower edge of the sleeve.

**TIP**  If your fabric has a tendency to fray, treat the cut edges of the flap with a liquid sealant. Test first to make sure it isn't visible on your fabric when dry.

**TIP**  To reduce bulk, cut the strip from the selvage edge of the fabric, so that you eliminate one of the ¹/₄ in (6mm) seam allowances. If you do this, there is no need to press this edge under before slipstitching it in place.

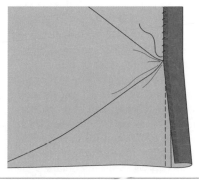

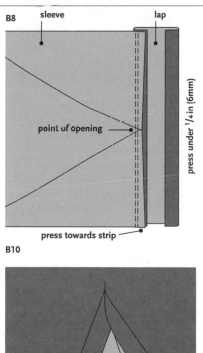

sleeve          lap
point of opening
press under ¹/₄ in (6mm)
press towards strip

## S THE SERGER METHOD

**C1**   Measure the length of the placket opening on your pattern tissue. Cut a 1in (2.5cm) wide bias strip of fabric that is twice the length of the placket opening.

**C2**   Reinforce and slash the placket opening as for the conventional method.

**C3**   With right sides together, pin the bias strip to the slashed edge so that the stitching line of the opening is ¼in (6mm) from the edge of the strip.

**C4**   Working with the sleeve on top, serge until the blade reaches the point of the slash. Be sure to keep the fabric in front of the blade clear. Rearrange the sleeve folds and continue serging. As you stitch, guide the bias strip under the needle with your right hand, while holding the placket edge straight with your left hand.

**C5**   Serge the remaining raw edge of the bias strip, trimming away about ⅛in (3mm) as you serge.

**C6**   Press the seam allowance toward the bias strip.

**C7**   Fold the bias strip to the wrong side of the garment so the edge of the strip extends ⅛in (3mm) over the line of the reinforcement stitching. Press and then stitch in the ditch using your conventional machine.

**C8**   Press the front portion of the lap to the inside and baste it in place across the lower edge of the sleeve.

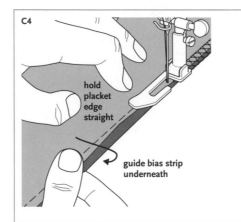

hold placket edge straight

guide bias strip underneath

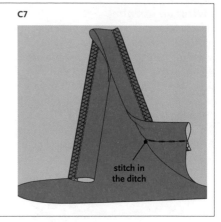

stitch in the ditch

## Attaching the cuff

Once the cuff is assembled and the sleeve opening is finished, you're ready to attach the cuff.

### THE CONVENTIONAL METHOD

Your pattern will probably tell you to attach the cuff in one of the following conventional ways.

**Technique 1:** Stitch the cuff to the lower edge of the sleeve. Working on the inside, slipstitch the facing in place over the seam allowances.

**Technique 2:** Stitch the cuff facing to the lower edge of the sleeve. Working on the outside, edgestitch the cuff in place over the seam allowances.

Although Technique 2 sounds much easier (and has a sportier look), you may find it more difficult to get neat results, particularly if this technique is new to you. You can substitute Technique 1 for Technique 2 and then go back and edgestitch the cuff on the outside.

> **TIP** When you are attaching the cuff to the sleeve, the pattern directions usually tell you to trim and grade the seam allowances. However, if you are using a sheer or loosely woven fabric, do not trim and grade. If you do, you may find that the first time you bend your elbow and rest it on a table, the strain causes the trimmed seam allowance to pull away along the stitching line.

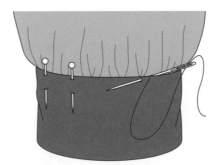

Technique 1.

Technique 2.

## S THE SERGER METHOD

**NOTE** This serged technique is successful only if your "placket" is an opening in the sleeve seam. On sleeves with a faced opening, a hemmed opening, a continuous lap or tailored placket, the cuff should be attached using a conventional machine.

**D1** With right sides together, pin the cuff to the lower edge of the sleeve, matching markings.

**D2** Roll the edge of the opening over the ends of the cuff and pin. Trim the corners diagonally before serging. This eliminates bulk at the corner once the seam is serged.

**D3** Serge the cuff to the sleeve and secure the thread ends.

**D4** Turn the lap edges of the opening to the inside. Press the seam allowance toward the sleeve.

## RIB-KNIT CUFFS

These cuffs are a good way to finish the legs or sleeves of a sporty garment. For more information, see Bands and Ribbing, pages 150–154.

## FOLD-UP CUFF

This type of cuff is often found on pants, particularly trouser styles, and short sleeves. Patterns styled this way include the extra length that's needed to form cuffs.

The traditional fold-up cuff includes some hand sewing. However, a shortcut machine method will save you time. If your machine has a free arm, it's even easier. Be sure you have marked the hem and cuff foldlines.

**A1** Turn the leg or sleeve inside out and press the hem up.

**A2** If necessary, finish the raw edge. Machine-stitch the hem in place. (These hem stitches won't show on the outside of the finished cuff.)

**A3** Turn the leg or sleeve right side out. Fold the lower edge up along the cuff foldline and press.

**A4** To keep the cuff in place, stitch in the ditch at the seams, through all of the layers.

### Mock fold-up cuff

If your pattern has straight, untapered sleeves or legs, and you want to add cuffs, there are two easy ways to fake it as described on page 168.

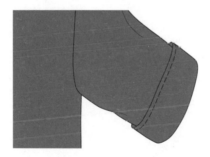

The mock fold-up cuff.

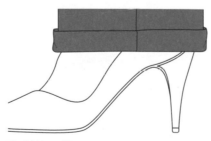

The fold-up cuff.

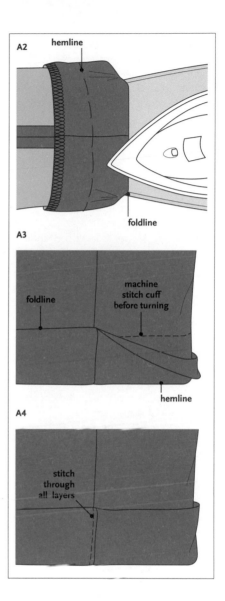

## THE CONVENTIONAL METHOD

**B1**  Before you cut out your garment, you'll need to alter the pattern. Cut the pattern apart along the hemline, spread it ¹/₂in (1.3cm), and pin or tape it to paper.

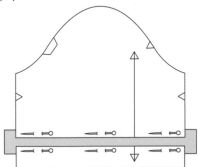

**B2**  When you're ready to hem the garment, fold the edge to the inside along the hemline and press.

**B3**  Fold the edge up again the same amount and press.

**B4**  Stitch ¹/₄in (6mm) from the second fold. This will create a tuck and encase the raw edge of the hem.

**B5**  Open out the sleeve or pants leg so that you can press the tuck up and the "cuff" down.

## ⓢ THE SERGER METHOD

It's easier to make this type of cuff before serging the underarm seam (on sleeves) or the inner leg seam (on pants).

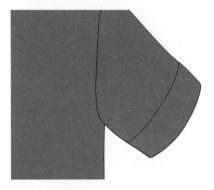

**C1**  Before you cut out your pattern make sure that the cuff allowance is twice the width of the finished cuff, plus ³/₄in (2cm). If necessary, lengthen the pattern at the lower edge.

**C2**  Measure up from the lower edge of the sleeve or pants a distance equal to the width of the finished cuff, plus ¹/₄in (6mm). Fold the lower edge of the garment section to the wrong side along this line; press.

**C3**  Now turn the folded portion of the garment back to the right side; press.

**C4**  Serge along this second fold, being careful not to cut the fabric.

**C5**  Press the cuff down.

**C6**  Beginning at the lower edge of the garment, serge the underarm or inner leg seams.

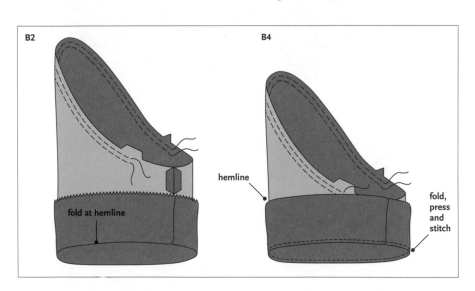

B2

fold at hemline

B4

hemline

fold, press and stitch

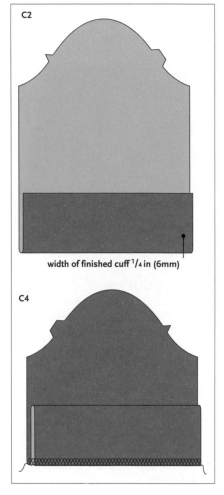

C2

width of finished cuff ¹/₄in (6mm)

C4

# SHOULDER PADS

Shoulder pads are an integral part of the stylish silhouette but, depending on the prevailing whims of fashion, their role may be a very subtle adjustment or a dramatic statement.

## As a fitting tool

In addition to enhancing the fashion look, shoulder pads can be a quick and easy way to enhance the fit of a garment.

### NARROW OR HOLLOW SHOULDERS

Shoulder pads can fill the natural hollow that occurs just below the shoulder. They can also add width to narrow shoulders.

### UNEVEN SHOULDERS

This is a common fitting problem that's easily corrected with different size shoulder pads. The shoulder that's lower gets the thicker pad. Don't try to get away with just one pad for the lower shoulder. The result will be a bumpy, lopsided appearance.

### LARGE BUST

By adding balance to the upper body, the addition of shoulder pads to your garment can minimize the appearance of a large bust.

## As a fashion tool

Shoulder pads are available in the traditional style for set-in sleeves, as well as in an extended shoulder style for kimono or raglan sleeves or dropped shoulders. The type of garment you're making determines the size pad you'll need as illustrated on page 170.

### FOR BLOUSES AND DRESSES

Use 1/4 in–1/2 in (6mm–1.3cm) pads. This size is occasionally used for jackets when a small pad is desired.

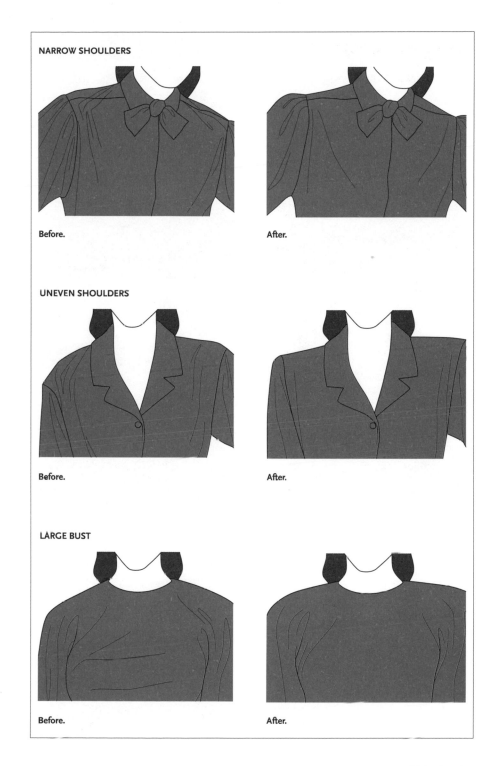

NARROW SHOULDERS

Before.

After.

UNEVEN SHOULDERS

Before.

After.

LARGE BUST

Before.

After.

## TYPES OF SHOULDER PAD

**TRADITIONAL JACKET PAD**

**TRADITIONAL DRESS PAD**

**EXTENDED JACKET PAD**

**EXTENDED DRESS PAD**

**FOR JACKETS AND COATS**
Use ½in–1in (1.3cm–2.5cm) pads. This size is occasionally used for dresses when an oversized look is the fashion focus.

## Attaching the shoulder pad

**ON SET-IN SLEEVES**
**A1** Pin the shoulder pad to the inside of the garment so that the largest layer of the pad is against the garment. The shoulder line of the pad should match the shoulder seam of the garment and the straightest edge of the pad should extend ½in (1.3cm) beyond the armhole seam (see illustration below left).
**A2** Try the garment on to check the pad placement before fixing.
**A3** Remove the garment. On the inside, loosely hand-tack the pad in place at the shoulder seam allowance and along the armhole seam allowance.

**ON DROP SHOULDERS,**
**KIMONO OR RAGLAN SLEEVES**
**B1** Try on the garment and slip the shoulder pad inside. Shift the pad over the shoulder until it looks right and feels comfortable. Pin it in place from the outside of the garment.
**B2** Remove the garment. On the inside, loosely hand tack the pad to the shoulder seam allowance.

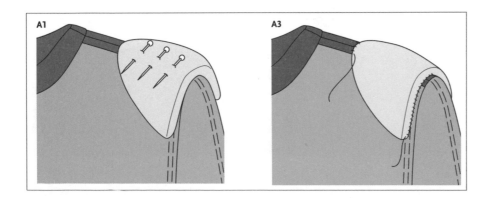

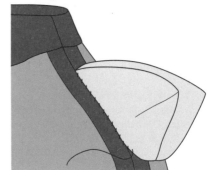

## Removable shoulder pads

If you need to remove the shoulder pads when washing or dry-cleaning, you can use self-gripping hook-and-loop fasteners to attach them to your garment. Removable pads can be easily transferred between garments so that you do not have to invest in multiple sets of pads.

**C1** Using the hook side of the fastener, hand-sew three dots or one long strip to the garment along the shoulder line or seam.

**C2** Try on the garment. Adjust the position of the pad until it looks right and feels comfortable. Pin it in place from the outside of the garment.

**C3** Remove the garment. On the pad, mark the corresponding position(s) of the loop section(s) of the fastener. Hand-tack them in place.

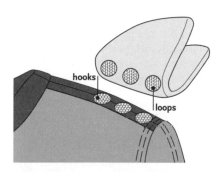

hooks

loops

**TIP** Keep an extra set of hook-and-loop fasteners around. Then, when you've removed the shoulder pads for cleaning, you can cover up the hook fasteners that are secured to the garment to prevent them from picking up bits of lint or snagging other garments during the cleaning process.

## Detached shoulder pads

If you're using covered shoulder pads on a dress or blouse, there is no need to even attach them to your garment. Just use this clever method and 1/2 in (1.3cm) wide strips of hook-and-loop fasteners.

**D1** Hand-sew the hook side to the top of the pad, along the shoulder line.
**D2** Position the loop side on top of the hook side and hand-sew the two sections together at the end nearest the neck edge.

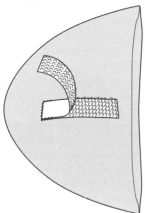

**D3** To wear the pads, open the fastener, position the pad on your shoulder under your bra strap, and close the fastener.

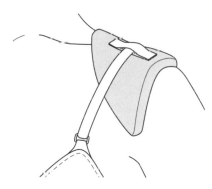

## Shoulder pad covers

Sometimes, particularly in the case of unlined jackets and coats, you'll want your shoulder pads to be the same color as your garment. And, if your garment is white or a light color, the shoulder pads will be a lot less noticeable if you cover them with a nude-color lining fabric. Shoulder pad covers are easy to make.

**E1** Cut a rectangle of lining fabric large enough to cover both sides of the pad, plus 5/8 in (1.5cm) all around.
**E2** Position the shoulder pad so that the straight edge is on the bias grainline.
**E3** Fold the lining over the pad.
**E4** Straight-stitch along the edge of the pad, trim the seam allowances to 1/4 in (6mm) and zigzag over the raw edge or serge the edges.

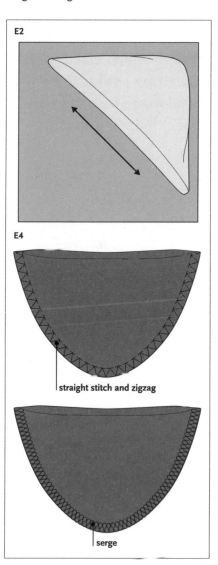

E2

E4

straight stitch and zigzag

serge

# WAISTLINES

**The waistline of a garment can be defined by a waistband made from a separate strip of fabric, or by creating a casing – a tunnel of fabric formed by parallel lines of stitching – through which elastic or drawstring cord is threaded. A well-made belt adds the perfect finishing touch.**

## WAISTBANDS

There are several different methods for applying and finishing waistbands. Your pattern instructions will include a method appropriate for your garment. You can follow those directions exactly or use one of the easy variations described in this section.

### Interfacing

Regardless of the construction method you choose, the waistband must be interfaced so that it retains its shape. For best results, interface the entire waistband, eliminating the seam allowances as described on page 133. If you're using a sew-in interfacing, add a row of basting on the facing side of the waistband, near the foldline. This will keep the interfacing from shifting.

### The no-bulk waistband methods

For most sewers, the biggest stumbling block to a smooth waistband is learning how to deal with all of the layers of fabric that converge at the waistline seam. Both of the following methods solve this problem by eliminating the seam allowance on the waistband facing. These methods are suitable for all fabrics, but are especially good for heavyweight or bulky fabrics. It's up to you whether you prefer machine stitching or hand stitching as your final step.

**STITCH-IN-THE-DITCH MACHINE METHOD**
The waistband can be prepared in two ways prior to attaching. Choose the option you prefer.

**Preparing the waistband, option 1:**
Cut out the waistband, placing the long, unnotched edge along a selvage, and eliminating ¼in (6mm) from the seam allowance. Fuse the interfacing in place.

**Preparing the waistband, option 2:**
Cut out the waistband. Apply fusible or sew-in interfacing. To finish the long, unnotched edge, serge, trimming off ¼in (6mm) as you stitch. If you don't

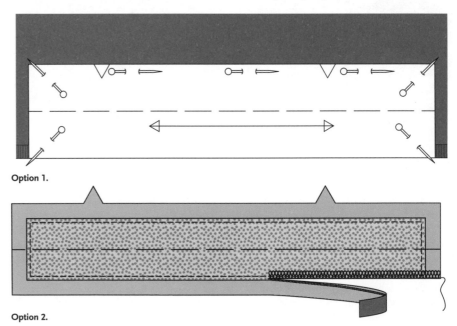

Option 1.

Option 2.

**TIP** Mark the stitching lines on your waistband pattern piece so it can serve as an accurate, see-through template for positioning the interfacing.

own a serger, trim off ¼ in (6mm) and then overcast the edge on your conventional machine.

**Attach the waistband:**

**A1** With right sides together, pin or baste the notched waistband edge to the garment, matching notches, centers and markings; stitch.

**A2** Press the seam allowances toward the waistband; trim the seam to ³/₈ in (1cm).

**A3** With right sides together, fold the waistband along the foldline and stitch the overlap end.

**A4** On the underlap, turn the waistband seam allowance down. Beginning at the fold, stitch the end to ³/₈ in (1cm) from the lower edge; pivot and continue stitching to the small dot marking. Backstitch to secure. Clip the seam allowances to the dot marking and trim the seams.

**A5** Turn the waistband right side out so that the finished or selvage edge extends ³/₈ in (1cm) below the waistband seam on the inside of the garment; press.

**A6** On the inside, fold the finished or selvage edge under diagonally at the zipper; pin. On the outside, pin the waistband layers together along the waistband seam.

**A7** On the outside, stitch in the ditch or groove of the waistband seam, catching the finished edge of the waistband and the diagonal turn-under. Remove the pins as you stitch.

HAND SEWING METHOD
Prepare the waistband using one of the methods described as you prefer.

**Preparing the waistband, option 1:**
Cut out the waistband, placing the long, unnotched edge along a selvage, eliminating the ⁵/₈ in (1.5cm) seam allowance. Fuse the interfacing in place.

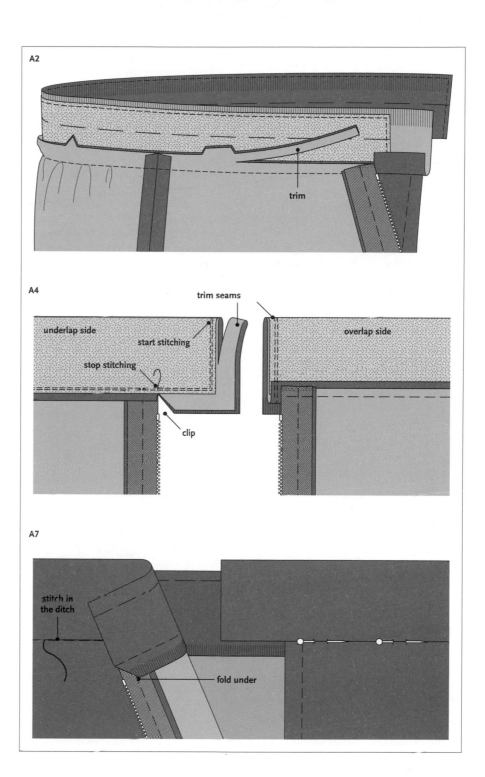

**Preparing the waistband, option 2:**
Cut out the waistband. Apply fusible or sew-in interfacing. To finish the long, unnotched edge, serge, trimming off the ⁵/₈ in (1.5cm) seam allowance as you stitch. If you don't own a serger, trim off ⁵/₈ in (1.5cm) and then overcast the edge on your conventional machine.

**Attach the waistband:**
**B1**  With right sides together, pin the notched waistband edge to the garment, matching notches, centers and markings; stitch.
**B2**  Press the seam allowances toward the waistband; trim to ³/₈ in (1cm).

**B3**  With right sides together, fold the waistband along the foldline. Stitch the seams at both ends of the waistband; trim the seam allowance.
**NOTE**  When stitching the underlap end, open out the fold that was created when you pressed the seam allowances toward the waistband.
**B4**  Turn the waistband right side out so that the finished or selvage edge meets the waistband seam on the inside of the garment and pin; press.
**B5**  On the inside, slipstitch the serged or selvage edge in place along the entire length of the waistband seams, including the underlap.

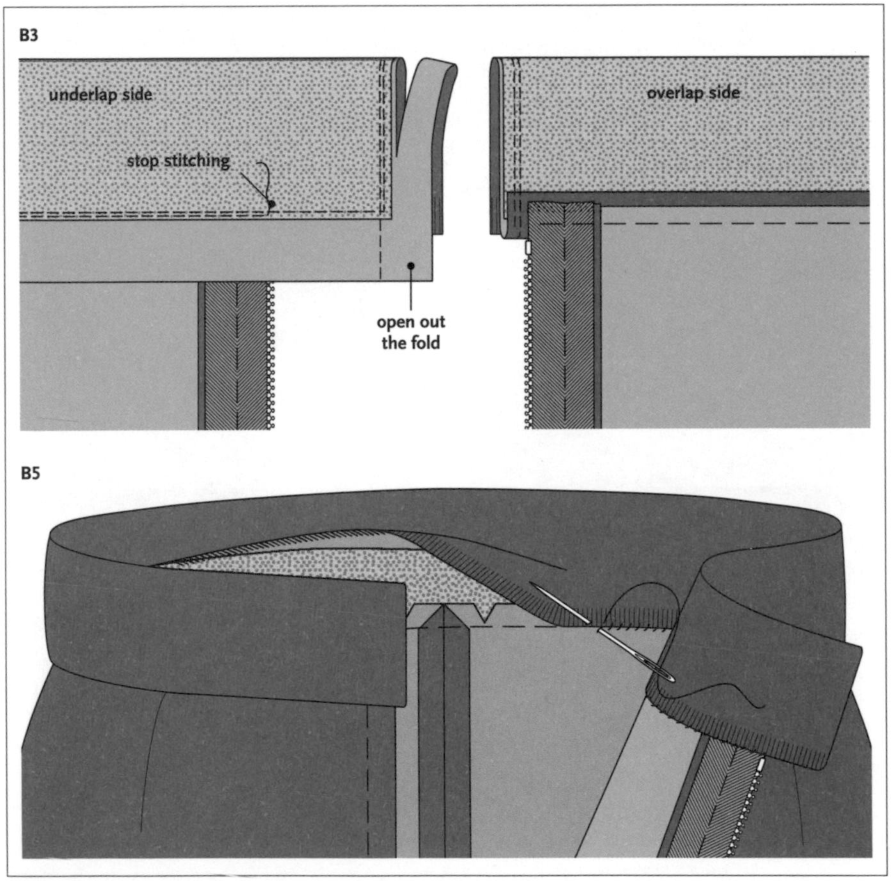

**ⓢ SERGER METHOD**
This is a quick way to attach a waistband and finish the raw edges in one step. It's an excellent choice for knits and light- to medium-weight fabrics.
**C1**  With right sides together, fold the waistband in half lengthwise. Using your conventional machine, stitch across the ends. At the underlap end, pivot and stitch along the waistline seam, ending at the small dot. Backstitch to secure.
**C2**  Clip to the stitching at the dot and then trim the seams (see illustration opposite).
**C3**  Turn the waistband right side out and press.
**C4**  Pin both cut edges of the waistband to the outside of the garment, matching notches, centers and markings.
**C5**  With the garment side up, and beginning at the underlap edge, serge along the waistline seams.
**C6**  Press the seam toward the garment and the waistband away from the garment. Hand-tack the seam allowance in place at the inside edges of the garment opening.

B3

underlap side

stop stitching

overlap side

open out the fold

B5

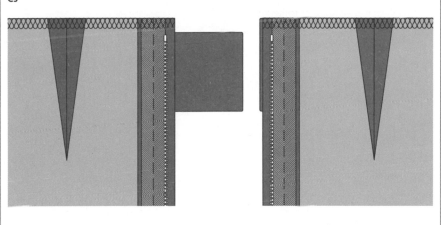

## CASINGS AND ELASTIC

When elastic or a drawstring is used to control fullness in a garment, it is often inserted into a tunnel of fabric called a casing. However, with some techniques, the casing is created at the same time the elastic is applied. This is called the direct application method. Elastic can also be applied directly to a garment edge with no casing at all. These exposed applications are commonly used on lingerie.

### Tunnel casings

There are three common types of tunnel casings: folded, applied and bias.

#### FOLDED CASING

As well as at waistlines, this can be seen at sleeve and pants leg edges. The pattern is designed with an extended garment edge that is pressed under ¼ in (6mm), pressed under again along the foldline and then edgestitched along both folds. To reduce bulk on a folded casing, the raw edge can be finished on a serger Instead of turning it under ¼ in (6mm).

**NOTE** Knits and firmly woven fabrics do not have to be pressed under and they don't have to be machine-finished either.

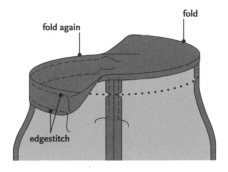

Working a folded casing.

## APPLIED CASING

This is a bias strip that is sewn to the edge of the garment, then folded to the inside and stitched close to both edges of the casing. When you're done, it looks like a folded casing from the outside of the garment. This technique is used in place of a folded casing if the garment edge is shaped or curved.

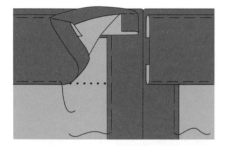

**TIP** Use a sheer tricot seam binding, such as Seams Great®, as a lightweight substitute for bias tape. There is no need to turn the raw edges under as they will not fray.

## BIAS CASING

This is created by applying single fold bias tape or a strip of bias fabric a specified distance from a garment edge. Bias casings are often used on the inside of a one-piece dress, a tunic or a jacket to create waistline definition. If the bias casing is placed a short distance in from a garment edge, a heading or ruffle forms at the edge once the elastic or drawstring is inserted.

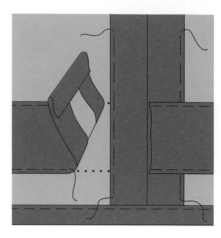

ABOVE **Working a bias casing.**
LEFT **Working an applied casing.**

Here a tunnel casing has been added just below the bustline for a decorative drawstring feature.

### TUNNEL CASINGS – GENERAL INFORMATION

✂ For accurate placement, be sure to mark necessary foldlines or stitching lines.

✂ For a drawstring opening that occurs at a seamline, reinforce the opening with small pieces of lightweight fusible interfacing or by adding small squares of seam binding when backstitching (see right).

✂ Purchase elastic that is 1/8 in–1/4 in (3mm–6mm) narrower than the casing to ensure ease of insertion.

✂ Before applying a bias casing, use steam to preshape the tape into a curve that matches the garment edge (see tip, page 148).

✂ If your fabric is too bulky, too scratchy or too loosely woven for a folded casing, make an applied facing instead. Use the casing foldline as your seamline.

✂ To keep elastic from getting stuck in the seam allowances as it's inserted, use fusible web or machine basting to anchor the seams to the garment within the casing area. Do this before you create the casing.

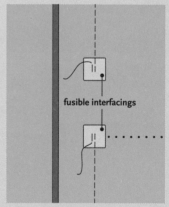

fusible interfacings

## INSERTING ELASTIC

**A1** Cut the elastic 1in (2.5cm) larger than the body measurement or according to the pattern guides.

**A2** Fasten a safety pin or bodkin to one end of the elastic and thread it through the casing opening.

**A3** To avoid accidentally pulling the elastic all of the way through the casing, before inserting one end of the elastic into the casing opening, use a safety pin to anchor the other end of the elastic to the garment just below the casing.

**A4** Overlap the ends of the elastic ½in (1.3cm), and stitch together in a square or with parallel rows of stitches.

**NOTE** If you have any doubt about the fit, try the garment on and pin-fit the elastic before permanently securing it.

**A5** Stitch the casing opening closed.

**A6** To keep the elastic from rolling and twisting during wear, stitch in the ditch (the groove) formed by each seam.

**TIP** To add waistline definition to a one-piece garment, make a bias casing. Center it over the waistline marking on your pattern and then insert elastic through the casing.

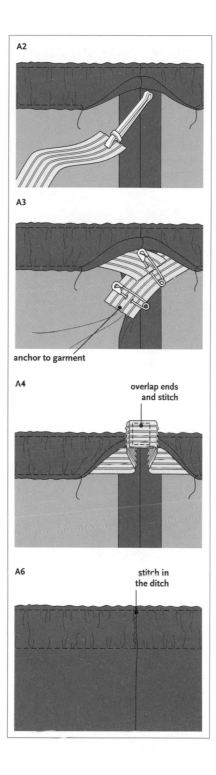

A2

A3

anchor to garment

A4 overlap ends and stitch

A6 stitch in the ditch

## Direct application methods

With the following methods, you stitch through the elastic so there's no chance of the elastic twisting or curling. Many of these elastic application methods suggest dividing and marking the elastic and the garment edge into quarters. However, if you're a beginning sewer, or if you're working on a long edge, you'll have an easier time if you divide and mark into eighths.

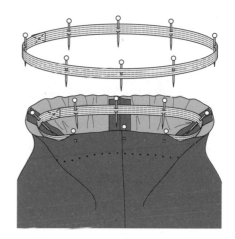

## HIDDEN ELASTIC,
## THE CONVENTIONAL METHOD

Use this quick technique to create a casing at the edge of a garment and apply the elastic at the same time. It's a no-twist method suitable for knits or wovens that won't unravel and for aerobic wear, swimwear and lingerie.

**B1** Cut the elastic the required length, generally 3in (7.5cm) smaller than the body measurement. Overlap the ends ¹/₂in (1.3cm) and stitch.

**B2** Trim the seam allowance on the garment edge to equal the width of the elastic.

**B3** Divide the elastic and the garment edge into quarters or eighths and mark. Pin the elastic to the wrong side of the garment, matching the markings and keeping the edge of the elastic even with the edge of the garment. Zigzag, overcast or straight stitch the elastic to the edge of the garment. Be sure to stretch the elastic to fit as you sew.

**B4** Fold the elastic to the inside of the garment. Stitch close to the raw edge of the fabric, through all of the layers, with a straight or a zigzag stitch. Again, stretch the elastic to fit as you sew. For increased stretch and recovery, use a straight stitch with elastic thread in the bobbin (see Using Elastic in the Bobbin) or a zigzag stitch with nylon thread in the needle and the bobbin.

### USING ELASTIC IN THE BOBBIN

✂ This technique is borrowed directly from ready-to-wear swimwear and aerobic wear.

✂ For the final row of stitches, put elastic thread in the bobbin and stitch with the right side of the garment facing you. For best results, use nylon thread in the needle.

✂ How you wind the bobbin threads depends on how your conventional machine is designed. If it has a self-winding bobbin, wind the elastic thread by hand, stretching it slightly. If you must remove the bobbin case to wind it, guide the elastic thread onto the bobbin while it's turning on the bobbin winder, being careful not to stretch it.

✂ If your bobbin case has a tension bypass hole, insert the elastic thread through it, replace the bobbin case and bring the thread up through the hole in the needle plate. This gives you a lighter bobbin tension.

✂ Set your machine for a straight stitch, 3mm long or 8 stitches per inch.

✂ Working on the right side of the garment, topstitch close to the inner edge of the elastic, through all of the layers.

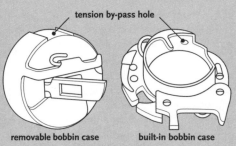

tension by-pass hole

removable bobbin case    built-in bobbin case

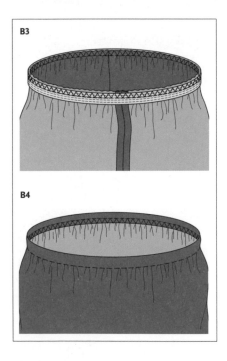

B3

B4

## ⓢ HIDDEN ELASTIC, THE SERGER METHOD

**C1** Adjust your serger to the appropriate settings (see Hidden Elastic Application chart, right).

**C2** Leave one seam open. Divide and mark the elastic into quarters or eighths.

**C3** Divide and mark the garment edge into quarters or eighths.

**C4** Pin the elastic to the wrong side of the garment, placing the inside edge along the foldline and matching the markings.

**C5** With the elastic side up, position the outer edge of the elastic next to the blade. Serge, holding the elastic next to the blade. Serge a couple of stitches to anchor the elastic. Be careful not to cut the elastic. Continue serging, holding the elastic up slightly off the fabric against the toe of the presser foot and stretching the elastic to fit between the pins. Remember to remove the pins before the presser foot reaches them.

**C6** Adjust your serger to a balanced stitch setting and serge the remaining seam up through the elastic.

**C7** Fold the elastic to the inside of the garment. Using your conventional machine, stitch close to the edge of the fabric, through all of the layers. To keep this row of stitches from popping when you wear the garment, use elastic thread in the bobbin (see opposite) or use a zigzag stitch and nylon thread in the needle and the bobbin.

## HIDDEN ELASTIC APPLICATION

| TYPE OF SERGER STITCH: | | 3 | 4 | MINE |
|---|---|---|---|---|
| Stitch length: | | 4mm–5mm | 4mm–5mm | |
| Stitch width: | | Widest | Widest | |
| Tensions | Needle: | Tight | Tight | |
| | Right Needle: | N/A | N/A | |
| | Upper Looper: | Normal* | Normal* | |
| | Lower Looper: | Normal | Normal | |

\* Can use wooly nylon thread.

### ⓢ THREE STEPS TO A SERGED HALF SLIP

This simple half slip will give you some practice on your serger. Using an old half-slip as a guide, cut a piece of tricot the desired width and length. Allow 1¹⁄₂ in (3.8cm) for side seams and ¹⁄₂ in (1.3cm) for the waistline seam.

✂ **Step 1:** Flatlock a piece of the flat lace to one end of the slip. (See Trims, page 209.)

✂ **Step 2:** Attach elastic to the other end using the flatlock method.

✂ **Step 3:** Adjust your serger for a balanced stitch setting and serge the side seam. For comfort, cover the seam in the elastic with a piece of ribbon. Use a dot of glue stick to hold it in place and then stitch it on your machine

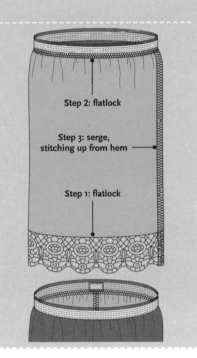

Step 2: flatlock

Step 3: serge, stitching up from hem

Step 1: flatlock

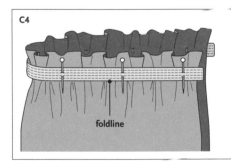

C4

foldline

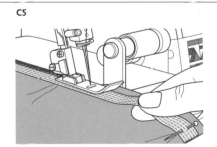

C5

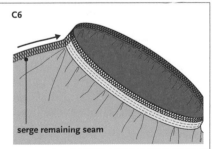

C6

serge remaining seam

**S** **FLATLOCK OR EXPOSED APPLICATION**
This professional one-step application
makes for fast sewing and comfortable
wearing. Because the elastic is exposed,
this technique is most frequently used for
lingerie. For the most attractive results,
use lingerie elastic, a soft, stretchy elastic
with one picot or decorative edge.

**D1** Adjust your serger to the appropriate
setting (see Flatlock Elastic Application
chart, right).

**D2** Leave one garment seam open.
Divide and mark the elastic into quarters
or eighths.

**D3** Divide and mark the garment edge
into quarters or eighths.

**D4** Position the elastic so that the
straight edge is along the foldline. If you
want the seam to be flat against the body,
with the ladder stitches on the outside,

## FLATLOCK ELASTIC APPLICATION

| TYPE OF SERGER STITCH: | | 3 | 4 | MINE |
|---|---|---|---|---|
| Stitch length: | | 3mm–4mm | 3mm–4mm | |
| Stitch width: | | Widest | Widest | |
| Tensions | Needle: | Very loose | Very loose | |
| | Right Needle: | N/A | N/A | |
| | Upper Looper: | N/A | Loose | |
| | Lower Looper: | Normal | Very tight | |

pin the elastic to the right side of the
fabric. If you want the seam on the
outside, with the ladder stitches against
the body, pin the elastic to the wrong side
of the fabric.

**D5** With the elastic side up, position
the straight edge of the elastic next to
the blade. Serge a couple of stitches to
anchor the elastic. Be careful not to cut
the elastic. Continue serging, holding the
elastic up slightly off the fabric, against
the toe of the foot. As you do this,
stretch the elastic to fit between the
pins. Remember to remove the pins as
you come to them.

**D6** Pull on the elastic until the picot
edge is up and the seam is flat.

**D7** Adjust your serger for a balanced
stitch setting and serge the remaining
seam all the way up through the elastic.

**S** **TIP** It is easier to serge elastic on
straight if there's a wide margin of fabric
for the serger's blade to trim away.
Before you cut out your pattern, check
that the distance between the foldline
and the cut edge of the garment is at
least $1/2$ in (1.3cm) wider than the width
of the elastic. For $1/4$ in (6mm) wide
elastic, a $3/4$ in (2cm) wide seam
allowance is required; for $3/8$ in (1cm)
wide elastic, at least a $7/8$ in (2.2cm)
wide seam allowance is needed. If necessary,
adjust the seam allowances before you
cut out the garment.

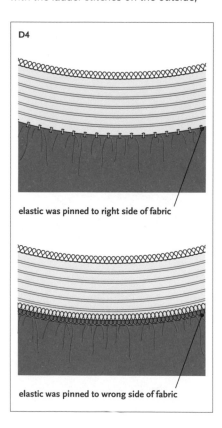

D4

elastic was pinned to right side of fabric

elastic was pinned to wrong side of fabric

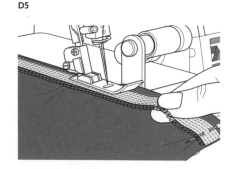

D5

## BELTS AND BELT LOOPS

Belts add the finishing touch to many ensembles. In fact, your local fabric store is probably a wonderful source for a wide array of gorgeous buckles.

### Covered belts

If you're going to make your own covered belt, check your fabric store for the stiffening material that is specifically designed to use inside belts. It's available in several widths and has the right blend of rigidity and flexibility necessary for a belt that is comfortable but won't curl. Do not be tempted to substitute several layers of interfacing – you'll end up with a belt that collapses into folds after several wearings. The stiffening material is sold by the yard/meter or in kits with an accompanying buckle to cover. If it's your first belt, buy the kit and follow its directions to cover the belting.

### Soft belts

Done on either the conventional machine or serger, this simple stitched-and-turned method can be used to make a fabric sash or a soft, crushed belt that's attached to a slip-through buckle at one end.

#### THE CONVENTIONAL METHOD

**A1** Cut a lengthwise strip of fabric that's equal to the desired length plus 1¹/₄ in (3.2cm) and twice the desired width plus 1¹/₄ in (3.2cm).

**A2** With right sides together, fold the belt in half lengthwise.

**A3** Stitch along the ⁵/₈ in (1.5cm) seamline, leaving an opening at the center back for turning. To secure the stitching, backstitch at the corners and at either end of the opening.

**A4** Trim the seams and corners. If possible, press the seam allowances open. Otherwise, press the top seam allowance toward the body of the sash.

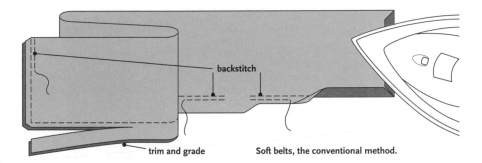

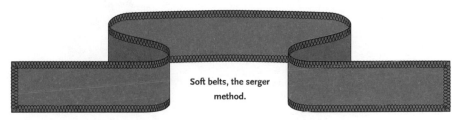

trim and grade    backstitch

Soft belts, the conventional method.

Soft belts, the serger method.

This ensures that your finished sash will have crisp edges.

**A5** Turn the belt right side out, press and slipstitch the opening closed.

> **TIP** Use a ruler to turn the belt right side out. Push one end toward, and out through, the opening. Repeat for the other end.

#### **S** THE SERGER METHOD

**B1** Cut a lengthwise strip of fabric that's equal to the desired length plus 1¹/₄ in (3.2cm) and twice the desired width plus 1¹/₄ in (3.2cm).

**B2** With wrong sides together, fold the belt in half lengthwise.

**B3** Serge around the outside edges. For fine fabrics, use all-purpose thread and a rolled hem. For heavy fabrics, try pearl cotton or ¹/₁₆ in (2mm) silk or rayon ribbon in the upper looper.

### Stretch belts

Stretch belting and elasticized trims are available by the yard/meter in a wide range of widths and styles, from solid colors to simple patterning to elaborately embellished surfaces. For the most gala evenings, there's even sequined or beaded stretch trim.

Purchase enough stretch belting or trim to fit comfortably around your waist, plus 2in (5cm). Buy a clasp buckle or interlocking buckle that fits the width of your trim.

**C1** To keep the ends of the belting from unraveling, seal them with Fray Check™, finish them on the serger or trim them with pinking shears.

**C2** Slip the ends of the belting through each half of the buckle and fold back 1in (2.5cm).

**C3** Pin and stitch the edges in place, backstitching to secure. If your stretch belting is sequined or beaded, stitch the edges by hand.

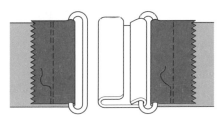

## Belt loops

No matter what type of belt you choose to make or buy, belt loops will help it stay put when you wear your garment. On a garment without a waistline seam they'll serve as anchors to keep the hemline from shifting and dipping as you stand up and sit down.

### PLACEMENT

A pattern that calls for fabric loops will include a pattern piece and markings for placement. If you're adding loops, center them over the waistline. Plan on at least three loops – one at center back and one at each side seam. If your belt has a heavy buckle, you might want to add them to the front. Depending on the style of buckle, position one slightly off center, so that it's hidden from view when the buckle is fastened, or add two, each one midway between the side seam and the center front.

### FABRIC LOOPS

If you want fabric loops, and the instructions aren't included in your pattern, follow these instructions.

**D1** Cut a strip of fabric along the selvage, three times the width of the finished loop. To determine how long this strip should be, add ³/₄ in (2cm) to the width of the belt and then multiply by the number of loops.

**D2** Fold the strip lengthwise in thirds with the selvage on top. Edgestitch along both folded edges.

**D3** Cut apart into the desired number of loops.

**D4** To attach the loops to the garment, press the short ends under ¹/₄ in (6mm). Position one loop at each marking. Topstitch it to the garment by machine or slipstitch in place by hand.

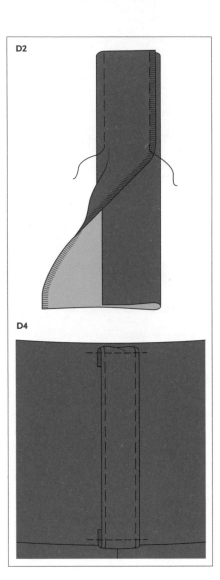

D2

D4

### MACHINE THREAD LOOPS, THE CONVENTIONAL METHOD

On many ready-to-wear garments, fine thread chains are used as belt loops or button loops at the cuffs or neckline. They are not bulky and they're almost invisible.

**E1** Take two or three lengths of fine cording, such as buttonhole twist, crochet cotton or tatting thread, and twist them tightly together.

**E2** Stitch over them twice using a close, narrow zigzag stitch.

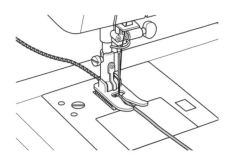

**E3** Cut the thread chain into loops. To make them easy to handle, each loop should be three times its finished length.

> **TIP** Use thread loops to help keep children from losing their winter gear. Sew buttons on the inside of a child's coat, at the sleeves and back of the neck. Sew loops onto mittens, hats and scarves and then button them in place.

### ⓢ MACHINE THREAD LOOPS, THE SERGER METHOD

**F1** Thread the machine with all-purpose sewing thread that matches the garment fabric. Set the tensions for general serging and shorten the stitch length so that the stitches lock into a tight chain.

**F2** Serge a chain that is three times the finished length of each loop. As you serge, pull tightly on the thread tails so that the chain comes off the stitch fingers smoothly.

**F3** Cut the chain apart into the desired number of lengths.

### ATTACHING THE CHAINS

Once you have made the chains, either by the conventional or serger method, you will need to attach them to the garment. This can be done in one of two ways.

**Option 1:** Make the belt loops first; then catch them in the seamline as the garment is sewn together.

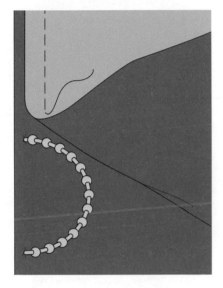

**Option 2:** Sew the garment together first. Then, thread the loop through the large eye of a needle. Insert the needle between the stitches in a seamline or between the threads of the fabric (if there is no seamline) and gently pull the tail of the thread chain to the wrong side of the garment. Knot to secure. Repeat for the other end of the loop.

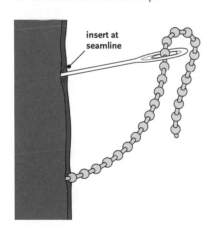

insert at seamline

# POCKETS

**Pockets should be more than just an attractive design feature. In order to be functional they should be constructed so that they can withstand the wear and tear of frequent use. The techniques for making patch, in-seam and front hip pockets are described here.**

## PATCH POCKETS

Patch pockets come in many shapes and sizes. They can be lined, unlined or self-lined. Your pattern will include only one of these techniques, but you can easily convert any patch pocket as you prefer.

### Unlined pockets

These are the easiest to make, and are most popular for children's and casual garments in light- to medium-weight fabrics. Creating the pocket facing is always the same, but completing the pocket will depend on its shape.

#### TO CREATE THE FACING

**A1**  Press under ¼ in (6mm) on the upper edge of the pocket and edgestitch. Alternatively, finish on your serger.

**A2**  To create the pocket facing, fold the upper edge to the right side along the foldline; press.

**A3**  Starting at the fold, stitch along the seamline, backstitching at either end.

**A4**  Trim the seam allowances in the facing area only to ¼ in (6mm). For bulky fabric, diagonally trim the corners.

#### FOR A CURVED PATCH POCKET, THE CONVENTIONAL METHOD

**B1**  Make a row of machine gathering stitches around the curved edges ¼ in (6mm) away from the first stitching line, within the seam allowance.

**B2**  Press the seams open in the facing area (use a point presser if available).

**B3**  Turn the facing to the wrong side pushing the upper corners out with a pin or a point turner.

**B4**  Pull up the gathering threads to shape the curve; then press under along the seamline, rolling the stitching to the wrong side. Press the facing seams and the fold. To eliminate bulk, notch out the fullness in the seam allowance at the curves to the gathering stitches.

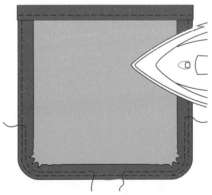

**B5**  To finish, edgestitch or topstitch the facing or secure with fusible web.

**⑤ FOR A CURVED PATCH POCKET, THE SERGER METHOD**

**C1**  Adjust your serger to the appropriate setting (see Curved Patch Pocket chart).

**C2**  Working on the right side of the pocket, serge around the pocket on the ⅝in (1.5cm) seamline, tightening the needle tension when you reach the curved areas. This will make the seam allowances curl to the inside, easing in the fullness. When you are past the curved area, loosen your needle tension to the normal setting.

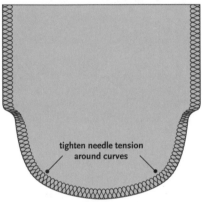

tighten needle tension around curves

**C3**  Press the seam allowances to the wrong side along the stitching line.

**C4**  To finish the patch pocket, edgestitch or topstitch the facing in place or secure with fusible web.

**FOR A SQUARE OR RECTANGULAR POCKET** Miter the lower corners, as described in Mitering, page 148.

## Lined pockets

There are times when a pocket lining makes a nice finish. You can add this touch even if your pattern doesn't include it.

**D1**  Once the pocket is cut out, fold the pocket pattern piece along the foldline to omit the facing. Use this new shape to cut the lining.

**D2**  Fold under along the upper edge of the lining. The width of this fold should be equal to half the depth of the original pocket facing. Press.

**D3**  With right sides together, pin the lining to the pocket, matching sides and lower edge. Turn the pocket facing down over the lining so that all of the raw edges match; pin.

**D4**  Starting at the fold, stitch along the seamline, backstitching at the ends.

**D5**  Trim the seam allowances and corners; notch any curves.

**D6**  Press the lining seam allowance toward the lining.

**D7**  Turn the pocket right side out and press, rolling the seam slightly to the lining side. (See the useful tip on the opposite page for how this can be made easier.)

**D8**  Slipstitch the opening in the lining to the facing.

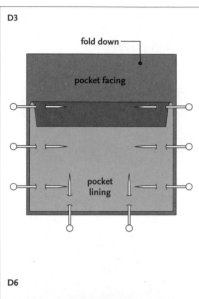

D3

fold down

pocket facing

pocket lining

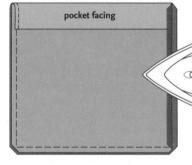

D6

pocket facing

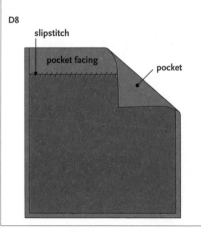

D8

slipstitch

pocket facing

pocket

| CURVED PATCH POCKET | | | | |
|---|---|---|---|---|
| **TYPE OF SERGER STITCH:** | | 3 | 4 | MINE |
| Stitch length: | | 3mm | 3mm | |
| Stitch width: | | Widest | Widest | |
| Tensions | Needle: | Normal to very tight | Normal to tight | |
| | Right Needle: | N/A | Very tight | |
| | Upper Looper: | Slightly tight | Slightly tight | |
| | Lower Looper: | Slightly loose | Slightly loose | |

**TIP** Trim ⅛ in (3mm) off the sides and lower edge of the pocket lining. Pin the lining to the pocket, matching the raw edges. The smaller lining will automatically cause the seams to roll slightly to the inside.

## USING A POCKET TEMPLATE

Another way to ensure a perfectly-shaped pocket is to use a template. You can make your own by tracing the shape of the pocket, minus seam allowances and facing, onto a piece of cardboard. Cut out the cardboard template. After the facing is turned and pressed, slip the cardboard under the facing; pull up the gathering threads and press the seam allowances over the cardboard. Or invest in a pocket curve template. This notion is a metal template with four different corner shapes and a clip to help the fabric conform to the appropriate curve for your pocket.

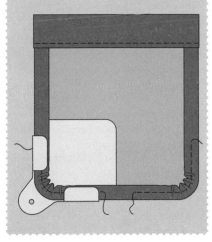

## Self-lined pockets

This super-simple way to line a pocket works best on lightweight fabrics. If your pattern does not utilize this technique, you can easily convert it.

**E1** When you cut out your pocket, place the pattern piece so that the foldline is on a crosswise fold of the fabric. (The facing part of the pattern will extend beyond the fold and will not be cut.)

**E2** To make the pocket, fold it in half with right sides together. Stitch, trim, clip and notch as for Lined Pockets.

**E3** Press one seam allowance toward whichever side you wish to designate as the pocket facing.

**E4** Cut a 1½ in (3.8cm) slash near the lower edge of the pocket facing.

**E5** Turn the pocket right side out through the slash. Press, rolling the seam toward the pocket facing.

**E6** Fuse a strip of interfacing or mending tape over the slash.

## Applying the pocket

The easiest way is to topstitch or edgestitch the pocket to the garment.

**F1** Pin or baste the pocket in place. Glue stick or double-faced basting tape also work well.

**F2** Edgestitch and/or topstitch ¼ in– ⅜ in (6mm–1cm) from the edge.

**F3** To reinforce the upper corners, backstitch or stitch a small triangle.

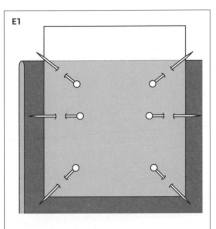

E1

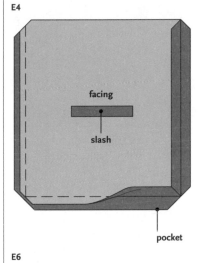

E4

facing

slash

pocket

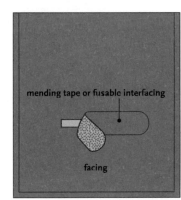

E6

mending tape or fusable interfacing

facing

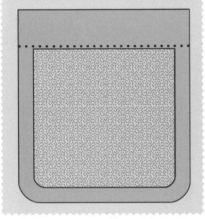
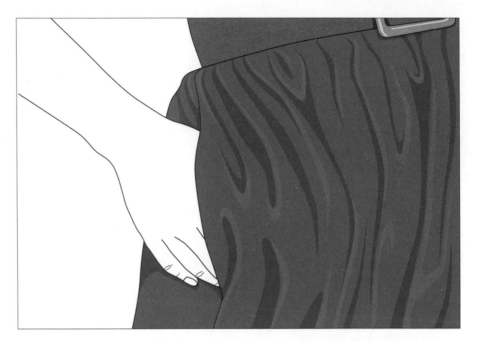

In-seam pocket.

### APPLYING THE POCKET BY HAND

On delicate or hard-to-handle fabrics,
such as velvet, it is easier to apply the
pocket by hand. To do this, pin or hand-
baste the pocket in place. Turn back the
pocket edge slightly and slipstitch it to
the garment. To secure, take several
small stitches at the upper corners of
the pocket.

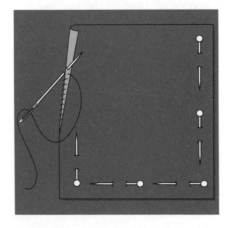

## IN-SEAM POCKETS

In-seam pockets can be found at the
side seams of dresses, skirts and pants.
Often these pockets are created from a
separate pattern piece which means that
the pocket can, if you wish, be cut from
a lining fabric.

### THE CONVENTIONAL METHOD

Your pattern instructions will tell you how
to make this type of pocket but there are
two important things to remember as
illustrated opposite top left.

**Reinforce the corners:** Shorten your
stitch length for about 1in (2.5cm) on
either side of each corner.

**Isolated clipping:** Clip the garment/
pocket back seam allowance only so
that you can press the side seams open
and the pocket toward the front of
the garment.

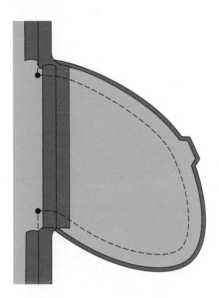

**Conventional method for in-seam pockets.**

### ⓢ THE SERGER METHOD

Use this technique for in-seam pockets on a skirt or pants. If the pockets are two separate sections, serge them to the garment front and back along the seamline.

**A1** With right sides together, pin the pocket/garment sections together at the side seams. On your conventional machine, and beginning at the waistline edge, stitch along the side seam to the first marking; backstitch. Machine baste to just below the next marking. Switch back to a regular length stitch, backstitch to the marking and then stitch forward for about 3in–4in (7.5cm–10cm).

**A2** Machine-baste or glue-baste the pocket sections together along the outside edges.

**A3** Serge the side seams, beginning at the hemline. (This is important as if you begin serging from the waistline, it is very difficult to serge around the lower edge of the pocket without cutting into the garment.)

**A4** As you approach the lower edge of the pocket, pull the pocket forward with

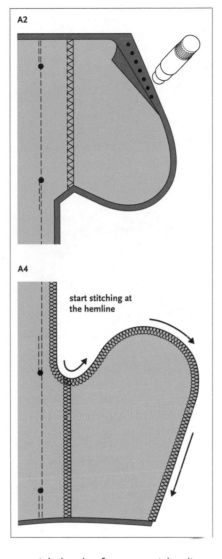

**A2**

**A4**

start stitching at the hemline

your right hand to form as straight a line as possible. At the same time, use your left hand to guide the stitches around the curve so they remain on the garment.

**A5** Press the pocket toward the center front, and then remove the basting stitches from between the markings.

### Cut-in-one pockets

Some patterns have the pocket shape built into the front and back pattern pieces. This saves time because you don't have to cut out the pockets separately or stitch them to the garment. If your pattern wasn't designed this way, you can adapt it to use this method – just as long as your fabric is wide enough to accommodate the expanded pattern piece.

**B1** Lap the pocket pattern piece over the garment front pattern piece, matching the seamlines and markings. Pin or tape together. Repeat for the garment back.

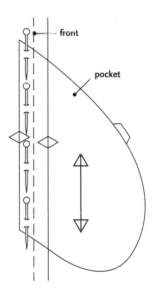

front

pocket

**B2** Cut out the front and back garment sections.

**B3** Sew the garment together on either your conventional machine or your serger, following the guidelines for in-seam pockets.

## FRONT HIP POCKETS

Many pants and skirts feature partially hidden hipline pockets, sometimes called slant pockets. The slanted opening may be straight or curved.

Front hip pockets consist of two different-shaped pieces: the pocket, which also becomes part of the main section of the garment at the waistline, and the pocket facing, which finishes the opening edge.

If your pattern features this style of pocket, the pattern instructions will tell you how to construct it. However, there are a few extra things you might want to do, depending on the type of fashion fabric you have chosen for your garment.

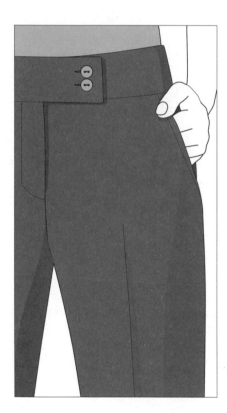

**Front hip pocket.**

**For heavy or bulky fabrics:** Cut the pocket facing from lightweight lining fabric in a matching color.

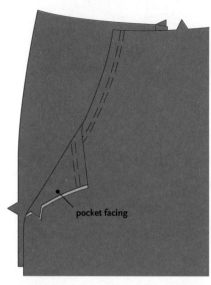

pocket facing

**For very stretchy or very delicate fabrics:** Cut a strip of interfacing 2in (5cm) wide and shaped to follow the opening edge of the pocket. Baste or fuse it on the inside, along the opening edge of the pocket.

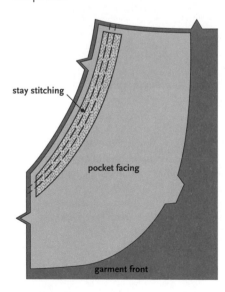

stay stitching

pocket facing

garment front

## S Creating a stay

Regardless of your choice of fabric, a front hip pocket will retain its shape better if the opening edge has a pocket stay which will reinforce it against the wear and tear it will endure. If you use your serger to create the stay, you'll also eliminate the need to interface the edge of the opening.

**A1** With right sides together, pin the pocket facing to the garment front along the pocket opening.

**A2** Serge the seam. As you do this, thread pearl cotton through the hole in the front of your presser foot, or guide it over the finger guard of the presser foot, so that it's caught in the stitching and acts as a stay in the seam. This technique is the same as for Gathering Over a Cord, page 143.

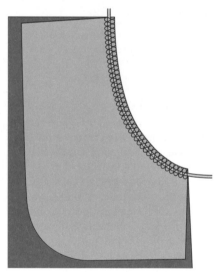

**TIP** In place of the pearl cotton, you can also feed twill tape under the presser foot as you serge.

# HEMS

Hems can be done by hand, by machine or simply fused in place. If you decide to hem by hand, the stitches should be invisible on the outside of the garment. If you decide to hem by machine, some stitching will appear on the right side so it is important to match the thread perfectly to the fashion fabric. This section covers all you need to know for perfect hemming.

## HEM BASICS

Regardless of which technique you choose, the basics of preparing the hem are almost the same. However, since some of these procedures vary slightly depending on the type of hems, read through this section and decide on your technique before you begin. For hemming pleats, see Pleats, page 141.

### Marking
When your garment is at the "almost finished" stage, when there's not much left to do but sew on the buttons and put up the hem, it's a good idea to let it hang for 24 hours. This gives the fabric grain time to "settle in" before you mark the hem. This rest period is particularly important for knit garments or for garments with a bias or circular hem. If you skip this step, your finished garment may develop mysterious hemline dips and sags after a couple of wearings.

Once your garment has rested, try it on. Wear suitable undergarments and, if possible, the shoes, belt, etc. that you plan to wear with it. These accessories will affect how the garment hangs as well as influence the visual proportions. With them on, it will be easier to determine the most flattering hem length.

The best, and easiest, way to mark a hemline is to enlist the help of a friend. For even results, you stand in one spot, with your feet together; the friend moves around you, using a yardstick or pin-type skirt marker to establish the hem length. Pins should be placed parallel to the floor about 2in–3in (5cm–7.5cm) apart.

### Trimming
Take the garment off, turn it wrong side out and place it over the ironing board or on a table. If you are working with a particularly bulky fabric, it is a good idea to trim the seam allowances that occur within the hem allowance before turning

up the hem. If this is the case, trim to ¼in (6mm) between the edge of the garment and the hemline.

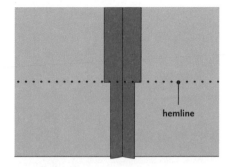

Turn the hem up along the pin-marked line. Matching the seamlines first, insert pins at right angles to the hemline, through both layers of fabric; then remove the pins that indicate the hemline. (Once the hem is pinned up, it's a good idea to try on the garment to check length and evenness.)

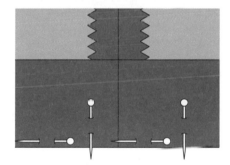

Hand-baste the hem about ¼in (6mm) from the folded edge, removing the pins as you go. (If you're making a machine-rolled hem or a narrow topstitched hem, skip this step.)

Measure and mark the desired hem allowance plus ¼in (6mm) for finishing. Trim away the excess. The type of hem you choose, as well as the shape of the hemline, will determine the depth of the hem allowance. On a straight garment, the hem allowance should be no more than 3in (7.5cm). On an A-line or flared garment, the hem allowance is usually 1¼in–2in (3.2cm–5cm).

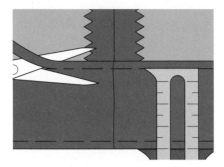

Press the hem. If necessary, put strips of brown paper between the hem allowance and the garment to prevent ridges as you press. Use a press cloth to protect your fabric.

## Easing

If the garment edge is slightly curved, the hem allowance will have extra fullness. Unless this fullness is eased so that the hem allowance lies flat against the garment, your finished hem will have ripples and ridges.

**THE CONVENTIONAL METHOD**
Easing is done after the hem allowance is trimmed but before the raw edge is finished.
**A1**   Ease-stitch ¼in (6mm) from the edge, remembering to loosen the needle tension slightly.
**A2**   Working on a flat surface, use a pin to draw up the bobbin thread wherever there is extra fullness. Pin to control the distribution of the fullness.

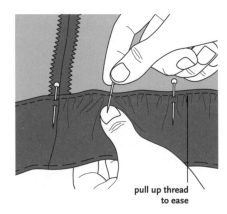

pull up thread
to ease

**A3**   Steam-press to shrink out some of the fullness.

**⑤ THE SERGER METHOD**
Use this technique to ease the fullness in the hem allowance on full, circular and A-line skirts and shirttail hems.
**B1**   Adjust your serger to the appropriate setting (see Easing chart).
**B2**   On the right side of the fabric, serge 3in–4in (7.5cm–10cm) along the edge of the hem allowance. As you do so, hold your forefinger behind the foot so that the fabric piles up. Release the fabric.
**B3**   Repeat, serging all around the raw edge. The hem allowance will automatically roll toward the garment.
**B4**   Working on a flat surface, pin to control the distribution of the fullness.
**B5**   Steam-press to shrink out some of the fullness.
**NOTE** Some fabrics may not ease up enough using this technique. For heavier fabrics, tighten the needle tension even more so that the fabric curls. This will enable you to adjust the gathers.

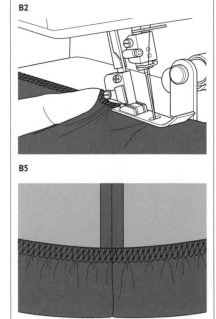

| EASING | | | | |
|---|---|---|---|---|
| **TYPE OF SERGER STITCH:** | | **3** | **4** | **MINE** |
| Stitch length: | | 2mm–3mm | 2mm–3mm | |
| Stitch width: | | Normal | Normal | |
| Tensions | Needle: | Tight | Tight | |
| | Right Needle: | N/A | Tight | |
| | Upper Looper: | Normal | Normal | |
| | Lower Looper: | Normal | Normal | |

## HAND-SEWN HEMS

With machine-sewn hems so quick and easy to achieve on your machine, the hand-stitched hem may not be your first choice; but, if it is, here are some good tips for getting the neatest results.

### Finishing the edge

If your fabric frays, it will be necessary to finish the edge; the stitch and pink, the zigzag/overcast and the bound seam finishes described on pages 97–98, are all excellent choices. Alternatively, use the serger technique on page 98.

Other good hem finishes include adding seam binding or stretch lace. Both these products are applied in exactly the same way, but seam binding is suitable for straight hems only, while stretch lace, because of its flexible properties, is best for knits and curved hems. To apply, lap the lace or binding ¼ in (6mm) over the edge of the hem allowance and edgestitch it in place.

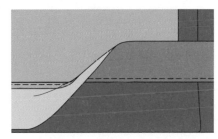
Seam binding.

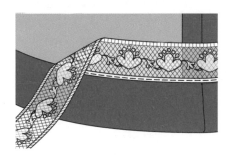
Stretch lace.

### Sewing the hem

Choose the blindstitch, the catchstitch or the hemming stitch (see Hand Sewing, pages 121 and 122). Use a thread that is the same color or one shade darker than your fabric as thread looks lighter when sewn. To make sure the finished hem is invisible, pick up only one or two garment threads with each stitch.

## MACHINE-MADE HEMS

Hems done by machine are a quick and easy alternative to hand sewing. Just be sure the machine technique you choose is suitable for your fabric.

### Machine blindstitch

Many machines have a built-in stitch that can be used for straight or nearly straight hems on medium-weight wovens and stable knits. It is particularly popular for children's playclothes and home decorating. A special foot is usually required. Check your sewing machine manual for details.

**A1** Turn up the finished edge of the garment to the desired hem depth.

**A2** Turn the garment over so that the hem allowance is underneath. Fold the fabric back, exposing ¼ in (6mm) of the hem allowance.

**A3** Place the garment under the foot with the folded-back edge along the hem guide. Adjust the foot, as indicated for your machine, so that the fabric fold is against the guide and the needle barely catches the fold as you sew.

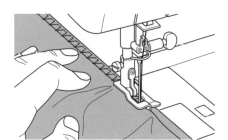

### Narrow topstitched hem

Suitable for sheer, lightweight or medium-weight fabrics.

**B1** Turn up the edge of the garment to the desired hem depth.

**For knit fabrics:** Press under along the hemline; trim the hem to ⅝ in (1.5cm).

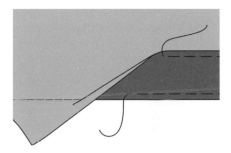

**For woven fabrics:** Press under along the hemline and then trim the hem allowance to 1in (2.5cm). Fold the raw edge in to meet the first crease and press again.

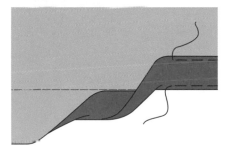

**B2** Working on the right side, topstitch close to the edge of the hem allowance.

**B3** If you wish, topstitch again, close to the edge of the garment.

**TIP** A decorative thread, such as buttonhole twist, turns a topstitched hem into a design feature. For balance, repeat elsewhere on the garment.

## Wide topstitched hem

This technique can be used on all fabrics and styles, except for very curved hems. If the hem is slightly curved, be sure to easestitch it before topstitching.

For the most attractive proportions, the hem allowance should be 1½in–2in (3.8cm–5cm) wide.

**C1** Press the hem up along the hemline. Ease in the fullness on any curves. For woven fabrics, press the raw edge under ½in (1.3cm). (It is not necessary to press the raw edge under if you are working on knit fabrics.)

**C2** Working on the wrong side of the fabric, stitch close to the edge of the hem allowance.

**C3** Stitch again, ¼in (6mm) away from the first row of stitching, within the hem allowance.

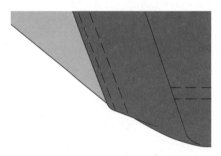

## Machine-rolled hem

This is a quick and easy way to achieve the narrow rolled hem look that is particularly attractive on sheers, lightweight silk and synthetic fabrics, and for hemming ruffles. For this type of hem, your garment must have at least a ⅝in (1.5cm) hem allowance.

**D1** Mark the hemline ⅛in (3mm) longer than desired. Fold the garment up along this hemline and then stitch as close as you can to, but not more than ⅛in (3mm) from, the fold. Do not press before you stitch. If the hemline is not on straight of grain, pressing first will distort the hem.

**D2** Using sharp embroidery scissors, carefully trim away the hem allowance above the stitching.

**D3** Fold the hem allowance up along the stitching line, rolling the stitching line just slightly to the inside of the garment; press.

**D4** Stitch close to the inner fold; press.

> **TIP** When making the machine-rolled hem on sheers, use long basting stitches for the first row of stitches and then remove them when the hem is completed.

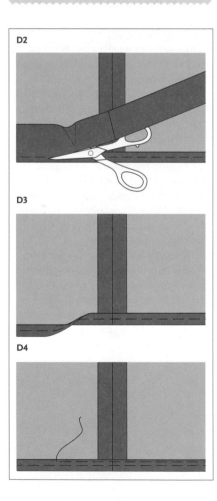

D2

D3

D4

## ⓢ HEMMING ON THE SERGER

Your serger provides you with an array of hemming techniques

### ⓢ Overcast hem

Overcasting on the serger is an easy way to finish the raw edges of your hem allowance.

Plan your hem allowance so there's at least ¹⁄₁₆in (2mm) extra that you can trim off as you serge. This ensures that your fabric "fills" the stitches and that, in time, the stitching won't pull away from the raw edge.

**A1** Adjust your serger to the appropriate setting (see Overcast Hem chart, opposite).

**A2** Serge along the raw edge for the hem allowance.

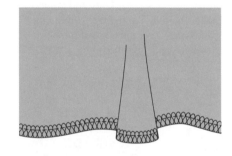

**A3** Secure the thread chains.

**A4** Complete your hem, folding up the hem allowance and using the appropriate hand stitches or topstitching on the conventional machine.

> **ⓢ TIP** The overcast technique can be used to create a finished hem. Using topstitching thread in both the upper and lower loopers, serge along the finished hemline.

## OVERCAST HEM

| TYPE OF SERGER STITCH: | | 2 | 3 | 4 | MINE |
|---|---|---|---|---|---|
| Stitch length: | | 2mm–3mm | 2mm–3mm | 2mm–3mm | |
| Stitch width: | | Normal | Normal | Normal | |
| Tensions | Needle: | Very loose | Normal | Normal | |
| | Right Needle: | N/A | N/A | Normal | |
| | Upper Looper: | N/A | Normal | Normal | |
| | Lower Looper: | Normal | Normal | Normal | |

### Ⓢ Blind hem

Because the stitches will show a little bit on the outside of the garment, this type of hem is more appropriate for children's wear, casual garments and home decorating. The serger finishes and secures the hem in one operation.

**B1** Adjust your serger to the appropriate setting (see Blind Hem chart, below right).

**B2** Prepare the hem allowance as for a handsewn hem; then fold the garment back ¼ in (6mm) from the raw edge of the hem allowance. Baste or pin in place. Press.

**B3** Serge along the raw edge so that the needle just catches the fold of the fabric.

**B4** Remove the pins or the basting stitches. Open out the garment until the stitches lie flat and then press on the wrong side to set the stitches and ease out the fullness.

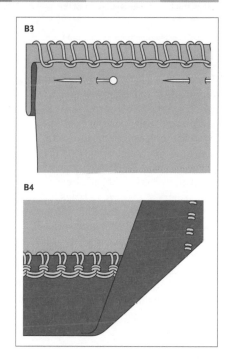

B3

B4

### Ⓢ Rolled hem

The rolled hem, sometimes referred to as a handkerchief hem, is the beautiful and durable finish found on the edges of scarves, napkins, tablecloths and ruffles. Although it is possible to recreate the effect using a rolled hem presser foot on a conventional machine, the serger makes it even easier to duplicate the rolled hem at home. For this type of hem, you should have at least a ½ in (1.3cm) hem allowance.

The best fabric choices for a rolled hem are silk or polyester crepe de chine, georgette, lightweight tissue faille and soft cottons. If you use a washable fabric, you'll get better results if you preshrink it to remove the sizing.

What gives the hem its finished appearance is the serger's ability to roll the fabric to the underside as the edge is stitched and finished. The thread you see in a rolled hem is the upper looper thread; the lower looper and needle threads are hidden inside the roll. As a first choice, use silk or wooly nylon thread in the upper looper. These threads have the stretch and recovery necessary to help the fabric roll, will lay smooth along the finished edge, and have a beautiful sheen. Use polyester serger thread in the lower looper and the needle. If you can't find the right color silk or wooly nylon thread, use the same polyester thread in the upper looper.

> **Ⓢ TIP** A special blind hemming foot is available for some sergers. Check your machine's instruction manual. Generally, only the right needle is used when the blind hem foot is attached.

## BLIND HEM

| TYPE OF SERGER STITCH: | | 2 | 3 | MINE |
|---|---|---|---|---|
| Stitch length: | | Longest | Longest | |
| Stitch width: | | Widest | Widest | |
| Tensions | Needle: | Loose | Very loose | |
| | Upper Looper: | N/A | Normal | |
| | Lower Looper: | Normal | Tight | |

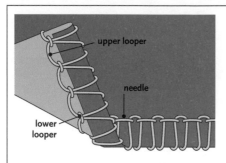

A perfect rolled hem.

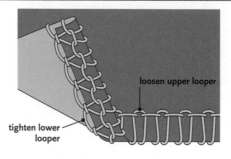

How to adjust if large loops form on the underside.

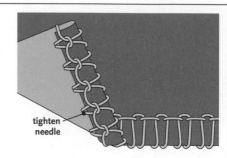

How to adjust if the needle thread is visible on the underside.

Adjust the serger to the appropriate setting (see chart below). Place a test swatch, right side up, under the presser foot; serge. Fine-tune the settings until the hem rolls perfectly (see above left).

**If the lower looper thread forms large loops on the underside:** Loosen the upper looper and tighten the lower looper (above center).

**If the needle thread is visible on the underside:** Tighten the needle tension (above right).

When recording your serger setting for a rolled hem, keep with the fabric swatch; settings may differ from fabric to fabric.

### Ⓢ Lettuce edge

This delicate edge finish works best on very stretchy knits, such as interlocks, tricots and knit ribbing, that are cut and serged across the grain or "with the stretch". You can also achieve good results on lightweight wovens if they are cut on the bias. The lettuce edge looks great on ruffles and lingerie hems, as well as neck and sleeve ribbings.

**C1** Adjust the serger to the appropriate setting (see Rolled Hem and Lettuce Edge Hem chart). Test the settings on a swatch of fabric cut "with the stretch".

**C2** Place the fabric under the presser foot, right side up, ½in (1.3cm) from the raw edge. Begin serging so the machine grabs the fabric for a couple of stitches.

**C3** Continue serging, holding the fabric firmly in front of the foot so that it is stretched before it's serged. The finished edge will curl just like the edge of a lettuce leaf.

**NOTE** If your knit runs, don't stretch the fabric before you serge. Instead, stretch it after the serging is finished

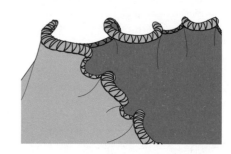

Ⓢ **TIP** If you can't get the proper look to the stitch, and your lower looper needs to be set higher than the tightest tension setting, wrap the thread around the tension dial twice. Just remember to rethread the lower looper before doing any regular serging.

### ROLLED HEM AND LETTUCE EDGE HEM

| TYPE OF SERGER STITCH: | | 3 | MINE |
|---|---|---|---|
| Stitch length: | | 1mm | |
| Stitch width: | | 2mm* | |
| Tensions | Right Needle: | Normal | |
| | Upper Looper: | Tight | |
| | Lower Looper: | Very tight | |

*Narrow the stitch width to 2mm or use the presser foot and needle plate especially designed for a rolled hem. Consult your serger manual for specific information about your machine.

## ⓢ Picot or shell hem

When you want a softer treatment, the picot or shell hem is a variation of the rolled hem that will provide a scalloped, decorative application. The more supple look is achieved by using a longer stitch length for less thread coverage. It is particularly beautiful on lingerie, as well as along the edges of silks, crepe de chines and soft, scarf-like fabrics.

Adjust your serger for the appropriate setting (see Picot Hem chart). For best results, use polyester thread. Follow the instructions for the Rolled Hem, page 193.

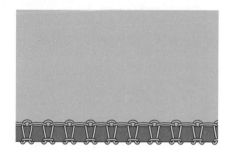

## ⓢ Narrow hem

Because the narrow hem is flat rather than rolled, it's better for heavier fabrics when a soft treatment is desired.

Adjust your serger for the appropriate setting (see Narrow Hem chart). Follow the instructions for the Rolled Hem, page 193.

## PICOT HEM

| TYPE OF SERGER STITCH: | | 3 | MINE |
|---|---|---|---|
| Stitch length: | | 3mm–4mm | |
| Stitch width: | | Narrowest | |
| Tensions | Right Needle: | Normal | |
| | Upper Looper: | Tight | |
| | Lower Looper: | Very tight | |

## NARROW HEM

| TYPE OF SERGER STITCH: | | 3 | MINE |
|---|---|---|---|
| Stitch length: | | 1mm-2mm | |
| Stitch width: | | Narrowest | |
| Tensions | Needle: | Normal | |
| | Right Needle: | N/A | |
| | Upper Looper: | Normal | |
| | Lower Looper: | Normal | |

## ⓢ Cover hem

The cover hem resembles a twin or triple needle straight stitch on one side of the fabric and a serger stitch on the other. You decide whether the needle threads or the looper threads appear on the outside of the garment. Consult the manual for the cover stitch settings.

**D1** Stitch around the hem, overlapping at the original starting point for about 2in (5cm).

**D2** Declutch the chain looper and pull off the threads (refer to the manual).

**D3** Cut the threads, leaving a long tail. Pull the threads to the underside; tie them in a knot. Apply a drop of seam sealant to the knot and lip the tails.

> ⓢ **TIP** You may experience skipped stitches as you serge over bulky steams. If this occurs, reduce the foot pressure when you reach the seam. Once you've serged past the seam, readjust the pressure to its previous setting.

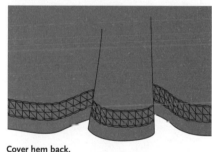

Cover hem back.

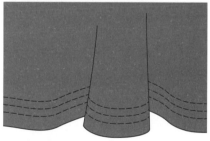

Cover hem front.

## FUSED HEMS

This no-sew method of hemming is suitable for all but very sheer or lightweight fabrics. Use packaged strips of fusible web or cut your own from web purchased by the yard/meter.

The strip of web should be narrower than your hem allowance. Sandwich the strip between the hem allowance and the garment, just below the finished edge. Fuse in place, carefully following the manufacturer's directions.

To make sure that no ridges appear on the right side of your garment, test the fusible web on scraps first. If ridges show, pink the edges of the web before applying and try not to rest the iron on the finished edge of the hem allowance.

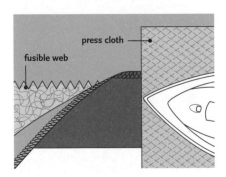

press cloth

fusible web

## ALTERING A HEMLINE, FACED HEM

The faced hem is a useful technique should you need to lengthen an item that has no spare fabric at the hemline. It can also be used to hem very bulky fabrics. Purchase packaged bias hem facing tape or make your own wide bias strips (see Making Custom Binding, page 144).

**A1**  Trim the hem allowance down to ¹/₂in (1.3cm).

**A2**  With right sides together and raw edges even, pin the facing to the hem allowance, lapping the cut edges. Stitch a ¹/₄in (6mm) seam.

**A3**  Press the seam allowances toward the facing. Turn the hem up ¹/₄in (6mm) below the facing seam. Sew the hem in place and slipstitch the ends of the facing closed.

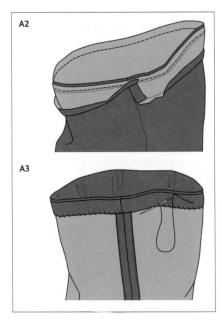

A2

A3

## ALTERING A HEMLINE

✂  You may need to alter a hemline to keep up with changing fashions, or growth spurts in children, or to adapt hand-me-downs to fit.

✂  To shorten a hem just remove the old stitches and proceed as if you were hemming the garment for the first time.

✂  To lengthen a hemline, you must first get rid of the old crease. A good steam pressing should do the job.

✂  For more persistent creases, make a solution of equal parts white vinegar and water. Apply it along the crease line using a small brush or an eyedropper, and then press. To be sure the vinegar won't affect the color of the garment, test this technique first on an inside seam allowance.

✂  If the crease still remains or the color has faded along the former hemline, consider covering the mark with a decorative trim that is compatible with your garment.

✂  For children's garments, adding a colorful trim may be the best option.

✂  If you don't have a deep enough hem allowance once you let the garment down, add seam binding or stretch lace, or make a faced hem (see Altering a Hemline, Faced Hem, left).

✂  To turn a faced hem into a decorative feature, use a wide band of contrasting fabric. Turn the hem under halfway across the width of the facing so a border of contrast fabric shows along the hem. Sew the hem in place on the reverse as normal.

# CLOSURES

One area where you can make a big difference to how a garment looks is in the kind of closure you choose. Closures can be as subtle or as obvious as you wish. Zippers and buttons can be selected in colors that match or contrast with the garment fabric, or they can be replaced by snaps, toggles, frogs, ties or self-gripping hook-and-loop fasteners, such as Velcro®.

Frogs (above) and toggles make a great alternative to buttonhole closures. For more see page 204.

## BUTTONS AND BUTTONHOLES

At one time, anyone who learned to sew had to struggle with learning how to make bound buttonholes. Thanks to the advances in sewing machine technology, this is no longer the case. Most modern machines have an automatic buttonhole function of some sort. Take the time to practice making buttonholes on your machine in a variety of fabrics. Read your sewing machine manual and learn what, if any, tension or pressure adjustments are required. Review the information in this section before you begin.

### Transferring buttonhole markings

Buttonhole placement should be marked on the right side of your fabric. You can do this during the cutting and marking stage, when you transfer all of the other markings, or you can wait until just before you're ready to stitch. Even if you carefully marked the placement lines when you cut out the garment, it's a good idea to recheck them when you're ready to make the buttonholes.

**TIP** Always make a test buttonhole first on a scrap of fabric. Use the same number of layers (fashion fabric, interfacing, facing, etc.) as the garment will have. If your fabric doesn't feed evenly through the machine, try using a piece of nonwoven stabilizer such as Trace Erase® or Stitch-n-Tear® underneath all the layers. If your fabric is very sheer or very fragile, put the stabilizer both on the bottom and on top. It's easy to tear away once the buttonholes are made.

### UNSATISFIED WITH YOUR BUTTONHOLES?

✂ Take your sewing machine to the dealer and get it serviced.

✂ Bring your sample buttonholes with you so the dealer can see where you are having problems.

✂ Find someone to make buttonholes for you; ask at your local fabric store and check out the Yellow Pages.

✂ Consider substituting with a closure that does not require buttonholes. Explore the alternatives in this chapter.

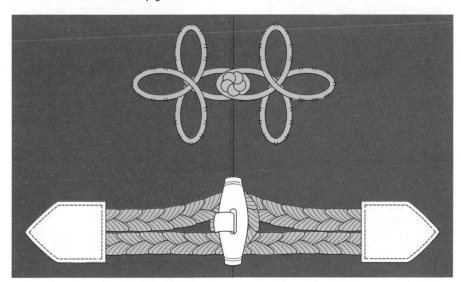

**A1** Place the pattern on top of the garment, aligning the pattern seamline with the garment opening edge.

**A2** Stick pins straight through the tissue and the fabric at both ends of each marking; then carefully remove the pattern without disturbing the pins.

**A3** If appropriate for your fabric, mark between the pins with a water-soluble or evaporating marking pen. Alternatively, place a strip of ¹/₂ in (1.3cm) wide transparent tape or masking tape alongside, but a scant ¹/₈ in (3mm) away from, the pins. (Tape marks some fabrics; test first on a scrap of the fabric.) Mark the position of each pin on the tape. When you make the buttonhole, stitch next to the tape, being careful not to stitch through it.

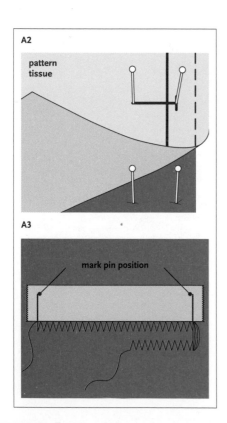

## Stitching the buttonholes

To make sure your buttonholes are accurately placed, begin stitching horizontal buttonholes at the marking closest to the garment edge; begin stitching vertical buttonholes at the marking closest to the upper edge of the garment.

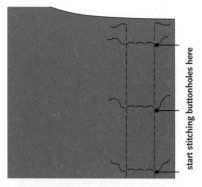

Horizontal buttonholes.

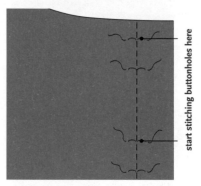

Vertical buttonholes.

**TIP** Stick to the button size that is recommended on the pattern envelope. If you can't find a button you like in the right size, don't go more than ¹/₈ in (3mm) larger or smaller. Otherwise, either the buttons will look out of proportion on the garment, or the buttonholes will have to be respaced.

**TIP** Many modern sewing machines have a buttonhole foot as standard, as illustrated on page 39. This has a slot to place the button in, with a stopper that slides to fit. When the buttonhole is being sewn, the stopper limits how far the stitching can go, automatically creating a buttonhole sized to fit the specific button.

## Determining buttonhole size

The buttonhole markings on the pattern tissue indicate the placement, not the size, of the buttonhole. Buttons are sized according to their diameter. However, it is a button's circumference that determines how large the buttonhole needs to be. For example, a ⁵/₈ in (1.5cm) flat button will require a smaller buttonhole than a ⁵/₈ in (1.5cm) domed button.

To determine a button's circumference, wrap a piece of narrow ribbon, seam binding or twill tape around the widest part of the button and pin the ends together.

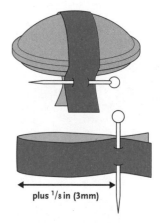

plus ¹/₈ in (3mm)

The length of your test buttonhole should be equal to half the button's circumference plus ¹/₈ in (3mm). If your button is very thick, you may need to increase the size a little bit more. Test the size before making any buttonholes on your garment.

## Cutting the buttonhole open

Once all of the buttonholes are stitched, cut them open using a razor blade, X-acto® knife and a cutting board, buttonhole cutter, seam ripper or a pair of small, sharp scissors. Start at the center and cut toward each end. To prevent cutting too far, put a straight pin at each end of the buttonhole opening.

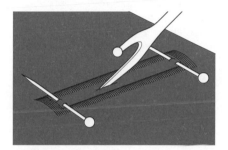

### CORRECTING BUTTONHOLE ERRORS

A liquid seam sealant, such as Fray Check™, is a great remedy for buttonhole errors. If you cut into the stitches, repair the damage with a dot of the seam sealant. If fabric "whiskers" develop along the cut edges of your buttonhole, trim off all of the loose threads and then treat the edges with a thin beading of Fray Check™. If the liquid comes out of the bottle too fast, apply it with a very fine paintbrush. Wipe off the bristles immediately or the brush will be too stiff to use again.

## Sewing on the button

Buttons come in two styles: sew-through and shank. The shank is designed to compensate for the thickness of the garment layers. On sew-through buttons, you'll need to use thread to create a shank. You do this at the same time as you sew on the button.

Sew through button.

Shank button.

### TO LOCATE THE BUTTON POSITION

After making the buttonholes and cutting them open, lap the garment edges, matching centers, so the garment looks buttoned.

**For a horizontal buttonhole:** Stick a pin through at the center front or back marking, 1/8 in (3mm) in from the end of the buttonhole.

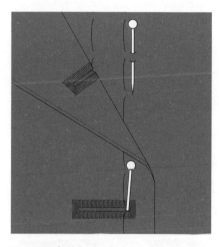

**For a vertical buttonhole:** Insert the pin 1/8 in (3mm) below the top of the buttonhole.

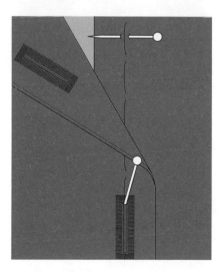

### TO SEW ON A SHANK BUTTON BY HAND

Thread the needle with a double thread. Take a few small backstitches to lock the thread at the point of the pin marking. Bring the needle through the button and back into the fabric. Repeat several times.

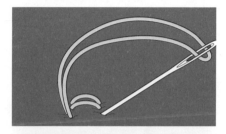

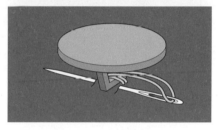

### TO SEW ON A SEW-THROUGH BUTTON BY HAND

To create a thread shank on a sew-through button, place a toothpick or wooden match on top of the button and sew over it. Sew back and forth several times, then remove the toothpick and wind the thread round and round the extra thread under the button. Stitch back into the fabric.

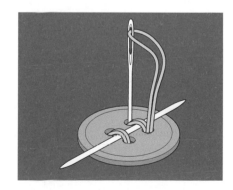

### TO SECURE A HAND-SEWN BUTTON

To avoid making an ugly knot on the underside of your garment draw the needle to the underside of the garment and fasten the thread with several small, tight backstitches. Insert the needle into the fabric and tunnel it between the garment layers for about 1in (2.5cm). Bring the needle out and clip the thread close to the fabric. If your garment is only one layer thick or if your fabric is sheer, clip the thread close to the backstitches instead of tunneling it.

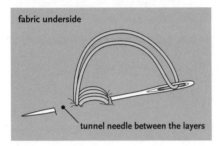

fabric underside

tunnel needle between the layers

**TIP** To sew on buttons super quickly, double your thread before passing it through the needle's eye. You'll be sewing with four strands instead of only two, so you'll need to take only half as many stitches.

### TO ATTACH A SEW-THROUGH BUTTON BY MACHINE

If your sewing machine makes a zigzag stitch, you can probably use it to attach sew-through buttons by machine.

**B1** Attach the buttonhole foot. Set the machine's stitch width to 0. Position the button and fabric under the foot so that the needle is in the center of the left hole. Turn the hand wheel to check the needle position, and then sew several stitches in place to secure the threads.

**B2** Adjust the stitch width so that the needle will swing from the left hole to the right hole. (Check your manual for information.) Sew 8–10 stitches.

**B3** To lock the stitches (unless this feature is programmed into your machine), set the stitch width to 0, reposition the needle over the right hole and sew a few stitches.

**B4** Remove fabric and button from the machine and clip the threads.

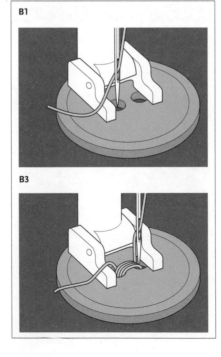

B1

B3

### TO ADD A SHANK TO A MACHINE-SEWN SEW-THROUGH BUTTON

Check your manual. Some machines have a small accessory plate that will raise the button. If not, place a pin or toothpick on top of the buttonhole foot before you begin to stitch. When you have finished stitching, leave a 10in (25cm) tail. Bring the needle thread down through one of the button's holes and wrap it around the shank several times. Using a hand-sewing needle, draw the needle thread to the wrong side of the fabric. Tie the needle and bobbin threads together in a knot.

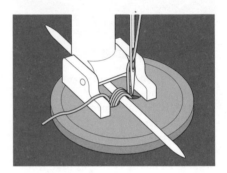

## ZIPPERS

Because zippers have a reputation for being difficult to install, many sewers – especially new or returning ones – unnecessarily avoid patterns that feature them. There really is no need for this as the little tricks that guarantee a perfect zipper installation are so simple that anyone can learn them.

### Zipper installation tips

There are four basic zipper applications: centered, lapped, fly-front and separating. Your pattern will give you instructions for the method appropriate to your garment. In order to easily follow those instructions, familiarize yourself with the Parts of the Zipper diagram opposite.

Consult your pattern instructions for when and how to put in the zipper. Always use a zipper foot when machine basting and permanently stitching the zipper. It can be positioned either to the right or the left of your needle, making the installation easier and your stitching straighter. To keep ripples out of your finished product, always stitch in the same direction – from the bottom of the zipper to the top. This rule holds true for both the machine basting and the permanent stitching.

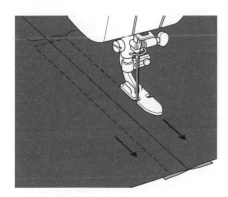

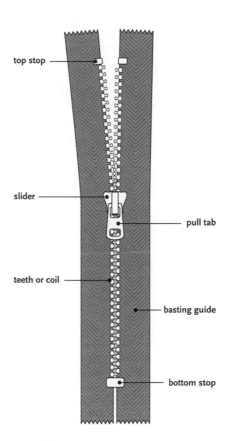

top stop

slider

teeth or coil

pull tab

basting guide

bottom stop

Parts of the zipper.

**When the garment seam is basted closed before the zipper is installed:** Use a long machine basting stitch. Then, before pressing the seam open, clip the basting stitches at the bottom of the zipper opening, as well as every 2in (5cm). This will make the basting easier to remove once the zipper is installed. At that point, if you have trouble grabbing the thread ends, use pointed tweezers.

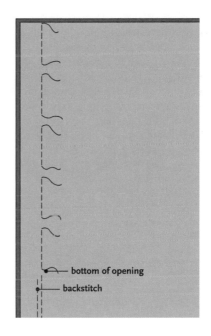

bottom of opening

backstitch

## ZIPPER FACTS

✂ Always check the back of your pattern envelope for the zipper length and type.

✂ Zippers can have either plastic, nylon or metal teeth, which are mounted on a colored tape. They come in a range of different lengths, weights and colors.

✂ Conventional zippers have exposed teeth; concealed (invisible) zippers have coils that roll inward and are hidden by the zipper tape.

✂ Closed-end zippers have a bottom stop at one end and are used for skirts, pants, and dresses.

✂ Separating (open-ended) zippers are used for the front opening of cardigans, coats, and jackets. A separating zipper splits open into two separate sections so you don't have to put on the garment over your head.

✂ Unless the zipper tape is 100 percent polyester, pre-shrink the tape by plunging the zipper into hot water for a few minutes.

✂ Before installing your zipper press the zipper tape to remove any packaging folds. Work on the wrong side and don't rest the iron on the teeth or the coils.

**When the zipper is going to cross a seam:** As, for example, a center back zipper on a dress with a waistline seam, you may need to reduce some of the bulk before basting the seam closed. To do this, make a clip in the intersecting seam allowances, 1in (2.5cm) in from each opening edge. Trim the seam allowances within the clipped section to ³/₈in (1cm) and press open, as illustrated right.

**When an alternative to machine basting is required:** Although machine basting is usually the suggested method for holding a zipper in place for permanent stitching, you may get better results with double-faced basting tape or glue stick. Put the basting tape along the outside edge of the zipper tape so you don't stitch through it. You can stitch through glue stick as long as you let it dry for a few minutes first, otherwise it will gum up your needle. You could also use masking tape, positioning the tape along the edge of the zipper tape so that you absolutely do not stitch through it.

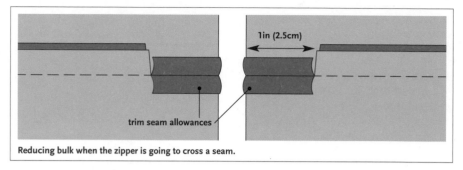

Reducing bulk when the zipper is going to cross a seam.

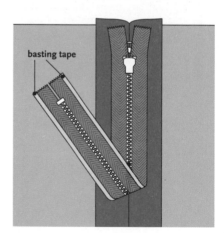

**When basting the zipper in place:** Keep the pull tab flipped up. Later on, this will make it easier to permanently stitch around the pull tab and the slider.

## TIPS FOR TOPSTITCHING

For a professional-looking zipper installation, the topstitching should be smooth, straight, and a consistently even distance from the edge(s) of the garment all along the length of the zipper. If you can't do this by eye, try one of the following methods.

**Use a ruler and a water-soluble or evaporating fabric marking pen:** Draw stitching guidelines on the right side of your fabric. Test first to make sure the ink is removable.

**Use topstitching or stick-on sewing tape:** This tape is perforated so that you can separate it into different widths. Stitch next to the edge of the tape and then pull it off.

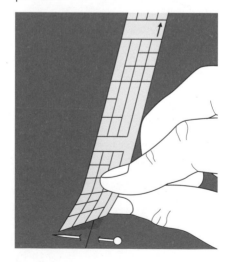

**Use ¹/₂in (1.3cm) wide transparent tape:** This is a great topstitching guide if you're inserting a lapped zipper.

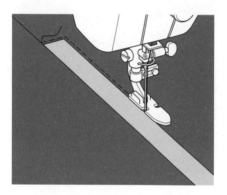

**Move the slider:** To avoid bumpy topstitching around the tab and slider, stop topstitching just before you get to the slider. Leaving the needle in the fabric, raise the presser foot and pull the slider down below the needle. (If you can't work it down gently with your finger, you may have to remove some of the basting that is holding the garment seam closed.) Lower the presser foot and continue topstitching.

**Use a longer zipper:** Another way to avoid stitching around the slider "bump" is to purchase a zipper that's longer than the pattern calls for. When you install the zipper, position it so that the pull tab and slider extend above the edge of the garment. Once the zipper is installed, slide the pull tab down and cut off the excess zipper tape at the raw edge of the garment. The intersecting waistband, seam, facing, etc., will act as the top stop for the zipper.

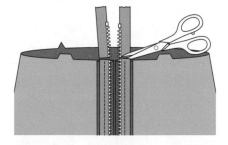

## The hand-sewn zipper

If your fabric is delicate or requires special handling (for example, chiffon, velvet or lace), consider doing the final row of stitching by hand. In addition, many people prefer the couture look of a hand-sewn zipper for tailored suits and dresses.

The final row of stitching is done with the pickstitch (see Hand Sewing, page 121). To keep the stitches straight, use a row of hand basting or any of the Tips for Topstitching opposite.

## The concealed or invisible zipper

This type of zipper is so named because after it is installed, it looks like a plain seam with a small pull tab at the top. Generally, if your pattern calls for a zipper, you can choose a conventional or a concealed (invisible) zipper.

A perfect installation requires a special concealed zipper foot (also known as an invisible zipper foot). It is available in the notions department where you purchase your concealed zippers. This inexpensive plastic accessory has one foot for zippers with polyester coils and one foot for zippers with metal teeth, as well as a choice of shanks. Following the instructions that come with the foot, you choose the shank that is suitable for

your sewing machine and then snap the appropriate foot and shank together. The foot is designed to hold the coil upright while positioning the needle so that the stitching crowds up close to the coil. The result is a "tight" – i.e. concealed – installation.

There are two important differences when installing a concealed zipper rather than a conventional one. The concealed zipper is installed first, before the seam is stitched; and all stitching is done from top to bottom. (Conventional zippers are stitched from bottom to top.)

### INSTALLING A CONCEALED ZIPPER
**A1**   Open the zipper and press the tape flat. Do not press the coils.
**A2**   Place the open zipper face down on the right side of the fabric so that the coil is along the seamline and the tape is within the seam allowance. Pin or glue-baste in place.
**A3**   Position the foot at the top of the zipper with the right-hand groove over the coil and the needle aligned with the hole in the center of the foot. Stitch to the slider, backstitch for a few stitches and knot the thread tails.
**A4**   Place the other side of the zipper face down on the right side of the adjacent garment section so that the coil is along the seamline and the tape is within the seam allowance. Pin or glue-baste in place. Position the foot at the top of the zipper with the left-hand groove over the coil. Stitch to the slider, backstitch for a few stitches and knot the thread tails.
**A5**   Close the zipper. Pin the seam together below the zipper. Using your machine's regular zipper foot, finish stitching the seam, overlapping the stitches at the bottom of the zipper.

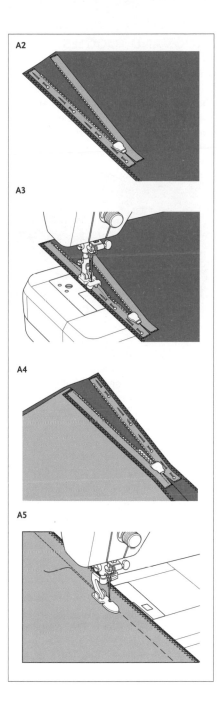

## FROGS AND TOGGLES

Your pattern may recommend these two-part closures, or you can choose them as a substitute for buttons and buttonholes. In general, toggles will add a sporty touch while frogs are more decorative.

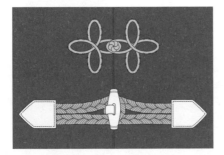

**A1**  Lap the garment edges so that the center fronts match, or make the edges meet if there is no overlap.

**A2**  Position the toggle or ball part of the closure on the left side of the garment and the loop part on the right, so that they close directly over the center front. (For men's clothes, the toggle part goes on the right and the loop part goes on the left.) Hold them in place with pins, double-faced basting tape or glue stick.

**A3**  Machine-stitch or hand-tack them in place, as appropriate.

## HOOKS AND EYES

Hooks and eyes may be used alone or in combination with another fastener, such as at the top of a zipper. They range in size from 0 to 4, for light- to heavyweight fabrics. Most hooks come with both loop eyes and straight eyes. Which eye you use depends on where the hook and eye fastener is placed on your garment.

### FOR EDGES THAT MEET

Use a hook and loop eye. On the inside, sew the hook ⅛ in (3mm) from the right-hand edge of the garment by making a few tacking stitches through the holes. Then sew across the end, under the curve of the hook. Position the eye opposite the hook, letting it extend slightly beyond the garment edge. Make a few tacking stitches through the holes. Take a few stitches along the sides of the loop to hold it flat.

### FOR EDGES THAT OVERLAP

Use a hook and straight eye. Sew the hook(s) to the inside of the garment on the overlap, ⅛ in (3mm) from the edge. Hand-tack in place, sewing through the holes, and then across the end, under the curve of the hook. Don't let the stitches for the hook(s) show on the outside of the garment. Close the zipper or other closures and then mark the eye position(s) with pins. Position the eyes on the outside of the underlap. Make a few tacking stitches through the holes.

> **TIP**  When attaching hooks and eyes, your stitches should never show on the outside of the garment.

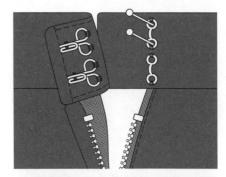

For a waistband, use two sets of regular hooks and eyes (above) or one set of the heavy-duty-hooks and eyes especially designed for waistbands (below).

### No-sew hooks and eyes

This type of waistband hook and eye requires no sewing – just hammer them or clamp them on. Use them on sturdy or firmly woven fabrics only. No-sew hooks and eyes should be applied before the waistband is finished, following the manufacturer's instructions.

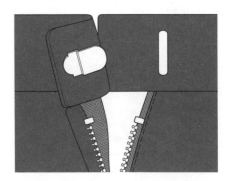

## SNAPS

Snaps are used when a garment edge needs to be held flat but where there is no strain. Decorative snaps can be used as a substitute for buttons on loose-fitting, casual garments.

Snaps, like hooks and eyes, come in many different sizes, for light- to heavyweight fabrics, and in sew-on and no-sew versions.

### Sew-on snaps
**A1** Sew the ball half to the inside of the garment on the overlap. Positioning it approximately ⅛ in (3mm) from the edge, make several tacking stitches through each hole. To keep the stitches from showing on the outside, pick up only one or two threads of fabric with each stitch and tunnel the needle between the layers of fabric as you go from hole to hole.
**A2** To mark the socket position, close the garment and stick a pin through the center of the ball to underlap.
**A3** Sew the socket half in place the same way as you did the ball half.

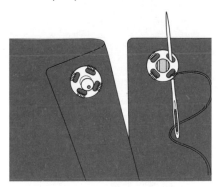

**TIP** Baste the snap sections in place with a dot of glue stick. Let them dry thoroughly before you sew.

### No-sew snaps
These sturdy, hammer-on snaps are a fast substitute for buttons and button-holes on children's garments and sportswear. Follow the package instructions to hammer them in place, or purchase a pliers-like tool which also comes with instructions.

### Snap tape
Available in a range of colors, this tape comes with the snaps already attached. To apply, preshrink the tape first in hot water. Then, using a zipper foot, edge-stitch the tape in place, turning the raw ends under. Sew the ball strip to the underlap and the socket strip to the overlap.

Snap tape fasteners are ideal for casual tops.

**TIP** Thread wrapped hooks and eyes are more attractive than metal ones. They can be used for lingerie or where the fastening is likely to be on show.

## SELF-GRIPPING HOOK-AND-LOOP FASTENERS

These flexible, two-part fasteners (e.g., Velcro®) have tiny, stiff hooks and soft loops that interlock when you press them together. They're an easy substitute for buttons or snaps and are ideal for children's clothes as small children who are learning to dress themselves will find these closures easier to maneuver than buttons and buttonholes. They are available in precut dots and squares or in strips. The light adhesive backing holds them in place for permanent stitching.

Position each part at least ¼ in (6mm) from the garment edge. The loop part goes on the overlap, the hook part on the underlap. To attach by machine, stitch the dots in a triangular pattern; edgestitch the squares and the strips.

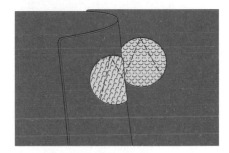

Alternatively, if you don't want the stitching to show on the outside of the garment, hand-sew the pieces in place all around the edges.

## TIES

If your pattern calls for self-fabric ties, here's a quick way to make them. The method varies slightly, depending on whether you're using a conventional machine or a serger. But, either way, the result is a neat, narrow tube of fabric that can be used for ties, belt loops, button loops or spaghetti straps.

### The conventional method

**A1**  Cut a piece of string twice the length of the finished tie, plus 5in (12.5cm).

**A2**  With right sides together, fold the tie in half lengthwise, placing the string inside the fold, as shown below.

**A3**  Sew back and forth across the top of the tie to secure the end of the string. Stitch along the length of the tie, being careful not to catch the string in the stitching. This will be easier to do if you use your machine's zipper foot.

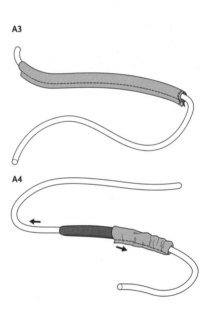

**A3**

**A4**

**A4**  To turn the tie, pull on the string.

**A5**  To remove the string, trim off the end where it is attached.

**A6**  To finish the ends, if required, tie them in a knot or tuck them into the fabric tube and then slipstitch the openings closed.

### ⑤ The serger method

**B1**  Serge a chain the length of the tie, plus 2in (5cm). Do not cut the chain. Pull the chain around to the front of the foot and center over the tie fabric with the right side facing.

**B2**  Fold the tie in half lengthwise. Serge the length of the tie, being careful not to catch the thread chains in the stitching.

**B3**  To turn the tie right side out, pull on the inside chain.

**B4**  Finish the ends as The Conventional Method, step A6.

**TIP**  Ribbon is a quick and easy substitute for fabric ties. Pick matching or contrasting ribbon. To prevent unraveling, notch the ends or cut diagonally. If necessary, apply a little bit of Fray Check™.

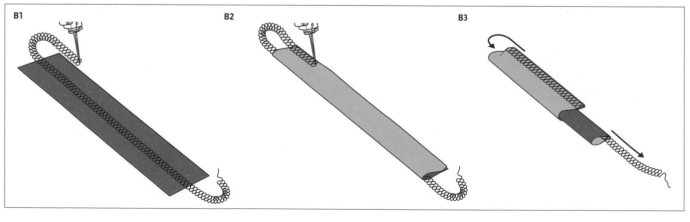

**B1**

**B2**

**B3**

# TRIMS AND DECORATIONS

Trims and decorations are the finishing touches that make your garment personal to you. This section will provide you with all the tips you'll need for applying store-bought trims as well as some useful techniques for making decorations of your own using both the sewing machine and the serger.

## TRIMS AND EDGINGS

You don't have to be limited by the trim recommendations on your pattern envelope. You can add trims to any garment as your personal preferences or the season's fashion dictates. Use them to highlight a seam or detail and bring it into focus. Trims with at least one decorative edge, such as fringe, piping and pre-gathered ruffles, can be applied in several different ways, depending on where they are located on the garment.

### Inserting an edging in a seam

**A1** With the wrong side of the trim to the right side of the fabric, place the trim along the seamline so that the decorative edge is toward the garment and the raw edge is inside the seam allowance. For pre-gathered ruffles or piping, place the binding edge just over the seamline; for rickrack, center it over the seamline.

**A2** Machine-baste the trim in place along the seamline. Use a zipper foot when stitching bulky trims, such as a piping or bound ruffles.

**A3** Pin the garment sections right sides together. Then, using your conventional machine or your serger, stitch just to the left of the basting.

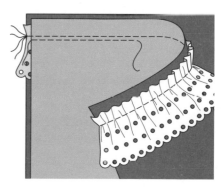

**A4** To finish, press the seam allowances to one side.

## Inserting pre-gathered trims in a seam

Pre-gathered trims require some special handling if they are inserted in a seam.

To get the trim to lie flat at a corner, some extra fullness is needed; take a tiny tuck in the trim at the corner before basting it in place.

If the trimmed edge will be intersected by another garment edge, such as on a collar or a cuff, taper the ends into the seam allowance, clearing the edge that will be stitched to the garment.

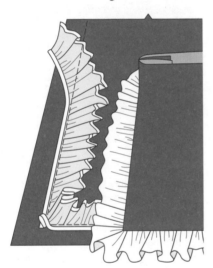

### ⓢ Gathering lace

Occasionally, you may want to use a coordinating straight lace and ruffled lace trim in the same garment. Since it's not always easy to find matching lace, use your serger to transform a piece of straight lace trim into a ruffled trim.

**NOTE** Because lace has a delicate, open weave, this technique differs slightly from the ones described in Gathers, pages 141–143.

| GATHERING LACE | | | |
|---|---|---|---|
| TYPE OF SERGER STITCH: | 3 | 4 | MINE |
| Stitch length: | Longest | Longest | |
| Stitch width: | Widest | Widest | |
| Tensions Needle: | Tight* | Tight* | |
| Right Needle: | N/A | Tight | |
| Upper Looper: | Normal | Normal | |
| Lower Looper: | Normal | Normal | |
| *For desnser gathers, tighten the needle tension.* | | | |

**B1** Adjust your serger to the appropriate setting (see Gathering Lace chart).

**B2** With the right side up, place the straight edge of the lace just to the left of the blade so that you won't cut the lace as you serge.

**B3** Holding your finger firmly against the back of the foot, begin serging. As you stitch, the lace will pile up behind the foot. Keep serging until you can't hold the lace any longer.

**B4** Repeat, until you've serged the entire length of the lace.

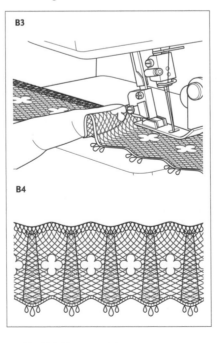

## Inserting an edging along an edge

### TOPSTITCHED METHOD

Use this technique on a finished garment edge or on a raw edge that has been folded under and pressed.

Lap the finished edge or the pressed edge of the garment over the straight edge of the trim and topstitch it in place. For rickrack, lap the garment edge so that only one set of points is visible.

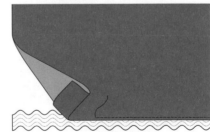

Trims with two decorative edges, such as scalloped braid or rickrack, can be positioned on the outside of the garment and topstitched in place.

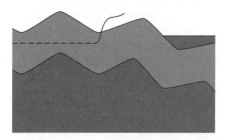

## THREE/FOUR THREAD METHOD

| TYPE OF SERGER STITCH: | | 3 | 4 | MINE |
|---|---|---|---|---|
| Stitch length: | | 2mm–3mm | 2mm–3mm | |
| Stitch width: | | Widest | Widest | |
| Tensions | Needle: | Normal | Normal | |
| | Right Needle: | N/A | Normal | |
| | Upper Looper: | Normal | Normal | |
| | Lower Looper: | Normal | Normal | |

## FLATLOCK METHOD

| TYPE OF SERGER STITCH: | | 3 | 4 | MINE |
|---|---|---|---|---|
| Stitch length: | | 2mm–3mm | 2mm–3mm | |
| Stitch width: | | Widest | Widest | |
| Tensions | Needle: | Very loose | Very loose | |
| | Right Needle: | N/A | N/A | |
| | Upper Looper: | N/A | Loose | |
| | Lower Looper: | Normal | Very tight | |

**ⓢ THREE/FOUR THREAD METHOD**
Use this method to apply lace trim with one straight edge to the raw edge of a garment. This technique also can be used with other straight-edge trims. However, always make a test sample first to make sure the finished effect is not too bulky.
**C1** If necessary, trim the raw edge of the garment so that there is a ⁵/₈ in (1.5cm) seam or hem allowance.
**C2** Adjust your serger to the appropriate setting (see Three/Four Thread Method chart).
**C3** Place the lace and the fabric right sides together, with the straight edge of the lace parallel to and ¹/₂ in (1.3cm) from the raw edge of the fabric. Use glue stick or pins to hold the lace in place.

**C4** Lift the presser foot and place the garment, lace side up, so that the straight edge of the trim is aligned slightly to the left of the blade; serge, trimming off the excess garment fabric.
**C5** Press the seam allowance toward the garment.
**C6** If desired, topstitch on your conventional machine.

**ⓢ FLATLOCK METHOD**
This technique can be used to apply lace with one straight edge to a raw edge or to a finished garment edge.
**D1** Adjust your serger to the appropriate setting (see the Flatlock Method chart).
**D2** Place the lace and the fabric right sides together, with the straight edge of the lace parallel to and ¹/₂ in (1.3cm) from the raw edge of the fabric. Use a glue stick or pins to hold the lace in place.
**D3** Lift the presser foot and place the garment, lace side up, so that the straight edge of the trim is aligned slightly to the left of the blade; serge, trimming off the excess garment fabric.
**D4** Gently pull on the lace and the fabric until the stitches are flat; press.

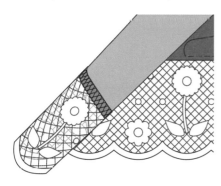

Three/four thread method.

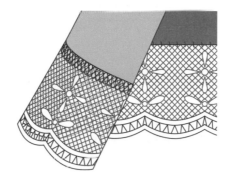

Flatlock method.

## ROLLED HEM METHOD

| TYPE OF SERGER STITCH: | | 3 | MINE |
|---|---|---|---|
| Stitch length: | | 1mm | |
| Stitch width: | | Narrowest | |
| Tensions | Needle: | Normal | |
| | Upper Looper: | Tight* | |
| | Lower Looper: | Very tight | |
| *Use wooly nylon or silk thread | | | |

### ⓈROLLED HEM METHOD

This technique can be used to apply lace with one straight edge to the raw edge of a garment.

**E1**  Adjust your serger to the appropriate setting (see Rolled Hem Method chart).

**E2**  Place the lace and the fabric right sides together, with the straight edge of the lace parallel to and ½in (1.3cm) from the raw edge of the fabric. Use a glue stick or pins to hold the lace in place.

**E3**  Lift the presser foot and place the garment, lace side up, so that the straight edge of the trim is aligned slightly to the left of the blade; serge, trimming off the excess garment fabric.

**E4**  Gently pull on the lace and the fabric until the stitches are flat; press.

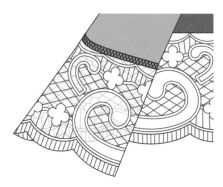

Rolled hem method.

## Applied trims

Bands or any other trim with two finished edges can be applied almost anywhere on the outside of the garment. Create borders by applying the trims in parallel rows. Create a checkered or woven effect by crisscrossing them on a bodice, yoke or cuff. Use narrow, flat trims, such as braid or yarn, to create intricate, curved designs.

#### FOR A WIDE TRIM

Apply before stitching the garment sections together so that the trim ends will be caught in the seams. Topstitch along both trim edges.

#### FOR A NARROW TRIM

Stitch through the center of the trim or along both edges, depending on the trim's width. For very narrow braid or yarn, use a special braid foot that has a groove to make the application easier.

## Insertions

See-through trims with two finished edges, such as lace or eyelet, are perfect for insertions on flat garments where there are no darts or curved seams.

Apply the insertions to the garment sections before seaming so that the ends of the trim can be included in the seam.

#### THE CONVENTIONAL METHOD

**F1**  With both fabric and trim right side up, pin the trim in place and topstitch close to both edges. For scalloped edges, stitch just inside the points, leaving the decorative edges free.

**F2**  Working on the wrong side of the garment, trim away the fabric to within ⅛in (3mm) of the seam. Press the seam allowances away from the trim.

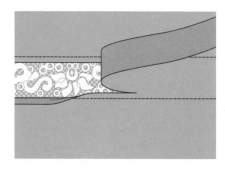

**F3**  Working on the right side of the garment, edgestitch close to the pressed edges, through all of the layers.

## THE SERGER METHOD

If your lace has two straight edges, you can insert it using either the Flatlock Method or the Rolled Hem Method described on pages 209 and 210.

Before you begin, use a fabric marker, dressmaker's carbon or any other appropriate method to mark two parallel trim placement lines. The distance between these lines should be ¹⁄₂ in (1.3cm) less than the width of your trim. Apply the lace.

**G1** Position one finished edge of the lace between the placement lines so that it overlaps the marking by ¹⁄₈ in (3mm).

**G2** Adjust your serger and serge, following the directions for either the Flatlock Method (page 209) or the Rolled Hem Method (page 210).

**G3** Match the other finished edge of the lace with the other placement line and serge.

**G4** Open out the garment section so the lace lies flat; press.

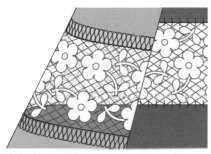

Flatlock method.

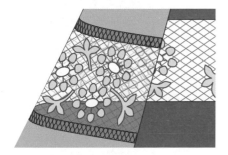

Rolled hem method.

## CUSTOM TRIM

| TYPE OF SERGER STITCH: | | 2 | 3 | MINE |
|---|---|---|---|---|
| Stitch length: | | 2mm–4mm | 2mm–4mm | |
| Stitch width: | | Widest | Widest | |
| Tensions | Needle: | Very loose | Tight | |
| | Upper Looper: | N/A | 0 | |
| | Lower Looper: | 0 | Normal | |

## Creating custom trim on the serger

Decorative threads can be used to create special effects with your serger (see page 105). Consider threading knitting ribbon (silk or rayon, but not 100 percent polyester) or pearl cotton through the upper looper and then serging around the edges of a wool cape or jacket. Imagine variegated pearl cotton used to serge the neckline, hem and sleeve edges of a dress or tunic. There would be no need for linings, facings, or hems.

To determine how much decorative thread you will need for your custom trim, measure the length of the project edge to be finished; multiply by 7 and add 6yd (5.5m) for testing. This is the amount required for each looper through which you are using decorative thread.

**H1** Thread the needle with an all-purpose thread.

**H2** Thread the decorative thread through the thread guides and the upper looper and/or the lower looper. (If you choose to, you can use all-purpose thread in one of the loopers.)

**H3** Adjust your serger to the appropriate settings (see Custom Trim chart).

**H4** Serge a test swatch of the garment fabric, feeding the fabric so that the seam/hem allowance is trimmed off. Adjust the tensions as necessary so that the decorative thread forms an even stitch. If you get an uneven stitch – or your stitches form an S or a zigzag

pattern – loosen the tensions even more or bypass the tension assemblies. If the thread still doesn't feed smoothly (a special problem with knitting ribbon), try bypassing the top thread guide of the upper looper.

**H5** If you're serging in a circle, stop stitching when the stitches meet and then overlap two stitches. Pull on the needle thread just above the needle so that there's about 3in (7.5cm) of slack. Lift the presser foot and pull the garment out from under the foot. Cut the threads. To secure the thread ends use a craft or yarn needle with a large eye and tunnel the threads back under the stitching on the wrong side of the garment.

**TIP** If you're using decorative three-thread stitching on a garment where both sides of the stitches will show, for example, a cape, poncho or reversible garment, consider using topstitching thread in the needle and the lower looper. The stitches will have a more polished look.

## SHIRRING

| TYPE OF SERGER STITCH: | | 2 | 3 | MINE |
|---|---|---|---|---|
| Stitch length: | | 2mm–3mm | 2mm–3mm | |
| Stitch width: | | Widest | Widest | |
| Tensions | Needle: | Very loose | Very loose | |
| | Upper Looper: | N/A | 0 | |
| | Lower Looper: | 0 | Very tight | |

### ⑤ Shirring

For a smocked, decorative treatment at the waistline or wrist, or on the bodice of a child's dress, use your serger, pearl cotton and narrow elastic cord. This is a quick and easy substitute for conventional smocking or shirring, as well as an attractive substitute for an elasticized casing.

**11** Adjust your serger to the appropriate setting (see Shirring chart).

**12** With wrong sides together, fold the garment along one smocking line.

**13** Thread pearl cotton, knitting ribbon or other decorative thread through the upper looper for three-thread stitching or the lower looper for two-thread stitching.

**14** Place the garment section under the presser foot, positioning the fold slightly to the left of the blade so that the fabric

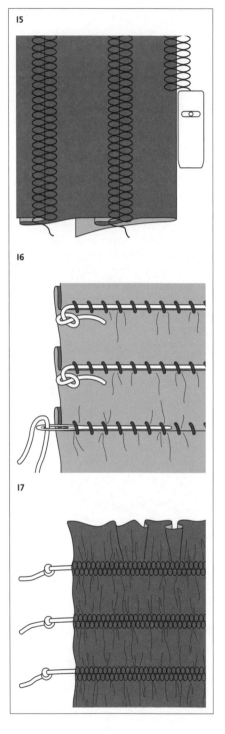

fills only half of the stitch. Serge, being careful not to cut the fabric.

**15** Repeat, flatlocking as many rows as desired. The shirring will look best if the folds are spaced about ³/₄ in (2cm) apart.

**16** If you own a long, thin loop turner, tunnel it under the stitches on the back of the fabric. Knot one end of a length of ¹/₈ in (3mm) elastic cord, attach the other end to the loop turner and pull it through the stitches. If you don't own a loop turner, thread the knotted end of the elastic onto a blunt tapestry needle and, working on the back of the fabric, gently work the tapestry needle under the stitching.

**17** Once the elastic is pulled through, adjust the shirring until the garment section is the desired width; then knot the other end of the elastic.

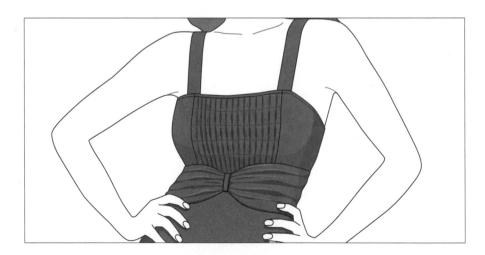

## FAGOTTING

| TYPE OF SERGER STITCH: | | 3 | MINE |
|---|---|---|---|
| Stitch length: | | 4mm | |
| Stitch width: | | Widest | |
| Tensions | Needle: | 0 | |
| | Upper Looper: | 0 | |
| | Lower Looper: | 0 | |

**S** FAGOTTING

Fagotting is a method of joining two pieces of fabric with visible decorative stitching while leaving a space between the fabric sections. Use it as a delicate, decorative way to join sections of the garment or to add a fine trim to dresses and blouses. For a rich, custom look, do all of your stitching in a thread that matches the fabric.

**NOTE** If the fagotting is purely decorative, you may find it easier to fagot the fabric first and then cut out the garment, rather than attempting to adjust your pattern to accommodate the fagotting.

**J1** Press under ¹⁄₂ in (1.3cm) on the fabric edges that will be fagotted together. If your fabric unravels, serge-finish the raw edges before pressing them under.

**J2** Adjust your serger to the appropriate setting (see Fagotting chart).

**J3** Place the fabric right sides together so that the folded edges are even. Insert the fabric under the presser foot to the left of the blade so that the needle just catches the fabric; serge.

**J4** Gently pull the fabric apart. There will be a ¹⁄₈ in (3mm) space between the folded edges that is filled with stitched thread. Press.

**J5** If you want to further embellish your garment, use your conventional machine to topstitch on either side of the fagotting. Use a straight stitch or a decorative stitch.

J3

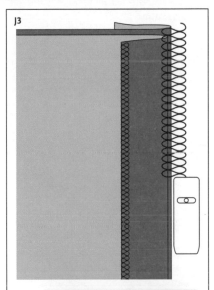
J5

decorative topstitching

fagotting

## RUFFLES

It's easy to make a decorative gathered trim or ruffle. A ruffle can add interest to hemlines, necklines and cuffs. The two most common types of ruffles are single ruffles and double ruffles.

Single ruffles have one hemmed edge; the other edge is gathered and then incorporated into a seam or attached to an edge.

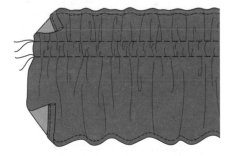

Double ruffles have two hemmed edges. The gathers can be placed along the center of the ruffle or near one edge. Then the ruffle is topstitched in place on the garment.

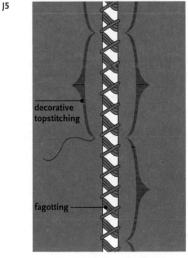

**TIP** Use ribbon as a substitute for a ruffle. Because the long edges are already finished, there's no need to hem the edge. For best results, the ribbon must be at least 1¹⁄₂ in (3.8cm) wide.

## Hemming

Since ruffles are usually made from very long strips of fabric, you'll want to use a hemming method that's fast and easy. Either the narrow topstitched hem or the machine-rolled hem on your conventional machine, and the rolled hem or lettuce edge hem on your serger are all particularly good choices. See pages 191–194 for information on how to do these hems.

## Gathering

After hemming, the fabric is gathered. Gathers in ruffles are handled the same way as gathers in any other part of a garment. (See Gathers, pages 141–143.) For double ruffles, put the gathering stitches along the lines indicated on your pattern pieces.

If you're making a double ruffle, do not use the technique for gathering over a cord. If you do, the zigzag stitches will be visible on the outside of your garment.

## Attaching the ruffle

### SINGLE RUFFLE IN A SEAM

**A1**  With right sides together, pin the ruffle to one garment edge, matching notches and markings. Adjust the gathers and machine baste in place.

**A2**  With right sides together, pin the ruffled section to the remaining garment section. With the ruffled section on top, stitch along the seamline, just to the left of the basting.

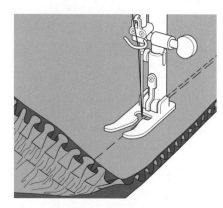

**A3**  Press the seam allowances flat and then press them in the direction indicated on the pattern instructions.

### SINGLE RUFFLE AT AN EDGE, THE CONVENTIONAL METHOD

**NOTE** If you're customizing your pattern by adding a ruffle, begin by trimming the garment hem allowance to ⅝ in (1.5cm).

**B1**  Press under along the hemline or seamline of the garment.

**B2**  Working with right sides up, lap the pressed edge of the garment over the raw edge of the ruffle so that the raw edges meet underneath. Pin, adjusting the gathers to fit and allowing for extra fullness if you are going around any corners.

**B3**  Edgestitch close to the fold through all of the layers.

**B4**  Finish the raw edges of the ruffle by zigzagging, machine overcasting or serging the edges together.

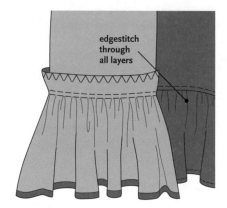

edgestitch through all layers

**TIP** If you're making a single ruffle from a lightweight fabric, you can eliminate the need to do any hemming. Cut the strips twice the desired depth, plus 1½in (3.8cm). Fold the strip in half lengthwise with wrong sides together and gather the raw edges with two rows of stitches

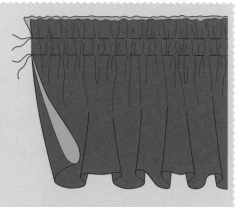

**TIP** Adding a single ruffle to the hem edge is a good way to lengthen a child's dress, particularly when there isn't enough hem allowance to let down. If the old hemline leaves permanent marks, cover it with ribbon or trim.

**NOTE** If you're customizing your pattern by adding a ruffle, begin by trimming the garment hem allowance to ⅝ in (1.5cm).

**C1** With right sides together, pin the ruffle to the garment edge, adjusting the gathers to fit.

**C2** Serge the seam and then press the seam allowances toward the garment.

**C3** Working on the right side, and using your conventional machine, edgestitch close to the seamline, through all the layers to hold them in place.

### DOUBLE RUFFLE

**D1** Pin the wrong side of the ruffle to the right side of the garment, matching all of the markings. Adjust the gathers to fit.

**D2** Topstitch over the gathering stitches.

**D3** Remove the gathering stitches or hide them with a trim, such as ribbon or rickrack.

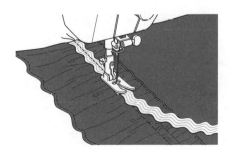

## Adding your own ruffles

You can add ruffles to your garment even if the pattern does not include them.

Ruffles can be cut on the straight grain or the bias. If the ruffle is very long, you'll probably have to piece it.

As a rule of thumb, the ruffle section should be two to three times the length of the area to which it will be attached. In general, the wider the ruffle or the more sheer the fabric, the longer the ruffle should be. This will result in a fuller, more attractive ruffle. Cut your ruffle the desired finished width plus 1½ in (3.8cm) for hem allowances and seam allowances.

## APPLIQUÉS

Appliqués are fabric motifs added to a background fabric, and they are a great way to decorate any type of garment. They are particularly popular for children's garments and are often included as a design feature on their patterns. But adult clothes, too, are great places for appliqués. Depending on the choice of fabrics and colors, they can add a playful touch to casual garments, such as sweatshirts and T-shirts, or a sophisticated accent to tailored garments and evening apparel. Playful or sophisticated, they can create wearable art.

### PURCHASED APPLIQUÉS

Purchased appliqués usually are finished with a tight overcast edge. Apply them with a zigzag stitch all around the edges, or with a straight stitch positioned along the inside edge of the overcast stitches.

### CUSTOM APPLIQUÉS

You can use a pattern or create your own. If you're not an artist, inspiration is all around you: coloring books, wallpaper, wrapping paper, greeting cards, stencils and computer clip art are just some of the sources. Printed fabrics often have motifs that can be cut out and used as appliqués.

## Basting

For successful results, the appliqué must be secured to the background fabric so that it won't shift during stitching. The two best methods are to use a glue stick or fusible web. (See Basting, pages 81–82.)

## Stitching basics

Set your machine for a narrow to medium-width zigzag stitch and a short stitch length. Position your project so that the appliqué is just to the left of the needle when the needle is in the right-hand position. Stitch slowly – it's the only way to achieve smooth edges and good control.

### STITCHING CURVES

**For outside curves:** Stop stitching with the needle at the right-hand position so that it is in the background fabric. Raise the presser foot, pivot the fabric slightly, lower the foot and continue stitching.

**For inside curves:** Stop stitching with the needle in the left-hand position so that it is in the appliqué. Raise the presser foot, pivot the fabric slightly, lower the foot and continue stitching.

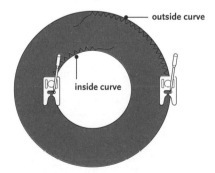

**For deep curves:** Stop and pivot at more frequent intervals than for shallow curves.

## STITCHING CORNERS

**For outside corners:** Stitch all the way to the end of the appliqué edge. Stop stitching with the needle in the right-hand position so that it is in the background fabric. Raise the presser foot, pivot the fabric, lower the foot and continue stitching along the next edge.

**For inside corners:** Stitch past the corner into the appliqué for a distance equal to the width of your zigzag stitch. Stop stitching with the needle in the left-hand position. Raise the presser foot, pivot the fabric, lower the foot and continue stitching along the next edge.

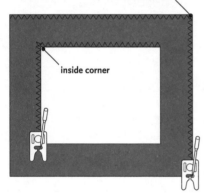

outside corner

inside corner

**TIP** For the best results, use your machine's satin stitch foot for machine appliqué. This foot is designed with a wide groove on the bottom so that it will glide smoothly over the build-up of thread that is created by the short zigzag stitch.

# TAILORING THE SPEED WAY

Today, speed tailoring techniques are synonymous with quality tailoring techniques, and the reason for this is fusible interfacings that have eliminated the need for padstitching and other tedious handwork. The following guidelines are for a woman's lined classic blazer. Although the style of your jacket may vary, the general principles will remain the same.

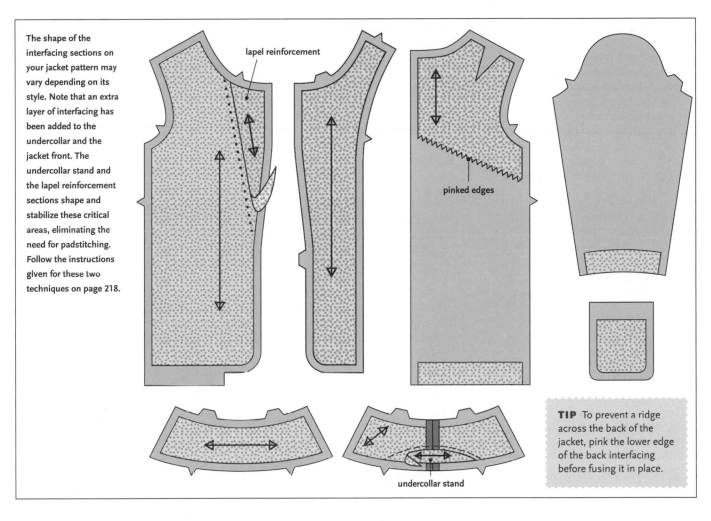

The shape of the interfacing sections on your jacket pattern may vary depending on its style. Note that an extra layer of interfacing has been added to the undercollar and the jacket front. The undercollar stand and the lapel reinforcement sections shape and stabilize these critical areas, eliminating the need for padstitching. Follow the instructions given for these two techniques on page 218.

lapel reinforcement

pinked edges

undercollar stand

**TIP** To prevent a ridge across the back of the jacket, pink the lower edge of the back interfacing before fusing it in place.

## CHOOSING YOUR FABRIC

If it's your first tailoring project, speed tailoring begins with making the right fabric choice. You should select one that is easy to work with. Because it can be easily steamed and molded into shape, your best option is either 100 percent wool or a blend that has a high percentage of wool. To hide any less-than-perfect stitching, choose a wool with a slight texture, such as tweed or double knit, or one with a brushed surface or slubbed yarns.

## APPLYING THE INTERFACING

Take a close look at the accompanying sketches of the collar, undercollar, jacket front, jacket back and facing sections of a classic blazer to see where the interfacing should go. For a softer look, you may want to eliminate the interfacing on the facing and the upper collar.

You may not want to use the same weight interfacing throughout the entire jacket. For example, you might use a fusible knit interfacing for the jacket back and a firmer woven or nonwoven interfacing in the rest of the jacket. If you wanted a soft look at the edges, you might choose a lighter weight interfacing for the hems.

Since most jackets are made from medium- to heavyweight fabrics, you'll need to keep the bulk in the seam allowances to a minimum. To do this, trim ½in (1.3cm) from the seam allowances of all of the interfacing sections before fusing them in place.

If the jacket front or back has darts, trim the interfacing away along the dart stitching lines before fusing.

## Undercollar stand

### CREATING THE PATTERN PIECE

**A1**  Trace the shape between the roll line and the neck edge on the undercollar pattern piece, eliminating the ⁵/₈ in (1.5cm) neckline seam allowance.

**A2**  Change the center back seamline to a "place on the fold" line, eliminating the center back seam allowance.

**A3**  Draw a grainline perpendicular to the foldline.

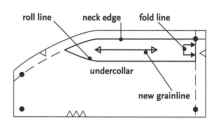

**A4**  Cut out the undercollar stand. Position it on the wrong side of the (already interfaced) undercollar, a scant ¹/₈ in (3mm) below the roll line, and fuse in place.

### PRESSING TO ADD SHAPE

Fold the undercollar down along the roll line. Using straight pins, fasten it to a tailor's ham the way it would rest on your body. Holding the iron several inches away, apply a generous amount of steam. Be sure the undercollar is thoroughly dry before your remove it from the ham.

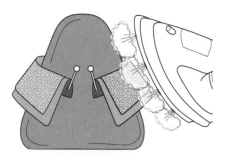

## Lapel reinforcement

### CREATING THE PATTERN PIECE

**B1**  Using the jacket front pattern piece, trace the shape formed between the roll line and the outer edge of the lapel, eliminating the ⁵/₈ in (1.5cm) seam allowances.

**B2**  Draw a new grainline that's parallel to the roll line.

**B3**  Fuse the front interfacing to the jacket front.

**B4**  Place the lapel reinforcement over the first layer of interfacing, positioning it a scant ¹/₈ in (3mm) from the roll line. Fuse in place.

### PRESSING TO ADD SHAPE

Put the jacket front, right side up, on the ironing board. Fold a hand towel lengthwise into several thicknesses and insert it under the curve of the lapel. Holding your iron several inches above the lapel, apply a generous amount of steam. Repeat for the other lapel. Be sure each section is thoroughly dry before you remove it from the ironing board.

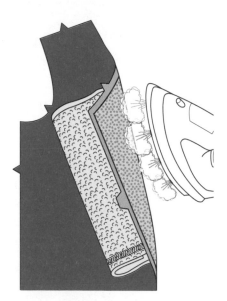

## ASSEMBLING THE JACKET

To continue assembling the jacket, consult your pattern instructions.

## SPEED LININGS

The traditional way to insert a lining in a jacket is by hand; the modern, speed method is by machine.

**A1**  Assemble the body of the jacket, but do not attach the upper collar or the facings or construct the hem.

**A2**  Sew the body of the lining together, including setting in the sleeves.

**A3**  Sew the jacket facings and upper collar together.

**TIP**  Suitable lining fabrics range from manmade polyester to lightweight silks, or for a more substantial fabric choose satin. Whichever lining fabric you select, make sure it has the same laundry care as the garment fabric.

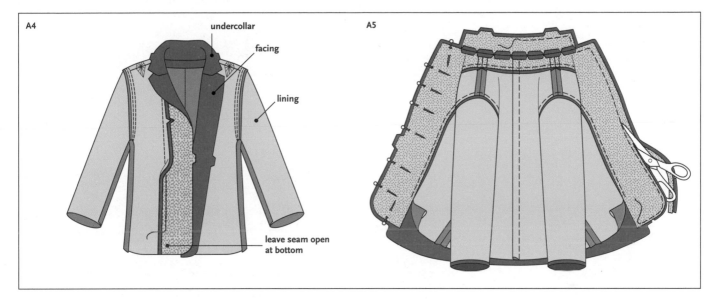

A4  undercollar  facing  lining  leave seam open at bottom

A5

**A4**  Sew the facings/upper collar to the lining, beginning and ending the seam approximately 5in (12.5cm) from the lower edge of the lining.

**A5**  With right sides together, pin the facings/upper collar to the body of the jacket, matching all of the markings; stitch. Trim, grade and press the seam allowances. Then turn the garment right side out and give it a thorough pressing. (To learn the secret of crisp, neat notches where the collar meets the lapel, see Achieving Crisp, Neat Notches, right.)

**A6**  Hem the jacket and then hem the lining by slipstitching it in place over the raw edge of the jacket hem allowance and the lower edge of the front facing.

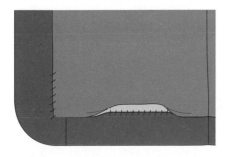

## Achieving crisp, neat notches

Make sure that the dot that indicates the notch is clearly marked on all of the sections – the collar, undercollar, jacket front and front facing. Now use the following stitching procedure.

**B1**  With right sides together, pin the facings/undercollar to the body of the jacket at the neck.

**B2**  Take one small hand basting stitch through only the jacket and the jacket facing at the notch marking. This will keep the layers from shifting during machine stitching. Don't catch the seam allowances, the undercollar or the upper collar in the basting stitch. Tie the ends of the thread in a square knot.

**B3**  Keeping the seam allowances free, and beginning at the notch marking on the collar/undercollar, machine-stitch from the dot to the center back of the collar and stop.

**B4**  Beginning at the notch marking on the jacket front/front facing, stitch from the dot to the lower edge of the jacket, keeping the seam allowances free at the notch marking. Tie the thread ends at the notch in a knot.

**B5**  Repeat for the other side of the jacket, overlapping the stitches at the center back collar.

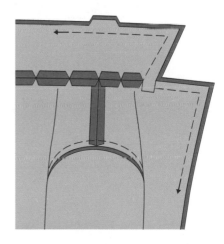

It is very important to follow the stitching procedure as outlined above. If you look carefully, you'll see that you have a small hole at the lapel notch where you started your stitching. Without it, there wouldn't be enough room for all of the layers of fabric that converge at the notch when the jacket is turned and pressed. The hole will magically disappear on your finished jacket.

# SEWING ON
# SPECIAL FABRICS

# INTRODUCTION

Have you ever bypassed a beautiful fabric because you were afraid it required some special sewing knowledge that you didn't have? In this chapter, we have gathered tips for some of our favorite special fabrics. With these tips and techniques in hand, stripes, plaids, satins, velvets, denims and more are transformed into sewer-friendly fabrics. To give yourself the confidence to sew on any fabric that catches your eye, take some time to look over the general guidelines, which should be applied whatever fabric you choose.

# GENERAL GUIDELINES

**When starting any sewing project, begin with the basics – good quality thread, a new sewing machine needle and a well-maintained machine. If you want successful results every time, there are a few other things you need to think about before you begin, so take the time to look over these general guidelines first.**

## THINGS TO CONSIDER

Before choosing and starting work with a fabric, there a few things you should take into consideration before getting underway with your sewing project.

### Fabric compatibility

Use the suggested fabric list on the back of your pattern envelope as a guide. If the fabric you have chosen is not listed, make sure it has a similar hand (body and weight) to those recommended.

### Cutting layout

When it comes to the cutting layout, the fabric you have chosen may require special attention. A single thickness cutting layout is preferred for most pile fabrics, including fake fur, velvet and heavyweight corduroy. Use the with nap cutting layout for one-way fabrics, including those that are shaded, have a pile or a directional motif. Review The Cutting Layout (pages 72–74) for layout options. If you have any doubt, use a with nap layout.

### Machine needle

Start each new project with a new needle. Sometimes problems such as skipped stitches or puckered seams need more help than just a new needle. Be sure the needle is the right size and type for your fabric; depending on the fabric you are using, you may need a special type of sewing needle. Machine needles come in European sizes 60 to 125 and American sizes 6 to 20 (for lightweight to heavyweight fabrics). The two most widely available brands on the market, Schmetz® and Singer® are described below. Keep a collection of needles in assorted types and sizes on hand.

#### SCHMETZ®

This is the most widely available European brand. European sizes are listed first, followed by a slash and the corresponding American size. This is then followed by a letter or letters that indicate the style of the needle.

✂ **H:** Indicates a universal point needle.

✂ **HS:** Indicates a ballpoint tip for stretch fabrics.

✂ **HJ:** Indicates the sharp point tip and stronger shank required for fabrics such as heavyweight denim.

#### SINGER®

This is the most common American brand and it uses a color band to indicate the needle style. For example, a Yellow Band indicates a ballpoint tip; a Violet Band indicates an extra sharp point.

### Machine settings

In addition to a special purpose needle, an out of the ordinary setting on your sewing machine may solve a stitching problem. Sometimes, a tighter or looser hold on the fabric is necessary. To accomplish this, you may need to increase or decrease the pressure on the presser foot, use a different foot or change the needle plate. Consult your sewing machine manual for assistance.

### Marking

You want to be sure that the marking method you choose provides accurate, visible markings, but that these markings will disappear once the garment is completed. Review Marking, pages 78–80. In addition to the marking techniques outlined there, there is one more you need to acquaint yourself with – the tailor's tack. These thread markings are useful for fabrics that have a particularly deep texture or for materials that are delicate and may be marred by any other technique. The tacks are made while the pattern is still pinned to the (single or double thickness) fabric.

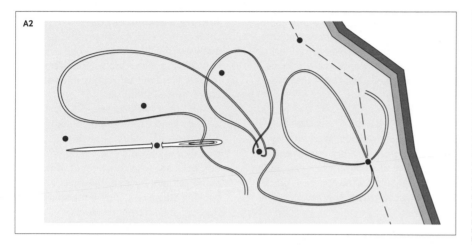

A2

## MAKING TAILOR'S TACKS

To transfer the dots from the pattern to the fabric, start with a long double strand of unknotted thread.

**A1** Allowing a 4in (10cm) tail, take a small running stitch at the dot. Take a second stitch to cross the first, leaving a 4in (10cm) loop between the two.

**A2** Continue to the next dot, leaving a generous loop of thread in between; make two more crossed stitches.

**A3** Clip the loops and the long threads between each marking.

**A4** Unpin the pattern tissue and gently remove. Carefully pull the fabric layers apart. Clip the threads between to leave small tufts of thread for each marking.

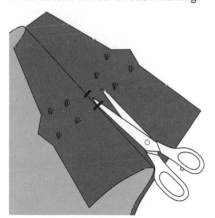

### Interfacing

Some fabrics are fusible-friendly; others are not. Review Interfacings, pages 131 and 133, and consult the chart on page 132. Then experiment on scraps of your fashion fabric before making a final decision regarding the type and weight of interfacing.

### Pressing

The Press-As-You-Sew Guide on page 119 will provide you with pressing guidelines. Experiment on scraps of your fabric before putting an iron to your garment sections.

**TIP** Start a notebook or an index card system for special fabrics. Along with a swatch of the fabric, record the pattern number and information regarding interfacings, machine needle, machine settings, marking technique, etc. This record will be a real timesaver the next time similar fabric catches your eye.

# STABILIZERS

Technological developments and increased consumer interest in embellishments have spawned a whole new category of sewing aids called stabilizers. These supply a firm, secure base to fabric for smooth, pucker-free results. Stabilizers may be just the magic ingredient that helps you to achieve the most professional finish.

## USES FOR STABILIZERS

Stabilizers are the secret behind professional looking results for just about any embellishment technique that utilizes thread and a sewing machine – computerized embroidery, free-motion embroidery, heirloom sewing, appliqué, quilting, monogramming, etc. And, on the utilitarian side, a bit of stabilizer underneath machine-made buttonholes can vastly improve their appearance. Stabilizer can also provide a smooth, temporary cover that can be valuable when sewing loopy fabrics such as mohair and terrycloth.

Some stabilizers are designed to function exclusively as a base – that is, placed underneath the project, between the feed dog and the fabric. Some see-through versions can also be used as a cover, either to protect the fabric or as a stitch-through template for the design. And some stabilizers are temporary backings, while others are permanent.

## The basic categories

The easiest way to categorize stabilizers is by how they are removed.

### TEAR-OFF STABILIZER

This type of stabilizer offers temporary support. Once the stitching is completed, the stabilizer is gently torn away. This category is generally recommended for stable fabrics. Most tear-offs are non-wovens. However, there are also several clear plastic tear-off films on the market.

### CUT-OFF STABILIZER

These are woven products that provide permanent support during stitching and throughout the life of the garment. They are suitable for most fabrics, but are particularly good for knits and stretch wovens, in areas such as under machine-made buttonholes or satin-stitched appliqués. After stitching, the excess stabilizer is carefully cut off close to the stitches. Sometimes the choice between a cut-off and a tear-off is merely a matter of personal preference. However since cut-offs are usually softer than tear-offs, comfort may be a factor if the stabilizer cannot be easily removed from all areas of the design.

> **TIP** Tear-offs and cut-offs come in different weights. When a heavier foundation is required, many sewing experts recommend two or more layers of a lightweight stabilizer. Each layer is removed individually, putting less strain on the stitches.

### WASH-AWAY STABILIZER

This category includes water-soluble films, liquids or sprays designed to be used as temporary support in washable fabrics. They are desirable when you do not want any traces of stabilizer left in the finished project. Liquids and sprays are generally more suited to lightweight fabrics, and they will require drying time before stitching. A wash-away stabilizer can be a great help when you are trying to hem a washable knit fabric that has a tendency to curl.

### HEAT-DISINTEGRATING STABILIZER

These stabilizers disappear when they are treated with a hot, dry iron. These are used in place of a cut-off when you don't want any stabilizer showing, or in place of a wash-away, particularly on dry-clean-only fabrics.

> **TIP** Water-soluble films and heat-disintegrating stabilizers are preferred if it is necessary for the stabilizer to be completely removed. They should be stored in Ziploc® bags. Unfinished projects should be similarly stored until the stabilizer is removed.

## Securing the stabilizer

It's not enough to simply place a stabilizer underneath the fabric. It must also be secured so that the stabilizer and fabric act as one during stitching. While pinning or basting often suffices, more secure methods will prevent slippage or off-register motifs when used for machine embroidery or monogramming.

A few stabilizers come with a variety of self-securing backings. Some can be temporarily ironed onto the fabric. Some have a pressure-sensitive backing, somewhat like Post-it® notes. If these stabilizers are removed carefully, they can often be used again. There are also temporary spray adhesives that can be used to transform cut-off, tear-off and water-soluble stabilizers into self-adhesive versions. Self-adhesion is particularly desirable if you need a cover stabilizer and you are working with velvet or some other fabric that cannot handle pins or ironing.

## Adding a stabilizer cover

Under some circumstances, the surface quality of the fabric needs to be changed in order to achieve professional-looking results. Here the solution is to add a cover layer of stabilizer.

This cover can be a tear-off, wash-away or heat-disintegrating stabilizer. If it is a tear-off, it should be one that pulls cleanly away from the stitching and does not leave any whiskers behind. If two stabilizers are needed, the cover and the backing stabilizers can be the same or they can be different products.

Water-soluble and clear tear-off film stabilizers are generally preferred for cover tasks. However, when the thread is dark, the stitches are dense and the fabric is light, such as an appliqué outlined with black satin stitches on white terrycloth, look for a stabilizer that is available in a color that will help camouflage the fabric behind the stitching.

> ### USES FOR A STABILIZER COVER
>
> ✂ To hold down the loops (terrycloth or mohair) or the pile (velour or velvet).
>
> ✂ To work together with a stabilizer backing to bridge the openings when embellishing on an open weave fabric such as mesh, netting or lace.
>
> ✂ To smooth out the surface of a textured fabric such as piqué or corduroy, particularly in the case of machine-made buttonholes.
>
> ✂ To provide a transfer surface for an embellishment design. (If the design can be traced onto the stabilizer, there is no need to mark the fabric.)
>
> ✂ To provide protection against hoop burn (friction marks caused when the inner and outer rings of a machine embroidery hoop rub against the fabric).

# SPECIAL FABRICS

One of the joys of doing your own sewing, whether you are making curtains or clothes, is the chance to use any fabric that takes your fancy. However not all fabrics are as easy to work with as, say, pure cotton. Some fabrics will have challenges and require extra time and attention, but if you follow the advice given here, you can be sure that you will always achieve the best possible results.

## DENIM

This is a heavy, durable cotton twill weave that has a colored warp and a white filling.

### Layout

✄ A double thickness cutting layout is fine, but take care to align the grainline arrows exactly. If they are not aligned, the fabric will twist when the garment is on the body. This characteristic is a result of the twill weave.

✄ Use a with nap cutting layout for brushed denim; a without nap layout for all others.

✄ Use a single thickness cutting layout for heavy denim.

### Marking
Use dressmaker's chalk, tracing paper or water-soluble fabric marking pens.

### Cutting
Use very sharp scissors or a rotary cutter. For very heavy denim, you should cut single thickness.

### Needle

✄ Use a needle with a sharp point for densely woven fabrics; a heavy-duty shank to resist bending or breaking.

✄ Choose a medium- to heavyweight size: 90/14 HJ to 100/16 HJ (Schmetz) or 14 to 16 Red Band (Singer).

### Interfacing
Sew-ins or fusibles, wovens or non-wovens are suitable.

### Seams and seam finishes

✄ **Seam options:** Almost any type of seam is suitable for denim fabric. However, it must be finished securely to prevent unraveling. The serged seam and the Flat-Fell Seam (see page 96) are popular choices.

✄ Denim has a tendency to unravel, so avoid clipping and notching seams.

### Topstitching
Use a medium length stitch and heavy-duty thread, polyester thread or jeans topstitching thread.

### Hems
Choose from the Wide Topstitched Hem (see page 192), the Fused Hem (see page 196), the Cover Hem (see page 195) and the Narrow Topstitched Hem for woven fabrics (see page 191).

### Pressing
Medium to high temperature; use a steam setting.

---

**SEWING OVER BULKY SEAMS**

To help prevent the presser foot from rocking (which can cause uneven stitches and jammed threads) when hemming over bulky flat-fell seams (or anywhere you encounter multiple layers), use a shim to keep the foot level. This shim can be as simple as a scrap of denim folded several times to the necessary thickness. Use the shim in front, in back or to the side of the presser foot, as required to keep it level. Stop stitching as often as necessary to reposition the shim. The Jean-a-ma-jig™ is a $1/8$ in (3mm) thick plastic notion that performs a similar task. Another choice is the Hump Jumper®, available in $1/8$ in (3mm) and $1/16$ in (1.5mm) thicknesses.

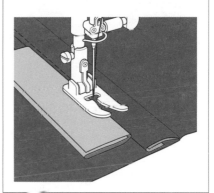

## SATIN

Satin is a woven fabric that has a shiny, slick surface. The reverse side is usually matte, or not shiny. It is a tightly woven fabric that can hold structured silhouettes and as such it is used mostly for special occasion dresses.

### Layout

✂ Use a double thickness cutting layout, right sides together.

✂ Use a with nap cutting layout as satins have a tendency to shade in different directions.

✂ Use fine pins, pinning within the seam allowances.

### Marking
Use dressmaker's chalk. Avoid fabric marking pens as they run and bleed into the fabric. Avoid wax dressmaker's carbon as it may leave spots.

### Cutting
Use scissors with serrated blades or a rotary cutter.

### Needle

✂ Use a standard universal point needle, usually in a lightweight size: 70/10 H (Schmetz) or 10 (Singer).

✂ If runs or pulls occur, try a Microtex needle with a sharp point in a lighter weight size: 70/10 HM (Schmetz) or 10 Violet Band (Singer).

### Thread
Use standard or fine cotton-covered polyester thread or lingerie thread.

### Machine settings

✂ Straight stitch, average length to slightly shorter than average (2mm–2.5mm or 10–15 stitches per inch).

✂ On some lightweight satins, increasing the pressure on the presser foot may be helpful.

✂ For lightweight satin, use a small, single-hole needle plate when sewing a straight stitch to prevent the fabric from being swallowed into the machine. A narrow straight stitch foot and/or flat-bottom presser foot may also be helpful. Alternatively, consider moving the needle to the far left to provide support on three sides of the fabric.

### Interfacing
Sew-in woven or nonwoven. Consider organdy or organza on lightweight satin. Avoid fusibles.

### Seams and seam finishes

✂ **Seam options:** Plain Seam (page 95); French Seam (page 96) on lightweight satins (not suitable on curved seams).

✂ When finishing seam allowances with a serger, use lightweight thread or wooly nylon thread. This will prevent thread imprint on the right side.

### Hems

✂ Avoid hand-sewn hems unless the garment is underlined. Without an underlining, the hem stitches will show on the right side.

✂ On lightweight satins, use the Machine-Rolled Hem (see page 192).

✂ Topstitched hems may pucker. However, by interfacing the hem and topstitching several rows spaced $1/4$ in–$1/2$ in (6mm–1.3cm) apart, you can create a design feature.

> **TIP** For satins, silk organza is a great underlining. It has a soft hand but will support the weight of a hem.

### Pressing

✂ Press with a warm dry iron, preferably on the wrong side of the fabric.

✂ When pressing on the right side, use a press cloth to avoid shine.

✂ Avoid steam as satin has a tendency to water spot.

✂ Press seams open over a seam roll or seam stick, or use strips of paper underneath the seam allowances. This will prevent ridges from forming on the outside of the garment.

**Satins have a lustrous surface making them ideal for evening wear.**

## VELVET

A broad term that applies to a warp-pile fabric with a soft, sturdy face created from dense loops that may or may not be cut. It is a luxurious fabric, originally made from silk, but now made from a wide variety of fibers.

### Layout

✂ Use a single thickness cutting layout with the wrong side of the fabric facing up.

✂ Use a with nap cutting layout.

✂ Do not allow the fabric to hang off the cutting table. The weight may distort the fabric, pulling it off grain.

✂ Pin within the seam allowances. Use extra-fine pins.

### Marking

Use dressmaker's chalk or fabric marking pens on the wrong side of the fabric only. If it is absolutely necessary to mark on the right side, make tailor's tacks using silk thread.

### Cutting

Use sharp scissors.

### Needle

✂ For woven velvets: Use a standard universal point needle in a medium-weight size: 70/10 H to 80/12 H (Schmetz) or 10 to 12 (Singer).

✂ For stretch velvets: Use a ballpoint or stretch needle in a medium-weight size: 70/10 HS to 80/12 HS (Schmetz) or 10 to 12 Yellow Band (Singer).

### Thread

Use cotton, polyester or cotton-covered polyester thread for general sewing, and a silk thread for tailor's tacks and hand basting.

### Machine settings

✂ Average length straight stitch (2.5mm or 15 stitches per inch) or narrow zigzag stitch with average length (0.75mm wide and 2.5mm long).

✂ Reduce presser foot pressure slightly.

✂ When sewing two layers together, a roller foot or even-feed foot will minimize velvet's tendency to "creep".

✂ Use silk thread to hand-baste each seam before stitching it by machine.

### Interfacing

✂ Use sew-in woven interfacing. Nonwoven interfacing may be used with stretch velvets.

✂ Avoid fusibles.

### Seams and seam finishes

✂ **Seam options:** Plain Seam (see page 95) with a Stitch and Pink, Zigzag or Tricot Bound seam finish (see pages 97 and 98).

✂ The serger is also a good choice when stitching seams, or to finish the edges of a plain seam.

### Hems

Choose a Hand-sewn Hem (see page 191), finishing the edge of the hem allowance with seam binding, stretch lace, or by overcasting it on the serger.

### Pressing

✂ Press with the velvet face down on a needle board; alternatively use thick terry-cloth towel or scrap velvet face up.

✂ Press velvet from the wrong side, keeping the weight of the iron off the surface of the fabric.

✂ Check the fiber content of the fabric. Acetate or rayon velvets may scorch or shine under heat and steam. Cotton velvets can withstand a slightly higher temperature and some steam.

✂ When pressing, put strips of paper underneath the seam allowances to avoid leaving an impression on the right side of the fabric.

A needle board is a good investment if you sew with velvet often.

> **TIP** As two layers are joined together, velvet tends to "creep" so that one layer ends up longer than the other. To avoid this, use silk thread to hand-baste each seam before stitching. Then, when you are stitching at the machine, stop stitching every 3in–4in (7.5cm–10cm). With the needle in the fabric, raise the presser foot, allowing the fabric to relax. Lower the presser foot and continue stitching. Repeat, stopping and starting, until you reach the end of the seam.

## FLEECE

Fleece is a unique knit fabric that has a little stretch and a highly-brushed surface. It has a plush soft feel on both the right and wrong sides, and it can often be difficult to tell which side of the fabric is the right and which the reverse. As it is a stable fabric, it is easy to work with and the cut edges don't unravel.

### Layout

✂ Use a double thickness cutting layout. For heavyweight fleece, use a single thickness layout.

✂ Always use a with nap cutting layout.

✂ If you can't see a difference between the right and wrong side of the fabric, pick one and stick with it. To help keep track as you sew, mark the chosen side.

> **TIP** To determine the right side of the fleece (or which grain is which), see how it curls. On the crosswise grain, fleece will curl to the wrong side. On the lengthwise grain or along the selvage edge, fleece will curl to the right side.

### Marking
Use dressmaker's chalk or fabric marking pens.

### Cutting
Use sharp scissors or a rotary cutter.

### Needle

✂ **Option 1:** Use a standard universal point needle in a medium-weight size: 70/10 H to 80/12 H (Schmetz).

✂ **Option 2:** Ballpoint or stretch needle in a medium-weight size: 75/11 HS to 90/14 HS (Schmetz) or 11 to 14 Yellow Band (Singer).

✂ **Option 3:** For windbreaker-style fleece, very sharp Microtex point needle: 70/10 HM to 80/12 HM (Schmetz).

### Machine settings

✂ Use a slightly longer than average straight stitch (3mm or 9–12 stitches per inch).

✂ Decrease the pressure slightly on the presser foot.

> **TIP** When stitching fleece to another fabric (such as a lining), stitch with the fleece against the feed dog. This will help keep the bulk and the stretch under control.

### Interfacing
Avoid fusible interfacing as it tends to flatten the fabric. Use a nonwoven, sew-in interfacing with a slight amount of stretch as support for collars and cuffs, as well as behind buttonholes and zippers.

### Seams and seam finishes

✂ **Seam options:** Double-stitched Seam (see page 95); Stretch Knit Seams (see page 95); or a serged seam.

> **TIP** If the seam allowances tend to curl, use the Topstitched Seam (see page 97).

### Hems

✂ Use a single hem with a slightly wider than usual hem allowance. If necessary, edgestitch or topstitch the hem to hold it flat.

✂ A hem allowance that is finished on the serger will keep the edge of the fabric from becoming wavy but still provide some stretch.

✂ Instead of traditional hems and facings, consider self-binding or contrast binding, as described below.

#### BOUND HEM
Review Bindings, pages 144–148. Because fleece does not unravel, single-layer binding made from matching or contrasting fleece is an option.

**A1** Cut crosswise strips of fabric that are twice the desired finished width of the binding.

**A2** With wrong sides together, center the binding over the garment edge. Edgestitch the binding in place using a straight stitch.

**A3** Turn the garment over. Wrap the binding around the raw edge. Edgestitch in place, using a straight stitch or a zigzag stitch and stitching through the garment and both layers of binding.

**NOTE** If you want only one visible row of edgestitching on your finished garment, use a water-soluble needle thread for the first row of edgestitching.

### Pressing
Avoid pressing. If it is absolutely necessary, use a press cloth. Often finger pressing will do just as good a job.

## MICROFIBERS

Microfiber is a synthetic fabric commonly made from polyamides, polyester, or a combination of the two. It is durable, soft, and easy to care for.

### Layout

✂ Use a double thickness cutting layout with right sides together.

✂ Use a with nap cutting layout. These fabrics shade differently in each direction.

✂ On lightweight microfibers, shift the pattern pieces slightly off grain (not more than 10 percent). This will prevent puckering on lengthwise seams.

### Marking

Use dressmaker's chalk or fabric marking pens.

### Cutting

✂ Use scissors with serrated blades or a rotary cutter.

✂ Use fine pins only within the seam allowance (regular pins may leave permanent pinholes) or pattern weights

### Needle

Use a Microtex needle with a sharp point and a slender shaft in light- to medium-weight: 60/8 to 80/12 HM (Schmetz) or 8 to 12 Violet Band (Singer).

### Thread

Use very fine cotton-covered polyester thread or lingerie thread.

### Machine settings

✂ Straight stitch, slightly shorter than average (1.75mm– 2mm or 12–25 stitches per inch).

✂ Increase the pressure on the presser foot to prevent puckers on lightweights.

✂ Also for lightweight microfibers, use a small, single-hole needle plate when sewing a straight stitch. This will prevent the fabric from being swallowed into the machine. A narrow straight stitch foot and/or flat-bottom presser foot may also be helpful.

### Interfacing

Avoid high temperature fusibles. Lightweight sew-in wovens or nonwovens are best. Organdy or organza fabrics are also an option.

### Seams and seam finishes

✂ **Seam options:** Plain Seam (see page 95); Topstitched or Welt Seam (see page 97). Choose carefully – topstitching may cause puckers.

✂ If you finish the seam allowances on a serger, use lightweight thread or wooly nylon thread. This will prevent thread imprint on the right side of the garment.

### Hems

Fused hems will be least conspicuous. Experiment with different fusing products and be careful not to use too much heat. A Topstitched Hem (pages 191–192) is a possibility. Experiment on scraps to determine the best hem allowance width before hemming your garment.

### Pressing

✂ Use moderate heat, preferably on the wrong side of the fabric. Use a press cloth on the right side of fabric to avoid shine. Avoid steam.

✂ Cover the holes in the iron's sole plate with a Teflon shoe so that they won't make an impression in the fabric.

✂ Press seams flat first, then open. Press over a seam roll or a seam stick so that the seam allowances won't create ridges on the outside of the garment.

## FAKE FUR

Fake fur, also called fun fur or faux fur, is material made of synthetic fibers designed to resemble fur.

### Layout

✂ Use a single thickness cutting layout, wrong side up.

✂ Always use a with nap cutting layout. Generally, the pile runs down. However, you might want to run a short pile up to add color depth.

✂ Use long pins (quilting pins) with large round heads. To avoid pins altogether, use fabric weights and/or trace the pattern onto the fur backing.

### Marking

✂ **Option 1:** Mark on the wrong side, using dressmaker's chalk.

✂ **Option 2:** Mark on the right side, using tailor's tacks.

### Cutting

✂ If the backing fabric is firm, trim the seam allowances on the pattern to 1/4 in (6mm) before cutting to reduce bulk.

✂ Use only the tip of the blades to cut through the backing only, separating the fur as you cut.

### Needle

✂ Use a standard universal point needle for fake fur with a woven backing; a ballpoint needle for a knit backing.

✂ For short pile fur with a medium-weight woven backing to long pile fur with a heavyweight backing: 80/12 H to 100/16 H (Schmetz).

✂ Medium- to heavyweight knit backing: 80/12 to 100/16 HS (Schmetz) or 12 to 16 Yellow Band (Singer).

### Interfacing

The backing on most fake furs provides enough support to eliminate the need for interfacing. However, for collars or other areas that need extra support, use a woven interfacing secured to the backing with pad stitches. Pad stitching consists of rows of blindstitches placed ¹/₂ in (1.3cm) apart. Cover the entire surface so that the interfacing is attached to the fur backing without disturbing the fur. Do not use fusible interfacing.

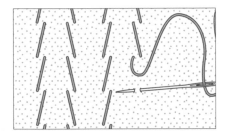

### Seams and seam finishes

✂ Before pinning and stitching a seam, brush long pile furs towards the center of the pattern section. This will prevent the ends of the fur from getting caught in the seam and will allow the fur to appear less interrupted on the right side.

✂ Use a roller foot attachment for long pile furs.

✂ **Seam options:** Plain Seam or Double-stitched Seam (see page 95). Disregard all references to pressing.

### Hems

Hand-sewn Hems (see page 191) are the best choice. Ease the hem, as necessary. If desired, finish the edge with a seam binding.

### Pressing

Avoid pressing. Many fake furs are made from fibers that are extremely heat sensitive and will become damaged when pressed.

## KNITS

- - - - - - - - - - - - - - - - - - - - - - - - - -

All knitted fabrics are constructed using one set of yarn running in the same direction – looping the yarn around itself holds knit fabrics together. Some knits have their yarn running along the length of the fabric, others have their yarn running across the width. Because of its construction, knitted fabric has some give in every direction, so it is ideal for figure-hugging garments.

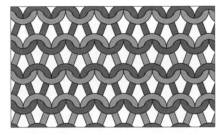

### Layout

✂ Use a double thickness cutting layout, except for sweater knits which require a single thickness layout.

✂ Use a with nap cutting layout. Knits frequently have one-way shading that may not be discernible until the garment is finished. Most sweater knits have directional motifs or cable designs.

✂ If the fabric has been folded, the crease may not be easy to remove. Try steam; if unsuccessful, refold the fabric or cut around the crease.

✂ Always position the pattern pieces on the fabric so that the greatest amount of stretch goes around the body.

✂ Use pattern weights rather than pins for sweater knits.

### Marking

Use dressmaker's chalk or fabric marking pens; tailor's tacks or small safety pins on sweater knits.

### Cutting

Use scissors or a rotary cutter for lightweight knits.

### Needle

Use a ballpoint or stretch needle in a medium-weight size: 75/11 HS to 90/14 HS (Schmetz) or 11 to 14 Yellow Band (Singer).

### Machine settings

✂ Narrow zigzag stitch (0.5mm width, 2.5mm length) or a stretch stitch.

✂ Decrease pressure on presser foot for heavy sweater knits; increase pressure for lingerie knits.

### Interfacing

Choose a lightweight nonwoven or stretch interfacing. Avoid fusibles. Apply interfacing to the facings rather than to the body of the garment.

### Seams and seam finishes

✂ **Seam options:** Stretch Knit Seam (see page 95). Because they build in stretch, clean-finish the edges and prevent curling, serged seams are ideal for knits.

✂ When appropriate, stabilize the seam (see page 95).

### Hems

Many different hems, including the Narrow Topstitched Hem, the Wide Topstitched Hem and the Serger Rolled Hem, are suitable; your choice will depend on the weight of the knit and the look you want to achieve. Review Hems, pages 189–196.

### Pressing

Use steam or a damp press cloth and a temperature appropriate for the fabric's fiber content. Do not over press.

## LACE

Lace is a special fabric that begins with a woven netting. The netting is then embellished or embroidered with an openwork pattern, usually floral. This fabric is lightweight, soft and sheer, and it almost always needs some form of lining for modesty when used in a garment .

### Layout

✂ Use a single thickness with nap cutting layout.

✂ A cutting surface with a contrasting color will help you get the best view of your lace.

✂ Plan the layout so that large motifs fall attractively on the figure.

✂ Consider using a decorative edge of the lace as a finished (straight) edge of the garment. This way you can eliminate hem allowances and/or facings.

✂ If pins prove difficult to use, pattern weights are a good alternative.

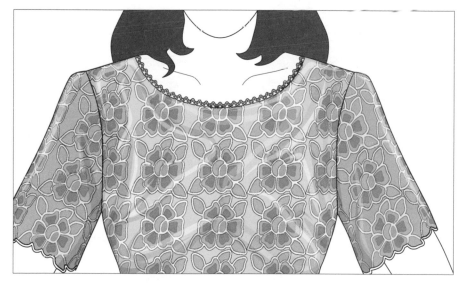

With lace garments, a lining is necessary for the sake of modesty.

### Marking

Use tailor's tacks or fabric marking pens.

> **TIP** If a pattern marking falls at a hole in the lace, put a piece of transparent tape over the hole, then mark the symbol with a pencil.

### Cutting

Use scissors or rotary cutter.

### Needle

Use a standard universal point needle, usually in a light- to medium-weight size: 70/10 H to 90/14 H (Schmetz) or 10 to 14 (Singer).

### Thread

Very lightweight lace may require an extra-fine polyester or cotton-covered polyester thread.

### Machine settings

✂ Straight stitch, slightly shorter than average (1.75mm–2mm or 12–25 stitches per inch); or use a short, narrow zigzag stitch (0.5mm width, 1.5mm length).

✂ On some lightweight laces, increasing the pressure on the presser foot may be helpful.

✂ On lightweight lace, use a small, single-hole needle plate when sewing a straight stitch. This will prevent the fabric from being swallowed into the machine. A narrow straight stitch foot and/or flat bottomed presser foot may also be helpful. If you do not have these machine attachments, consider moving the needle to the far left to provide support on three sides of the fabric.

### Interfacing

✂ Eliminate interfacing whenever possible. If additional body is needed, use tulle or netting to maintain the open quality of the fabric. For a semi-opaque look, consider using a sheer voile, organza or organdy instead of commercial interfacing.

✂ An underlining (a layer of lining fabric basted to the main garment sections and sewn as one with the lace) in a skin tone can be used to maintain the open look while eliminating the see-through qualities, and this will provide an anchor for attaching the interfacing.

### Seams and seam finishes

✂ Double-stitched Seam, Stretch Knit Seams (page 95), using a very narrow zigzag stitch (0.5mm width, 1.5mm length), or a narrow serged seam.

✂ The overlapped seam is useful when you don't want to break up the flow of the motifs at prominent seams, such as the center front, the center back or the shoulder seams.

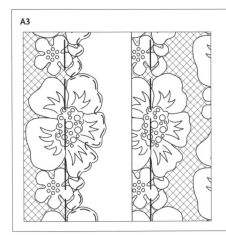

**THE OVERLAPPED SEAM**

Preliminaries for this type of seam begin when you are cutting out your garment.

**A1**  Draw in the seamlines on your pattern pieces.

**A2**  Position the first pattern piece so that the dominant lace motifs are balanced within the seamlines. Thread-trace along the seamlines. Using a different color thread, thread-trace around the motif outline as it extends beyond the seamline. Carefully cut out the garment section along this second traced line.

**A3**  Remove the pattern tissue. Lap the pattern piece for the adjacent garment section over the cut-out section, matching the seamlines. Trace the overlapping motif onto the pattern tissue. Pin this pattern piece to the fabric, matching the traced motif to the fabric underneath. Thread-trace the seamlines. Cut out the garment section.

**A4**  To construct the seam, overlap the first garment section onto the second one, matching the thread-traced seamlines. Stitch along the edge of the overlapping motifs, using small slipstitches (see page 121) or a short, narrow machine zigzag stitch. For the latter, a stabilizer may be required (see page 223).

**A5**  Once the seam is stitched, use embroidery scissors to carefully cut away the excess underlap.

## Hems

✂  If the hemline is on the straight grain and the lace has a decorative edge, you can eliminate the hem allowance and use the decorative edge as the finished edge of the garment.

✂  If the lace does not have a decorative edge, hand or machine stitch a strip of coordinating lace trim to the right side of the fabric along the hemline. Cut away the excess lace underneath.

✂  For a conventional approach, use Hand-sewn Hems (see page 191).

## Pressing

Always use a press cloth. To prevent flattening lace with raised motifs, place the fabric face down on a terrycloth towel and press lightly.

> **TIP** Sheer tricot seam binding can substitute for a facing at both straight and curved edges of a garment.

Hemming with a coordinating lace trim.

## PLAIDS AND STRIPES

These are designs that must be matched at the seams, and to achieve this you need to take some special measures.

### Layout

**NOTE** Review Designs That Must Be Matched, page 75 first. Before deciding on a cutting layout, it is important to determine whether you have an even or uneven plaid or stripe. In an even plaid or stripe, the arrangement of bars/stripes is the same on both sides of the main bar. In an uneven plaid or stripe, the arrangement of bars/stripes is different on either side of the main bar. Fold your fabric on the center of a main lengthwise bar; see if the design and colors repeat evenly on either side of it. Do the same for the main crosswise bar. If all the bars on both fabric layers match, the fabric is even; if not, it's uneven.

#### EVEN PLAIDS OR STRIPES

Use a without nap cutting layout unless the fabric surface is brushed or napped. You may fold and cut through a double layer of fabric if you align and pin the bars together first.

#### UNEVEN PLAIDS OR STRIPES

Use a with nap cutting layout and cut a single layer at a time. An uneven plaid can be made to proceed around the figure in one direction or in opposite (mirror-image) directions from the center.

**To lay out the plaid so it goes around the figure:** Fold fabric at the center of a main bar or group of bars. Position the pattern pieces that must be cut on the fold. Then cut the remaining pieces from a single layer of fabric. For fly-front openings, place the foldline on the center of a main bar. Be sure to place sleeves so that the plaid moves in the same direction on both sleeves.

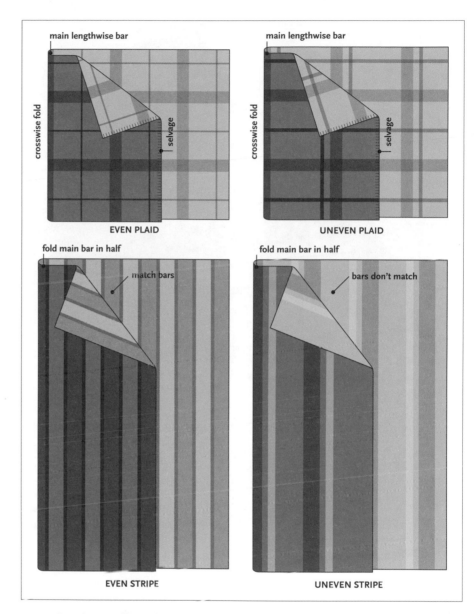

**For a mirror image effect:** The pattern must have a center front and back seam or closure. Work with a single layer of fabric. The main pieces (garment front and back) must be cut once, then reversed and turned upside down before they are cut again. Place center seams or center front lines along the center of a main bar or group of bars. Position the center of the sleeve along a main bar and cut it out. Then, to cut out the second sleeve, reverse and turn the pattern piece. Match the direction of the plaid on the right sleeve to the right side of the bodice front; on the left sleeve to the left side of the bodice front.

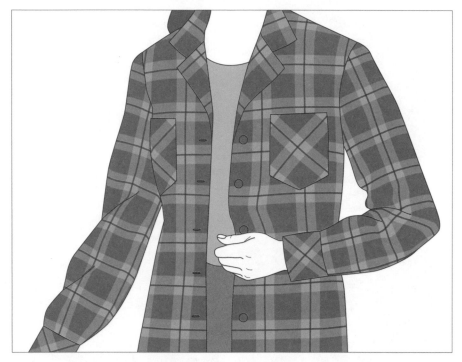

To eliminate some of the matching – and add visual interest to your garment – cut small detail sections, such as collars, cuffs, pockets and yokes, on the bias.

about ³/₈ in (1cm) to the left of the previous stitch.

**A3** Continue to slip baste the seam in place.

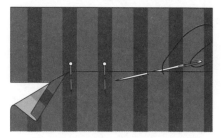

**A4** To sew the seam, remove the pins, open out the fabric, and machine stitch along the basting line.

**S** SERGING

**B1** Pin the fabric layers, right sides together with pins at right angles to the seamline and matching the bars as you go. Alternate each pin so that the one above the dominant bar or repeat is pinned from right to left and the one below the repeat pinned left to right.

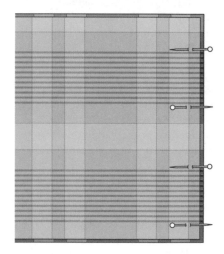

**B2** Serge slowly, remembering to remove the pins before they reach the serger knives.

## Machine settings

✂ Average length straight stitch (2.5mm or 15 stitches per inch).

✂ Decrease the presser foot pressure slightly.

✂ When sewing two layers together, consider using a roller foot or even-feed foot to minimize shifting.

## Seams and seam finishes

✂ **Seam options:** Choose a seam and seam finish that is appropriate to the fiber content and the fabric weight and construction.

✂ No matter what type of seam you use, it is important to match the color bars and keep them from shifting as you sew. Basting tape or glue stick are two

excellent options. Alternatively, hand slip baste (see Slip Basting, below).

✂ The serger is a great choice when sewing seams in plaids. Because the serger sews without feed dogs, the fabric won't shift or crawl as you serge, helping you to keep the bars aligned. The trick is in the pinning (see Serging, right).

### SLIP BASTING

**A1** Press one seam allowance under along the seamline. Lap it over the adjoining section, matching seamlines and fabric design. Pin at right angles. Bring the needle and thread through to the right side at the folded edge, through all three layers.

**A2** Insert the needle just opposite the fold, through the single layer of fabric, and bring it back up through the fold,

## SHEERS

Follow this advice when working with semi-transparent and flimsy fabrics such as chiffon, organza and voile.

### Layout

✂ Use a single or double thickness cutting layout with right sides together.

✂ Use a without nap cutting layout.

✂ Use a cutting surface with a contrasting color to your sheer.

✂ Soft sheers will easily slip off grain. Use pushpins to anchor the fabric to a padded cutting surface. Insert the pins along the selvage and across the cut edge along the crosswise grain.

✂ Pin only within the seam allowances, especially on crisp sheers. Extra fine pins are suitable on crisp sheers but may easily fall out of soft sheers. Insert pins at more frequent intervals than usual.

### Marking

Use tailor's tacks or an evaporating fabric marking pen. Avoid dressmaker's chalk and wax dressmaker's carbon.

### Cutting

Use scissors with serrated blades or a rotary cutter.

### Needle

Use a standard universal point needle in a light- to medium-weight size: 70/10 H to 80/12 H (Schmetz) or 10 to 12 (Singer).

### Thread

Standard or fine cotton-covered polyester thread or lingerie thread.

### Machine settings

✂ Straight stitch, average length to slightly shorter than average (2mm–2.5mm or 10–15 stitches per inch).

✂ On some lightweight sheers, increasing the pressure on the presser foot may be helpful.

✂ Use a small, single-hole needle plate when sewing a straight stitch. This will prevent the fabric from being swallowed into the machine. A narrow straight stitch foot and/or flat-bottom presser foot may also be helpful. If you do not have these machine attachments, consider moving the needle to the far left to provide support on three sides of the fabric.

### Interfacing

✂ Eliminate interfacing whenever possible.

✂ In place of a commercial interfacing, choose organza for soft sheers and organdy for crisp sheers. These fabrics are compatible with the transparent qualities of a sheer.

✂ Never use a fusible interfacing.

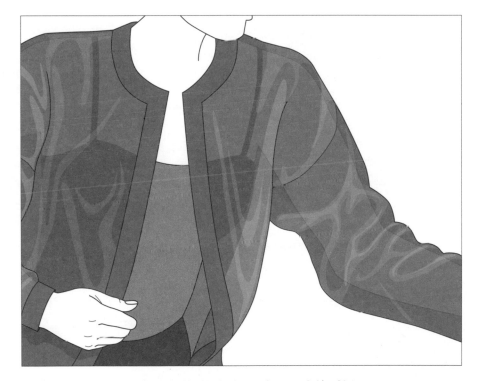

On sheer fabrics, edges can be finished with a bias binding cut from your fashion fabric.

> **TIP** On faced edges, consider substituting bias binding for both the facing and interfacing.

### Seams and seam finishes

✂ **Seam options:** Double-stitched Seam (page 95); French Seam (for straight not curved seams, page 96); the three-thread or four-thread serger seam. The Narrow Seam (below) is a variation of the narrow hem that works well as a seam technique for sheers.

✂ Sheers can be seamed quite successfully on the serger. Test first to be sure you are happy with the amount of thread that shows through.

**NARROW SEAM**
When making a collar from sheer fabric, seams should be as inconspicuous as possible. To achieve this, use one of the following two seam techniques. (These techniques work equally well for cuffs.) Note that clipping, grading and understitching are not necessary.

**The conventional method:** Stitch along the seamline over a filler cord of pearl cotton or crochet thread, using a fine zigzag stitch. Trim the seam allowance close to the stitching; then turn and press the collar.

**Ⓢ The serger method:** Set the machine to make a narrow seam (see Narrow Seam chart below). Serge along the seamline; then turn and press the collar.

### Hems

✂ Choose the narrow Machine-rolled Hem (see page 192) or the narrow serger Rolled Hem (see page 193). If you are using the latter, test first. If the serger stitches are too dense, the hem may pull away from the fabric.

✂ On crisp sheers, the Narrow Topstitched Hem or the Wide Topstitched Hem (see pages 191 and 192) are also good choices, particularly if the hemline is on the straight grain of the fabric.

### Pressing
Press with a warm, dry iron.

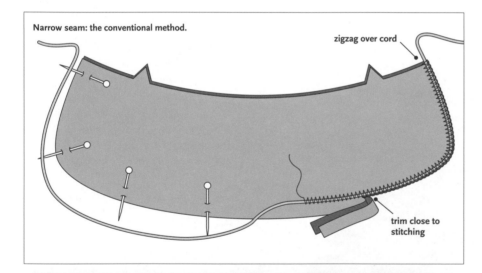

Narrow seam: the conventional method.

zigzag over cord

trim close to stitching

| NARROW SEAM | | | |
|---|---|---|---|
| **TYPE OF SERGER STITCH:** | | 3 | MINE |
| Stitch length: | | 2mm–3mm | |
| Stitch width: | | Narrowest | |
| Tensions | Needle: | Normal | |
| | Upper Looper: | Normal | |
| | Lower Looper: | Normal | |

# LEATHER AND SUEDE

Leather is a material created by tanning the hide of an animal, usually cows or sheep. It has one fuzzy side and one smooth side. Suede is a type of leather that is fuzzy on both sides.

Cowhide comes in heavy and medium weights and offers a wide range of colors and finishes. Lambskin is similar in texture to cowhide but finer and generally more expensive; it too is available in many colors. Pigskin may be an option when a light to medium-weight leather is required, but as pigskins are usually small (about 5–7 square feet/50–65 square centimeters), they are generally used for smaller items such as belts or trims.

## Layout

✂ The maximum size of a piece of leather or suede is limited to the size of the original animal. If piecing is necessary, try to work out the lines of patching so that they form an integral part of the design.

✂ Some areas of the animal skin will be thinner than others, so when planning out a project avoid letting these fall where they will be subject to strain.

✂ Use a single thickness with nap cutting layout, wrong side up.

✂ Do not pin the pattern pieces in place as this will leave permanent holes in the fabric; you should use pattern weights instead.

## Marking

Mark on the wrong side, using dress-maker's chalk.

## Cutting

Use scissors with serrated blades or a rotary cutter.

## Needle

Use a leather needle with a specially shaped shaft (the sewing point is shaped a little like an arrowhead to pierce through the fabric's surface cleanly).

## Thread

Use a general-purpose polyester or a polyester-covered cotton.

## Machine settings

Stitch length will vary according to fabric thickness, but generally a larger than usual stitch is required (3mm or 9–12 stitches per inch minimum); if you make your stitches too small, the leather will be punctured too close together, which will cause tears.

## Interfacing

✂ Use crisp or soft canvas; sew-in medium-weight nonwoven or woven.

✂ For suede a fusible interfacing can be used, but do not use fusibles on real leather.

## Seams and seam finishes

✂ **Seam options:** Plain Seam (see page 95); Lapped Seam (see page 96).

✂ Once leather or suede has been stitched the holes made by the needle are permanent, so it is important to make sure your pattern fit is accurate before stitching. It makes sense, therefore, to do all fitting and pattern checking in a fabric toile first.

✂ Always leave long threads at both the start and end of the seams so you can tie them off by hand.

✂ As you are sewing leather garments, you might experience skipped stitches. The use of a nonstick foot, which is designed to glide over the fabric's surface, can help to avoid this.

✂ When stitching round corners, you should make the corner blunt rather than very pointed.

✂ All points of possible strain on the garment, such as the neckline and underarms, should be staystitched with tape to reinforce and prevent tearing. This will also be more comfortable for the wearer.

✂ When seams are finished, stick the seam allowances down with a liquid adhesive suitable for leather.

## Hems

✂ With right side facing, topstitch ½ in (1.3cm) from the folded hem. The hem can be held in place for stitching with double-sided tape or paper clips.

✂ For an invisible finish at the hem you can turn the edge under and stick it in place with no stitching at all.

## Pressing

To smooth out wrinkles, creases, and stretched out bumps, use a lukewarm iron on the wrong side. Do not use any steam.

**TIP** To hold garment pieces together or the hem in position prior to stitching use paper clips (pins will leave permanent holes). However, you should never try to stitch over a paper clip.

PATTERNLESS
PROJECTS

# INTRODUCTION

Whether your goal is to try out some new techniques or polish up some rusty sewing skills, this chapter has a few projects that require no pattern to get you started. For the novice sewer, the instructions are organized in an easy-to-follow sequence, from Material Needs to Cutting Directions to Sewing Directions. You can concentrate on becoming familiar with your sewing machine and developing your basic sewing skills before moving on to a commercial pattern. For those new to serger sewing, some of these projects offer the opportunity to integrate serger techniques with conventional techniques.

# JEANS SKIRT

There is no better way to begin sewing than to recycle existing items of clothing. So, if you have a pair of jeans that are worn out at the knees, why not turn them into a funky jeans skirt instead. All the hard stitching is done for you; all you need to do is cut off the jean legs and insert a panel of a contrasting or a cute printed cotton fabric at the back and front.

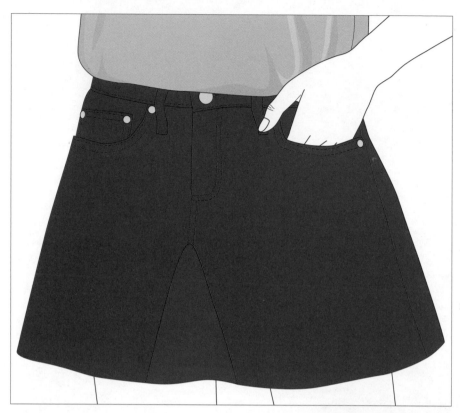

## MATERIAL NEEDS

- Old pair of jeans
- 1yd (1m) of 45in (115cm) or 60in (150cm) wide cotton fabric
- Seam ripper
- Matching or contrasting thread

## SEWING DIRECTIONS

**A1** Decide on the length of the finished skirt; add 2in (5cm) to this measurement and cut off the legs at that point. **NOTE** The extra 2in/5cm ensures that you will be able to trim the skirt without worrying that it will be shorter than you want – you can always cut away extra, but you can't add it back on.

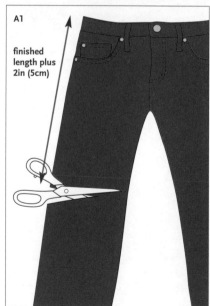

A1

finished
length plus
2in (5cm)

**A2** Using the seam ripper, open up the inner leg seams from the cut legs all the way up to the crotch. On the FRONT, continue until you reach the bottom of the fly. On the BACK the opening should end at the lower end of the back yoke; if your jeans don't have a back yoke, the opening should end about 5½in (14cm) from the waistband.

**A3** Lay the skirt with the FRONT facing you on a flat surface. Lap the left crotch over the right crotch and pin it in place. Stitch right over the original topstitching to hold it permanently together. Repeat this step at the BACK of the jeans. Now you have a skirt shape that's missing a wedge-shape at the front and the back.

**A4** Slide a piece of cotton fabric underneath the wedge-shaped opening at the FRONT and pin. Stitch in place sewing about ⅜in (9mm) from the edge of the jeans. Trim the fabric to match up with the hem of the denim. Repeat this step in the BACK.

**A5** Trim the skirt hem so that it's straight and even. You can turn up the hem ½in (1.3cm) and stitch it in place, or leave it raw for an edgy look.

A2

BACK

FRONT

open inner leg seam to the back yoke

open inner leg seam to the fly

**TIP** If you have some cotton fabric leftover, add a ruffle to the skirt hem by cutting a strip of fabric that's twice the total width of the skirt hem and 3in (7.5cm) wide. Fold the strip in half, gather the top and lay it underneath the skirt hem. A quick machine stitch along the hem will hold it in place.

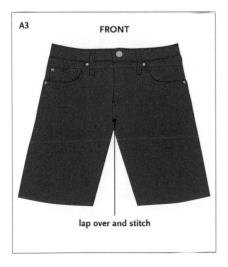

A3

FRONT

lap over and stitch

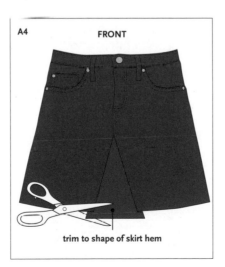

A4

FRONT

trim to shape of skirt hem

A5

BACK

# KIMONO

This versatile kimono can be made in a Misses' hip-length or dress-length version, or for Girl's and Boy's sizes. As sized for the Misses' figure, it fits up to a 42in (107cm) bust; for Girls, sizes 7–14; and for Boys, sizes 7–12. Change the length and/or the fabric and the kimono silhouette translates into a coat, a casual jacket, a bathrobe, a karate jacket or even a geisha costume for a fancy dress party.

One simple pattern, two great looks. To the left, made from a comfortable jersey, this smart hip-length jacket is perfect for the office. To the right, made from a soft-to-touch fabric, such as terrycloth or velour, the basic kimono pattern can be customized to your favorite bathrobe length.

**TIP** Except for the Cutting Diagrams and the measurement differences indicated in Sewing Directions, Steps A3 and B1, the procedures for making the Misses' and the Girl's/Boy's versions are exactly the same.

## MATERIAL NEEDS

- - - - - - - - - - - - - - - - - - - - - - - - -

**FOR MISSES' HIP-LENGTH JACKET**
✂ 2¹/₂yd (2.3m) of 45in (115cm) or 54in (138cm) fabric

**FOR MISSES' DRESS-LENGTH ROBE OR COAT**
✂ 3yd (2.8m) of 45in (115cm) or 54in (138cm) fabric

**FOR GIRL'S OR BOY'S HIP-LENGTH KARATE JACKET**
✂ 2yd (2m) of 45in (115cm) or 54in (138cm) fabric

**FOR GIRL'S OR BOY'S KNEE-LENGTH ROBE**
✂ 2¹/₂yd (2.3m) of 45in (115cm) or 54in (138cm) fabric

**FOR GIRL'S ANKLE-LENGTH GEISHA COSTUME**
✂ 3yd (2.8m) of 45in (115cm) or 54in (138cm) fabric

✂ Thread

✂ Chalk marking pencil or fabric marking pen

✂ Yardstick or T-square

✂ Glue stick (optional)

The versatile kimono can be used for a boy's karate jacket or a girl's fancy dress costume.

## CUTTING DIRECTIONS

Place your fabric, single thickness and right side up, on a large, flat surface or cutting board. Using the appropriate cutting layout diagram (see pages 244–245), plot out and cut the following sections of the kimono.

✂  One BODY

✂  Two BELTS

✂  Two SLEEVES

✂  One NECKBAND

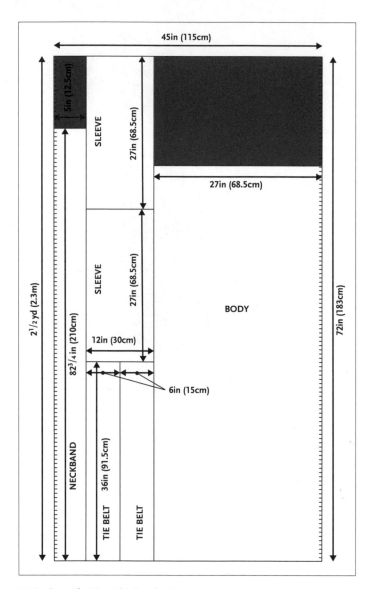

Cutting layout for Misses' hip-length jacket.

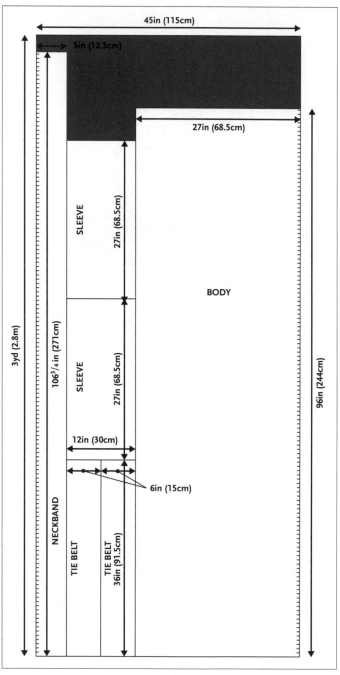

Cutting layout for Misses' dress-length robe or coat.

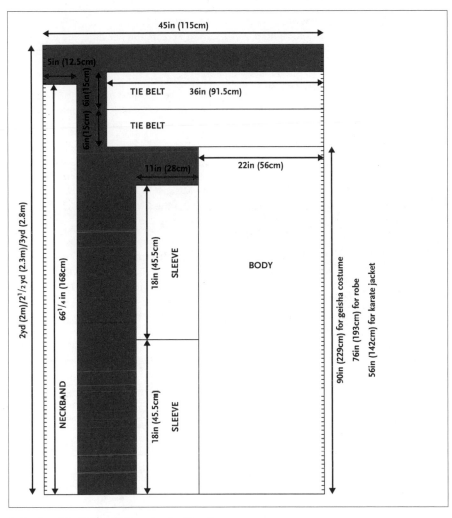

The diagram contains the following labels:

- 45in (115cm)
- 5in (12.5cm)
- 6in(1.5cm)
- TIE BELT — 36in (91.5cm)
- 6in(1.5cm)
- TIE BELT
- 11in (28cm)
- 22in (56cm)
- 18in (45.5cm) SLEEVE
- 18in (45.5cm) SLEEVE
- BODY
- 66¹/₄in (168cm)
- NECKBAND
- 2yd (2m)/2¹/₂ yd (2.3m)/3yd (2.8m)
- 90in (229cm) for geisha costume
- 76in (193cm) for robe
- 56in (142cm) for karate jacket

Cutting layout for Girl's or Boy's versions in all lengths.

## SEWING DIRECTIONS

**NOTE** All seam allowances are ⁵/₈in (1.5cm). The hem allowance is 1in (2.5cm) at the lower edge.

### Establish the neckline and center front opening

**A1** With right sides together, fold the BODY in half lengthwise and mark the fold. This is the Center Front/Center Back line.

**A2** Unfold the BODY and refold it in half crosswise, right sides together; mark the fold. This is the Shoulder line.

**A3** The point where the Center Front/ Center Back line and the Shoulder line intersect is the starting point for establishing the neckline curve as is described in more detail on page 246.

**TIP** Draw one side of the curve, then fold the BODY along the Center Front/Center Back line and use dressmaker's carbon and a tracing wheel to transfer the curve to the other side.

**FOR THE MISSES' KIMONOS ONLY**

✂ On the Center Back line, put a mark ³/₄in (2cm) from the intersection point.

✂ On the Center Front line, mark 10in (25cm) from the intersection point.

✂ On both sides of the Shoulder line, put a mark 3in (7.5cm) from the intersection point.

**FOR THE GIRL'S OR BOY'S KIMONOS ONLY**

✂ On the Center Back line, put a mark ³/₄in (2cm) from the intersection point.

✂ On the Center Front line, put a mark 9in (23cm) from the intersection point.

✂ On both sides of the Shoulder line, put a mark 2³/₄in (7cm) from the intersection point.

**FOR ALL VERSIONS**

✂ To create the neckline, draw a line, as shown on the diagrams, connecting these four marks. Gently curve the line to get rid of the corner at the point where the neckline meets the Shoulder line. Be sure that the left side of the neckline matches the right side.

✂ Beginning at the lower edge of the Center Front line, cut the BODY apart until you reach the 10in (25cm) mark of the Misses' BODY or the 9in (23cm) mark of the Girl's or Boy's BODY, then cut around the neckline.

### Attach the neckband

**B1** To establish the Center Back and Shoulders on the NECKBAND, fold it in half crosswise and mark at the raw edges. This is the CB marking.

**FOR THE MISSES' KIMONO ONLY**
Mark along the raw edges 4³/₈in (11.2cm) from the Center Back on each side for the Shoulder markings.

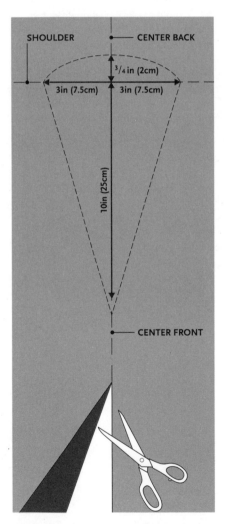

Marking and cutting the Misses' neckline.

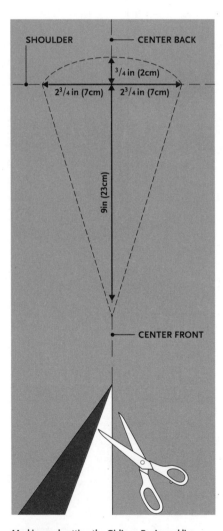

Marking and cutting the Girl's or Boy's neckline.

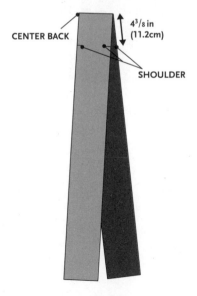

Marking the Misses' neckband.

**FOR THE GIRL'S OR BOY'S KIMONO ONLY**
Mark along the raw edges 4$\frac{1}{8}$in (10.5cm) from the Center Back on each side for the Shoulder markings.

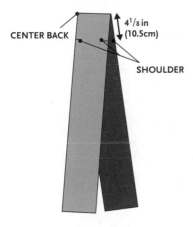

Marking the Girl's or Boy's neckband.

**B2** Staystitch the BODY neckline. Clip the seam allowances just to, but not through, the staystitching all around the neckline.

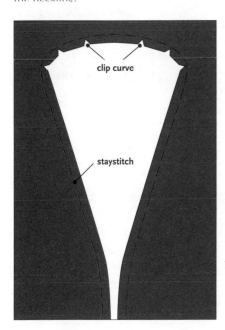

**B3** With right sides together, pin the NECKBAND to the BODY, matching the CB and Shoulder markings. Be careful not to stretch the band; instead, ease it carefully around the curves. Stitch, trim and clip the seam, or serge the seam on the serger.

**NOTE** Depending on your fabric and how much easing you have to do, the NECKBAND may extend beyond the lower edges of the BODY. Trim off the excess before hemming the kimono (see Step E2).

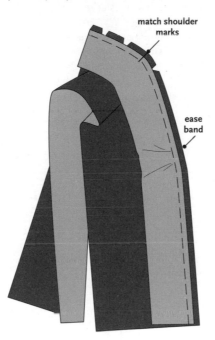

**B4** Press the long raw edge of the NECKBAND under ⅝in (1.5cm). Then fold the band to the inside of the kimono so that the folded edge just covers the seamline. Hand-baste or glue-baste in place, easing it carefully around the curves. Slipstitch in place.

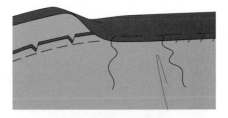

**B5** Working on the outside of the kimono, edgestitch the NECKBAND close to the seamline, through all thicknesses.

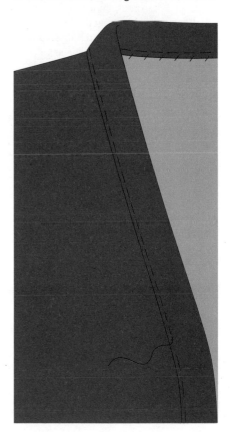

## Attach the sleeves

**C1** To find the Shoulder line, fold each sleeve in half crosswise and mark. Then, along one 27in (68.5cm) edge of each Misses' SLEEVE or one 18in (45.5cm) edge of the Girl's or Boy's SLEEVE, mark ⅝in (1.5cm) in from each outer edge.

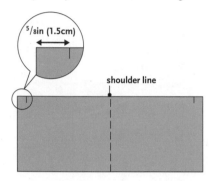

**C2** With right sides together, pin the SLEEVE to the BODY, matching Shoulder lines and raw edges. Stitch the seam, beginning and ending the stitching at the ⅝in (1.5cm) marks. Repeat for the other sleeve; then press both sleeve seams open.

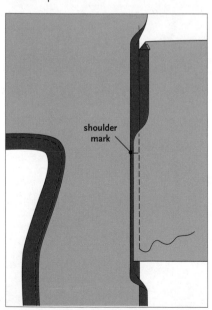

**S TIP** Both the sleeves and the lower edge of the kimono can be finished on the serger, then turned up and top-stitched in place.

## Stitch the side seams

**D1** With right sides together, pin the BODY front and back together at the side seams and underarm seamlines.
**D2** Beginning at the lower edge of the BODY, stitch the side seam. End the stitching when you reach the sleeve seam, keeping the sleeve seam allowances free.
**D3** Beginning at the lower edge of the SLEEVE, stitch the underarm seam. End the stitching when you reach the ⅝in (1.5cm) markings, keeping the sleeve seam allowances free. This break in the stitching at the underarm is what makes this seam lie smooth on the finished kimono.
**D4** Press the side and the underarm seams open.

## Hem the kimono

**E1** Make a narrow hem on the lower edge of the sleeves, following the directions for the Narrow Topstitched Hem on page 191, and changing the hem allowance from 1in (2.5cm) to ⅝in (1.5cm) as illustrated opposite.
**E2** Mark the hem at the lower edge of the kimono, then press up along the hemline. Trim the hem allowance to 1in (2.5cm). Finish, following the directions for the Narrow Topstitched Hem, page 191, or serge-finish the edge and topstitch, as shown opposite.

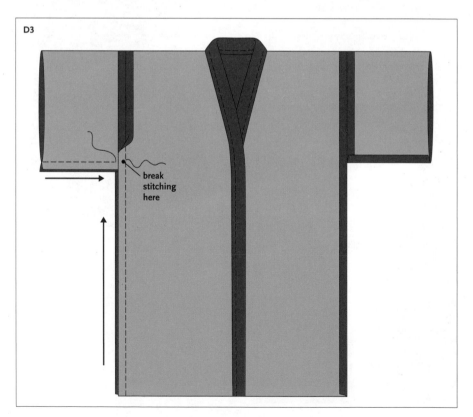

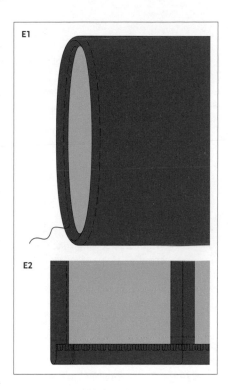

# TOTE BAG

This roomy tote bag can hold everything, from portable sewing projects to beach supplies. Its generous proportions and practical pockets make it the perfect carryall for shopping, office or beach gear. Use a sturdy medium- to heavyweight fabric, such as denim, canvas, sailcloth, synthetic suede or quilted fabric. If you're looking for a great teach-someone-to-sew project, this is it.

## Construct the belt

**F1** With right sides facing, serge or stitch the two BELT sections together along one 6in (15cm) end.

**F2** You can finish the belt on the conventional machine or the serger, following the directions for Soft Belts, page 181.

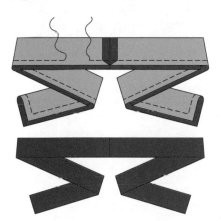

The finished size of this roomy tote is 9¹/₄ in x 17³/₄ in x 21¹/₄ in deep (23.5cm x 45cm x 54cm deep).

## MATERIAL NEEDS

✂ 1¼ yd (1.2m) of 45in (115cm) fabric without a nap or one-way design

✂ Thread

✂ Chalk marking pencil or fabric marking pen

✂ Iron-on monogram letters (optional)

✂ Glue stick (optional)

## CUTTING DIRECTIONS

Place your fabric, single thickness and right side up, on a large, flat surface. Using the cutting layout diagram, plot out and cut the following sections of your tote bag.

✂ One BAG

✂ One BOTTOM

✂ Two POCKETS

✂ Two HANDLES

## SEWING DIRECTIONS

**NOTE** All seam allowances are ⅝in (1.5cm). Since you will be sewing through four or more layers of heavy fabrics, the right size sewing machine needle is essential. Use a size 16/100 or 18/110. You may find it easier if you choose a wedge-point needle (the type designed for leather or vinyl) rather than a general purpose needle.

### Prepare the pockets

**A1** Using chalk or a fabric marking pen, mark 6¾in (17cm) in from each end on both long edges of each POCKET.
**A2** Connect each set of marks for the Handle Placement lines.

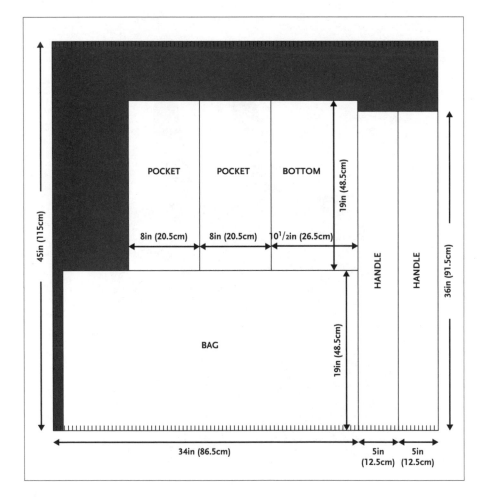

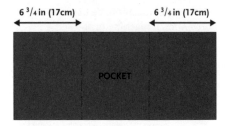

### Create the pocket facings

**B1** Finish one long edge of one POCKET. For the conventional method, turn the edge under ¼in (6mm) and topstitch close to the fold. For the serger method, serge along the edge, trimming off ¼in (6mm).
**B2** Fold the finished edge 1in (2.5cm) to the inside and press.

Cutting layout for the tote bag.

**B3** Topstitch ³/₄in (2cm) from the fold.

**B4** Repeat Steps B1–B3 to create the facing on the other POCKET.

## Mark the pocket placement lines
**C1** Mark 12¹/₂in (32cm) in from each end on both long edges of the BAG.
**C2** Connect each set of marks.

## Finish the edges of the bag
Finish the 19in (48.5cm) edges of the BAG. For the conventional method, turn the edge under ¹/₄in (6mm) and top-stitch close to the fold; or serge along the edge trimming off ¹/₄in (6mm).

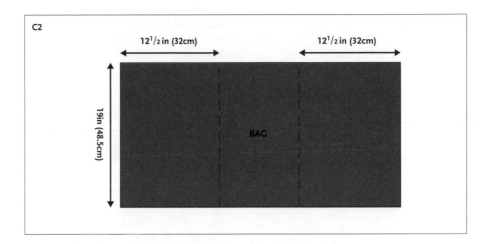

## Baste the pockets
**D1** With the wrong side of one POCKET to the right side of the BAG, position the POCKET so that its long raw edge extends ⁵/₈in (1.5cm) beyond the Pocket Placement line; pin.

**D2** Baste the POCKET to the BAG along the sides and lower edge of the POCKET, and continue basting along the Handle Placement lines.
**D3** Repeat Steps D1 and D2 for the other POCKET.

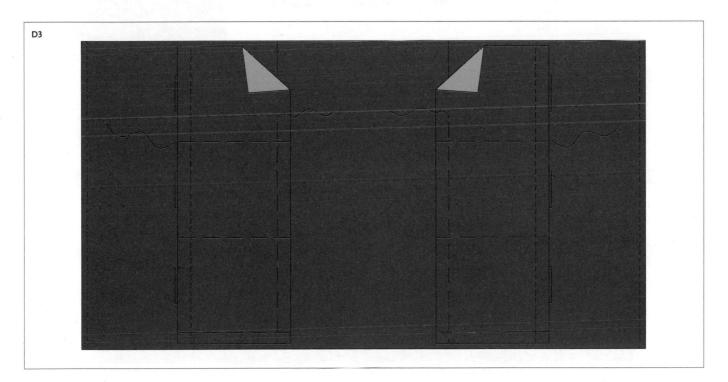

## Make the handles

**E1**  Fold each HANDLE in half lengthwise, wrong sides together; press.

**E2**  Unfold one HANDLE and turn in each long edge so that the raw edge meets the fold; refold and press again. Edgestitch along both outer edges, through all four layers of fabric. Repeat for the other HANDLE.

## Attach the handles

**F1**  Position the HANDLES on the outside of the BAG over the Handle Placement Lines so that the raw edges of the HANDLES and the POCKETS are even. Pin or glue-baste in place.

**F2**  Topstitch each handle to the POCKET and BAG over the edge-stitching. End the topstitching at the upper edge of the POCKET; backstitch to reinforce.

## Apply the monogram (optional)

Following the manufacturer's instructions, apply the iron-on monogram to one center pocket between the handles.

## Attach the bottom section

**G1** Press under ⅝in (1.5cm) on both long edges of the BOTTOM. With the wrong side of the BOTTOM to the right side of the BAG, position the BOTTOM so that the sides are even and the folded edges just cover the Pocket Placement lines; pin or glue-baste in place.

**G2** Topstitch close to the folded edges of the BOTTOM, catching the POCKETS and HANDLES in the stitching.

**G3** Baste the BOTTOM and BAG together along the remaining edges.

## Stitch the side seams

Fold the bag in half, right sides together, so that the edges match. Serge the side seams. Alternatively, for the conventional method, stitch the side seams. Stitch again ¼in (6mm) from the first line of stitching, within the seam allowance. Trim close to the second stitched line.

¼in (6mm)

Stitching the side seams using the conventional sewing method.

G1–G3

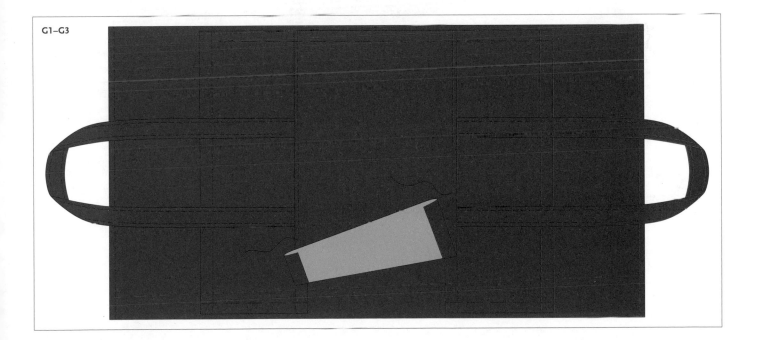

### Finish the bag

**H1** To form the BAG facing, fold the finished edge of the BAG 1½in (3.8cm) to the inside and press. Folding the handles out of the way, topstitch the facing to the BAG 1¼in (3.2cm) from the fold.

**H2** On the outside of the BAG, topstitch the HANDLES to the rest of the BAG. To keep the stitching lines smooth and connected, start stitching about 1in (2.5cm) below the top of the pocket, directly over the previous stitching. To reinforce the handles, backstitch at the upper edge of the bag.

**H3** For a flat bottom bag, fold the bottom corners up and slipstitch in place.

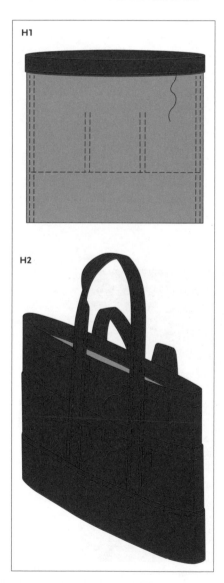

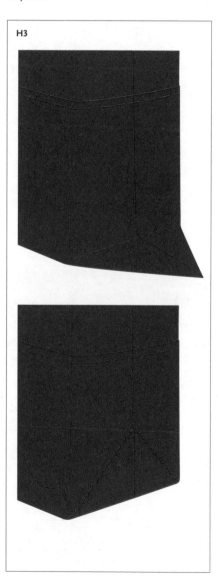

# TOILE PILLOW

Home decorating projects are a practical way to work on your sewing skills. Give your home an elegant update with this beautiful banded pillow. The design showcases a classic toile print. Choose your border and backing fabrics to coordinate with the toile panel. A lace-fringed trim and decorative buttons finishes it off to perfection.

## PILLOW TREATMENTS

✂ A knife-edge pillow is made by sewing two panels together and then stuffing. The front panel can be decorated in many different ways.

✂ Apply ribbons and/or flat trims in an interweaving pattern for a mock plaid design.

✂ Antique laces, including doilies and handkerchiefs, can be fashioned into interesting appliqués.

✂ Use a wide ribbon to create a mitered border.

✂ Use different fabrics for the front and back of the pillow. Try pairing lace with satin, tapestry with velvet, oversize prints with miniprints.

## MATERIAL NEEDS

✂ 1yd (1m) of 45in (115cm) wide print fabric

✂ ⅝yd (0.6m) of 45in (115cm) wide solid fabric

✂ ¼yd–⅜yd (0.25m–0.35m) of 45in (115cm) wide toile fabric

✂ 1⅝yd (1.6m) of narrow fringe or eyelet trim

✂ 2yd (1.85m) of cording with lip

✂ Four ¾in (2cm) diameter buttons

✂ 16in (40cm) square pillow form

## CUTTING DIRECTIONS

✂ **From the print fabric:** Cut four 3½in × 17½in (9cm × 45cm) strips for the OUTER BORDER. Cut one 17½in (45cm) square for the pillow BACK.

✂ **From the solid fabric:** Cut four 3½in × 14½in (9cm × 37cm) strips for the INNER BORDER.

✂ **From the toile fabric:** Cut one 8½in square (22cm), centering the design for the CENTRAL SQUARE. (This may require more than the recommended yardage of toile fabric.)

## SEWING DIRECTIONS

**NOTE** All seam allowances are ½in (1.3cm).

### Make the front panel

**A1** With right sides together, stitch one INNER BORDER strip to each side of the CENTRAL SQUARE, mitering the corners (see Mitering, page 148).
**A2** Trim the excess length of each border strip at the corners to form a new perfect square.
**A3** Sew a button at each corner of the central square.
**A4** With right sides together, stitch one OUTER BORDER strip to each side of the newly-enlarged square, mitering corners and trimming excess.
**A5** Place the straight edge of the trim along the seamline between the INNER and OUTER BORDERS, with the decorative edge of the trim facing towards the pillow front CENTRAL SQUARE. Stitch in place along the straight edge.
**A6** Pin the cord with lip to the right side of the pillow front around the entire perimeter, matching the edge of the lip with the cut edge of the front panel.
**A7** Using a zipper foot, stitch the cord to the pillow front as close to the cording as possible. To ensure smooth corners, clip the cording lip at the corners.

### Assembling the pillow

**B1** With right sides together, pin the front panel to the pillow BACK, matching cut edges and encasing the cord.
**B2** Using a zipper foot, stitch as close to the cording as possible, leaving a 10in (20cm) opening for turning and stuffing.

### Finishing the pillow

Turn the pillow right side out. Insert the pillow form and slipstitch the opening closed, turning the cut edges to the inside.

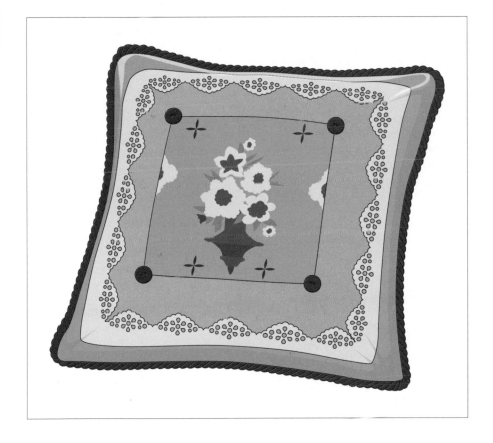

# GLOSSARY

**adjustment** – refers to a change made on the pattern tissue before the garment is cut out.

**alteration** – refers to a change made on the actual garment.

**appliqué** – additional fabric or motif attached to a background or base fabric in a decorative design. Appliqué can be done by hand, machine or with fusible web. Appliqué is a great technique to cover stains, rips or other problem areas on a larger fabric area.

**backstitch** – when machine sewing, this describes stitching in reverse for a short distance at the beginning and end of a seam to prevent the stitching from coming undone. Backstitch is also a hand stitch that creates a row of stitches set end-to-end, looking from the right side like machine stitching, but with the end of each stitch overlapping the next on the wrong side. It is a useful mending stitch and can be used to hand-stitch short seams securely.

**bagging** – a method of backing a fabric item that involves sewing the back and the front, right sides together, around three edges but leaving a gap in the fourth side. The item is turned right side out through the gap, which is then stitched closed.

**ballpoint needle** – needles with a slightly rounded tip that will slide between the fabric threads rather than piercing them; used for jersey and stretch fabrics.

**bar tack** – several short stitches worked parallel and very close together to reinforce the end of an opening, such as at the ends of a buttonhole.

**basting** – long stitches used to hold layers of fabric together until they are permanently machine stitched. Basting stitches are removed when the stitching is completed. Basting can be done by hand or by machine, using the longest stitch setting.

**bias** – the diagonal direction across woven fabric at an angle to the warp and the weft. Fabric cut on the bias stretches and must be handled with great care. Bias tape allows binding to be carried out around curved edges without pleating. *See also* **true bias**.

**bias tape or strip** – a long thin length of fabric cut on the bias and used for binding.

**binding** – a strip of fabric sewn over raw edges to finish and/or decorate the edge. Normally a binding is s ewn onto one side, then brought over the edges to the other side and slipstitched in place. Binding can be straight or it can be cut on the bias.

**blind hem foot** – a special presser foot attachment for the sewing machine that forms blind hems and tucks.

**blind hem stitch** – a method of machine hemming using zigzag stitch, so that only the very point of the zigzag catches the front piece of fabric and the stitching hardly shows on the right side.

**blindstitch** – hand stitch used for hemming and finishing; invisible on the right side of the fabric.

**bobbin** – a small spool for holding thread. Sewing machines use two threads to make a stitch: the needle thread coming downwards from the top of the machine, and the bobbin thread coming upwards from under the needle plate. Bobbins can be top-loading (the bobbin is dropped into the bobbin case through a sliding or hinged panel in the needle plate) or side/front-loading (the bobbin is placed into the bobbin case outside the machine, and the filled bobbin case is then inserted into the machine at the front or side through an opening door).

**bobbin case** – the metal case with tension plates on the side, which holds the bobbin. The bobbin case is removable, but on top-loading machines it is normally left in place unless removed for cleaning or to change it for a spare or special bobbin case, for example to adjust bobbin tension for free-motion work. On side/front-loading machines the bobbin case is taken out of the machine before the bobbin can be removed from it.

**bodice** – the upper body section of a garment.

**bolt** – a length of fabric wound onto a round tube or a flattened oval cardboard form. Wider fabric is usually folded lengthwise, right sides together, before being wound onto the bolt. Wholesale fabric stores sell fabric by the bolt or by the cut length – the amount in a bolt can vary according to the manufacturer and the type of fabric.

**border** – a strip of fabric, usually in a contrasting or complementary color, sewn to the outer edges of an item to serve as a frame for the interior or to enhance the design.

**bound edge** – a technique using bias binding that neatens a raw edge.

**box pleats** – pairs of pleats with each pair pointing towards each other to create a flat, tailored look.

**casing** – the tunnel through which elastic or drawstring is fed and pulled up.

**catch stitch** – *see* **blind hem stitch**.

**clipping** – to cut a short distance into a seam allowance with the point of a pair of scissors. Clipping is used in areas such as curved seams and square corners to remove excess fabric, allowing the seams to lie flat when pressed.

**composition** – the percentage of each material that a fabric is made from; this information is normally given at the end of the fabric bolt and it is important to know so that you can care properly for the finished item, particularly when it comes to laundering.

**cone** – thread can come wound into a cone-shape on a long spool. A cone contains far more thread than an ordinary spool of thread, and cones are often used on embroidery machines and sergers because both get through large amounts of thread quickly.

**continuous binding** – binding that runs round four sides in a single length with miters at the corners and only one join at the start/end of the strip of fabric.

**cording** – this is piping that has a cord enclosed within the narrow tube of fabric to give it a more rounded appearance. It is used to trim seams and edges for decoration. Also known as corded piping.

**coverstitch** – a serger stitch created with two or three needle threads and one looper thread, and the cutting blade disengaged, to create a hem for stretchy fabrics.

**crosswise grain** – the crosswise grain of a woven fabric is at right angles to the selvages and has more stretch than the lengthwise threads. Also known as the cross-grain, weft or width.

**cutting line** – the outermost solid line on a pattern piece, which indicates where you cut out.

**dart** – a triangular, stitched tuck running horizontally or vertically in from the edge to shape a flat piece of fabric around the curves of the body. A double-pointed dart runs vertically down the fabric piece, going from a point, widening out, and then back into a point again.

**directional print** – fabric with a printed pattern that has a definite direction or grain. Care must be taken to match the direction when joining different lengths. *See also* **nap**.

**double hem** – a hem in which the fabric is folded under to the wrong side twice, so the raw edge is completely enclosed. The hem is stitched in place along the upper foldline.

**drape** – the property of fabric to fall into folds. If it falls gracefully, it is said to drape well or to have good drape.

**drop feed** – a term used to describe the process by which the fabric is normally fed through the sewing machine. When the needle moves upwards and withdraws from the fabric, the feed dog comes up through slots in the needle plate and the serrated top surface grips the material, which is held firmly against it by the presser foot. The feed dog moves horizontally backwards, so the fabric is dragged backwards into position for the next stitch. The feed dog is then lowered again and returns to its original position while the needle makes its next pass through the material. When the needle is in the material, there is no feed action.

**dual feed** – an enhancement to drop feed on a sewing machine in which a moving upper foot (separate from the presser foot) clamps the fabric against the feed dog and moves in sync with it to move the fabric creating an effect similar to an even-feed (or walking) foot. It also covers some of the functions of the differential feed on a serger.

**ease** – to make two edges of different lengths fit together in the same seam. One piece may have to be stretched a little, or bunched up slightly, so that the edges are adjusted to the same length.

**easestitching** – machine stitching used to very slightly gather the length of an edge to reduce it so it can be joined to a slightly shorter edge without visible folds.

**edgestitching** – a line of stitching made close to a seamline, foldline or a finished edge, which is visible on the right side of the fabric. It is not necessarily deco-rative, although it can be worked in a contrasting color to make it so. The main purpose of edgestitching is to keep the line crisp.

**embellish** – the addition of decorative stitching, appliqué and trims.

**even-feed foot** – this machine presser foot draws the top and bottom layers of fabric along at the same speed, preventing multiple layers or very slippery fabrics from being pushed out of alignment by the action of the feed dog. Also known as a walking foot.

**faced hem** – a hem with a separate strip of fabric stitched on the hemline right sides together and then turned to the inside along the hemline. The raw edge of the facing is either turned under and hemmed, or zigzag stitched and machine stitched into place.

**facing** – a shaped piece of fabric stitched on the seamline, right sides together, and then turned to the inside to create a finished edge.

**fagotting** – a decorative technique that joins two pieces of fabric leaving a space in between filled with stitches.

**feed dog** – the serrated teeth below the needle plate that grip and move the fabric through the machine. If the feed dog is dropped the fabric can be moved freely under the needle for free-motion quilting, machine embroidery or for sewing on buttons.

**finger pressing** – using your fingers to press a seam or fold into fabric.

**finish** – the surface treatment on a fabric, usually added after the fabric is woven.

**flat bed** – this type of sewing machine has a base that sits flat on the work surface for its full length, so it may be hard to stitch narrow cylindrical items. The alternative to a flat bed is a free-arm.

**flat-fell seam** – a seam designed to give a strong join on heavy-duty fabric that is subject to a lot of wear and traditionally used on jeans. The seam is stitched wrong sides together. One seam allow-ance is trimmed back, and the other seam allowance has the edge folded under and is then pressed flat to cover the trimmed seam allowance. The upper seam allowance is stitched in place along the foldline, giving a double line of stitching on the right side of the fabric and a join line with a parallel line of stitching on the reverse.

**flatlock stitch** – a serger stitch created with one needle thread and two looper threads, used for butted or lapped seams and decorative stitching.

**foldline** – a line marked in fabric by folding over and pressing along the fold.

**foot pressure** – the weight applied to the fabric by the presser foot when it is in the down position. A machine with adjustable foot pressure will allow you to reduce the pressure when sewing very thin fabrics, or increase it when stitching through many layers.

**free-arm** – a sewing machine that has the base cut away at the needle plate end, to give an "arm" raised above the work surface. Narrow cylindrical items can be threaded onto the arm for easier stitching. The free-arm is often brought into use by detaching a piece on the base , leaving the arm protruding. The alternative to a free-arm is a flat bed.

**French curve** – a tool used to create smooth curves in pattern design.

**French seam** – a seam in which the fabric is stitched together wrong sides together first, then folded back along the seamline and stitched again right sides together, so the raw edges are fully enclosed. It is ideal for sheer fabrics, where the raw edges of a normal seam would be visible on the right side.

**frill** – a length of fabric gathered along one long edge and stitched to a flat piece. Also known as a ruffle.

**fusible interfacing** – *see* **interfacing**.

**fusible web** – an adhesive web that can be ironed onto a fabric to adhere two layers of fabric together, for easier appliqué for example, or for hemming.

**gather** – reducing the length of a piece of fabric by stitching down one edge and then pulling the fabric up along the stitching thread into unstructured pleats.

**gathering foot** – a special presser foot attachment for the sewing machine that quickly creates soft gathers in fabric.

**grading seams** – trimming the seam allowances down to different widths after a seam is stitched, to eliminate bulk.

**grain** – the direction of the lengthwise (warp) and crosswise (weft) threads of a fabric. The lengthwise grain, parallel to the selvage, stretches least and should be used for borders whenever possible. The crosswise grain, at right angles to the selvage, has slightly more give.

**gusset** – a small, shaped fabric piece set into a seam for added width and ease.

**hand wheel** – a wheel to the right-hand of a sewing machine or serger that can be turned by hand to raise or lower the needle. On some models the hand wheel can only be turned in one direction.

**hem** – a method of neatening a raw edge by turning the edge under once or twice and stitching in place.

**hem allowance** – the width of fabric from the hemline that will be turned up to create a hem.

**hemline** – the bottom edge of the hem.

**hemming stitch** – a hand stitch used to secure a hem, showing only small inconspicuous stitches on the right side.

**hook and bar** – a type of fastening stitched on opposite sides of an opening. If the hook is paired with a circular eye it is called a hook and eye.

**hook-and-loop tape** – a flexible, two-part fastener; one side has tiny soft hooks and the other has loops, which interlock when the two sides are pressed together.

**hook cover plate** – on a top-loading machine, this is a removable section in the needle plate that covers the bobbin in its casing.

**hook race** – the circular route around the bobbin that the hook travels to loop the needle thread around the bobbin thread.

**in-seam buttonhole** – the simplest type of buttonhole, a gap within the length of a seam.

**interfacing** – a compressed synthetic fabric used as a backing to the main project fabric, particularly in dressmaking and tailoring, to give extra body, shaping and support. An interfacing can either be sew-in or fusible.

**interlining** – a fabric placed between the lining and the main fabric. It is used in heavyweight garments, such as coats, to give added warmth or bulk.

**inverted pleats** – two pleats folded towards each other, meeting in the center, with an inlay of contrasting or self-fabric beneath

**invisible stitching** – sewing that does not show on the right side of the item, usually achieved by taking a very tiny stitch from the back through only a single thread of the fabric.

**Kimono sleeves** – sleeves that are cut as an extension of the bodice.

**knife pleats** – a series of single pleats made to the same width and all pointing in the same direction.

**lapped seam** – a type of seam in which the edges are overlapped and stitched, used to join pieces with minimum bulk. It is ideal for interfacing, interlining and thick fabrics that do not fray.

**lettuce edge** – an edge finish in which the fabric edge is stretched as it is overcast, creating a ruffled effect. It is usually created on a serger by using the differential feed function.

**lining** – fabric used to finish the inside of a garment to hide seam construction.

**lint** – the dust and tiny pieces shed from thread and fabric while sewing, which builds up as fluff around the hook race, bobbin casing and feed dog mechanism. It should be cleaned away regularly to ensure that your sewing machine keeps working smoothly.

**lockstitch** – the stitch performed by most modern sewing machines. One thread comes down through the needle and a second thread comes up from the bobbin. The needle takes a loop of thread through the fabric and down through the hole in the needle plate, where it is caught by a rotary hook and looped around the thread from the bobbin. The needle thread and bobbin thread each stay on their own side of the fabric, but interlock in the middle creating a stitch that looks the same on both sides.

**looper** – a serger uses one or more loopers instead of a bobbin. The looper threads lock around each other and are linked together with the needle thread to form the stitches.

**Microtex needle** – a needle with a very slim acute point for easy piecing of very fine or densely woven fabrics. It is used for silk, microfiber, coated materials, foils and artificial leather.

**mitered corner** – a corner (usually of a border) that is joined at a 45-degree angle, like a picture frame. It is achieved by stitching and cutting excess fabric on the diagonal from the corner.

**mock flat-fell seam** – a seam stitched wrong sides together, with the lower seam allowance then trimmed back, and the upper seam allowance pressed flat to cover it and stitched in place. For neatness, the raw edge of the upper seam allowance can be finished with an overcast or zigzag stitch before it is stitched down. Also known as a welt seam.

**mock French seam** – a seam in which the fabric is stitched together right sides together, then the two raw edges of the seam allowance are folded inwards to the seamline and hemmed together along the foldline, to give the look of a French seam. *See also* **French seam**.

**mock safety stitch** – a serger stitch created with either two needle threads and one looper thread, or two needle threads and two looper threads, and used for seams on stretchy fabrics. *See also* **safety stitch**.

**monogram** – a design, usually embroidered, made up of intertwined initial letters.

**motif** – a single design element in a printed pattern on fabric or a patch used for appliqué.

**nap** – a soft fabric surface, made by brushing all the short fibers in one direction. Depending on which way the light falls on the fabric it can look lighter or darker, so items would normally be constructed with the nap running in the same direction on each adjacent piece, unless the play

of light and dark is being used as a design feature. Achieving this often requires more fabric, particularly in dressmaking, because pattern pieces cannot be reversed to fit in with each other, and so get them closer together, when laying them out on the fabric. *See also* **pile**.

**needle plate** – the removable plate that fits over the feed dog and the bobbin, with a hole that the needle passes through. The plate often has a series of lines etched on it that show different distances from the needle, which can be used to stitch accurate seams.

**notch** – triangular mark on the cutting line of a pattern, used to determine how pieces join together; cut around the notch's outer edge when cutting out.

**notching** – *see* **clipping**.

**notions** – a general term covering small sewing items used in the construction of projects, such as thread, needles, pins, zippers, buttons, fastenings, trims and bindings. Also known as sewing notions or haberdashery.

**overcasting** – a hand stitch, such as a long whipstitch, worked over the raw edges being stitched together to neaten the edges and prevent them from fraying. Sergers overcast; it can be done on a conventional sewing machine by using a close set zigzag stitch near to the edge, but a special overcasting foot is normally required to prevent the fabric edge from curling in as it is stitched.

**overlap** – the edge of a garment that extends over another edge.

**overlock stitch** – a serger stitch created with one needle thread and one or two looper threads, and used for finishing edges and for seams.

**overlocker** – *see* **serger**.

**pattern layout** – diagrams used to show how pattern pieces should be laid onto the fabric.

**pattern repeat** – *see* **repeat**.

**pickstitch** – decorative hand stitch that can be used as an alternative to top-stitching. Also known as half backstitch.

**pile** – raised threads or loops on the surface of a fabric. Pile fabric often also has a nap. *See also* **nap**.

**pilling** – the tendency of fibers to work loose from the fabric surface and form balled or matted particles attached to the surface of the fabric; the better the quality of fabric, the less it will pill. Also known as bobbling.

**pin tuck** – a very fine, narrow tuck in fabric. Pin tucks are usually worked in groups of three or more.

**pinking shears** – cutting tool with serrated blades; can be used on fabrics that do not have a tendency to fray to neaten a seam.

**piping** – a strip of flat, folded fabric inserted into a seam for decoration. *See also* **cording**.

**pivoting** – to lift the presser foot and turn the fabric on the machine needle without lifting the needle from the fabric; the presser foot is then lowered to continue stitching.

**placket** – a finished overlapping opening, often leading to a pocket, a concealed zipper or other fastener, or in the sleeve at the cuff. The term can also refer to the flap of fabric often found behind such an opening.

**pleats** – folds in fabric that are usually only held in place at the top, with the length of the pleat pressed in a straight line to the bottom edge.

**point presser** – a tool for pressing seams and points in small areas such as a collar.

**point turner** – this tool has an angled point used to push out collar points, for example, for a neat, sharp finish.

**preshrunk fabric** – fabric that is treated in the manufacturing process so that it will not shrink when cleaned.

**press cloth** – a cloth placed between the fabric and the iron when ironing to offer protection, prevent unwanted shine and facilitate pressing at higher temperatures.

**presser foot** – on a sewing machine, the piece of metal or plastic that sits below the needle and can be lowered to hold the fabric in place against the feed dog so that it doesn't move about as it is stitched. The actual foot section can usually be removed and there is a range of special presser feet for different tasks.

**Princess seam** – a seam joining two different-shaped edges, to shape out an area of a garment, over a bustline for example, to create a fitted garment. Also known as a curved seam.

**raglan sleeves** – this type of sleeve begins at the neck with a long, angled seamline from the neck edge to the armhole, which gives the garment a relatively undefined shoulder. Raglan sleeves are often used on leisure and sportswear for more flexible movement and greater comfort.

**raw edge** – a cut edge of fabric that has not been finished off in any way.

**repeat** – measurement between the centers of identical motifs running in a straight line lengthwise along printed or woven fabric. A half-drop repeat fabric is when the motifs are identical but staggered, so the motifs in one row crosswise fall halfway between the motifs in the rows above and below.

**rickrack** – a type of flat braid made in a zigzag design.

**rolled hem** – a very narrow hem made by rolling the edge of the fabric over just until the raw edge is enclosed, then stitching in place. Rolled hems can be hand or machine stitched.

**roller foot** – a machine foot that has rollers built into it to allow it to feed smoothly on fabrics with an uneven surface, such as velvet.

**rotary cutter** – a cutting tool with interchangeable round blades used to produce precise, straight edges when cutting fabric. It should always be used with a self-healing cutting mat.

**ruffle** – *see* **frill**.

**running stitch** – a hand stitch most often used to join flat layers of fabric together.

**safety stitch** – a serger stitch made using four or five threads. For a four-thread safety stitch, a double chain stitch is formed with one needle and one looper and an overlock stitch with another needle and looper simultaneously. For the five-thread version an extra looper is used. *See also* **mock safety stitch**.

**seam allowance** – the width from the raw edge of the fabric to the stitching line of the seam.

**seam roll** – tool used to help when pressing shaped garment areas.

**seamline** – the line of stitching on a seam.

**self-bound seam** – a technique in which one edge of the seam allowance is folded over to encase the other edge.

**selvage** – the outer edges of a length of fabric, which is usually more tightly woven and so is normally cut off and not used. There is often manufacturer's information on the selvage.

**serger** – a machine that makes overcast seams and can cut off the excess seam allowance automatically as it stitches. Also known as an overlocker.

**set-in sleeves** – a sleeve joined to the body of a garment by a seam starting at the edge of the shoulder and continuing around the armhole. The rounded sleeve cap (the curved portion at the shoulder) is slightly larger than the armhole it fits into to enable it to fit easily over the arm.

**sewing bed** – the bottom section of a sewing machine, which houses the bobbin and forms a base to work on.

**sharps** – small, thin hand sewing needles with a really sharp point that pierce the thread of woven fabrics easily. Available in sizes 8/60–14/90, they are a good choice for straight stitch sewing.

**shirring** – gathering with several rows of stitching across the fabric to take in fullness.

**single binding** – binding an edge with a single thickness strip of fabric.

**single hem** – a hem in which just one layer of fabric is pressed to the wrong side and stitched in place. The raw edge can be neatened with zigzag stitch first.

**sleeve board** – used to press seams and narrow sections of a garment under construction.

**sleeve cap** – the rounded section at the top of a sleeve which is intersected by the shoulder seam.

**slipstitch** – a hand stitch used to join two folded edges together, or to secure a folded edge to a flat piece of fabric.

**snap tape** – a two-part tape that has small round fastenings running along it, one side of which has a little knob (the ball) and the other a sprung hole (the snap).

**spindle** – the pin that holds the bobbin when winding thread onto it.

**spool** – the reel that holds the thread.

**spool holder/cap** – a removable plastic disk on some machines that is pushed onto the spool pin over the thread spool, holding this steady so the thread unwinds smoothly during stitching.

**spool pins** – the pins to take the thread spools or cones.

**stabilizer** – a firm gauze used to support fabric, particularly when it is being machine embroidered. It can remain in place permanently, but is usually cut-away, tear-away, heat-away or wash-away.

**staystitching** – a single or double line of straight stitching within the seam allowance through only a single thickness of fabric, made to stabilize stretch fabrics or curved lines and prevent them from stretching.

**stitch-in-the-ditch** – stitching directly in the seam when you do not want your stitching to show. It is usually done in a thread color to match the fabric.

**stitch selector** – on more basic sewing machines, this is often a dial that allows you to select from a small number of different stitch types. On computerized machines, selection from a wide range of stitches is made by pressing a key pad.

**stitch tension** – for even and balanced machine stitching, the threads must be at the correct tension relative to each other. The tension on each thread can be adjusted individually to achieve this.

**straight grain** – straight along the lengthwise (warp) grain of the fabric. *See also* **bias**.

**straight stitch** – the most basic type of machine stitching with the stitch length set at around 2–3 and the width at 0.

**swatch** – a small piece of fabric used as a color sample.

**tacking** – *see* **basting**.

**tailor's board** – *see* **point presser**.

**tailor's ham** – tool, rather like a tightly stuffed pillow, used for pressing curved areas, such as collars and waistlines.

**tailor's tacks** – used to transfer symbols from a paper pattern to several layers of fabric at the same time.

**tension mechanism** – the adjustable plates on a sewing machine or serger that the thread must go through to place it under tension, so that the stitch can be formed correctly. *See also* **stitch tension**.

**thread count** – the number of threads per inch (2.5 centimeters). The higher the thread count, the finer the fabric.

**thread guides** – the guides that take the thread from one point to the next along the threading run on a sewing machine.

**thread take-up lever** – a lever with an eye on the front of a sewing machine that moves up and down with the needle and controls the amount of thread needed for stitching.

**threading run** – the route of the thread from spool to needle or looper.

**ties** – strips of fabric or lengths of fabric tubing set on either side of an opening and tied in a bow to close it.

**topstitching** – an extra line of stitching made parallel to a finished edge, usually done in contrasting thread.

**tracing wheel** – used together with dressmaker's carbon paper to transfer pattern markings to fabric.

**true bias** – the 45-degree diagonal edge formed when fabric is folded so that the length-wise and crosswise grains match. Fabric has the greatest amount of stretch along the true bias.

**tuck** – a fold in fabric that is stitched in place along its full length.

**underlap** – edge of a garment that extends under another edge. *See also* **overlap**.

**underlining** – a layer of lining fabric basted to the main garment sections and sewn as one with the fashion fabric.

**understitch** – a line of stitching through lining and seam allowances invisible from the right side, which helps the edge seam to roll naturally to the wrong side and lining to lie flat.

**universal needle** – these sharp pointed needles can be used for most general sewing applications and can be used on the majority of fabrics including jerseys and synthetics.

**walking foot** – *see* **even-feed foot**.

**warp** – the long threads in woven fabric that run from top to bottom in the length of the material, parallel to the selvage. The warp is also sometimes known as the floating yarn/thread.

**weft** – the shorter threads in woven fabric that run from side to side. The weft is also sometimes known as the filling yarn, the filler or the woof.

**welt seam** – *see* **mock flat-fell seam**.

**whipstitch** – a strong overedge hand stitch, worked diagonally, and used to join two flat edges together.

**with nap** – refers to a fabric that has a texture or design that must run in one direction on the finished garment. Fabrics with nap can look different depending on which way you hold them, though sometimes the difference might be a very subtle variation in color. Examples of with nap fabrics include velvet and corduroy, satin, knit fabrics and toile designs.

**without nap** – refers to fabrics that do not have a particular one-way texture or design. If you are unsure whether your fabric has a nap, use the with nap layout.

**zigzag** – machine stitching in which the needle moves from side to side to create a double-pointed line. The stitch width controls the width of the line of zigzag, and the stitch length controls how tightly together the stitches are.

**zipper** – a linear fastening with plastic, nylon or metal teeth, available in different types, weights and lengths.

# INDEX

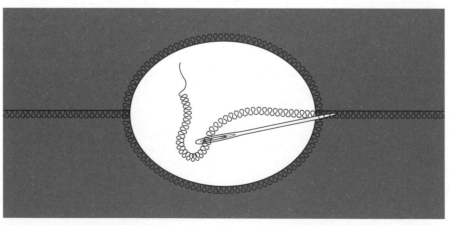

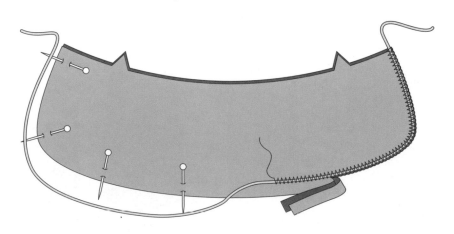

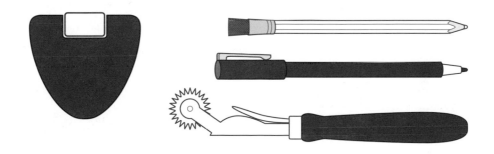

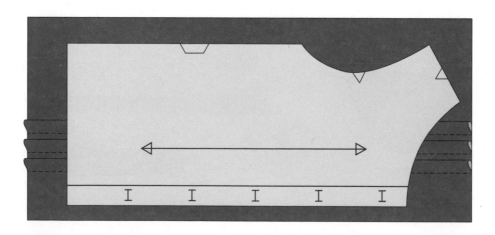

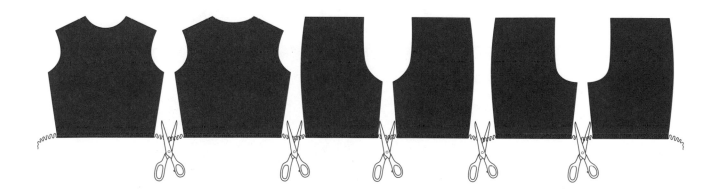

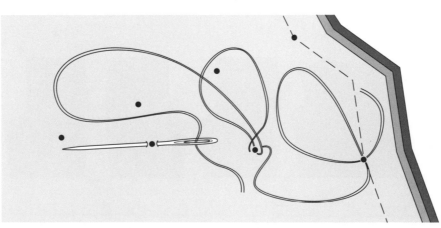

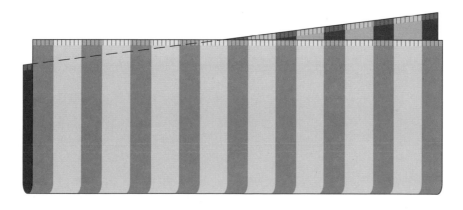

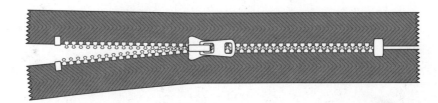